Jeffrey "Loner" Gray

Find your adventure!

Jeffry "Loner" Gray

SHADOW ARCHER
P R E S S
110 Johnson Street, Suite #1060, Pickens, SC 29671

PAINTED BLAZES – Hiking the Appalachian Trail with Loner

Cover design: Vicente A. Mendoza P.

Published by:
Shadow Archer Press LLC.
110 Johnson Street Suite #1060
Pickens, SC 29671 U.S.A.

Official Website: www.PaintedBlazes.com

Publisher: www.ShadowArcherPress.com

Email: Loner@ShadowArcherPress.com

Library of Congress Cataloging-in-Publication Data
ISBN-13: 978-1545166314
ISBN-10: 1545166315

Printed in the USA.

Disclaimer: Prices of hostels and other services are provided as a reference of general costs. Most prices have changed, and unfortunately, some business may be closed or no longer available. The author or publisher assume no liabilities arising from this book or its content.

*Author's note: Highlights from my Appalachian Trail hike can be found posted on YouTube. They closely follow the book contents and may help you better visualize some of the people and places.
http://youtube.com/c/Loner2012AT/.

Praise for Painted Blazes

Trail magic for the eyes... Loner won us over on YouTube, now he tops it off with an awesome book. The AT book mold has been broken. This book is a great read for day, section, thru-preppers and seasoned sole-burners. It should be in the hands of anyone who loves the AT. **Sam I Am**

I think this is one of the best on the subject... It gives a look into trail life and some very interesting facts on the trail. The best part is the author is a great guy. My husband and daughter watched his thru hike videos on YouTube in 2012. These videos were one on the reasons my husband and daughter (13 years old at the time) hiked the A.T. in 2013. **Hiker Mom**

I am reading this excellent book in synch with a third viewing of Loner's YouTube series. This was the beginning of my fascination with the AT. His narratives provide a unique insight to the experiences of the journey by someone who does not fit stereotypical notions about AT through hikers. **Larry Vickery**

Just finished this book and absolutely loved it! I couldn't put it down for long. Jeff goes into detail about his journey on the AT that took place in 2012. This is a must read of the highs and lows of months on the trail! **Harvey Brooks**

This is a good book for new hikers as well as, seasoned ones. There are details about the trail that really are not anywhere else. Loner give "tips" that are informative and funny. I would place it in the top 10 of Appalachian Trail books. It holds its own up against Bryson's "A Walk in the Woods". If you are looking to get a feel of what a "thru hike" is like, then "Painted Blazes" is the book you want to read. **Hike Hunter**

Map of the Appalachian Trail

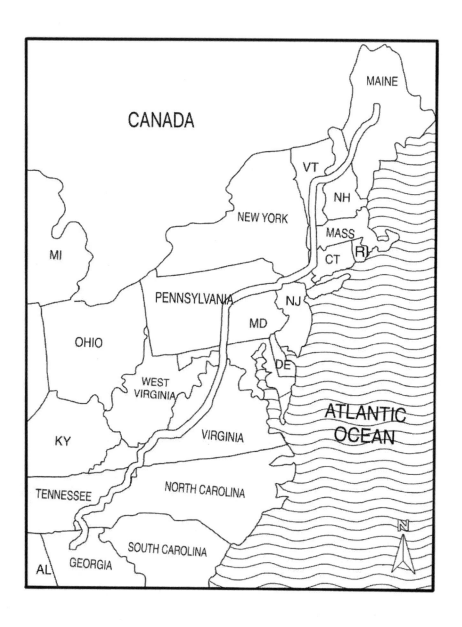

Table of Contents

Dedication

For my mother, who taught me to live life to the fullest.

Mom and Loner, April 7th, Amicalola Falls State Park.

Forward

April 7th, the day before Easter, Kendall, my granddaughter, and I dropped off my son, Jeffrey, at Amicalola Falls State Park, Georgia, for his 2,100 plus mile hike of the Appalachian Trail (AT). As his mom, I must admit I've been frantic since he left.

Jeff chose his trail name, Loner. Although mostly English, Irish, Polish and Russian, I would have given Jeff a Native American trail name from the Algonquin's who are in his ancestral line on his father's side, dating back to his great-great-great grandmother, from the time when one of the British Grays of Gray, Maine, married an Algonquin girl. In their language, the most fitting name for Jeff would be, Enkoodabaoo, which means "one who lives alone."

Jeff wanted us to hike with him to see the majestic Amicalola Falls. Families of all nationalities were cooking out, having Easter egg hunts and playing badminton. I had expected a quiet, rather sacred send off and couldn't quite wrap my head around all the colorful frivolity and activity. Unfortunately, Kendall was in flip flops and had to walk with her feet stretched out so as not to go careening in backward somersaults, bowling over large families of East Indians, Asians and Hispanics, causing them in turn, to execute backward somersaults resulting in an avalanche of international proportions.

While I was tremendously excited for Jeff, it was bittersweet to see him wave goodbye on that switchback trail and wondered if I would ever see him again. On the way home I attempted to drive serenely through the countryside while my granddaughter fell happily into a three-hour Dramamine doze. Finally, I couldn't hold it together anymore. Volumes of tears cascaded down my cheeks, enough to rival Amicalola Falls.

I wanted to picture what he was doing. *Where did he sleep? Were his socks wet? Did he have enough food in that ridiculously tiny backpack? Who did he meet? What are their trail names? Has he met any crazy people?* Whew! Time to take a breath...

While Jeff is a quiet guy, his dad's family riled-up his adventurous spirit. Every man Jeff knew - great-grandfather, grandfather, dad, uncles - all drove racecars. Most in the late models of their day. His dad specialized in figure eights. Jeff, at ten months old, sat on my lap with earplugs in his ears.

When we moved to South Carolina, Jeff was bummed out having to leave our picturesque lakeside village, Dracut, Massachusetts, at age 10 and moving to Greenville, a relatively large city. But he found his niche when he started skateboarding in the early 1980's, going from the street, to half-pipe ramps he built in the backyard, to jumping over cars in competitions.

Jeff also spent a lot of time in the woods. My then boyfriend, Steve, a mountain man to be sure (he caught rattlesnakes for Clemson University, in pillowcases as we hiked) would often take us to the Blue Ridge Mountains. Jeff then started collecting arrowheads and still walks farmer's fields and explores lakes in his kayak - but that's a whole other story.

Still, Jeff couldn't resist driving a racecar and started building cars in the backyard at age 16. He was a shy guy, in rough pits where drinking was almost the rule and fights broke out often. Jeff doesn't drink alcohol, but he was still respected by the other rather rowdy drivers because during the first race his car went airborne (not by Jeff's design) - just like on The Dukes of Hazard, and everyone thought he did it just to show off.

I then thought he was feeding his adventurist side enough when he went back to skateboarding, in a big way, while in his thirties. Founding his own skateboard company, he traveled throughout the southeast filming his team's road trips. But I guess that still wasn't enough.

If you meet him at any one of the hostels or shelters along the trail, you'll never guess he's done all these things. You'll meet a quiet, unassuming guy; a deep thinker in touch with the world on a natural level, like the Native Americans. His whole life, he's navigated the Jungian approach without knowing it, learning who he is. Even beneath the shy surface and droll sense of humor, he quietly and with dedication, goes after his dreams and makes them come true. He has lived a minimalist lifestyle for many years - and when I say minimal, I mean it. All his worldly belongings would fit in a couple of trunks. My daughter, Beth, and I have a terrible time trying to get him to hang onto things like photos. We kind of do that for him.

Now, he's taken another spiral on his quest over the 39 years of his life, as he's been circling around this unknown goal for many years in the wide range of activities with which he's become obsessed - all of which, I imagine, has taught him skills and given him the mental tools for this most unique experience yet.

Gail Gray, Loner's mom.

*Gail Gray is a self-taught artist, photographer and author best known for her gothic novel, **Shaman Circus**. She has also written two books of shorts stories: **Memories & Monsters** and **Dark Voices**, in addition to seven books of poetry and multiple DIY books related to the SCA (Society for Creative Anachronism, a medieval re-enactment organization). She was the editor of two magazines: **Fissure**, a magazine of experimental art and writing, and **The Howling**, a goth literary magazine. Gail founded Shadow Archer Press in 1993, which continues to publish books on a variety of subjects.

"Loner." Pencil portrait by his mom, Gail Gray.

Chapter 1. White Blaze Fever

Loner reaches the first white blaze atop Springer Mountain.

2,178 miles in all, the Appalachian National Scenic Trail, or AT for short, stretches from Springer Mountain, Georgia, all the way up the Southeastern United States to Katahdin, Maine. I had already been studying and training for months when I finally made the announcement to my family during Christmas: I was going to attempt a northbound thru-hike of the Appalachian Trail, and my goal was to walk the entire distance in a single hiking season. My reasons for attempting this? Maybe I needed to take a break from "real life," and wanted to live in the adventure of it all. Also, to experience the satisfaction from learning everything I can about a fixation, then making it a reality. This would be my most ambitious undertaking yet.

Out of fear, most people's first reaction is almost always, "No!!! You'll die!!" Just the thought of it evokes images of grizzly bear maulings, ritual murders, avalanches, dueling banjo hillbilly hostage situations and rabid diseases, like 'lock-jaw night vision.' Never do they first think of nature, adventure, community, or personal and spiritual growth, when, in fact, hiking and living on the trail can be a very positive, life changing experience and probably safer than sitting in your own backyard.

To her credit, my mother understood immediately why I would take on such a feat. And although she expressed concerns and would literally worry herself sick while I was away, she embraced her support role: keeping an online blog, paying my bills while I was away and sending many resupply boxes to help keep me going. On the other hand, my sister, Beth, thought the trip sounded exciting, but said I was out of my mind (her same reaction to other life decisions I've made), but she supported me in her own way. Condescending friends thought I was stupid for not taking a gun, or at the very least, a machete, with which to defend my life. Others criticized me for doing something foolish, "just for fun," that didn't earn money. These people had no imagination or sense of adventure.

Mom and my nine-year-old niece, Kendall, drove me from Greenville, South Carolina, to the southern terminus of the AT, Amicalola Falls State Park in Georgia, 80 miles north of Atlanta. Our drive only took three hours. Many travel much further, even from faraway countries, to start their hikes here. We enjoyed Chick-Fil-A, my "last supper," in Dawsonville, Georgia, a small town made famous by a local boy 'done good,' former NASCAR championship driver Bill Elliott, also known as "Million Dollar Bill." The road to Amicalola goes right by the old Dawsonville Pool Room, where they rang a bell every time he won a race. They rang it a lot.

Entering the park after paying a $5 parking fee, we explored a small museum that featured AT history, a short informational video and a life-size display of animals and reptiles that hikers might encounter along the way: Black bears, coyotes, rattlesnakes and others. These were just harmless taxidermy examples, but still intimidating.

There is also a gift shop where you can buy AT logo shirts, hats, bandanas with a printed map of the AT and other items. A squished penny machine sat in a corner and I still have a flattened coin with "Amicalola Falls" impressed on it. They also sell official AT guidebooks, but don't count on them being in stock. There are two guidebooks to choose from, and both are updated every season...

• **The Thru-Hikers' Companion** from the staff of the Appalachian Trail Conservancy (ATC). $14.95. A 'Digital Companion' App offers GPS-coordinated maps and photos of every shelter. A PDF version is also available.

• **The A.T. Guide** from David Miller, more commonly known as the 'AWOL.' $15.95. Kindle $1.99.

> *HIKER TIP: Thinking about thru-hiking? Purchase a guidebook to study and become familiar with. Collecting items for your adventure, even years away, can create a great deal of momentum.*

As tradition, I weighed my backpack on the park's "official" fish scale. Containing a four-day supply of food and everything else I needed to survive, my total pack weight was just 13.5 pounds. This shockingly low number is a little misleading, as I carried 2 bottles of water in the pockets of my shorts, so tack on an additional 4 or so pounds, as one of the first things hikers concerned about pack weight will learn, water weighs 2.2 pounds per liter. In comparison, most people's packs weigh between 30 and 50 pounds. However, I would see some much larger.

Next, I signed in at the ranger's station and was assigned hiker number #801 of about 3000 hopefuls to start this year. The ranger told us 20 others had already registered that same day with intentions of thru-hiking. An after-hours kiosk can be found outside if the main building is closed.

> *HIKER TIP: Amicalola Falls State Park offers long term parking for AT hikers across from the visitor center. Only $50 for up to 6 months. That's a great deal! Register at the ranger's station.*

Approach trail - to do, or not to do? I bet these are the most talked about 8.5 miles in all of hiking - and it's not even officially counted as the AT. Doing these 8 "extra credit" miles is barely a drop in the bucket compared to the full 2100-some odd miles. Not to mention all the uncredited mileage spent getting in and out of trail towns for supplies. So, it's not like you're saving any real time by skipping it. This park is also a safe and convenient place for family or friends, who may be sending you off, to learn more about the trail, see an actual shelter (AFSP Shelter is located just behind the visitor center) and even walk a little way with their hiker. In support, my mother and niece hiked with me as far as they could, through the archway and up the blue blazed trail.

Poor mom, hunched over and walking with an Ozzy Osborne shuffle, earned the trail name "8th Mile." Not an intentional play on Eminem's rap movie, but because that's how far she could walk! Kendall walked slightly less, so we called her "Almost an 8th Mile." The gesture still meant a lot. Stopping at the foot of the stairs that zigzag steeply up beside the waterfalls, we all hugged and said our goodbyes. As I walked away, Mom made a note the time was 3:30 p.m. Months later, my niece told me Mom cried all the way home, convinced she would never see me again.

> FUN FACT: A season 5 episode of 'The X-Files' featured a fictional National Forest, "The Apalachicola," where FBI agents Mulder & Scully searched for a Bigfoot-like creature.

Stairs. I've never seen so many stairs. 803 in all. The seemingly endless wooden risers, steps and short walkways leading to the top of the falls were very rigorous and hard on unconditioned and conditioned hikers alike. By the halfway point, I had to take several breaks to catch my breath and massage my calf muscles. What had I gotten myself into? On the assent, I spotted a rusty bumper sticking out of the ground, an errant car part dramatically described on the Amicalola Falls website as "...part of a moonshine truck that tumbled down the mountain during the Prohibition Era." (If you have a sharp eye, a door and other debris can be found on adjoining trails.)

Seeing this artifact, my mind imagined sirens blaring and screeching tires. A farmer, wearing old blue coveralls and in his hopped-up pickup, is trying to outrun the "revenooers." Checking on a dozen mason jars of white lightning clanging around in a box of straw next to him, he slides off the twisted mountain road, flips over and rolls down the hill. The sheriff gets out and throws down his hat in anger as the bootlegger escapes to carry on the Blue Ridge tradition of brewing harmless corn into intoxicating, illegal spirits, using makeshift stills made of barrels, car radiators and copper tubing. This was only the first evidence of this old-time southern art that remains abandoned, hidden in plain sight at springs and streams along the AT, this side of the Mason-Dixon Line.

The falls themselves get their name, "Amicalola," from a Native American Indian word meaning "tumbling waters." The Cherokee lived here until 1832, when they were forced to march west into the Ozarks as part of the Trail of Tears. Local settlers knew of only one Indian, a woman, who defiantly remained here up until the 1850's. The falls themselves are breathtaking. At 729-feet, they are the tallest in Georgia. Standing on an observation deck only a few feet away, I could feel the mist and power this downfall of water creates.

I found all this very exciting but signing-in, the stairs, the rusty bumper, the waterfalls...none of this is required and many hikers just bypass the park and its approach trail altogether. You can drive to within a mile of the actual starting point on top of Springer Mountain, but the one lane park service road to the top is all dirt and gravel and a long drive out of the way.

A few miles in, I placed my simple camera on a log, pressed the record button, and filmed an awkward introduction that would become the first video in a series posted on YouTube - with a couple weeks delay. Although the video was meant for family and friends, I was happy and excited when many others began following along, asking questions and posting comments of support. Some would even come to my rescue when the going got tough.

That first day and evening, I hiked the approach trail marked with blue blazes painted on trees, all the way to the top of Springer Mountain. This spot was chosen in 1958 to be the new southern terminus of the Appalachian Trail. Before then, from 1937 until 1958, the original starting point was Mount Oglethorpe, about 20 miles south. The start was moved here because of smelly and unsightly chicken farms that sprung-up along the unprotected route. Curious, the exact reason why this peak was renamed "Springer" is unknown. Locals still call it "Penitentiary Mountain," although they don't seem to know why they call it that, either. It never housed a jail of any kind. Whichever, the buildup of excitement, approaching the first white blaze by foot, was intense. I found it a beautiful hike and an accomplishment in itself.

A nice couple on an overnight hike, used my camera to take a picture of me kneeling at the first white blaze. You can see the anticipation on my face. Stained green with age, a copper plaque was embedded into the outcropping of stone and a logbook, enclosed in a stainless steel box, was tucked inside a rock under a straggly looking tree. Wrinkled pages were full of names and messages left by other hikers like me, embarking on this very same journey - some of whom I would cross paths with in the coming days, or months. The sky was almost dark, but colors of the fading sun made everything feel more special.

> FUN FACT: The plaque reads: "A footpath for those who seek fellowship with the wilderness." There are at least four similar markers scattered along the AT. Hiking the trail? See how many you can find!

Setting up my hammock by headlamp in the trees out front of Springer Mountain Shelter, I could hear the murmur of dozens of people. Even as late as April, the first shelter on the official AT was completely full of pilgrims staying the night, and many more tents dotted the overflow area all around the main clearing. Altogether, there must have been at least 25 people camping, plus several of their trail dogs. Every hook hanging from the bear cables had two or three food bags suspended from it.

Even though I was sleeping just 70 yards away from the Appalachian Trail, it was still hard to believe I was actually here and going to attempt this. Almost overwhelmed, I laid awake, thinking about all the interesting places ahead of me, wild animals I might see and the people I would meet. I was leaving home, my j-o-b, family, hobbies and starting a whole new way of life, for half a year, that if successful, would take me thousands of miles away. But was I ready?

The previous year, I took my pre-hike preparation very seriously. I slept through winter nights with the windows open and no heat, to get my body conditioned to the bitter cold I would face on the AT, only allowing myself to use the sleeping bag and clothes I would carry. Almost daily kayak jaunts, where my feet were cold and wet for extended periods of time, helped toughen my feet. Trekking hundreds of miles during shakedown hikes, I learned to make fires and practiced using my camp stove to cook meals. Instead of the customary tent, I chose an ultralight hammock system and with lots of trial and error, perfected my equipment. Twice weekly skateboard sessions improved my balance and endurance. That was until I badly injured a calf muscle that took almost six months to heal completely. To make matters worse, I reinjured it twice during my recovery period, trying to be more active than the healing process would allow. I came very close to postponing my hike for another full year.

During my downtime, I gained a lot of weight due to inactivity and depression. Being heavy at the start, almost 250 pounds, seemed like a disadvantage, but I hoped my extra "bulk" would prove a benefit, keeping me warm and burnt off as fuel.

My recovery time was invested reading books about the AT. The first one I picked up was 'AWOL on the Appalachian Trail' by David Miller (the same author who now publishes the 'AWOL' guidebooks). Naïve and new to long distance hiking, I was confused whenever he referred to northbound and southbound. Never having been on the AT before, I'm embarrassed to say I envisioned two dirt lanes with a median of trees or bushes, like an interstate highway. Of course, I soon learned you could simply hike going in either direction on the same path. Insert Homer Simpson voice, "DOH!"

Furthering my backcountry education, I watched every AT video or series I could find on YouTube. There were many going back several years. Favorites: Tuts, Cleanshave and Hover. I watched some of these video blogs in real time, as they were posted from the trail and followed each one, with great interest, all the way to the end. A couple of my predecessors even watched my videos while I was hiking!

I also ordered several DVD documentaries, including '2000 Miles to Maine.' I watched it at least 10 times before my hike, motivating myself to get my act together before leaving. It was also very exciting when I visited shelters or other places shown in the movie. Another good one was 'America's Wild Spaces: Appalachian Trail,' by NatGeo (National Geographic). It only followed a few hikers, but the sweeping helicopter shots were stunning.

> HIKER TIP: Going solo? You're never really alone if you hike in peak season and making friends is easy on the trail. You already have many things in common and chances are, others are looking for buddies too.

Waking up before daylight after a restless sleep, I walked back to the first white blaze to watch the sunrise from atop Springer Mountain, 3,780'. The view was impressive and uninhibited by leaves, as trees had not leafed out yet. The only other person there was a ridgerunner, who climbed onto a low branch to watch as well.

Ridgerunners are paid employees of the ATC, usually experienced long distance hikers, who now travel up and down assigned sections, interacting with hikers. They're not hall monitors, but keep an eye on things, do light trail maintenance and report problems. Ridgerunners also encourage hikers to minimize impact on the environment, especially in heavily used areas. My favorite slogan is "Leave No Trace - Bigfoot's Been Doing it for Years!" Advertising material features a fluffy, blue Bigfoot waving sheepishly. He makes me chuckle every time I see it. This particular ridgerunner was much younger than I expected, and rag-tag looking, wearing torn shorts and a shirt with a faded "AT" logo.

Seeing me with my headlamp turned on, he called me "The Night Hiker" and suggested the nickname with a grin on his face. I ignored this gimmicky trail name disaster as, thankfully, no one else was there to hear it! This was only the first of several assigned monikers that I rejected.

Trail names. It's a fun tradition, and part of this subculture, that hikers earn, use, and answer to trail names, usually bestowed by another hiker, born from any number of reasons: some humorous mistake, an odd habit, resemblance to a famous person, a reflection of your personality, favorite snack, and so on. Sometimes it happens the first day on the trail, other times it can take weeks, even months. Once given, most people keep their trail names for life, but they can be modified, compounded, or changed altogether. I know of at least one hiker who had three different trail names during his three years on the AT

(DDoods, Tech and Navigator). Some names get used again and again every season, or belong to more than one person.

Affectionately, "Trail angels" and other nice folks we interact with along the way, are also awarded trail names from time to time. On the other hand, uncooperative "townies" may be fixed with unflattering ones. Trail dogs usually get new names too ("Trouble," "Chaser," etc.). Sometimes, there are nicknames for unusual gear or backpacks, ("Big Bertha," "The Monster.") It's a rite of passage to earn your trail name spontaneously and I had the privilege of handing out a few myself. One fellow, who you'll meet later in this book I christened "Psychic." And, although we only met twice, the naming created a bond.

> FUN FACT: *Even the very first thru-hiker, Earl Shaffer, had a self-dubbed trail name - "The Crazy One." The name fit - in 1948 when he did his thru-hike, the AT wasn't even fully connected yet!*

I chose a name for myself, mostly because I had created a YouTube channel before leaving and wanted to avoid confusion. There was also the chance I might be fixed with one I didn't like. For example, "Ass Trumpet" or "Chunky Monkey" - both real trail names! But I would have probably been given the same one I have, anyway: "Loner." The name fit. I have always been painfully shy - I mean, really shy. During school, every lunch I sat by myself and put my head down on the table to pretend I was sleeping. Like a frightened turtle, I rarely came out of my shell to try talking to some pretty girl I had pined over for months, only to be broken hearted. Years later, after quitting a succession of jobs, I paid the rent by selling my vintage toy collections at flea markets. If I wanted to sell anything, I had to talk people up. Over time, I became good at both, adopting this nomadic lifestyle to support myself. But old habits die hard, and perhaps I subconsciously chose the trail name "Loner" as a way to keep strangers at arm's length.

> HIKER TIP: *Before starting your hike, take "before" pics, weigh yourself and trace your feet. Do the same again "after" you finish - to compare. You'll lose a lot of weight and feet can grow several shoe sizes.*

Officially setting off, I met Mountain Squid at the gravel parking area a mile north of the shelter. Cold drinks and snacks were arranged on the tailgate of his truck - my first trail magic! Mountain Squid is a prolific trail maintainer who also takes it upon himself to keep track of hiker counts and posts the stats he collects on the Whiteblaze.com message board, an online forum with vast amounts of info about the AT. He had already been here for weeks, meeting potential thru-hikers as he counted, and said I was at the end of the "large bubble." Hikers had come before me, starting early as January, and many more would trickle through during the rest of the month.

Setting up camp later that evening, I worked very hard to hang my food bag safely from a tree branch - high as I could. Only to find jagged, thin lines carved into a tree nearby - bear claw marks...fresh, too, by the look of it. Kind of scary, but I couldn't hike any farther, and certainly wasn't going to pack everything up in the dark and move.

What a view! This was the payoff for climbing all those stairs.

Chapter 2. Tourist Trap

Blood Mountain Shelter, 4,458'. Built in 1934, it's the oldest on the AT.

Hiking from dawn to dusk, I struggled to complete a day over 15-miles by the end of the first week. Even this distance isn't recommended for beginners, and I was lucky not to have injured myself. My calves were sore the first couple of evenings, then my knees; later, my ankles. But these pains were never so great that they couldn't be fixed with a good night's rest, and I woke up each morning rejuvenated and ready to go again.

Spring had yet to take hold and the magical "green tunnel" I had read about was actually grey and barren. Skeleton arms of rhododendron and mountain laurel branches reached above, creating a narrow passageway. I also snuck past a log that, if you used your imagination, looked like an alligator's head with eyes and a long snout, waiting in the brush to attack the next person to walk by!

Temps were chilly in early April - in the low 30°s, so I wore most of my layers of clothing to stay warm. On a clear day, Gooch Gap had faraway views of the Atlanta skyline. Grey shadows of giant skyscrapers, resembling dominoes, stood in a row waiting to be pushed over with a brush of the hand.

Wearing a big cowboy hat, Lone Star was a smiling Spanish fellow from Texas. After initial introductions, he asked if we could walk together for a while, and I agreed. Honestly, I didn't know what to expect, having never hiked with anyone before. After all, I was a loner, but enjoyed his company. Also, both of us were interested in learning about Native Americans and took time to explore several stone overhangs that could have been used as primitive shelters.

Back home, Lone Star was a professional marathon runner and alternated between wearing his dayglow-colored, spandex racing suit, covered in sponsor logos, and another outfit consisting of a work shirt and khaki pants with lots of pockets. New to hiking, his huge backpack must have weighed at least 50 pounds. Friends and neighbors from his hometown had donated a lot of the equipment for his hike - most of it bulky and heavy. He even carried a full-size, old school 35mm camera, its case, multiple lenses and enough film and batteries to last the entire trip! Lone Star explained that he brought this rig along because it took great pictures, and, it was all he had. Even with the hefty weight penalty, he was a very strong hiker.

We were soon joined by another backpacker, Flatlander (an overused trail name for folks from Florida). A section hiker, this retired gent was diligently working to complete the entire trail in bits and pieces, over a period of years. Lone Star and I peppered him with questions, and Flatlander sensei schooled us with exciting stories from prior seasons. Several times, as we were walking along, we heard an odd mechanical sound, like someone starting up a generator in the middle of the forest. The beats started out slowly, then became faster and grew louder. I was puzzled, but Flatlander knew right away what was making the noise - ruffed grouse, a wild bird from the chicken family. Males drum their wings against their side to impress the ladies. Later, I saw one directly on the trail - a pretty bird, much fancier and more colorful than any chicken. In no hurry to get out of my way, it let me get very close before jumping out of reach.

Another topic of conversation was how to avoid "Giardia Lamblia," a protozoan parasite that can be ingested in food or water. Infection is common in third-world countries and unkempt daycare centers, but also present on the AT and known in the hiker community as "Giardia," for short. The name sounds scary, and it is. Symptoms include stomach cramps, fatigue and projectile vomiting resulting in dangerous dehydration and nutritional loss. These very unpleasant indications may not show up for a few days, but can last three weeks or more. Even hosts with no signs of infection can become carriers, and Giardia can be transmitted person-to-person or by touching contaminated soil or objects. Hikers weakened with Giardia are better off waiting it out in a hostel or cheap hotel. Otherwise, plan on walking only about three miles a day, basically tree-to-tree ("brown blazing"). Medications are available to speed up treatment, but the infection will usually run its course in time. The easiest way to avoid most illness is by simply washing one's hands often or using hand sanitizer. Clean water is also very important: Filtering, boiling, or adding a chemical treatment before drinking or cooking, should make it safe.

> HIKER TIP: Expensive Nalgene bottles made of thick material don't flex. Thrifty hikers use common Smart Water bottles to carry H2O. Flexible and slender, they fit easily into most backpack pockets.

Clean water. Native Americans believed water was cleansed after passing over the seventh rock in a stream, but to be on the safe side, thru-hikers need to treat or filter water for drinking. Directions can be found on the Internet for the DIY (do it yourself) inclined to make their own water treatment, using small amounts of bleach. But most hikers were using water filtration systems that require hoses (some as restrictive as drinking straws), a syringe, two thick plastic bags and a handpump. I found these too much trouble and too bulky for my minimalist style. Plus, these items need to be cleaned with dishwashing liquid and are known to freeze or even crack in cold temps. Most important, you absolutely must keep track of which hoses and bags are "clean," and which are "dirty," or it defeats the purpose altogether. In addition, chemical treatment is still recommended in some states.

At first, I used iodine tablets, the lightest way to carry water treatment. But these gave the water a funky flavor that I can only describe as tasting like watered down ice tea and stale potato chips - mixed together. Gross! Also, the pellets turned my water a nasty brown color and more than one person asked why my water looked weird. Adding a second tablet would have reversed these effects but for the sake of weight, I chose not to carry the additional glass vile. Later, I learned these salt tablets can cause liver problems if used for prolonged periods of time, and a couple weeks into my hike, I switched to Aquamira, basically a very low dose of chlorine dioxide. Store bought kits cost about $15 for 3 oz. - enough to treat approximately 30 gallons of water, though sometimes difficult to find in trail towns and you have to carry 2 small plastic bottles. To use, I dip my bottles into a water source to fill, count 7 drops of each into a bottle cap (per liter), and then pour them into my bottle and let mix for 20 minutes before drinking. Also, make sure to splash a little of the treated water around the threads of the bottle where you put your mouth.

When using questionable or low quality water sources, I would sometimes filter using a bandana, or my T-shirt, to catch what I jokingly called, "floaties" or "amoebas." Crystal Light, Kool-Aid, or other flavor packets mask the faint chlorine taste, add a few calories and felt like a luxury after a few days in the woods.

Technology keeps improving and the most popular systems today are the Sawyer Squeeze and Sawyer Mini water filters. These small plastic cylinders can be used by twisting them onto a water bottle, bladder, or placed inline if you have a camel-back hydration system built into your backpack. Resembling a gun silencer screwed onto your water bottle, the Mini weighs a mere 2 oz., can filter up to 100,000 gallons, and only costs $20. The company claims: "Removes 99.99999% of all bacteria, and all protozoa, such as giardia." You can also drink right away with no waiting. If I were to do it all over again, I'd probably go with this method.

> HIKER TIP: Don't lose your bottle caps! After helplessly watching one float down a creek, I started carrying an extra. Some caps are interchangeable with other brand bottles, and may also fit Platypus or HEET bottles.

"Rangers Lead the Way." Camp Merrill, and its 290-acre campus, is close to the trail and shares the Chattahoochee National Forest with hikers. If you spend the night at Hawk Mountain Shelter, you may even be awoken at 3:00 a.m. by "Reveille" being played on a trumpet. The 5th U.S. Army Ranger Training Battalion is based at the camp, where aspiring Rangers undertake the "mountain phase," the second of three training stages necessary to become an elite U.S. Army Ranger. One-eighth of the earth's surface is covered with mountains, and missions here are designed to improve mountaineering and survivor skills. Several stories were going around that soldiers, covered from head to toe in camouflage and dark face paint, sneak in and out of hiker's tents without waking anyone up, as a test. Seeing several loud helicopters flying just above the treetops, and hearing booming bomb blanks exploding in the distance, made things more exciting. Yet, my only interaction with any military training was watching a convoy of heavy-duty military trucks and trailers, drab green, slowly pass by as I waited to cross a dirt road. A dry section with few water sources, Army Rangers stationed a trailer with a big tank on top, known as a "water buffalo," where hikers could find it.

Shelters. An impressive system of about 260 of these little buildings can be found all along the AT. Built for hikers to camp in or around, they are spaced roughly a day's walk apart, and usually located near a dependable water source. Most were purposely built where they stand. A few were constructed elsewhere, then dropped in place by heavy lifting helicopters. Others may be former fire warden's cabins, repurposed dwellings, and in one case, a historic old tobacco barn. Most of these sanctuaries are called "shelters;" however basic shelters in the Shenandoah Mountains are known as "huts." So are lodge-like buildings in the White Mountains, not basic at all. In the 100-mile wilderness, shelters are designated as "lean-tos." You may also find these modest safe havens referred to as "cabins," "lodges," or "Adirondacks." The smallest could sleep about 4 people and the largest over 30. First come - first serve.

Most shelters are very simple, 3 walled affairs. Others are more elaborate and feature lofts, porch swings, skylights, fireplaces, solar showers and other amenities. No two are exactly alike and all have their own special charm. More than once, I ventured off the trail just to check out a shelter's design.

Privies. Each shelter usually has its own bathroom, known as a "privy," and designs can be as simple as a wooden box over a hole in the ground (with a view), traditional as an outhouse with a ¾ moon carved into the door, or even fun restrooms with unexpected amenities. One example had double thrones with a checkerboard in the middle! Just make sure to bring your own toilet paper (TP).

Blood Mountain Shelter was one of those special historical landmarks that I looked forward to visiting. Climbing Picnic Rock, a giant boulder equally famous as the iconic shelter it sits next to, affords breathtaking views and is an excellent photo opportunity. The shelter was built by the organization: Civilian Conservation Corps, brainchild of President Franklin D. Roosevelt, and part of his "New Deal," providing jobs to young men during the Great Depression.

Besides constructing over 800 nature parks, CCC employees built rural roadways and planted 3 billion trees. Also, support buildings of all shapes and sizes were erected using local trees for lumber and native stone as foundations that blended in with the surrounding environments. Utilizing native resources had numerous benefits: no-cost materials, their removal cleared additional acres of land for roads or trails, and these materials didn't have to be transported over long distances - a very efficient system like that used by frontiersmen.

> *FUN FACT: Beautiful examples of CCC craftsmanship and architecture are visible up and down the AT and become easy to recognize. An astatic now known as "National Park Service rustic" or "Parkitecture."*

Over the years, Blood Mountain Shelter had weathered and decayed, its roof made weaker by people jumping onto it from Picnic Rock, and every single stick of wood trim (shutters, windows sills and door frames) had all been sacrificed by visitors needing to fuel the fireplace on cold nights. In 2010, the shelter was restored. Thirty-two round trips were made by trained pack animals, horses and donkeys to deliver pre-cut rafters and joists that were assembled, on site, using only hand tools.

It was fun exploring, but there was still no glass in the window openings and a once cozy fireplace was filled with concrete, supposedly to make it inoperable. Fires are banned altogether throughout the Blood Mountain section, but there was a fresh pile of grey ashes on the hearth. The air felt cold and the stone floor hard and uneven. Still, it's tempting for hikers to camp here, which is not allowed unless you have an approved, plastic bear canister to safely store your food. Some brave (or uninformed) souls stay here anyway and pay the price.

> *HIKER TIP: "Bear Vault" is a popular brand of bear canister. A 4 day food supply weighs 2lbs. 1oz. and a seven-day size weighs 2lbs. 9oz. $68. Bear's sharp claws can't grip the slippery plastic.*

A late-night visitor had terrorized two hikers we met; the black bear didn't enter the shelter, but a young man showed us his nylon food bag, and it looked like Freddy Kruger had shred it. Another hiker, who did use a bear canister, also had his food stolen. He had wedged the storage device in between some rocks the night before, but even expensive bear canisters are not much good if you leave them where a bear can just carry off the whole thing. When we arrived at Mountain Crossings later that day, the manager said they had already replaced 21 food bags that season!

> *HIKER TIP: DO NOT DISREGARD BEAR WARNINGS! We saw fresh claw marks on trees, thick hair stuck to branches and tree bark, logs or rocks that bears had overturned and piles of poo with candy wrappers in it.*

Hikers look forward to the first stop in civilization, so it's hard to pace yourself, but the steep trail that led us down the north side of Blood Mountain was no joke! All downhill and difficult, with lots of rocks and roots, a natural garden along the way featured several fascinating balancing rock formations. Boulders, as big as compact cars placed one on top of another by nature and glaciers, looked like circus elephants standing on beach balls. Finally, Lone Star, Flatlander and I started hearing cars on US HWY-19/129 and knew we were getting closer to Neel Gap.

Mountain Crossings Hostel and Outfitter, also known as "Walasi-Yi Center," is a mecca for hikers. The beautiful stone building was built in 1937, also by the CCC. The trail leads hikers right through the building's breezeway, the only covered area along the entire length of the AT, if only for a moment. Out front is a Superman-sized old-school phonebooth that no longer works and the infamous "boot tree," with dozens of discarded old boots hanging from its many long branches. A ritual for hikers giving up or trading in their tires.

Once an inn and dining/dance hall for sightseers, the main building is now a gift shop where car tourists can buy little rocks with their names painted on them, games with golf tees for playing pieces and other Cracker Barrel type knick-knacks, bric-à-brac, what-nots, do-dads and dust collectors.

A smaller backroom of the store is for serious hikers and carries name brand gear, at name brand prices. I enjoyed a couple of hotdogs, a bag of chips and found a green poly shirt on sale for $15. The black one I started out with was now too small for me after bulking up over winter, like a bear before going into hibernation.

For thru-hikers, Neel Gap is the first big milestone they reach. It's said that if you can physically make it this far - mile marker 31.7 - you can make it all the way. However, it's also said that 20% give up by this point. Former owner of Mountain Crossings, Winston Porter, used to sit in a lawn chair on the roof of his building and watch budding thru-hikers emerge from the woods. He claimed to be able to tell which ones would make it all the way, and which will fall by the wayside, just by what they were carrying.

An extremely helpful service provided here is a FREE gear shake down. An employee will go through your backpack, piece-by-piece, and make suggestions to help lower overall weight and bulk. A scale is used to get a baseline and final tally. Between 400 and 500 shakedowns are done each year, and thousands of pounds of unneeded gear gets shipped home. By this point, you should have a better idea of what you use and what you don't. Your back will thank you for it!

> HIKER TIP: Also offered; a "Virtual Shake Down" utilizes a video conference tool to go through your pack by way of a webcam. Cost is $100, but can be redeemed as store credit within 48 hours (*online purchases only).

On the ground floor of the former inn is a small hostel set-up like a fun clubhouse with board games, books, a BBQ grill and other creature comforts. However, I hear the high elevation can make it bitterly cold for winter guests, as the heat doesn't work very well. The hostel was looked after by a guy named Pirate, a tall, scruffy man who lived under the stairs (sounds like a bad horror movie). He's a living legend who has hiked up and down the AT a total of 10 times! I had planned to use the computer here to post my first update video, but Pirate had recently destroyed it with a baseball bat because of people bickering over whose turn it was. I did get my first shower of the hike. It only cost $4 to feel like a new man! There is also a washer and dryer to clean your clothes. Additionally, I picked up a drop box of supplies ($1 charge) that I had mailed to myself before leaving home, to avoid going into town for resupply. Otherwise, Dahlonega, an interesting former gold mining town, is 16 miles away.

My favorite thing about Mountain Crossings was the atmosphere. Hikers we had never seen were milling about, also taking care of chores. One pair, who I dubbed the "High School Crew," looked young enough to be playing hooky. The taller of the duo was a boy with bushy red hair who I called "Big Red," and the skinny one looked like comic Jim Carrey. When standing together, they reminded me of the movie 'Dumb N' Dumber.' Not at all prepared, each wore blue jeans and cotton T-shirts and shared one small tent and a single quilt from home. It had been nippy at night, and I pictured them all huddled up together, shivering in the cold like Harry and Lloyd.

Sadly, the Blood Mountain area was in the news a few years earlier for tragic reasons. Meredith Emerson, despite having some martial arts training and walking with her dog, was kidnapped nearby. An extensive search was initiated and police sketches of an older man, last seen with the young woman, were printed on the front page of a local newspaper. Finally, there was a tip from a gas station attendant who recognized the man cleaning out his van. Police arrested Gary Michael Hilton, but were too late. Leading investigators to her body, the killer said he couldn't bring himself to kill her dog. A memorial can be found on a spur trail off the AT where Meredith Emerson had been abducted. She was only 24.

Unsettling, Hilton had previously written 'Deadly Run,' a straight-to-video horror cliché about a man who kidnaps young women, sets them loose in the secluded Georgia Mountains, and hunts them down, complete with Casio music and a steroid weightlifter who flexes in every scene, playing the lead.

Lone Star and I said goodbye to our friend Flatlander. He had rented a nearby cabin for the night, then planned to continue the following day. Blood Mountain Cabins & Country Store is just off the AT. Each cabin is named after a different animal: chipmunk, racoon, bobcat, etc. Rates are $79-$99 a night, and each bungalow can accommodate up to 4 adults. No pets.

When hiking out of Mountain Crossings, the next stop for most hikers is Whitley Gap Shelter. Unbelievably, it's a very long, mile and a half off trail - each way! Forget that - I don't depend on shelters like most hikers, and just make camp wherever I like. Lone Star was just ahead, and the next morning, I found him making coffee and watched him add a bite sized Snickers bar to his cook cup. We skipped stopping in Helen, Georgia, as I've visited there before. The town has a gimmicky German alpine village theme and is popular with AT hikers looking for beer. There are several hotels, but no hostels.

Heading into Hiawassee, Lone Star and I were moving along when a guy and his girlfriend, both of whom had dreadlocks and smelled of reefer, passed us. They didn't even take the time to exchange trail names. How rude! Next, High School Crew raced past us on the long downhill coming into Dick's Creek Gap. It didn't take long to figure out what was going on. Neither team said so, but they were afraid all the motel rooms in town would be full and wanted to beat us to it!

Downhills kill. Soon, we repassed Big Red. Now wounded, he was dragging one foot on the ground behind him like a zombie from the TV show 'The Walking Dead.' After all the cat and mouse, the six of us still ended up at the trailhead at the same time. No one could get cell signal, not even when putting an aluminum hiking pole up to one ear, and a cellphone to the other. Team Dreadlock, the most eager of us, tried in vain to catch a ride to town, while the rest of us watched, using our backpacks as makeshift recliners. A few cars and beat-up pickup trucks crested the mountain, but none stopped, and it became comical watching these unlikely hitchhikers get more and more frustrated. We had been warned of a man named Matt, described as a "rogue shuttle guy" who lurks around trailheads trying to dupe unsuspecting hikers in exchange for rides. Reminiscent of the fare charged to hitchhikers in 1970's slasher movies: "Ass, cash, or grass?" At this point, our dreadlocked comrades looked willing to pay the price!

Finally, the still healthy of the High School Crew walked back to the top of the mountain he had just run down and got a call through to the hotel. In the guidebook, the inn lists "free pick-up at trailhead" as an incentive. However, they were unwilling to drive up the mountain for just 6 measly patrons. The profiteer did call an independent shuttle guy for us. Another half hour later, a gentleman in a black SUV with hiking stickers all over its back windows, showed up. Our chauffeur had to make two trips, but got everybody delivered to the bottom of the mountain. After another half hour wait, and splitting the charge of $20 per carload, Lone Star and I arrived at our destination.

> HIKER TIP: Phone signal can be very spotty in the mountains. Use your guidebook to make calls from the highest point preceding a planned town stop. Also, try sending text messages when phone calls won't go through.

There's a lot of competition among hostels in the south, even though there are more than enough hikers to go around. When visiting Hiawassee, if money isn't an issue, Holiday Inn Express is top of the line at $69.99 (hiker rate.) The most wholesome choice would be The Blueberry Patch. Lennie, and her husband, Gary (AT Class of '91), have a small organic farm/petting zoo with goats, chickens and a donkey. Famous for their homemade pancake breakfasts with fresh blueberry syrup. *Update: Now closed.*

Regrettably, we picked another place. This glorified motel's full name: "The Hiawassee Budget Inn, owned by Ron Haven's Appalachian Trail Hiker Services." Already settled in, the High School Crew was excited to have scored  the "BIG" room for $50, and showing off, invited us to check it out. It was indeed big with two king beds, a giant thrift store TV stand, two antique wooden dressers (nonmatching) and a full-size refrigerator. The celebrity owner, for whom the hotel is named, was not present, and some other dude was running the show. He must have been watching out his window, because he came running into the room and said I had to pay - like I was trying to sneak in. I guess that's understandable, as hiker trash are famous for "sharing" rooms. We then went back outside and negotiated. Reasonably, he said the 4 of us could all split the BIG room, so long as 3 of us paid the $5 EAP fee (each additional person.) Just then, Big Red slowly closed the door to their room as if to say, "Nope." He was sitting on the sidewalk, icing his sore knee while drinking a beer whose logo matched his T-shirt.

On a strict budget, a week was much too early in the hike for me to spring for a hotel. My original plan was to take the "free" shuttle to town, get some grub, wash my clothes, upload a video to the Internet and hang my hammock in the yard of the hotel. Camping space and a shower were advertised in the guidebook for $10 a night. In-and-out for 20 bucks - tops. WRONG. I was then informed of a loophole rule that you can't pay to camp here unless ALL the rooms are rented. There was still one left. Thankfully, Lone Star, nice guy that he is, offered to share his room but our visit to the "Budget Inn" wasn't such a bargain after all.

Our suite was along a poorly lit back alley of the building, and each doorway had walking sticks and stinky boots out front. The little room had a 20-year-old TV with only 4 grainy channels, stained carpet and sticky Scratch-N-Sniff wallpaper you didn't want to touch. The shower felt good, but after being in the woods for a week, I was taken aback by a heavy chlorine odor that made my eyes sting.

It was late, but we did what chores we could. Lone Star got busy cleaning out his heavy backpack and gave lots of things away to other hikers: machete and sheath, a silver multi-tool that looked like a giant Swiss Army knife, a three-piece cook set, an army folding shovel, etc. He also put a bunch more things in the hiker box.

Hiker boxes are a place for anyone to put unneeded, but still usable, gear, food, or supplies for other hikers to find. Right in front of me I actually saw a guy who worked at the hotel rifle through the new additions, take out a sealed 24 count package of AA batteries, place it on the counter and put a $10 post-it-note price tag on it. Yes, anything in a hiker box is up for grabs, but that was just plain sleazy.

To my surprise, a closet that served as the hotel laundry was locked at 7:00 p.m., "So no one messes it up." Another trick, using the machine was free, but economy detergent cost $5. There was no heat and Lone Star, only wearing his plastic raingear, nearly froze waiting for his clothes to dry. I found him disco dancing and doing jumping jacks to stay warm, so I loaned him my vest as the temps were dipping below freezing. The inn will hold mail (for guests only), but will not forward or return them, and must be picked up in person - "No Exceptions."

Our room only had one small bed. Sorry...I don't share beds with dudes, and was more than happy to sleep on the floor. But Lone Star insisted that HE be the one to sleep on the floor. The very last thing I wanted to do was put anybody out, especially since it was his room! We peacefully argued about this for more than 5 minutes. At one point, I even suggested that neither of us use the bed, and both sleep on the floor - negating my original protest of sharing the bed in the first place! Finally, I relented and took the bed so we could both just get some sleep.

The next morning, a dozen or so of us waited for someone to unlock a little shed outside the motel, a satellite of Three Eagles Outfitters (TEO), located in nearby Franklin, North Carolina, (45 minutes by car). Here, selection was limited because of the size of the building but had everything you might need and I bought stove fuel by the ounce to refill my bottle. AT hikers get a 10% discount. I was very impressed listening to the guy running the place assist a hiker who was having trouble with his complex water filter. The owner explained, in layman's terms, exactly what was being done wrong and how to use it correctly. He was also familiar with the next trail section, and gave us some pointers.

Even with the frustrations, Lone Star and I still had fun checking out Hiawassee, an official trail town endorsed by the ATC. We scarfed down some Mickey D's, our first taste of fast food since the start of our hikes. Lots of fellow travelers were also in town, and the sidewalk looked like a conveyer belt of hikers. They were easy to spot, each wearing brightly colored puffy jackets and week-old playoff beards.

Once again, the "free" shuttle ride back to the trail was falsely advertised, as the driver, "Shuttles", who could speak but hardly spoke, had handwritten, "PLEASE TIP YOUR DRIVER," across his trucker's hat. Once inside the van, we found more graffiti-like notices with the same obnoxious suggestion, "PLEASE TIP YOUR DRIVER." It was written across the back of the driver's shirt, on both sun visors, and just in case you can't take a hint, written on the back of every single seating position in the extra-long passenger van. I wasn't the only one put-off by being guilt-tripped into shelling out more money. There were at least 20 guys and 20 guys' worth of gear stuffed into that rusty tin can.

It bounced up and down the mountain, while we were all exposed to near-lethal exhaust fumes - manmade and mechanical.

At the top of the hill, I took my turn putting a $5 bill into a soiled 'Big Gulp' soda cup. At $5 a pop - these guys were making a killing off FREE shuttle rides! I felt like Chevy Chase in one of those corny 'National Lampoon's Vacation' movies, where poor Clark Griswold and his family are stuck in some rundown tourist trap, being charged extorted prices for every little thing. I knew right then and there that my budget to hike to Maine for $1 a mile was never going to cut it. Incidentally, I never saw the High School Crew again.

My trail runners hitting the dirt, it was fun starting off with a big group of hikers, amid jokes and chatter. This is how hiker bubbles start: the shuttle dropped everyone off who stayed the night in town, at the same time. Most people can hike approximately the same distance and, the way shelters are spaced, end up making camp together again. At the same time, everyone behind us bunched up and took their turn in town, to then get dropped off at that trailhead the next morning, and camp at the second shelter... and so on. Today, a few jackrabbits leapt ahead, and a tortoise or two hung back. Lone Star, his backpack lightened, sprinted ahead. The rest of us formed a conga line of sorts and made our way along the trail, like a giant human caterpillar with many legs.

Chapter 3. Dragon's Tail

Sign (and pipe) marking the state line between GA and NC. Mile marker 78.5.

First state down! Marking the Georgia/North Carolina state line, was an unassuming tree with a piece of metal plumber's pipe embedded into the bark. Maybe I was expecting more... as far as I know, the rusty pipe has no purpose. Wild Bill and his buddy Detective were the only onlookers. They were just sitting on a rock watching as hikers commemorated finishing their first state by posing for pictures - first, one-by-one, and then big group shots of everybody together. Others made video blogs, etc. We looked like a bunch of Japanese tourists, with all our cameras out snapping pics of the same thing.

Just as the Three Eagles Outfitters guy had warned, the first mountain in North Carolina was very steep and gave us a not-so-warm welcome that kept on giving. I took a breather about halfway up and talked to a man named Atlas (two hikers used that trail name this season). He was even bigger than me, at least 400 lbs., with a colorful tattoo of a globe on one leg. Panting and out of breath, we both thought we would never make it to the top! Atlas volunteered that he was stopping for the night at the next shelter about a mile away, even though it was only just past noon. Five miles a day was his max, but he had a great attitude and reasoned he'd just do what he could. Continuing, all hikers pass a twisted oak tree on Bly Gap. Other trees had metal signs indicating this area was a North Carolina Bear Sanctuary.

At last, I made it to Muskrat Creek Shelter. What's this? Oddly, leaning against a tree was a blue and silver crumpled up piece of aluminum that resembled the wrecked fender of a car. An older dude making lunch said it was a piece of wreckage from a Cessna airplane that crashed here in the 1970's. More wreckage can be found hiking up nearby Ravenrock Trail, which I hear is a great place to watch the sunset. Also, I met One Lung at the shelter. He was from Greenville, South Carolina, the same town where I live.

Numerous lookout towers, originally used to spot forest fires from high vantage points, make this section even more interesting. Atop Albert Mountain, we come across the first one. Built in the 1950's, a ranger lived in the small cabin on top while on duty. Usually locked, you can still get great views by climbing the stairs. This summit also marked the AT's 100-mile mark, resetting my personal world record for a long-distance hike. And I was just getting started!

Always a big NASCAR fan, it was Sunday so I was jonesing to at least listen to the race. Even a small FM radio might do the trick. To keep pack weight down, I had chosen not to bring one from home, but now decided to take a detour to Franklin, North Carolina. I had a free ride with a day hiker all lined up, but he canceled at the last second when we got to the trailhead parking lot. A friend picking him up had unexpectedly brought along a huge dog that took up the whole backseat and had his ginormous, drooling, barking head sticking out the back window of the compact car. Still determined, I tried hitchhiking for the first time.

Hitchhiking is a necessary part of life for thru-hikers. Some people have a gift and barely throw out a thumb and score rides straightaway. Others, like me, could stand there looking stupid for an hour before a motorist even thinks about tapping the breaks. A few cars did pass by on US-64. Some drivers waved, and one honked the horn, but no rides. Feelings of rejection grew with each passing car, and I now understood how Team Dreadlock felt the other day. After about 10 minutes of humiliation, I began questioning myself. Was I doing this wrong? Does it matter which thumb is out - right or left? Should I try moonwalking like Michael Jackson...lay down in the street pretending to be a hit-and-run victim... or do some other foolish thing to get attention? I felt like a hooker on a bad street corner.

> HIKER TIP: Hitchhiking. I really don't have much advice here, but no matter how frustrating it gets, flipping drivers the bird and cursing probably won't help. When you do get a ride, be polite and respectful.

I decided to try walking. Maybe if people saw I was trying, someone would take pity on me. Finally, about a mile down the highway, another of those long shuttle buses pulled over. It was a relief to get a ride, but didn't count as a successful hitch - as I had to pay. Prices are not cut-and-dry with these shuttle guys, and I negotiated a deal with the grey-haired old-timer, for $20, to run me to town and back.

Also belonging to "Ron Haven's Appalachian Trail Hiker Services," the same outfit that took my hard-earned cash back in Hiawassee, this van was stationed at one of their Franklin locations. Unlike the last driver, this one was talkative and, interestingly, an expert on Native American Indian mounds. He even drove me by a historical example, right in downtown Franklin, while giving me the grand tour.

Cherokee Indians built Nikwasi Mound during the Mississippian period over a thousand years ago. The obviously man-made, dome-shaped hill covered in green grass looked out of place in town next to a gas station. This mound is unique in that it has survived when many more were destroyed by excavation, construction, or flattened for agriculture. Earlier that same morning, I had found a little diamond-shaped arrowhead made of white quartz, with the tip broken off. Back home, I'm an avid collector of Indian artifacts, so all of this was a real thrill! In addition, I didn't ask, but the driver swore up and down he had seen Bigfoot in this area twice over the years!

Franklin had the ambitious town motto: "Gem Capitol of the World." You guessed it - tourism is the town's biggest industry, and features a dozen locations where you can buy buckets of dirt, *"salted"* with raw gems, to sift through. There are also a few real mines, where you can really get your hands dirty. Precious stones found here: sapphires, moonstone, garnets, crystals and ruby. The Macon County *"Gemboree"* (clever, huh?) is held here twice a year.

Town was bigger than expected, and I was surprised to learn that there are over 100 restaurants and fast food joints, including my favorite: Taco Bell! After scoffing down a couple burritos and buying a blue plastic portable AM/FM radio with ear buds for $6.00 at the dollar store, I rushed back, as instructed, to meet the van driver at the Franklin Budget Inn. But when I arrived, there were at least 20 other hikers waiting outside for the shuttle back to the trail.

Ron Haven's wife helps run everything, and with almost not enough room for everyone, got ticked-off at me for not being a guest and still wanting a ride. Ron Haven gets used municipal transit buses, donated from the county to promote the town, that have *"NC Tourism"* and *"Trail Angels"* lettered on the sides, but will only shuttle paid guests of his hotels? Lame. But my driver was a silver-tongued talker and smoothed things over with Ron's missis and everybody squeezed in for the 10 mile ride. But then, the long sliding door on the side got stuck shut and wouldn't open, trapping several people already inside. A hiker, sitting shotgun (there were two), jumped out and yanked on the handle so hard it broke off in his hand! For his superhuman strength, our rescuer should have been named after The Incredible Hulk. It took a few moments, but someone used a tire iron to pry the door open.

It was disappointing not getting to meet Ron Haven. He's the Donald Trump of trail towns and owns a chain of basic hiker hotels: 'Hiawassee Budget Inn,' 'Franklin Budget Inn,' 'Sapphire Inn' (*"...affordable rates and cheap budget discount lodging..."* 8% discount midweek) and the 'Penny Pincher Hiker's Den $ Resupply' (yeah, he spells it with a money sign. $20). What most folks don't know is that he's also a Macon County Commissioner (District 2).

> FUN FACT: Ronnie Haven, besides being a hiker hotel mogul and regional politician, is also a local professional wrestler. "The Masked SuperStar" wore a black, breast-exposing leotard with gold stars. He was also half of the Demolition Tag Team, Ax and Smash.

Unexpected shuttle ride tip requests by his employees aside, Ron has a good heart and has helped countless hikers over the years. He's one of the characters that make the trail what it is, and without him, wouldn't be the same. Ron is also known for an entertaining tongue in cheek town tour when he does the driving.

Once we arrived back atop the mountain, everyone grabbed their gear from the back of the van, and a couple of guys started freaking out about how small my backpack was. Others were laughing and making fun of the ski poles I used instead of high-dollar, telescoping, name brand hiking sticks. One scrawny dude yelled, "No one (meaning me) steal my $200 Black Diamond trekking poles!" Getting irritated, I wanted to tell him if he was so worried about it, he should write his name on them like a 4th grader does to his school lunch box.

After the van pulled away and everyone else took off walking, excited, I started getting the new FM radio ready to try out. Assuming the batteries my camera took would fit the radio as well, my heart sank when I found the gadget used smaller 'AAA' batteries! Disgusted with myself for not double-checking, I considered leaving the useless dead weight at the trailhead for someone else. Instead, I carried it with me. It would be almost a week before I learned Denny Hamlin, #11, used fuel strategy to win the race I missed.

Only a half-mile up the trail, I came across a wounded hiker, Pinwheel. He had one of those windmill toys on a stick, blue and sparkly silver, hooked to his enormous backpack. Socks and bulky army-style boots lay tossed to the ground, and there were red blisters on almost every toe, top and bottom, and on both heels. I'm not exaggerating. Pinwheel said he had already lain up in town for a week to heal, but his friends were almost 100 miles up the trail. Giving up, he resolved to hitch back to town and then home. It felt very strange just leaving him lying in the woods, but there was nothing else I could do. His troubles made my frustration over a powerless radio seem petty.

Fog lay low on the ground the next morning as I followed a cobblestone walkway to the John Byrne Memorial Fire Tower. The trail leading to the top of Wayah Bald is a little tricky where you meet a paved drive, and many hikers take a wrong turn. The CCC built this beautiful National Historic Landmark with native stone in 1937. With several incarnations over time, the original tower had been much taller, over 4 stories high, with an enclosed lookout at the top.

Underneath, there is a room with no door, but people have spray painted graffiti on the walls and it smelled like a bathroom. I guess you could still hunker down inside in the event of bad weather. Standing at a lofty 5,342', the tower was a perfect spot to take in the view. Even through the fog, mountains jutted up out of the earth, and the terrain ahead looked quite intimidating. *Update: Wildfires in 2016 have burnt the wooden roof off the tower.*

Just 10 miles away, another tower location, Wesser Bald, 4,627', was originally a fire tower, but ironically, was destroyed by arson in 1979. It was replaced with this modern viewing deck in the early 1990s, and affords 360° panoramic views of The Smoky Mountains and Fontana Lake. Here, I met Wrench & Pocahontas from Virginia. Recent high school graduates, they reminded me of the High School Crew only because of their age and statures. But where the High School Crew were novices learning as they went, Wrench & Pocahontas were bona-fide Eagle Scouts. Later, they showed me their trick hammock rigs and even taught me a few knots to improve set-up time.

Wrench was a mechanic back home and Pocahontas' trail name had also been his nickname as a kid ("Hurry up, Pocahontas!"). Both experienced hikers, they seemed surprised, even stunned, every time they saw me. One evening, soaking his feet in a stream, Wrench asked, "Man, what kind of miles are you doing?" I replied: "17, 19 and 18 the last few days." He shook his head, astounded that an old, fat dude like me could keep up with them. To be honest, we probably made about the same mileage, except it took me 12 hours to do what they did in 8!

Also in the area was ezNOMAD, from San Diego, California, a cool dude I would see from time-to-time and who always had a smile on his face. We were both 40 years old, short and stocky, but he was much fitter than me. He had sold his car and moved out of his condo to make his hike happen. Back home, he operated his own web-based business, and continued to work from trail towns with the help of a small laptop and his own mobile Wi-Fi hotspot.

The next morning, everyone was staged at a clearing to hit the Nantahala Outdoor Center, but I was craving hot food and pushed hard to get there before dark. However, the 'Companion' guidebook which I depended on, had incorrect info and everything had closed at 8:00 p.m., not 9:00 p.m. as listed!

The NOC (pronounced "knock"), sixteen miles outside Bryson City, is one of the largest outdoor recreation companies in the US, hosting over a million guests each year. First opened in 1972, this outpost is one of several now operated by the NOC. Covering over 500 acres, the giant playground for adrenaline junkies offers all kinds of adventure sports: zip lines, mountain biking, white water rafting and whatever else you can think of. Out back, dozens of brightly painted school buses were on standby, waiting to transport scores of thrill seekers to their various activities.

For lodging, you have your choice of a bunkhouse, basecamp, semi-private, or private cabins. With accommodations for up to 122 people, basecamp prices start at $39.99. Their website advertises: "Spend the night where the Appalachian Trail hikers stay!" Guests share a community building with kitchen, dining hall, grill and shower stalls. I avoid crowded bunkrooms so didn't stay there. Instead, I hiked an 8th of a mile up the next mountain and found an amazing stealth camping spot, hanging over a rock bluff, right above the NOC - just in time to watch a beautiful sunset. I had the same exact view, or better than, luxury cabins below, costing between $199-$599, for one night!

> HIKER TIP: If you start your hike early in the season, most services at the NOC will still be closed. Also, the small quick mart, Wesser General Store, had limited selection and some items were sold out.

First light, I hiked back down to the NOC and took a hobo bath in a sink inside the huge central bathroom complex, then hung out at the NOC all afternoon checking things out. The outfitter store is the first thing you see when you emerge from the woods. Selection was high-end, and employees working there were way cooler than me, but friendly. I put my high-dollar, name brand rain jacket into the hiker box. It fit fine during pre-hikes, but not anymore. So I replaced it with a much lighter, one size fits all, el cheapo poncho for $6. I also bought 'AAA' batteries for my radio, and found it received strong signal at least half the time. Out in the middle of the woods, I listened to many hours of music, weather reports, news, local programs of interest and of course, NASCAR races. Perfect! Just don't let it get wet (sad face).

Outside the outfitter, I met a tower of a man trail named "I'll Try." Well over 6 feet tall, he worked at the ATC in West Virginia. He was doing a "flip-flop," hiking north from Springer to Harpers Ferry, then starting over in Maine to hike south until he reached Harpers Ferry again.

River's End Restaurant had at least a dozen backpacks lined-up on either side of the foyer. Even though it was a chilly morning, hikers stink and were asked to leave their backpacks outside before being seated on an outside balcony. Still, I enjoyed a giant breakfast burrito and prices were about what you would expect to pay in a decent 'Applebee's' type establishment. Other interesting dishes: Sweet potato pancakes and trout cake sandwich. Sadly, an older lady from England sat crying as she told me she was getting off the trail because of a bad knee, even though her husband had continued.

Our booths were almost hanging over the river and the AT leads hikers over a bridge, right across the Nantahala River. Here, future Olympians are coached to represent the USA in kayak events. It was fun watching cute tattooed freestyle kayak girls doing their thing, executing spins, front flip moves and doing roll-overs where they completely submerge themselves underwater. Very impressive! Some were even carving waves, surf style. Gold medalists Joe Jacobi and Scott Strausbaugh both trained here, and are the only Americans to have won paddling C-2 (Barcelona, Spain, 1992). Watching the kayakers made me miss my almost daily, though much less acrobatic, kayak trips back home.

After lunch, I hiked back into the mountains to continue, and found a granite memorial for forest ranger Wade Sutton. Dated December 7th, 1968, "He gave his life suppressing a forest fire, so that you might more fully enjoy your hike along this trail."

Next was Jacob's ladder, part of the original AT and the most challenging section I had encountered thus far. Steep inclines, with several hand-over-hand rock climbs and lots of narrow ridgeline walking, surprised me. Honestly, I wasn't expecting that tuff stuff so soon.

Heavy rain showers that evening turned the trail into a stream. Thankfully, the new poncho worked well, as I walked in the storm for at least an hour before setting up camp. Hanging a hammock in the rain isn't as difficult as it sounds. I just put up my tarp first so there was a dry area to set everything up underneath and get out of my wet clothes. This hop was only 30 miles or so from the NOC to Fontana Village, our last chance for resupply before entering The Great Smoky

Mountains. Hiking along, I kept seeing something grey through the still barren trees, but couldn't figure out what it was. Getting closer, I realized the big grey blob was the massive Fontana Dam.

Arriving at a small boat marina on Fontana Lake, a bunch of hikers were sitting around waiting. One couple included an attractive younger woman named Gluten Puff, from Colorado, who was hiking with a much older dude. I overheard him talking about posting video updates to the Internet. Wanting to do the same thing, I simply asked how he uploaded them. He became very skittish around me after that, as if I was going to rob him of his fancy pants iPhone or something. Whatever, dude. Also, everyone here had their wet tents and damp sleeping bags spread out on the ground, draped over fences and hanging from tree branches to dry-out in the sun. Passersby probably thought Jacques Cousteau was having a yard sale.

Restrooms at the marina had some unexpected amenities: real indoor plumbing, a soda pop machine and power outlets that were all plugged with phone chargers. Also, hanging on the wall was a landline telephone direct-wired to the nearby resort. It's a free call, just dial "0" and someone will come collect you, answer questions and show you where everything is. The 2-mile shuttle run costs $3 each way.

While we waited our turn, out of nowhere, a police car sped by with lights flashing. Then another, and another; at least a dozen in all. A black SUV with darkened windows even did a 180° spinout right in front of us, then took-off in the opposite direction, just like Sheriff Rosco P. Coltrane chasing after "them Duke Boys" in the General Lee. We wouldn't find out until later what all the excitement was about.

Formally named "Welch Cove," Fontana Village was originally built to house the many construction workers who erected the dam. Now a totally self-contained resort, within walking distance you'll find a lodge, hotel, cabins, its own dedicated post office, laundromat, general store/grocery, ice cream shop and three restaurants. The most popular joint is called "The Pit Stop," an old gas station converted into a diner, serving hotdogs and hamburgers. If you're here during off-season, it may be the only thing open.Fontana Lodge has hiker rates if you ask: $70 rooms fit up to 4 people. That's a good deal for hikers who don't mind sharing beds. Also, Fontana General Store had a good selection of resupply – but at three-times grocery store prices. They also carry first aid and name brand socks.

Drop boxes. At the post office, I picked up a pair of boxes that Mom sent. In the case of Fontana Dam, I recommend having your box mailed to the lodge itself ($5). That way, you can retrieve it anytime, even after hours or on Sunday. You don't have to be a guest to do so. Some hikers use the food drop method for resupply instead of buying food in town. They either make up boxes before their trip or have a support person buy supplies and mail them as needed. Others do a little of both.

• **Advantages:** Choosing exactly what you want to eat. Also handy if you are vegetarian or require a special diet. Some hikers also make their own freeze-dried entrees beforehand.

• **Disadvantages:** Having to wait for post offices to open, or race to towns before they close. But if you don't open the box, you can have it forwarded (bounced), for free, to any other post office you specify.

> HIKER TIP: Organizing food drops is a great way to prepare, but leave boxes unsealed in case you need to add something before sending. Examples: A replacement pair of eyeglasses or a different food you're craving.

What was in my drop box? Most important was a new trash compactor bag to line my backpack. With these, I never had one single drop of water get into my stuff. Just roll up the top and you're good-to-go. Try and find the unscented kind so you don't smell like trail mix and roses. I tried to change it out at least once a month. To save weight, I never carried a pack cover - I just covered my pack with the back of my poncho if it was raining hard. It really won't matter if the pack itself gets wet on the outside.

> HIKER TIP: Mint candy is an excellent multi-use item. Candy satisfaction doubles as a breath freshener and is also a natural aid for upset stomachs.

Other items included: TP (toilet paper), a pair of socks, rubber bands, Ziploc bags (for repackaging) and small quantities of lip balm, aspirin, Vitamin I (Ibuprofen), and Benadryl. Edible staples consisted of the four hiker food groups: Ramen noodles, Pop Tarts, rice sides, and instant mashed potatoes. Also indispensable: tortillas, single serve containers of peanut butter, Slim Jims, candy, pepperoni, etc.

Enclosed in the second box: a letter with news from home, a self-addressed stamped envelope with blank paper to send notes back, wet-wipes, Cheez-Its, oatmeal, candy, Clif Bars and some small bags of cereal to mix with powdered milk. Mom also sent cheese dip and a jar of salsa to enjoy in town. A few of the things not used...

- **Moleskin:** I only used a little piece of moleskin, once, and it came off making a sticky mess. Unlike others, I was lucky and hardly had trouble with blisters.
- **Wet-wipes:** Everyone carries these, but I dislike their strong fragrance and don't want to be woken up getting French kissed by a bear. They are also dense, unfriendly to the environment and should be packed-out. It's easy to spot backcountry bathrooms because they are littered with "Charmin daisies," little wads of white toilet paper and wipes. Later in the hike, I did carry travel-size wipes and found them refreshing to clean my face and arms before going into towns.

> HIKER TIP: When shopping for food drop items in a grocery store, a good rule of thumb is anything not in a cooler or refrigerated machine of some kind should be safe to store and mail in a drop box.

To go with the salsa, I had to buy a two-pound bag of "Fontana Village Tortilla Chips" at the general store. One of the oldest tourist trap tricks in the book - they only carry the house brand, and it only comes in one size - HUGE. The bag was over two feet long! "Cha-Ching!" There goes another $8.00. A hiker girl was doing laundry, too, and it happened to be her birthday, so I gave her half the chips and the unopened dip. A little trail magic, hiker-to-hiker. After, I went to the beautiful lodge and used their lobby computer to thank Mother for the goodies. She asked if I wanted anything special in the next maildrop, so I asked her to send me a meatball sandwich!

After getting dropped off by the shuttle service, I was walking the road toward the dam when a parade of vintage Mini Coopers raced by all, in a row. Each of the British micro cars had white tops with the bodies painted a different color: green, blue, red and so on. Part of a car club staying at the resort, preparing for the biggest annual Mini Cooper rally in the country, with over 800 cars attending. Activities culminate with a midnight parade up and down "The Dragon's Tail."

Sports car and motorcycle enthusiasts come from all over to tackle this 11-mile stretch of US-129. A mountain road with over 300 sharp curves, blind hairpins and "...no intersecting roads or driveways to hamper your travel." Like trail names, some turns have earned imaginative monikers, such as "Hog Pen Bend," "Copperhead Corner" and "Gravity Cavity," just to name a few. Dangerous, every single mile of The Dragon has claimed at least one life; the majority were daredevil motorcycle riders pressing their limits. After 204 crashes and 6 fatalities within a 2-year period, the speed limit was reduced from 55 mph to just 30 mph, and trucks over 30 feet long are no longer allowed. The iconic winding road has also been featured in the cult classic car movies 'Thunder Road' (1958) and 'Two-Lane Blacktop' (1971).

The Fontana Hilton, compared to all the other shelters we've seen, was, by far, the nicest and sits right on the lake with a gorgeous view. The unique design is open on 2 sides and has double-decker bunks - enough to sleep 24 hikers. Only a few feet away, you'll find real flush toilets, a free hot shower, trashcans and even a solar-powered 'Power Up' station to charge your cell phone. But, because the shelter is so close to the road, it's notorious for drunken parties and police visits.

I hiked together that day with Yosemite, named after the famous national park from his home state of California. He was an easygoing, hippy-looking dude who wore a red Willie Nelson bandana. White blazes led us directly across the top of Fontana Dam, 480 feet, the tallest dam in eastern North America and 6th largest in the whole US. Built by the TVA (Tennessee Valley Authority) in the 1940's to produce electricity at the height of WWII, the massive hydroelectric dam is on the Little Tennessee River. Its construction completely inundated 4 towns and over a thousand homesteads. Cemeteries full of graves and miles of roads had to be relocated. A blue VW camper bus sat in the parking lot that I would see in many trail towns on the southern end of the Appalachians. Peeking inside, a huge map of the AT was glued to the interior roof. (This was a unique business enterprise where, Rock Ocean (Ryan) would follow the heard of hikers north and provide shuttles as needed. Unfortunately, the van suffered a blown radiator before it got out of the south.)

Hiking is free in the GSMNP. Camping is not. Thru-hiker permits cost $20 (non-refundable) and are required to camp overnight in the backcountry here. It's a huge pain, as you must fill out, beforehand, exactly which shelters you will be staying at each night. Keep a paper copy on you at all times, or risk a $125.00 ticket. Rangers do check.

Their website defines a thru-hiker as "...someone who begins and ends his/her hike at least 50 miles outside Great Smoky Mountains National Park and only travels on the AT within the park." Additionally, thru-hikers are expected to complete all 70 sum-odd miles and be out the other side of The Smokies within 8 days (not counting town stops). The general store was all out of forms and the visitor center was closed, so several hikers had to backtrack and print their forms at the lodge. I had already gotten mine from the marina kiosk and dropped them into a deposit box at the shelter. To be on the safe side, you can have the application sent to your email to print out within 30 days of your anticipated arrival; just make sure to read the directions and fine print:

www.smokiespermits.nps.gov/index.cfm?BCPermitTypeID=2/.

Yosemite and I were very excited to begin hiking the Great Smoky Mountains, but found the road to the trailhead blocked by the dozen cop cars we had seen earlier, and policemen were standing guard at the welcome sign. We were certainly not expecting to be greeted by uniformed men wearing bulletproof vests and carrying machine guns. Let the man-hunt begin!

Upcoming Shuckstack Fire Tower. Miler marker: 170.5.

Chapter 4. Top of the Carolinas

Clingmans Dome, 6,655'. Highest point on the AT.

Thru-hikers have followed painted blazes, through The Smokies, from one end to the other, since before this mountain range had even been mapped. I was also surprised to learn this is the most visited National Park in the Nation. Really! Almost 10 million people visit The Great Smoky Mountains National Park each year, twice the number of 2nd place. You might have heard of it... The Grand Canyon.

But today, all was not well in the GSMNP. Armed forest service employees checked our backcountry permits as a young woman sat on a rock, crying. Of course, Yosemite and I asked our inspectors what was wrong and were bluntly told, "Nothing to worry about." Roadblocks and police cars, swat team guys, a crying woman? With all this, they must be looking for someone. Someone dangerous. With no info to go on, we didn't know if a homicidal maniac was going to jump out of the bushes, or even what said maniac might look like. Every hiker we came across was as equally tense as we were. We traded info in bits and pieces and approached everyone with caution, wondering if they were the wanted person, or persons. These innocent day hikers probably thought the same thing about us.

After a tough 2,000+ foot climb back up into the mountains, we finally reached Shuckstack Fire Tower. All that was left of the old ranger's cabin was a crumbling stone chimney, and the tower itself was rundown and spindly. It took some nerve just to climb the rotten wooden stairs to the top. Once inside, it was scary with broken windows and big gaping holes in the roof, but 360° views were worth the risk. Yosemite didn't go up and I'm honestly surprised the tower is not condemned. Hurrying along, we watched the sun turn all kinds of entrancing colors as it descended, shining through the trees like a prism.

Tired, Yosemite and I managed to make it to Birch Spring Campsite before dark. Crowded, there were lots of tents already set-up, and I had to look hard to find a place to hang my hammock. Several other campers were all excited after just seeing a mama bear and her two cubs right on the trail. Firefighter John showed us some pics on his cell phone. Dang, we just missed it!

Out of nowhere, a sheriff, forest rangers and men wearing black riot gear and bulletproof vests descended onto the camp, some trying to hide assault-style rifles they were carrying. I was horrified by all this, as I don't care to be around guns, at all. I've never even seen weapons like these except in Hollywood movies. After checking our IDs and permits (again), they began asking questions. A couple of people didn't have permits at all and had to pay for them on the spot.

> HIKER TIP: If swat teams are searching for you with teargas and machine guns - you're just not doing it right and need to go home.

The sheriff running the show was an overweight, beer-belly guy gasping for air, and his shirt was sweat-soaked, like he had just run 10 miles. During a smoke break, he told us what all the excitement was about. And he did it with all the gusto and colorful language of Hank

Schrader from the TV show 'Breaking Bad,' except with a thick country boy accent. Finally, we learned the target of their search was a disturbed young man with the trail name... Lazy Susan.

Though underage, Lazy Susan was given wine at the Fontana Hilton the night before. He got stupid drunk and made offensive comments to the female hiker we saw crying earlier. Several men, also staying at the shelter, told him to knock it off but when the boy kept being overly rude, they called the police. As belligerent drunks do, he responded by threatening them with a knife and said, "I'll kill anyone who calls the cops!" Backed-up by TVA police, the sheriff told us they found the boy in his sleeping bag. Tackling him, they had to spray him with mace, because he wouldn't stop fighting. After getting the situation under control, they handcuffed Lazy Susan and hauled him off to jail. End of story, right? Wrong!

The young woman gave the kid a break and didn't press charges, so police had no choice but to release Lazy Susan the next day. However, before doing so, a judge forbade him from going near this woman again and he was also banned from the AT on all federal property, including the entire GSMNP. But of course, as soon as the man was released, he hitchhiked right back to the trail, found this innocent woman and threatened her yet again. This time, he added that he would kill any cops that came after him. Threatening to kill police is a felony, and to do so on federal property, just after being released on condition that you stay away is even worse. Lazy Susan was in big trouble.

Before the sheriff left, he also bragged that he'd been up and down this trail section many times. Once, he was even dropped onto the roof of the Shuckshack Fire Tower, hanging from a rope out of a helicopter! It sounded like a script from some cheesy 1970's TV cop show. Also, during the night, the bear that everyone else saw was still snooping around. She seemed to be circling the outskirts of our encampment, but never came too close.

Besides psychopaths, AK47s, police interrogations and killer bears, camping here was fun and everyone was friendly. One group of section hikers were visiting for the week, all the way from Indiana. Their leader carried a huge food bag, at least 40 liters, full of stuff! For comparison, my whole entire backpack was just 20 liters. This gentleman cooked Yosemite and I each a big Mountain House breakfast (a brand of freeze-dried meals) with ham and cheese on a wrap. MMM! Soon, I was all packed-up and ready to go, but Yosemite hadn't even gotten started yet. As things go, we just said, "See ya up the trail."

Just a few years ago, rangers counted over 1,800 bears living within the park boundaries. Today, it's estimated that less than 600 bears still make these mountains their home. But with a population density of approximately one per square mile, many hikers still see their first bear of the trip on this section. But don't get too close - it's against federal law to approach within 150 feet of a bear in the park. To keep bears and humans separated, some shelters have ugly, cyclone chain-link fences, called "bear cages," hanging across the open front wall. It must feel like sleeping in a dog kennel.

No bears for me, yet, but during the day, I did see a flock of wild turkeys and a hollow tree big enough to stand inside of. Somewhere around here, thru-hikers also cross into our third state, Tennessee - "The Volunteer State" - but we'll still wander back and forth over the state line for a couple hundred miles more.

On top of these ridges, the trail is well graded and makes for good hiking. The sky was cloudy most of the time, but I still caught a few fleeting peak-a-views and could just make out Clingmans Dome in the distance. I also had to dodge several big piles of gooey poo right on the trail and later found who was leaving all the mess - a nice couple, horseback riding. Horses are allowed in the GSMNP, but dogs are not. Thru-hikers must kennel their fury friends and make plans to pick them up on the other side. If you're caught with a dog in the park, you'll be escorted off the property and have to pay a $500 fine.

Another dumb rule is that you can't camp wherever you want. Here in the GSMNP, you MUST sleep in provided shelters; there are 12 along the roughly 70-mile stretch. The only exceptions: If "fancy hik-ers" with paid reservations show up, lowly thru-hikers have to give up their spot, OR, if the shelter is already full, then - and only then - are you allowed to pitch a tent or hang a hammock just outside the shelter. Some people like me can't physically sleep in a tiny, dirty room crowded with strangers - to the point I might have a panic attack.

To avoid this enormous inconvenience, I always dragged into shel-ters late after everyone else had already staked out their spots for the night. The sun was setting over Derrick Knob Shelter when I arrived, and as predicted, was packed. Some had already been hanging out for hours, and to keep from getting bored, made up word games to play. Settling into bed for the night, a mouse climbed into the hammock with me and scurried across my top quilt - twice! Each time I sent him flying and heard a thud in the leaves.

First to break camp in the AM, I was rewarded by seeing a pair of deer having breakfast on some green saplings. The entire GSMNP is a protected area with no hunting allowed. Because of this, wildlife has no reason to fear humans, and I stood and watched the 2 deer, just feet away. They looked up at me from time to time, but seemed almost tame and just went about their business. There were a few deer sightings back in Georgia, but they always ran away. Being this close to these wild animals, without them being afraid, was a special feeling.

"It's all downhill from here." That was the big joke after reaching the highest point on the entire AT: Clingmans Dome. Cherokee Indians believed the White Bear lived on top of this mountain, Great Chief over all bears. American settlers called it "Smoky Dome," and in 1859, it was officially named after Thomas Lanier Clingman, a General in the Civil War who explored this area for years. The massive concrete observation tower was constructed in 1959 to attract tourists and rises an additional 45 feet above the high summit of 6,655'.

Today was foggy, but it was still exciting to climb the long ramp that reminded me of a supersized Hot Wheels track. Photos are displayed on top so you can see the view - the one you would have seen in good weather. On a very clear day, you can see over 100 miles in every direction and into 7 states! Unfortunately, most days are hazy, as air pollution can choke viewing distances down to a mere 20 miles.

The foggy evergreen woodlands below smelled amazing, but Fraser Firs and Red Spruce here were dying off, due to acid rain pollution and attacks by a microscopic, non-native insect from Japan: The Balsam Woolly Adelgid. The Adelgid injects harmful toxins into the trees, cutting off vital nutrients and causing them to starve to death. There is a new method to try and save trees using a different kind of teeny-tiny beetle that preys on the Adelgid; collected from California, shipped here and placed on trees one by one - at a cost of $5 per bug!

Sightseers were milling about, and seeing my backpack, some asked, "Where did you start?" or, "How far are you going?" One lady even took my picture! Again, I just missed seeing a bear. It had crossed a half-mile long asphalt path leading down to the ranger station/gift shop. At the store, I bought a couple of GSMNP labeled candy bars and a Coke. That's about all they had for snack stuff. Chemical toilets can be found in the large parking lot and you can hitch out, if needed. I also quickly filled-out some stamped postcards that the rangers canceled with a special postmark. A cute ranger girl, with thick glasses, was wearing a green forest service coat at least two sizes too big. I developed a crush on her in about two seconds flat. She gave me an apple and said she loved thru-hikers! That made my day and caused me to blush.

Finishing up the Lazy Susan fiasco: Passing a ridgerunner going the other way, I stopped him and asked, "Have they found the trouble maker yet?" Giving me a puzzled look, he replied, "Do you know this person?" I said, "No." He asked again, "Are you sure?

Why does every single person I meet with an ounce of authority, act like this is a big secret? How frustrating! Finally, the ridgerunner gave me the cryptic, non-answer: "The young man has calmed down." I wanted to yell:

"If there's a dangerous psychopath running up and down the trail like a wild Indian, I would just like to know about it!"

Only a short time later, I stopped at the next shelter for lunch and got a surprise when I pulled back the large blue tarp covering the entrance. Sitting there was a young man who looked up at me with purple, puffy, crazy eyes. Lazy Susan! Of course, I skipped lunch but did speak with him for a moment. He had, indeed, calmed down and instead seemed sleep deprived and lethargic. He wanted to know if I had seen any police and said he was going to sue them for roughing him up. He also expected an apology from the state. When sober, the boy, barely weighing 100 lbs., didn't seem at all dangerous and even pointed me to the spring. Still, I didn't feel comfortable being alone with him and got the heck out of there.

Walking a fast pace to make distance between the boy and me, I grew very angry. First, the stuck-up ridgerunner could have at least told me I might run into the fugitive just ahead. What would have happened had I opened that tarp, not knowing it was Lazy Susan inside, and blurted out something like: "Did you hear about that crazy nut-case wanting to kill everybody?"

Then, I got angry at Lazy Susan, who frightened that poor girl and otherwise made everyone on-edge. Police finally picked him up when he entered the clearing at Clingmans Dome. Unfortunately, the young woman he threatened had already left the trail, out of fear. I filmed video updates about all this drama, but never posted them to YouTube, as I didn't want my mother and sister to worry. They were scared enough already, and had warned me about situations like this, which I shrugged off. Turns out, Mom had read about the search on Whiteblaze.com, anyway, and sent me an email warning, not knowing I was right in the middle of it.

The trail is full of wonderful people; unfortunately, a few bad eggs can ruin it for everyone. I guess you can say that's true about any-where, but I had envisioned the AT as maybe the one place where peo-ple could still go to escape the violence and intimidation of the "civi-lized" world. Guess I was wrong. With Lazy Susan back in custody, I didn't have to look over my shoulder all the time, but there was a new hindrance: chilly rain, and lots of it. To stay warm, one afternoon I sat on a damp log and cooked Ramen noodles in the pouring rain.

> FUN FACT: When Mark Sanford, South Carolina Governor 2003-2011, went "missing" for seven days, handlers said he was hiking on the AT. In reality, he was with his lover in Argentina. Sanford is still active in politics.

Crossing a fenced-in enclosure, I learned this was one of many sites in GSMNP designed to protect native plants from non-native wild boar. I personally didn't see any boar while on the AT, but they are abundant in the South and compete with indigenous black bear for food. Big game hunters, who released them into the wild for sport, first introduced "razorbacks," the fury feral ancestors of domestic pigs gone wild. Swine run together like packs of dogs and can really dig up some dirt. Prehistoric looking tusks can do damage, but, like most wildlife, are usually only aggressive toward humans during rutting season, or if they feel threatened. They don't see or climb very well, so if you're charged, try hiding behind a bush, or scrambling on top of something.

Fred is dead. An 11-year-old boy in Alabama, using a 50-caliber revolver with infrared laser sight, supposedly killed the largest wild boar ever, nicknamed "Monster Pig." It measured 9 feet long and weighed a whopping 1,051 lbs. Living up his 15 minutes of fame, the preteen prize hunter did TV interviews, was offered a camo role in the low-budget horror movie, 'The Legend of Hogzilla,' and was congratulated by country music superstar Kenny Chesney! Then, it was discovered the photos were fake and used forced-perspective to exaggerate proportions. If that wasn't low enough, the "aggressive wild boar" turned out just to be a domestic pig named "Fred," purchased and released on a commercial hunting preserve, a ploy called a "canned hunt." Former owners even said they let Fred play with their grandkids and "He craved sweet potatoes as a treat."

Per the permit I filled out, my next stop was Mount Collins Shelter, a half-mile off trail - and a half-mile back. No way was I going to hike a mile extra-credit to sleep in an overcrowded shelter, so I found a secret spot off the trail and hid out of sight. I'm not sure what the fine is for stealth camping in the GSMNP, but I took the chance and got away with it by setting up after dark. About halfway through the Smokies, with snow storms rolling in, most everyone was going to Gatlinburg.

Already a foggy and gloomy morning, it was a somber feeling reading a "Missing Person" flyer stapled to a signpost. Derek Joseph Lueking, age 24, of Tennessee, entered the GSMNP and was never seen again. Photos showed a smiling young man. Family members were in the area trying to locate him when they spotted his car at Newfound Gap. In the car, they found his wallet, credit cards and camping gear he had just bought, including a tent, sleeping bag and maps of the park. Most unsettling, they found a note reading: "Don't try to follow me."

Park Rangers took control of the investigation and determined Derek entered the woods carrying only a rain jacket, pick axe, a few pages torn from a survival manual, headlamp, granola bars and a 'Bear Grylls' multi tool. Not gear enough for freezing nights at high elevation. Park employees and dog teams covered 70 miles of trail, and AT hikers were asked to keep an eye out. It's entirely possible Derek simply hitched out to start a new life somewhere else, or, he's still in the woods.

Continuing into the parking lot area of Newfound Gap, a group of section hikers had just been dropped off. One blew a few ceremonial notes into a 6-foot long bullhorn, their tradition before beginning a hike. I only stood in the drizzle a few minutes when the group's driver picked me up. My first real hitch! The twisty road ran along a beautiful creek and through several tunnels carved out of the mountainside.

My trail angel suggested The Grand Prix Motel, famous for being hiker friendly. I was a little concerned, seeing some boarded-up windows and a "FOR SALE" sign out front, but a neon sign flashed "vacancy." Still, Princess Diana, a heavy set but very nice woman, had bad news. She had just rented out the last room. Just then, I heard someone yell "LONER!" It was my buddy, Lone Star, and he offered to again share his room with me. This time, our pad had a big TV, kitchen with full size refrigerator, stove, pots and pans and a dining room table. Most important - two queen-size beds. We split the bill for just $17 each!

Once an impressive hotel built by the billionaire Hiltons in the 1960s, The Grand Prix had fallen on hard times. The neatest feature was a shamrock shaped swimming pool ("Deepest in Gatlinburg"), now drained of water. Our Grand Prix was definitely in the rundown part of town, hence the price. If you're looking for something nicer, the Las Vegas-like strip has all manner of hotels (over 100) and price ranges from which to choose - ghetto to luxury. *Update: After many years of hosting thru-hikes, The Grand Prix has now closed forever.*

There were a couple of computers in the office, but I found a line of hikers already waiting their turn to play solitaire or look-up weather forecasts, so I decided to take the bus to Wally World and check prices on laptops. The bus makes regular stops at the front door of the hotel. Adding to the gimmicky town vibe, the fleet of 24 green and yellow buses resembles old-time trolleys. This brought back memories, as my Papa rode them for hours when we visited here when I was a kid. Even with several transfers, it was fun traveling to nearby Pigeon Forge, and I saw lots of the area this way. The two towns are next to each other and are like the Myrtle Beach of the mountains, with many over-the-top attractions and activities: go-cart tracks, putt-putt, waterparks, country music halls, etc. Most interesting was a life-size Titanic and a science building built upside down like a tornado had tossed it.

In contrast, Wally World looked the same as in any normal town. I bit the bullet and bought the smallest laptop they had. Dropping $300 was not in the budget, but I was desperate and it was a huge relief to finally get videos online to share with family, friends and anyone else who wanted to follow along.

Waiting for the bus, I pigged out on CICI's pizza buffet. This turned out to be my only chance to indulge my favorite pizza place during my time on the trail. I also ran into the kid who cracked on my ski poles back in Franklin. He was getting off the trail because he had just gotten news his girlfriend back home was pregnant. I bet his $200 Black Diamond Trekking poles, his pride and joy, were the first thing sold to pay for baby stuff.

The next morning, it was 9° at Newfound Gap, and we could see snow on the mountaintops. A few brave hikers did try to go up to the trail, but came right back down because the wind was blowing sideways. We didn't blame them one bit and stayed in Gatlinburg another night. My first real zero day! There was also a story going around about a family of hikers, including several small children, The Rainforests, who had to be rescued because their parents were unprepared and brought cheap equipment. This family had gotten most of their funding for their thru-hike attempt through a "Go-Fund-Me" type donation website, and many donors were ticked-off when the family left the trail without a word or refund, and posted Facebook photos of everyone having fun at Disney World instead!

The next day I took the trolley back to the post office and packed my PC in a Priority box, using free advertising newspapers. I bounced it up the trail and would use it again and again. The cost to do this was about $10 every 2 - 3 weeks. After, Lone Star and I set off to explore town, but first we enjoyed a huge breakfast of pancakes and steak rancheros. Yes, I ate two plates full of food and took a picture to prove it (when hungry hikers take photos of food, it's called "hiker porn.") The strip had more than enough crazy, sensory-overload stuff to see without paying to go inside the attractions. Several museums are owned by 'Ripley's Believe It or Not,' with creepy talking robotic figures, like those found singing and dancing at Chuck E. Cheese.

• **Hollywood Star Cars** featured Herbie the Love Bug, Batmobile, Ghostbusters Ecto-1, 'Back to the Future' DeLorean and more.

- **Ripley's Aquarium:** It was fun watching penguins through an outside window, play around on the ice. You can even pay to "sleep with the sharks" in hotel rooms/fish tanks with glass walls.
- **World's Largest Amazing Mirror Maze:** Something fun to do for under $10. 3D glasses extra.
- **Bubba Gump Shrimp:** Restaurant inspired by 'Forrest Gump.'
- **Cooter's Place:** This free museum was full of toys and memorabilia from the 1980's TV show, 'The Dukes of Hazzard.' The centerpiece was a real, orange General Lee car! The Dukes, now politically incorrect, is no longer on TV. What? Everyone loves Daisy Duke!

> FUN FACT: Stars John Schneider and Tom Wopat left the Dukes briefly due to disagreements over merchandise royalties. When ratings tanked, they returned and their clone cousins were written out by the first commercial.

That afternoon, I walked with Lone Star, Cat in the Hat, ezNOMAD and others for the shuttle ride back up to the trailhead. Lone Star, further lightening his backpack, started knocking off huge 30 mile days, and this would be the last time I would see my friend. He was a good guy who took pictures of everyone he met. Once, I even saw him give 2 section-hiking college girls all his food because they had run out. He had made plans to have his high-end racing bike sent to Maine when he finished the trail, so he could pedal home to Texas, but there was no sign of him after Hot Springs. Long live Lone Star!

During peak season, Cherokee Transit bus, operated by the Eastern Band of Cherokee Indians, picks up hikers in Gatlinburg twice a day, 6 days a week, and carries them back to the trail, for $5 each. Just for fun, I took the roundtrip down the other side of the mountain to check out Cherokee, North Carolina. Our driver happened to be a former thru-hiker named Mountainside, and told lots of funny stories. A pair of grey-haired old ladies, heading to the casino, laughed their heads off the whole way. Besides slot machines and blackjack, Harrah's Casino offers luxury suites and lots of buffets. There are little motels, too, if you want a different day off without the Las Vegas lights of Gatlinburg, and I saw a few hikers walking around. I asked my driver about the skateboard park and, ahead of schedule, he dropped me off there for a half-hour. Borrowing a board, I took a few easy runs in the beginner section and had fun hanging out with locals until my ride pulled up and honked the horn.

It was getting late and the usually crowded parking lot at Newfound Gap was deserted. I admit it felt weird walking back into the quiet woods after being in town for 2 days. I was also welcomed with snow! Most had melted but it was still fun hiking in it as I enjoyed a custom trail mix I made with peanut M&Ms, almonds, cashews and gumdrops.

Ice Water Spring Shelter was clouded-in and very cold at high elevation, 5,939'. As usual, I set up my hammock, then retreated inside the shelter for a bit. Hiker rule - he who sits closest to the fire must tend to it. I fulfilled my job by poking the sticks around every once in a while. There was a big, green tarp over the front of the shelter to keep heat in, and good conversation with a whole new hiker bubble. A friendly fellow from Florida, Blue Sky, was the only other person to brave the elements, sleeping in his tent outside.

> HIKER TIP: Sleeping bags are NOT electric blankets and only work by insulating body heat. I cheated by filling drinking bottles with warm water to use as makeshift hot-water bottles. Just make sure caps are tight!

Overnight lows dropped to around 17°, the coldest I would experience during my trek, but I stayed warm and toasty. Snowflakes softly collected on my tarp, but I only had to knock the buildup off a few times. Early birds, starting in February or even March, can find temps below zero, and may have to posthole through knee-high snowdrifts. They must take special precautions by carrying warmer clothing, lower rated sleeping bags, insulated boots and even crampons (ice spikes). Ice storms can be very dangerous, too, because rain turns to ice as it falls, blanketing the ground, trees and branches.

A short side trail led to Charlie's Bunion. This rocky protuberance is rare in these otherwise forested mountains, and is part of a range called "The Sawteeth." At 5,565', views are some of the best in the GSMNP. Mountaineer Horace Kephart named this pointy bump after his friend's...foot problem. Kephart was a very interesting person in his own right, and led the crew that built the original AT through this section and was inducted into the Appalachian Trail Hall of Fame, 2016.

Johnathan was the unofficial leader of a big group who had become friends, including: Jumanji, Crocatowie, Samson and others. Very enthusiastic, he led the way navigating over trees knocked down by the weekend snow storms. Johnathan didn't have a trail name, but I always called him "Fire-fighter John." That was his profession back home in Georgia.

Snow still survived in a few shady places, and someone left a tiny snowman, about the size of a soda can, on top of a tree stump. Setting-up camp outside Tri-Corner Knob Shelter, 5,911', I still had a few miles left in the tank, but was restricted by the permit system.

Come morning, I had all my gear packed up, backpack on and was about to leave when a heavy hailstorm began. I ducked for cover under the shelter's porch, just before quarter-sized balls of ice bombarded the old tin roof, making a loud racket. Jumanji, a Native American gentle giant originally from North Dakota and now living in Wisconsin, braved the pelting hail to retrieve a big chunk so I could get a picture, but it turned out just to be a rock. This turned out to be the first of three hail storms that day, and ice cube-sized hail hurt when they hit you in the head!

During the day, I stumbled upon rusty metal and green pieces of pop-riveted aluminum strewn over a large area. Some parts were as big as cars and had stenciled numbers. After a few moments, I realized this was debris field of a crashed airplane. I wasn't expecting this and had no idea when it happened. No one could have survived. Later, I asked other hikers if they knew anything about it and everyone else had walked right by. YouTuber Webrider321 provided this info: "We think it is from an Air Force C-141B that crashed 31 August, 1982, from Charleston AFB, SC. Nine crewmembers were never recovered and there is no monument."

Raining off-and-on most of the day, I wore my poncho over my head, but the radio still got wet and never worked again. Even worse, somewhere along the way, I made a wrong turn and hiked down a side trail for at least a half hour. Everyone gets lost at some point or another, and it's tempting to keep going, thinking white blazes will show up again. Getting worried, I finally turned around and found my way.

> HIKER TIP: The AT is marked both North and South. If you don't see a white blaze for a while, look on the opposite side of trees. If lost, backtrack up the path you are on. NEVER start bushwhacking. You can't get lost in the woods, if you don't go in the woods.

I still managed a respectable 17 mile day, but because of the detour, I was the first person to leave Tri-Corner Knob and the last to arrive at Davenport Gap Shelter, also known as the "Smokies Sheraton." Here, a pipe delivered fresh spring water into a little pool. I was covered in mud up to my ankles and hosed myself off in the freezing water, feet and all. Firefighter John joked, "It's bad when the best thing to do after hiking in the rain is pour more cold water on yourself!"

The next day, it was a huge relief to make it to the road marking the official property boundary of the GSMNP. I sat down with Firefighter John's crew waiting for others in their group. We clapped and cheered like fans watching a marathon as each emerged from the woods, one by one, running and yelling with their hiking poles raised over their heads. Crocatowie, this stocky fellow long-jumped across the imaginary finish line, threw down his backpack and extended his middle finger toward the mountains we had just conquered.

Chapter 5. Dancing with Rattlesnakes

Camping on big bald. The crazy thundercloud missed us.

Almost on cue, a pickup truck from Standing Bear Farm pulled up. Seeing our celebration, Rocket Man & Maria grinned and asked, "Anybody wanna slackpack?" Slackpacking is hiking without carrying your heavy backpack; in this case, hikers reunited with their gear at the hostel 3 miles away. Running and jumping over fallen logs, the others made a game of it and each sped past with big smiles on their faces! Everyone went for it, except me, but there's no shame in slackpacking. When asked about this, my friend Fatherman (FM) would say, "I hiked all 2,185 miles - my backpack didn't." It can make hiking more fun and is especially useful for injured hikers to get in some light miles while recovering.

> HIKER TIP: Purists insist on walking by every white blaze of the official AT without skipping sections, no matter how small. Blue blazers joke - "Purists are hikers who can't read maps."

Crossing Pigeon River over a crumbling, little-used bridge, a few of us watched inflatable rafts pass beneath us filled with white-water rafting tourists. Hardly more than a dingy, one was outfitted by a crew of amateurs wearing white helmets and bright orange life vests. Bobbing up and down while doing continuous 360's, their helpless river guide yelled instructions in vain. After crossing Interstate 40, up a tall stone stairway and along a gravel road, we finally arrived at Standing Bear where we were welcomed with open arms.

A "must see" stop on the AT, Standing Bear is considered a rite of passage for thru-hikers. Once a turn of the century homestead, this hippy commune-feeling hostel offers country accommodations and a great atmosphere: board n' batten planked cabins, hand-press washing machine, $15 bunkbeds and a wishing well next to the fire pit where everyone hangs out, usually while someone plays guitar. A stand-alone cottage, straddling a creek with water rushing underneath, was also available for rent. Adding to the ambiance, there is an outdoor shower if you're not too shy. I chose the indoor stall. Not the cleanest in the world, it was lit only by trippy sunlight beer bottle art built into a wall, handiwork of Rocket Man. It even had an AT logo incorporated into the design.

Perched on a hill, Maria's resupply room was had goods and supplies displayed on shelves and in showcases with old windowpanes for doors. Fair prices and you pay by the honor system (just check the dates.) Used jackets and a few bits of gear hung on the walls, but I'm not sure why they stocked canned goods - way too heavy to carry. Another hiker bluntly asked our host for marijuana as casually as one might ask for Pop-Tarts. She said no but I got the feeling he may have been more successful, or at least pointed in the right direction, had he been a little more discreet.

DiGiorno pizzas are the traditional treats here, and there was even a little square oven just big enough to hold one pie. Operating instructions were written on the wall, and an arrow pointed to a dedicated breaker box marked "PIZZA SWITCH." I wanted a pie, but they take 15 minutes to cook and 3 others were already waiting in line. Jumanji at least let me take a picture of his pizza. It looked delicious covered in pepperoni and melted cheese. I settled for microwave corndogs.

A common area had books to borrow and binders full of summit photos from past visitors. A pieced-together ghetto computer was stored in a small shed the size of an overgrown phone booth. The computer had stickers and graffiti covering both sides, was missing the compartment doors and had lines strobing up and down the screen. It still worked - very slowly. This was my first chance to see if anyone was watching my videos, and I enjoyed reading and replying to comments and questions. I paid $5 to rent the computer for an hour, but as usual, another hiker soon came knocking. I was encouraged to stay the night but kept on trucking.

> HIKER TIP: Dogs are not allowed in the GSMNP, so the nice folks at Standing Bear also kennel pets. They can pick-up or drop-off your fury friends at Fontana Dam and board them for up to 7 days. Cost: around $240.

The next afternoon, I picked up the pace when a southbound day hiker told me there was trail magic at the next gap. There, I found trail angels had set up 3 large tents, a grill, lawn chairs, multiple coolers...you name it - so much stuff it took a truck and a double-axle trailer to haul it all! Our hosts, Ox and Rat Patrol, were both former thru-hikers who told funny stories to the dozen or so of us gathered around. I enjoyed cheeseburgers, baked beans, chips, Girl Scout cookies, root beer and fresh strawberries. All delicious! I had heard of trail magic (TM) before but never expected all this.

"Trail magic" can be full-on hiker-feeds, a cooler of drinks left at a trailhead, or something as simple as an apple. "Trail Angels" are anyone who help hikers along by providing food, a ride to town, directions, etc. I've even heard of trail angels picking up stinky hikers they've never met, driving them to their homes for dinner, letting them shower and stay the night - then returning them to the trail in the morning. Conversely, "Trail Devils" slow thru-hikers down. They may also have good intentions, but usually suck you in with beer and partying. Angels and magic, these terms originated from when long distance hikers needed real help to complete thru-hikes, but are now commonplace. "Real trail magic" does still exist, like when a car picks you up in the pouring rain the second you pop out of the woods.

Next stop: Max Patch, 4,629'. Granddaddy of a series called the "Southern Balds." Our narrow path across this long clearing has been made bare by thousands of hikers following white blazes painted on wooden posts. Instead, I kicked off my shoes and gave my tired feet a break, walking in the cool grass. With perfect weather, there were sweeping vistas in all directions. It's said Native American Indians first created these balds with fires that drove wildlife down the mountainsides toward awaiting hunters. Until recently, they remained clear after decades of livestock grazing, a practice no longer permitted by North Carolina forestry regulations. Now, a large tractor and mower keep this enormous bald... well... bald.

During the previous winter, vandals on ATVs broke through a locked gate and tore deep ruts into the grass, causing damage that took over 300 man-hours to repair. A 24-year-old man was sentenced to 90 days in jail and ordered to pay restitution. Thanks to this loser and his loser friends, there are now further restrictions for all visitors to this magical place. Once a popular venue to watch sunsets and sunrises, overnight camping has been outlawed.

Now out of the Smokies, there seemed to be dogs everywhere. Most were friendly and well-behaved. But not all. Even though camping is illegal on Max Patch, there was a tent that looked like it had been there for a while, as heavy cast iron cooking pans sat near a smoldering fire (also prohibited here). Not the sharpest knife in the drawer, with 392 acres of green grass to choose from, the occupant made camp literality inches from the tread way. Walking by minding my own business, I startled an unseen white pit bull. It lunged at me barking furiously! Thankfully, it was on a rope tied to a stake in the ground. Still, it scared the heck out of me. The owner yelled at the demon dog, but didn't bother getting up, and probably cussed every hiker that walked by - like we're the assholes.

Sadly, I saw a news story about a young woman who was killed here by lightning while day hiking, only moments before her boyfriend planned to propose. He was injured also, but put the ring on her finger as paramedics tried to revive her.

Roaring Fork Shelter's logbook contained an entry left by my buddy, Lone Star. He always wrote his name, one word over the other, and with a star in the middle like a sheriff's badge.

Logbooks and pen are located at each shelter for anyone to sign when camping or just passing through. Logbooks may also be found at hostels or other places hikers visit. Leave your trail name, date and what direction you're headed: SOBO for southbound, NOBO for northbound (some thru-hikers prefer GAME for Georgia to Maine, or MEGA for Maine to Georgia.) Write something interesting about your day, leave notes for friends, report problems on the trail, post info about water sources, etc. It can be as long or short as you like. Sometimes logbooks, or word of mouth, are the only way you can communicate out here.

I found these personal reflections interesting and fun to read and often scanned old pages, some dating back to the start of the hiking season. Besides using journals to read about how friends up and down the trail, are managing, these records can be helpful clues, if someone gets lost, by pinpointing his/her last known location. This register also had entries about the poor condition of the dirty shelter and a mice infestation. Many complained that it was hard to sleep here, with owls screeching all through the night, waiting for a meal. In fact, I did see a small owl flying low overhead in this area, using the clearing of the trail to navigate through the forest, thick with trees.

> *HIKER TIP: Some hikers leave their unique mark in logbooks, drawing cartoons, writing jokes, or preaching bible verses. Others carried colored markers, ink stamps, or preprinted stickers.*

My campsite that night was obviously a former home place with foundation stones, old tin cans and remnants of a leather shoe. Weather looked clear at sunset - no clouds and lots of stars - so there was no need for my tarp. I slept like a baby.

On a large rock, a bronze marker similar to the one on Springer Mountain, welcomed us to Hot Springs, North Carolina. At first glance the two plaques look identical, but upon closer inspection, you'll see this one features a much woollier man with a long beard and larger backpack.

You can't miss Laughing Heart Hostel, Chuck Norris, who runs the business with his wife, Tigger, called at me like a carnival barker. His tactic worked as I was nursing a sore ankle and ready for a rest. I had broken it skateboarding 10 years before and it was giving me some trouble.

Laughing Heart. A brief history: the beautiful castle-looking lodge was built in 1892. Changing hands, the Jesuits Catholic Society used the property as a sanctuary for over 50 years until this season, when the property was sold again. The lodge is now a yoga retreat, and the hostel, first started in 1970, reopened to board hikers. There wasn't even time to list it in the guidebooks for their opening season; but it is there now. Alcohol free, the hostel had a quiet atmosphere. I rented a barebones private room and a pillow for $30 (bring your sleeping bag), but the $20 bunkroom would have been cheaper. Sorry to sound antisocial, but, as a loner, I prefer a room to myself. I did enjoy meeting other boarders; among them: JK & Navigator - a friendly middle-aged couple from Florida recovering from bad colds, a homeless man doing work for stay while on a bicycle trip, and a fella trail named: Six-Six - the answer to a common question, "How tall are you?" There was time to work on my shoes, adding duct tape to a few holes and cutting down the sunshade I used for foot insulation. I then die-cut the excess material into a pair of custom shoe insoles. Yes, better ones can be bought for $1, but that's how I roll. I did buy a replacement radio and correct batteries.

Known as "Warm Springs" until 1886, the town is famous for natural pools of bubbling water, with temps up to 100° - the only of its kind in North Carolina. Proof Cherokee Indians visited in earlier times, local residents often find clay pottery shards and other artifacts in their flower gardens. Travelers still come from all over, looking for rest and recuperation, and the population swells with weary hikers every spring. It's an official ATC trail community, with silver diamond-shaped markers cast into the sidewalk, leading hikers down Bridge Street. The only thing missing is a full-blown grocery store, making this a perfect candidate for a mail drop, or you can buy resupply at the dollar store.

Unfortunately, this area has a dark history as well. When World War I was first declared, 2,700 German naval officers were unlucky to be docked in N.Y. Harbor. Transported to Hot Springs by train, they were interned at the spa's hotel, leased to the US government. Oddly, a succession of 4 fancy hotels have burned down here over the years.

Hot Springs Resort has been a health spa for many years. Typical rejuvenation treatments once lasted 3 weeks and included baths in the hot springs with daily therapeutic massages. Today, the average hiker stays in town a day or two, enjoying the spring's magical mineral waters, now piped into modern hot tubs. Cabins $50-$72 + $5 EAP.

Another option for a place to stay is Elmer's Sunnybank Inn, also known as "The Balladry House," a beautiful white Victorian dating back to 1840 and on the National Registry of Historic Places. Elmer Hall purchased the Inn and has maintained it since 1978. ezNOMAD stayed the night. A rock musician during college, he was looking forward to the "music room," but found some of the instruments in poor condition. Cost: Shared rooms $20 per person, home cooked organic vegetarian meals: breakfast $6, dinner $10. Sunnybank has been open to hikers since 1948 when the very first thru-hiker, Earl Shaffer, stopped for a rest.

Shaffer was a remarkable man. The seed to thru-hike the AT was planted when he read an article written by Myron Avery, who declared, "It is impossible for any hiker to complete the entire trail in one trip." After watching his best friend die on Iwo Jima, Shaffer "walked the Army out of his system." Wearing his old army boots, using primitive gear and having to bushwhack much of his way, Shaffer became the very first person to complete a successful thru-hike of the AT, from one end to the other.

At first, this unprecedented accomplishment was met with disbelief, but later confirmed, after submitting his diary and photos from his trip, including landmarks and trailhead signs. It's exciting to think this was perhaps the very first AT blog! Long before today's technology of GoPros and YouTube, smartphones and Trail Journals, hikers documented their adventures with paper and pencil, 35 mm cameras (without a screen to review pics) and film that might not be developed for 6 months to even see if the pictures came out!

Earl returned in 1965 to complete a second thru-hike, walking south, and again in 1998. At age 79, this made him the oldest person to thru-hike the AT (since surpassed in 2004). Shaffer has been inducted into the AT Hall of Fame and chronicled his adventures in his book, entitled, 'Walking with Spring.'

> FUN FACT: In 1936, 6 boy scouts from New York claimed THEY were the first to complete a thru-hike of the AT by walking from Maine to Georgia in 121-days. This was never verified and most certainly a hoax.

Making a few more stops...The Wash Tub is where everyone does their laundry. A yellow piece of construction paper on the door warns:

"Absolutely <u>NO</u> <u>ALCOHOL</u> or <u>DRUGS</u> on premises. <u>This</u> <u>means</u> <u>you!</u>"

Besides that, it was hiker friendly and there is even a hiker box inside, usually found at hostels. While using some duct tape, I watched a local man park his truck outside, walk in to check the box, take some heavy mountain climbing rope & carabiners, then leave.

Like most trail towns, Hot Springs is also popular with the motorcycle culture. One bike I saw was decorated with a colorful ceramic tile mosaic. Scary-looking, the rider smiled and was happy to pose for a picture. All the bikers I met on my trip were friendly and just doing their own thing.

Smoky Mountain Diner's décor included AT related newspaper articles, posters and summit photos. Best of all was the awesome food. So good, I ate there twice! For dinner, I devoured a salad with grilled chicken and came back again for bacon and scrambled eggs the next morning. Super nice people, too. I saw that classic Bahama Blue VW bus again, this time parked in front of Bluff Mountain Outfitter's. The store was well stocked, but my only purchase was a Popsicle in the shape of Homer Simpson. There was also a cool, whitewater rafting-themed pinball machine upstairs. Outside, I said goodbye to Angie, a pretty girl my age from Asheville, North Carolina, that I had met a few days before. She was hiking with her puppy, Maggie, but their hike ended in Hot Springs, and were waiting for their ride.

Hikers were dropping like flies. I heard Wrench broke his foot climbing the mountain out of town, and his much smaller buddy, Pocahontas, had to carry him back down. Also, I didn't know it at the time, but it would be a long time before I would see Firefighter John again and what was left of his crew. I was sorry to hear Jumanji left the trail, but instead took his family to Las Vegas. Great guy! Then, at Hot Springs Library, a man - all the way from Australia - was printing out his plane ticket home because of troublesome knees. Leading up to Hot Springs, he had done two 20 mile days in a row. Too many miles, too soon, for the terrain we'd been encountering. He had already rested here for almost a week before giving up.

It's easy to get a Superman complex and push those macho, big mile days before we're fully conditioned for it. I've seen it before and have done it myself during pre-hikes. The knees are the largest joint in the body, and almost every hiker experiences knee pain at some point, many of which, unfortunately, end many thru-hikes. Some tips...

- **If you feel pain,** take a rest and consider stopping for the night.
- **If pain continues,** or the knee becomes swollen, apply ice.
- **Hot showers,** tobacco and alcohol increase swelling.
- **Wrap** with elastic bandage to prevent swelling (not support).
- **See a doctor** if you need to use the wrap for more than 72 hours.

> *HIKER TIP: A swollen knee is not going to heal itself by doing more hiking.*

Involuntary peer-pressure. Injuries can happen even easier if you're hiking with friends, because you can't just stop when you feel something is wrong. No one wants to be "that guy" who slows down the entire group. Your buddies don't want you to fall behind, or injure yourself. But, on the other hand, we're all on this mission to make forward progress. Also, it may seem early to think about, but rangers do close the trail up Mount Katahdin in mid-October. Any of these deadlines can influence the pace of the whole crowd. It's nothing personal, but sometimes the pack continues without you, and feelings do get hurt. Not wanting to lose your friends, you may try to "gut it out" and keep pace. Don't do it! Pushing through pain can do real damage that may end your thru-hike for good, or worse, require surgery. If the pain continues, take a few days off to heal. A constructive way to use this downtime may be to inventory your gear and jettison excess pack weight. When ready, you can then resume hiking, and build up your trail legs at your own pace. However, if the group aspect is most important to you, skip up the trail to meet your buds. You can always come back later and make-up that skipped section - or not. Honestly, lots of hikers have been awarded "2000 Miler" patches, who, for whatever reason, missed a few white blazes.

Leaving town after waiting for a cargo train to cross the road, a flyer on a telephone pole presented a new challenge...

"Appalachian Trail Angels, Sam's Gap I-26 (only 43 miles away!) Wednesday, May 2, 10:00 - 3:00 Hamburgers, Hotdogs, Drinks, Chips, etc. All Hikers Welcome!"

At first, 43 miles in 2½ days by lunchtime sounded farfetched, but after studying my guidebook, it looked almost possible. And the race was on! Crossing the French Broad River, stealth camping spots can be found along the river banks; just pay attention to the white blazes. I ended up way off trail and had to backtrack again. Halfway up the mountain, I stopped at Lover's Leap Rock for a break. The view from the cliff - overlooking Hot Springs - was a good place to reflect on my time in town.

Rattlesnakes. Back on my way, I had my first encounter with a rattlesnake. Thank you to whoever left sticks blocking the trail so the next hiker wouldn't step on this rattler having his chipmunk lunch! Patterns on the snake's skin blended-in perfectly with leaves until a few rattles of his tail pinpointed his location. Like staring at those optical illusion magic eye puzzles, it stuck out clearly when you knew where to look. Not wanting anyone else to come by, not expecting it or even kill it, I used my hiking pole to toss the stunned chipmunk off trail, and the snake followed. The hikers were safe...the snake was safe...the chipmunk, was not safe.

Eastern timber rattlers are common along most of the AT, but far rarer in northern states. I would see 5 during my hike, but I have never heard of an AT hiker being bit by one. Snakes would prefer to never interact with humans at all; it is us who are encroaching on their territory. Adults weigh up to 10 lbs. and grow more than 30 inches long, with the record being a reported 74 inches. Snakes hibernate during winter months, in dens, sometimes with other snake species. For food, they eat rodents, small birds, frogs and even other snakes. Long fangs and potent venom makes rattlesnakes potentially dangerous. However, they usually alert you to their presence, and give you plenty of warning, by rattling buttons on their tails. Be especially careful of a coiled-up snake - they can strike amazingly far and much faster than you can jump out of the way.

Injury can include puncture wounds, severe swelling, vomiting, paralysis and even death. Victims may show no symptoms at first, then suddenly go into shock or have difficulty breathing, so anyone bitten by a poisonous snake should get to a hospital immediately. Advice on the Internet differs, but here's some general info...

- **Move away** from the rattlesnake in case it strikes again.
- **Stay calm**. Increased heartrate spreads venom faster. However, if alone, it's more important to seek help.
- **Carry the victim** out if possible.
- **Remove constrictive** clothing or jewelry around swelling.
- **Keep the bitten area** below your heart.
- **Only suck out venom** if you have a specially made device.
- **Do not consume anything,** including water or medications.

A short blue blaze led to Rich Mountain Fire Tower, 3,643', built by the US Forest Service in 1932. After ascending flights of stairs - 33 feet up - I found great views and a resourceful hammock camper. Almost giddy, this young man looked very excited to be spending his night at the top! In the next section, I met a cute red headed girl who was asking around where he was. She had even yellow blazed up the trail to catch up to him. Ah, trail love.

What is blazing? Here are some examples...

- **Blue blazing:** Using side trails as shortcuts.
- **Yellow blazing:** Bypassing trail miles in a vehicle.
- **Aquablazing:** Skipping miles by canoe, kayak, etc.
- **Pink blazing:** Rushing to follow a potential love interest.
- **Brown blazing:** Hiking privy to privy with stomach problems.
- **Beer blazing:** Hiking to the next quick mart, bar, or party.
- **Green blazing:** Taking "safety meeting" breaks to smoke pot.
- **Gold blazing:** High roller fancy hikers who blow money.
- **Red blazing:** Hiking while bleeding or injured.
- **Rescue blazing:** Getting helped off trail to safety.

Spring Mountain Shelter is where I met D-Tour for the first time. This laidback fellow was from New Jersey. He had started his hike a couple of weeks before me, but had just returned after taking time-off to heal a sprained ankle. He was hoping to catch up to friends he met at the start. That night, my hammock and tarp were situated perfectly to watch the lightbulb of the moon traveling in an ark across the dark sky.

In the morning, Spring was finally upon us, and hikers were greeted with green grass and tiny white flowers - thousands of them - on either side of the trail. Also taking a walk was a thick centipede-looking bug, yellow and black with many legs and a hard shell like a beetle. After taking my first break near an abandoned tobacco barn covered in vines, I tackled the exposed ridgeline trail over Whiterock Cliff. Very narrow and always windy, an alternate blue blazed trail skirts lower around the mountain and still counts as official AT miles during bad weather. Passing a rock with "300 miles" carved into it, the incentive of TM helped me make my first 20-mile day!

During the American Civil War, divided loyalties caused a lot of heartbreak in these hills. Just north of Big Butt Mountain is Shelton Graves. Carved gravestones, placed here by the War Department, mark the burial site of William and David Shelton, who, although they lived in Madison County, North Carolina, joined and fought alongside the Union Army. While traveling home to visit family in 1863, they were ambushed and killed by Confederates - possibly neighbors - who resented their fighting for the Yanks. Millard Haire, the Shelton's 13-year-old cousin, who may have been scouting their way across the range, was also killed; his headstone was left by relatives. The fictional movie 'Cold Mountain,' staring Nicole Kidman and Jude Law, was partially based on real events that happened here.

Tired, I made camp in the large clearing within sight of the burials, but a respectful distance away. Trying to sleep, I kept hearing spooky whistling noises with the breeze. *What is that sound?* I even got up twice in the middle of the night to investigate. By morning, I found out the creepy noise was a whirligig American flag. I'm not sure if this place is haunted at night, but if it was, I slept right through it! I do have a few ghost stories to tell, that I'll share up the trail.

Getting up early and retrieving my food bag from a tree, my Snickers bars were frozen solid, so I put them in my pocket to thaw because I needed the extra energy. There was still 15½ hard miles to the TM, including several big ups and downs. Fifteen miles is a big deal for me on a good day, and I had it all to do before lunch! Having seen the posted signs, all the other hikers who passed that day were also talking about the trail magic. Speed walking, I was making good time until I hit Frozen Knob, 4,579'. This one slowed me down bigtime and really had me doubting myself. Hot, tired and ready to give up, D-Tour found me taking a break and winded, but encouraged me that we could make it, and hiked the last few miles together.

We made it! At Sam's Gap, walking under the US- I-26 highway overpass toward the crowd, we could see how large a hiker bubble we were in. Enjoying the hiker feed were at least 2 dozen people. These were all NOBO thru-hikers, most of whom had just tossed their backpacks into one big pile and dug into the grub. Pushing those extra miles was worth it as our trail angels had made hotdogs and hamburgers with all the fixings, and everybody pigged out until we were stuffed! Those who already had their fill were lying down in the grass like beached whales, rubbing their bellies. Others traded stories, or played guitar. Our angels even had bags of trail mix and candy made-up for us to carry and enjoy later. Very thoughtful.

After, I took a long break on top of the next hill, just resting in the grass, using my backpack as a pillow. I was hoping to make it to Big Bald that evening, still another 7 miles away, but was very relaxed watching clouds drift by. Chatty Kathy and his girlfriend Sacagawea came along and asked me to take their picture. They both had long dreads and made a good match. Chatty Kathy was from here in North Carolina.

Worn out, I was the last to arrive at the large, round grassy summit. Looking like a National Geographic expedition team, many ultralight tents, of different styles and colors, already dotted the mountaintop. Some hikers played Frisbee, ezNOMAD was taking pictures and D-Tour and High-gear were setting up their camps. Big Bald, 5,516', had amazing 360° panoramic views with no trees to obstruct our view. Weather and timing were perfect to catch an amazing sunset - maybe the most spectacular of the whole trip! This thunderhead formation resembled a mushroom cloud left by an atomic bomb, but upside down with changing colors within the layers.

By the bonfire, guitars and ukuleles jammed late into the night. I wanted to hang out and get to know everyone, but they were passing around a colorful glass pipe and I got some dirty looks because I didn't partake, so I just hung-out by myself, loner style.

> FUN FACT: Big Bald is also famous for bird watching. Every year, tens of thousands of native and migrating birds can be spotted in the area: Gray Catbird, Dark-Eyed Junco, Song Sparrow, Blue and Red Headed Vireos, etc.

Cowboy camping under the stars. I could have kept hiking and found trees to hang my hammock, but was excited to spend the night here, as I wanted to camp out on a bald at least one night during my adventure. Making a nest, I put down my plastic poncho, then my sleeping bags over-top. This worked fine, and I slept well, but not great. My bed was kind of in a hole, and my down sleeping bag got covered in dew during the night, so I put the tarp over me. I still had to dry the bag in the sun during lunch the next day. My reward for all of this was a killer sunrise. Low-lying white clouds filled in between the mountains and made peaks look like islands in an ocean. These descriptions can't come anywhere close to doing it justice. I encourage everyone to come here and see it for yourself! It was a night I'll never forget.

Chapter 6. Tennessee Turnpike

This rusty bicycle looked like someone left it here - a hundred years ago.

***Looking forward to visiting Erwin**, Tennessee, I camped on a bluff just outside town. From my lofty perch, I watched trains cross bridges over Nolichucky River, below. On my way, I examined a crazy centipede-looking insect, about 4 inches long, with pinchers! Super-size this bug and it would look at home in any old Godzilla movie.

Only 50 feet off the trail, you can't miss Uncle Johnny's Hostel & Outfitters. Opened to hikers in 1997, this 100-year-old house sucked hikers in like a magnet with a sign advertising "40¢ SNICKERS." I took the bait and stood in line with a half-dozen others, waiting to claim our prize, but woefully, only two per customer at this low introductory price. Here we go - Hiwassee all over again!

Every little thing here costs money. Want to call and order pizza? Sure, there's a payphone at the front desk, $1. Want to borrow a bike and run to town? No problem - $3. On a budget and just want to share a tent in the yard? Ok, but it'll cost ya, $10 <u>per person</u>. Most of these necessities are included at other hostels. Surprisingly, the cramped outfitter room was packed full of quality gear. Their specialty? Alcohol stoves made from used beer cans. There was a big box to choose from, some with logos still visible.

Strike 1. Scouting out the accommodations, I found that there was no toilet paper in the dirty community bathroom and a sign said the shower's hot water was broken.

Strike 2. Next, I found a shirtless hiker sitting face down at a picnic table, surrounded by beer cans, passed out, at 8:00 a.m.

Strike 3. I usually get along with everyone I meet, but for some reason, Grim, the guy running the place and I butted heads right off the bat. Asking if they had a private room, his answer: "You have to call ahead to reserve a room." I don't carry a phone so that was of no help. Then, asking if they had Internet: "Sit on the front porch and it works pretty good." My laptop was waiting at the post office and I had lots of videos to work on. I didn't want to rent a $20 bunk just to sit outside all night where everyone smokes. Grim then gave me a nature boy speech about how the trail is no place for computers. This coming from the "You have to call ahead to reserve a room" guy.

Feeling unwelcome and deciding not to stay, I politely asked to pay for the non-guest shuttle to town, as offered in the guidebook. This turned into a 5 minute interrogation on why I didn't want to stay in this wonderful hostel. After all of this, he did finally drop me off down the road when he drove his paid guests to some remote dive to get breakfast. That short ride cost me $7, and I still had to walk another 2 miles! Thanks for the hospitality, bud. To be fair, everyone else I talked to had a great time at Uncle Johnny's and was surprised Grim and I didn't find lots in common, as he was an expert on minimalist backpacking. I encourage future visitors to check all hostels out for yourself, as your experiences may be different.

Next to the restaurant was a rundown motel, The Dixie Inn (since renamed the more politically correct, Best Southern Motel.) The owner said the Internet wouldn't work in the cement block building and suggested I go to the Super 8, in town. Fine. It was a little unusual for a proprietor to recommend a different establishment, but I thought nothing of it. Getting frustrated, I tore out the page with a map of town, from my guidebook to find my way. Homes got much nicer closer to town and I stopped for breakfast at the Corner Grill, a little restaurant in a 2-story house. The kitchen was hidden behind a folding partition and meals were served on foam plates, but my gravy biscuit with hash browns and bacon was delish.

After an hour or so, I finally arrived at the suggested motel. The SAME EXACT MAN was standing behind the check-in desk, this time wearing a shirt with Super 8 logos! Feeling like I was in some wacky Seinfeld episode, I asked if we had just spoken. The man nodded yes, so I questioned why he didn't offer me a ride if we were going to meet here anyway!? He simply answered that the hotel's shuttle car was broken, without further explanation or apology. It was like pulling teeth paying anyone for services in this town! Defeated, I paid the $69.99 (ouch!), but room #128 was the most luxurious I would enjoy on my trip. "Life's great at Super 8!"

> *HIKER TIP: Instead of packing "town clothes," I bought a snazzy shirt and shorts for just $4 at a thrift shop. This allowed me to wash all my clothes and look decent walking around town, a trick I used several times.*

A sign advertising an "A.T. Film Fest" (and free pizza) caught my attention, and by chance, I was in town on the very night! Held at Town Hall, vehicles in the parking lot included the rusty white shuttle van from Uncle Johnny's, Miss Janet's famous burgundy "Bounce Box" shuttle car and that baby blue VW camper that seemed to be following us everywhere we went. A table was setup with ATC application forms, maps and fun temporary tattoos with AT logos. Our host, Miss Janet, brought plenty of Little Caesars pizzas to go around and invited us to raid a refrigerator full of generic brand sodas.

Miss Janet, former hostel owner-turned full-time shuttle driver, is well known in hiker circles and is an official AT ambassador. Interestingly, she "collects" trail names and has an amazing ability to remember every variation she's ever heard. She was the only person who ever asked if I was a "loner," who hangs out by himself, or a "loaner," who loans things. This double meaning hadn't occurred to me.

Turnout was good, with a crowd made-up of hikers, local townspeople and even an attractive newspaper reporter wearing a long summer dress. I sat in a group next to a tall, slightly overweight younger man playing video games on the latest high-dollar tablet. Gifted money to hike the AT for graduating college, he was talking about going on vacation in Hawaii instead! A punk rock girl with faded pink hair agreed with him and said, "Yeah, camping sucks." She was also quitting - not to go on holiday, but because she only had $40 left to her name.

Going around the room, we all took turns telling everyone our trail names...High Life & Red Fury were a young couple from Michigan. The pretty girl was small, with big hiker boots and bright red hair. They hiked along to heavy metal music played on a tiny boom box they carried. Documenting their experiences on TrailJournals.com, they abruptly stopped updating in Virginia. I could only assume they had given up. Feeling better, JK & Navigator were here, too. Others in the room: Running Water from Columbus, Ohio, Zena from Missouri, and Clint Eastwood from...Georgia. Then there was Salamander; this young man accidently carried a bowie knife on his hip into the county courthouse! In the process of hiding it in a desk drawer, he found the official gavel and begun hammering the podium and calling, "Order in the court!" to our group of misfits.

Projected onto a screen were films made by previous thru-hikers and footage of Miss Janet's own hiking attempt. She always said she had no interest in hiking the trail she loved, but gave it a try and had lots of fun even though she had almost as many zero days as she had hiking days. Another video called, 'Green Tunnel - A Six Month Journey in Five Minutes' - featured first-person hiking clips, fast forwarded and showing all the states and seasons.

> FUN FACT: "Blue Ridge Pottery," up to 1957, cranked out 324,000 hand painted plates each week! Today, Erwin's largest employer is Nuclear Fuel Services, producing enriched uranium for submarines.

Main Street was cordoned off and vintage cars lined both sides. Always a car guy, my favorite was a 1957 Chevy hot rod. Also on the main drag was The Capital, an old school movie theater, popular with hikers. Playing that week: 'The Avengers,' with a free collectible plastic cup offered as a promotion

Town is about relaxing, but also a time to do chores. Eight new videos were edited and uploaded, and I picked up another drop box from home, even though Erwin has a real grocery store within walking distance. The high priced Super 8 didn't have coin-op washing machines, so I ended up at Erwin Laundry & Tanning with blue waves and green palm trees painted on the windows. Inside, I treated myself to Ms. Pac-Man. Another game: 'Bay Watch' pinball, had graphics featuring Pamela Anderson in a red bathing suit.

A printed advertising flyer for Miss Janet's Bounce Box hung on the wall. For a moment, I considered taking it as a souvenir, but instead took a picture. In the meantime, women came in and out to use the tanning beds in the rear room. After changing back into trail gear, I left my town clothes in a hiker box. There was some frustration getting settled into Erwin, but it's a must stop for thruhikers and I enjoyed my stay; so much so that I have visited several times since. Every time I drive up I-26, I look for that big Super 8 sign.

Hiker Challenges. Starting where I left off, back into the woods I went. At the next shelter, someone had proposed a challenge. These usually involve food, alcohol, or both. Other times, these tests of endurance require completing a section within a certain amount of time. In this case, "...should you choose to accept," instructions were written on the shelter structure itself... *The Curly Maple Gap Pizza Challenge*.

- Two hikers may only take 1 pack.
- The hikers must not leave before 5:00 p.m.
- Said hikers must remain together. No splitting up!
- You must return with at least 2 pizzas and 24 beers.
- No delivery, no preorder (4.2 miles - each way).

Continuing, up ahead I saw something moving out of the corner of my eye. At first I thought it was a big black dog, but a few steps closer realized it was a bear, weighing around 100 pounds. It sniffed around then jumped into the brush a hundred feet in front of me. There wasn't even time to get my camera out, but very exciting!

On top of Unaka Mountain, 5,180', you'll find another bald, Beauty Spot. Today was drizzly with no chance of views, but I was eager to move along anyway. This is an uneasy section, with a long-standing animosity from landowners toward hikers because some of this corridor was confiscated by the US government to secure the AT's route. Monkey-wrenchers have been known to hang fishing line across the trail and paint fake white blazes leading nowhere. ATC warning sign:

"Recent vehicle activity on Beauty Spot has caused safety concerns. Hikers are urged not to camp on or near the top of Beauty Spot."

Locals can get a little rowdy. In fact, the scary incident hinted at, above, happened only days before I passed through. A group of 5 thru-hikers were camping on the bald when a drunk man pulled up in a truck. Waving around a loaded gun, pretending to be a game warden, he made everybody get down on their knees and searched them for drugs. But he picked the wrong crew to mess with. Two of them just happened to be U.S. Coast Guard officers, and they turned the tables on their assailant. Bravely, one punched the armed man, knocking him to the ground. They then took his gun away and hogtied him with

paracord until police arrived. Marcus F. Birchfield, 40, of Roan Mountain, was charged with 5 counts of aggravated kidnapping and 1 count each of unlawful possession of a loaded weapon (9mm pistol), criminal impersonation (of a game warden), possession of a Schedule II drug (oxycodone) and possession of drug paraphernalia (straws and rolled-up dollar bills). Posting bond, of course he didn't appear for his plea hearing. When he was finally picked up...he was only sentenced to...probation. What?! Not only that, he was also granted "judicial diversion," meaning if he completes his probation with no more problems, his record will be wiped clean as if it never happened. No wonder he has a goofy grin in his mugshot!

This was not the first time there has been big trouble in such a peaceful place. Although not related to the AT, another shocking crime was committed here in 1967. Earl Hill Jr. randomly shot a couple sitting in their car. The husband, a policeman, was killed and his wife left for dead. Nicknamed "The Beauty Spot Killer," the murderer is currently serving 2 life sentences, plus 1 year. The extra year is for escaping prison in 1977, along with James Earl Ray, the man who assassinated Dr. Martin Luther King, Jr. Hill still comes up for parole every 6 years.

The next day, I found, taped to a tree, a map to Greasy Creek "Friendly" Hostel. I had forgotten to refill my stove fuel, so decided to make the trek. Confusing, all downhill and basically a long mud slide, the poorly blue blazed half-mile ATV trail (aka ditch) has been described by others as a "scavenger hunt." Coming here, just make sure you knock on the correct door (covered with AT stickers). A truly unruly man next door causes a lot of trouble. He's been known to take down hostel signs at the trailhead and put up closed signs instead, citing illness or a death in the family for the reason. This is such a problem that Connie, aka Cee Cee, (the sweet owner who makes an awesome taco salad) offers a 10% discount if you bring her a bogus sign. He's also left lawn mowers running all night, destroyed surveillance cameras and even dug up her water pipes! She's been to court at least 5 times. Still, she asks hikers to just ignore him and "live and let live." This place was also kind of sad, as a couple of hikers had been stranded here for days, sleeping on a pair of couches in the living room - because of injuries that looked fatal - for a completed thru-hike. $10 bunkhouse; hiker/pet couches on the porch; indoor accommodations $15 and up. *Update: Cee Cee's website now reports: "No more neighbor issues!!!*

Roan Mountain is famous for its flowering rhododendron, ancestors of colorful gardens that once surrounded a luxurious health resort built in 1885, by John T. Wilder, Civil War general turned entrepreneur. Cloudland Hotel and its 6,285' elevation attracted health conscious patrons, including European royalty, who traveled here by train from far and wide. They enjoyed modern marvels of the day, such as steam heat and copper bathtubs. Rooms started at only $2 a day, but the hotel was eventually abandoned and auctioned off for lumber. Today, all that's left is a few stonewalls and even though most of the lush rhododendron were dug up and sold for landscaping, the few that remained spread and now cover over 600 acres, the largest wild gardens of rhododendron in the world.

Even rainy, cloudy days were beautiful and I felt alive in the wilderness. Breathtaking, the conifer forest I walked through next was inhabited by massive Christmas trees and miniature critters. Dwarfed red squirrels jumped from branch to branch, squeaking and waving their tails, and a bird's nest at ground level housed teeny-tiny eggs. This was an interesting ecosystem with an alpine-like environment and some rare plant species (usually only found on higher elevations of New England and Canada) were here collected by ambitious explorers and botanists of the 1700's - among them, American John Bartram and Scotsman John Fraser. I carried a little pinecone to plant when I got home, but lost it somewhere along the way.

Near the summit of Roan High Knob, a primitive stone fireplace had a white blaze painted on it. Nearby is a former fire warden's cabin built by the CCC in 1933, and then renovated in 1980 to accommodate hikers. Unfortunately, it's become rundown and my guidebook noted that the loft leaks. This is the highest shelter on the entire AT, 6,275', and has a rare door to close. The lookout tower is long gone. Interestingly, this also marks the highest elevation NOBO thru-hikers will be until we reach Mount Washington in New Hampshire - months away.

After crossing Carvers Gap, the Roan Highlands turn into miles of vast, grassy balds that roll like a green magic carpet and the AT became a thread stretched out in front of us with little specks bouncing along, hikers in the distance small as ants. Knief, with a red backpack was easy to spot, an excited kid from Switzerland who hiked huge mile days. Also in the area: Honest Abe and a girl named Stich.

Looking behind me from the dome of Little Hump (128 feet shorter than Big Hump, 5,587'), I could see a red roof nestled in the trees. Overmountain Shelter.

> FUN FACT: Overmountain Shelter was featured in the 1989 movie 'Winter People,' starring Kurt Russell. This old tobacco barn now serves as a hiker shelter and its two stories have room for at least 20 people.

This shelter was located down a blue blazed trail off Yellow Mountain Gap, part of the 'Overmountain Victory National Historic Trail,' a path once used during the American Revolutionary War. In 1780, Major Patrick "Egg Shell" Ferguson, a Scott in the British Army, threatened southern patriots that he would "...hang their leaders, and lay waste the country with fire and sword." Defiantly, farmers and common people formed a militia, using their own horses and supplies: The Overmountain Men. Nearly 2,000 soldiers camped near this barn (including Davy Crockett's father, John) on their way to South Carolina where they fought in the bloody, Battle of Kings Mountain.

In the end they were victorious when Ferguson was killed, causing his men to surrender. Among the dead was Virginia Sal, Ferguson's mistress. They were buried together on the battlefield. Theodore Roosevelt wrote, "This brilliant victory marked the turning point of the American Revolution." I've visited Kings Mountain in the past so I found all of this very interesting. If that wasn't history enough, this whole area was terrorized for almost 20 years by the fierce Cherokee War Chief, Dragging Canoe, and his 1,000 followers. Violently opposed to tribal lands being sold to the white man, they swore to remove all European settlers from these mountains. I had planned to see the barn myself, but rumbles of thunder told me it was best I get over the next few humps to lower elevation. Chilly winds swirled mist and grey clouds around me, floating like banshees.

I was moving along the next day when another hiker walked up behind me - Pocahontas! He's the Eagle Scout who had to carry his injured friend Wrench down a mountain near Hot Springs. Wrench was still back home, recovering from a broken foot, and Pocahontas was doing double time after taking a week off. I was surprised he made up all that ground so quickly.

Just a half-mile west on Highway US-19E was Mountain Harbour B&B and Hostel. I never pass up the opportunity to get an ice cream sandwich and top-off my food bag. Plus, each hostel is like a clubhouse for grownups, and I wanted to check things out. With more wet weather coming in, the charming barn loft (horses live underneath) was at full capacity and pricey at $20 bunk/$40 semi private (semi private means there's a curtain). Even the large tenting greens (horse pens) and the very limited hammock area (two trees) were occupied, but I never understood paying to camp when the woods are free just a few steps away. "Relatively clean pets allowed."

Most guests stay to enjoy the home-cooked $12 breakfast. Food in the fridge was by the honor system and had bags of homemade trail mix ready to go. Microwave popcorn was the popular treat here, with a DVD collection and large TV. The Waterboy was about to open up a can of whoop-ass on Colonel Sanders... "AaaaHaaaaaaa!!"

Appropriately named, Tail Dragger was a large man with a slow pace. He was here hiking for a week with his college-aged daughter and her friends. Of course, the youngsters walked a lot faster, and whenever they took a break, they would wait for him to catch up. But once he arrived, or even came into sight, they would all jump up and take off again. Poor Tail Dragger would have to sit down and take his breaks alone. Panting, he told me he was quitting at the next road because he hardly saw his daughter anyway. Also, a vegan thru-hiker named "Nelson" (from 'The Simpsons' TV show) had latched onto a pretty girl in the group. When you saw one, you saw the other.

Nelson was kind of a pain. One time, he ran out of water and expected some of mine. I obliged, but asked why he hadn't tanked up at the last spring? He snapped back, saying he drank it all already. Basically, he only wanted to carry 1 water bottle - not enough for this level of physical activity, even with plentiful water sources. During that same conversation, he also asked to borrow a cellphone. Telling him I didn't have one, which was true, he rolled his eyes like I was lying. Nelson was a way stronger hiker than I, with energy to spare, but last time I saw him, he was going off to explore some unidentified blue blaze, looking for water again.

Scenery in this section included a river that made a rare 45° turn, Mountaineer Falls and its 20-foot plunge, a 400-mile marker written in pebbles and a falling down tobacco shed that could be used as an emergency shelter - unless you're afraid of snakes.

Sitting on a random park bench on the side of the trail, I found an older gent named Funnybone. A retired orthopedic surgeon from Indiana, I'm sure he answered lots of hiker's questions about foot problems and inspected plenty of blisters during his flip-flop. Also close by was Vango/Abby Memorial Hostel, a nudist/alternate-lifestyle friendly bunkhouse where everyone is welcome. I found it funny you could choose heated or unheated bunkrooms.

One thing you realize when hiking a long distance trail, is that it rains a lot. For normal people in civilization, just getting a little bit wet can be a nuisance. Afraid they're going to melt, they scurry inside the nearest store or wait it out sitting in a car. But out in the woods, there's nothing to...get under. When it rains, all we can do is try to keep our vital equipment dry. Still, no matter how rugged a mountain man or woman, prolonged rainfall will wear anybody down. After 3 days and nights, I had been looking forward to at least cooking lunch inside a dry shelter, but when I arrived at Moreland Gap, people sat all in a row, blocking the entrance. Cookie cutter day hikers, dressed head to toe in matching plastic rain suits of assorted colors: yellow, blue, green, clear, red. Had I been in a better mood, I may have joked they reminded me of the new wave band DEVO. But these people just gawked blankly as I sloshed by, with no effort to make an inch of room.

Happily, Black Bear Resort was a wonderful place where I was greeted with a dry towel. That's service! This stop wasn't planned or in the budget, but I had to dry out. Mary, the owner, told me they bought this place with no idea hundreds, even thousands, of hikers passed by along the AT every year until they started showing up in droves. Now, the hiker community is their bread and butter, and they have embraced us whole-heartedly. Accommodations for every budget: camp sites, hotel style-rooms, cabins and even a honeymoon suite. Prices double on holidays and when NASCAR comes to nearby Bristol Motor Speedway, but bunks for thru-hikers are always $18 including shower and laundry (get in line early.)

My little 12' x 12' one room cabin had a porch decorated with birdhouses but was sparse inside. It was still cozy, with a space heater and a real mattress to sleep on (covered only in clear plastic). Some cabins sleep up to 6, so you could share a room and split the bill. My cabin, #4, cost $40 but was dry and that's all I cared about.

Hungry or thirsty? The resupply store/office had everything you'd need, and I downed 4 Hot Pockets, a 2-liter Dr. Pepper and a full-size bag of chips. They also have loaner poles and good fishing, as the resort's property has a quarter mile frontage on Laurel Creek, with decks hanging over the water. It was getting late when a slightly buzzed, yet very enthusiastic woman rang the "last call" bell and rung it right off the pole! There was a lot of beer and even some moonshine floating around but didn't get too loud. Bears Den was the main social area, with a computer and large screen TV with folding chairs arranged like a theater. Hiker's choice this time was 'Spaceballs,' a campy Mel Brooks 'Star Wars' parody, starring John Candy. Amusing, one group would watch it, then another group would find it already in the DVD player and watch it, and so on. I watched parts of 'Spaceballs' 3 times during my stay, and the whole room laughed at the same goofy jokes every time. Including me! "May the Schwartz be with you!"

Famous Kincora Hostel (and treehouse) is also on Dennis Cove Road, but in the opposite direction. It's been open to thru-hikers (exclusively) for at least 15 years. The owner, former airplane mechanic Bob Peoples, has hiked all over the world and is a tireless friend of the AT who spends 300+ hours a year maintaining 133 miles of trail he nicknamed "The Tennessee Turnpike." Bob encourages others to give back by doing trail maintenance, and every volunteer gets to paint a white blaze. Cool reward! Suggested donation for a bunk is only $5, but get there before 10:00 p.m. It's also "a dog free establishment" (he has a lot of cats). Bob doesn't want anyone quitting on his watch, so there's a 3-day limit. No website, but the phone number is (423) 725-4409. Chuck Norris-inspired sayings left on shelter walls...

- "Bob Peoples gives his boots blisters."
- "Every time Bob builds a switchback, an angel gets its wings."
- "Bears hang Bob Peoples' food bag for him."
- "Bob Peoples once night hiked, the whole AT."
- "A venomous snake bit Bob Peoples. After days of pain, fever and hallucinations, the snake died."

Another AT legend, Warren Doyle, also lives in the area. Beginning in 1972, he's hiked the entire AT more times than anyone - 17 in all! That's 36,000 miles, over 9 complete thru-hikes and 8 section hikes. I've wanted to meet the eccentric Mr. Doyle ever since I'd seen old VHS footage of him doing an interview. The ultimate thrifty hiker, he was wearing athletic tube socks and talked of buying used tennis shoes at thrift stores for $1 a pair and once hiked the entire AT spending a grand total of $6 on footwear! He could also survive eating only bargain bags of generic cookies. I've been compared to him several times for some of my cost saving techniques (aka cheap).

In 1982, Warren founded the ALDHA (Appalachian Long Distance Hikers Association), who works closely with the ATC to maintain the trail. He has also organized and successfully led 9 groups on complete thru-hikes. 'The AT Circle Expedition' is a huge undertaking where members form a nomadic community dedicated to encouraging each other. Their goal: To walk the entire AT in 140 days, all starting and finishing at the same time and on a specific date. A support van carries supplies and camping equipment, while members hike day-long sections and meet up at road crossings each night. Suggested $1,000 donation per person covers expenses, but this amount doesn't include gear, food, or lodging. I've met Warren several times since; when not hiking, he enjoys being a traditional Contra dance caller.

The next morning, finally dry, High-Gear and I hiked together for a few hours. A native Virginian, he had interesting stories to tell. All I had to do was keep up and listen. This section led us over wooden bridges and through deep gorges with towering stonewalls as the sound of an upcoming waterfall echoed through the woods. Laurel Fork Falls, 55 feet tall, is beautiful but dangerous. The same season I hiked, two section hikers from Louisiana, a father and his 15-year-old son, tragically drowned there, trapped by undercurrents below the base of the falls, their backpacks next to the trail where they left them. Twenty rescue members and volunteers helped in the recovery.

Carefully, we skirted along natural stone walkways hanging only a foot above the fast-moving river, then found myself going in circles for at least a half hour trying to get to Hampton, Tennessee, to retrieve a mail drop. Thankfully, a hippy family, apparently living in a tent, pointed me in the right direction. Once on the road, I happened upon a vintage car rally being run on public streets. Antique sports cars with numbers on the sides went racing by, including Jaguars, Fiats, a vintage Mercedes and an Aston Martin just like James Bond drives, except painted red. Orange arrows duct taped to telephone poles and guardrails advised drivers which turns to take. I even saw a silver Rolls Royce pull out and pass four cars at once! Seeing all this reminded me of the 'Cannonball Run' movies!

After more hiking, the trail rambles around man made Watauga Lake, built to make hydropower and control flooding. Still, the beach area is prone to overflow, causing detours. I watched tiny black and yellow chicks following momma duck on a swim while hikers braved chilly water up to their ankles. Beneath the lake still lies the town of "Old" Butler, where Native Americans traded peacefully with white settlers, and where frontiersman Daniel Boone rested between exploits. Next, hikers cross Watauga Dam, completed in 1948, 318 feet high, 900 feet across.

From here to Damascus was smooth sailing and a good place to put down some miles. Springtime was here, with green leaves on every tree and grass up to your knees on either side of the trail. It was fun checking out Iron Mountain Shelter, 4,125'. Like others in the area, it was built of ugly concrete blocks and dating the age of faded yellow paint were several "Free OJ" messages. Apparently, some have nothing better to do than draw on these buildings. Some fun examples...

Also on Iron Mountain, and within sight of the trail, is another old stone fireplace chimney, a makeshift gravestone for "Nick the Hermit." Uncle Nick Grindstaff, a shy man but also known for his kindness, lived here for over 40 years in a crude, 8' x 8' log cabin with no windows and only a 3-foot-tall door opening. A rattlesnake came and went through holes in the walls, and Nick was distraught when an unknowing visitor shot and killed the friendly pet. Nick's epitaph reads: "Born Dec. 26, 1851, Died July 22, 1923. Lived alone, Suffered alone, Died alone." But I disagree: He chose a life of solitude in this beautiful place. Besides, he had his loyal dog by his side to the very end. Panter died soon after, and was buried by Nick's side.

Chained to a tree was an orange, industrial toolbox with crosses cut into it with a blowtorch. Inside were waterproof Tupperware boxes filled with treats and drinks provided by Nelson Chapel Baptist Church GA's (Girls in Action.) My favorite, Hostess Chocolate Peanut Butter Bars! There was also first aid and a logbook.

Next, I came upon the nomadic-like Camp Riff-Raff. Out of respect for their privacy, I didn't take any photos, but it was impressive, with a half-dozen pop-up tents, camp chairs and coolers. Starting in 2006 with only 6 members, this family of friends has grown large and even have their own logo T-shirts featuring a skull wearing a cowboy hat and trekking poles for crossbones. They were celebrating, "Pre-Days," a 10-day trail magic gathering leading up to the rowdy 'Trail Days' festival in Damascus, still 20 miles away. These trail devils hooked us up with homemade cake and sodas, or beer, if you preferred.

All about having fun, these guys and gals played an elimination style Frisbee drinking game, where both members of your team knock empty beer cans off the tops of hiking poles stuck into the ground. I don't drink and thus was declared ineligible, but ezNOMAD sensed a calling to become Beer Frisbee's next World Champion. Even though we had talked about attempting a Damascathon - hiking 26.2 miles all the way to Damascus, I went on alone and wouldn't see my buddy again for several months!

The trail rolled along fields and past barns until it came to a fence-crossing stile. One of hundreds that all AT hikers scale during the duration of our trips. Imagine climbing an A-frame ladder, with narrow 2' x 4's for steps, over a barbed wire fence. Then 5 feet off the ground, awkwardly turn around on top and back down the other side - with your pack on. Dogs go under. Sometimes we find 3 or 4  pair a day. More than once my backpack's counterweight forced me off balance, almost sending me to the ground. Once inside the fences, you may be surrounded by a dozen cows directly on the trail. Most wagged their tails like giant dogs; others grunted or walked away.

McQueens Knob Shelter, aka "The Holiday Inn," was the smallest on the trail and its unchinked, lopsided walls made it look like it was built of oversized Lincoln Logs. Constructed in 1934, there's no water and only room for about 4 hikers, but it's left here in case of emergencies. Hiking late, I stumbled upon a couple of black bears! These fury critters were having their supper of green leaves and didn't notice me, at first. But as I tiptoed closer, they came to attention. Then, all at once, they took off! The small one climbed 6 feet up a tree, then jumped down and followed his buddy. Very agile, they run way faster than you might think. I've seen bears before, and it's always a heart pumping experience.

American black bears are present in almost every state along the Appalachian range and most thru-hikers will see at least 1 on their trip; some may see a dozen, and one hiker I read about counted 22! Adults weigh 200 to 600 lbs. and can grow 6 feet long. Living up to 20 years, some spend winters dormant by cutting their metabolic rates in half, although those in the South may not hibernate at all. Usually shy and non-aggressive, they would prefer not to have any interaction with us at all. When they do see or smell a pesky human, they usually just run away. Most tend to stop after a few yards (as do deer) to get a better look, then take off again. Black bears may roam up to 80-square-miles, foraging on grass, roots, berries, nuts and insects. Others have grown dependent on human foods and garbage, which can cause dangerous conflicts with humans.

• **When you see a bear,** take the long way around.
• **Always give extra room** to a mama bear with cubs.
• **Bear spray.** Some hikers hang these bulky cans from their packs. But if you're close enough to use it, you're already in danger.
• **If you don't want to see a bear,** sing to yourself, whistle, wear a cowbell and get parked in camp early.

> *HIKER TIP: Bear spray is strong pepper spray meant to deter aggressive bears' "undesirable behavior." To use, stand 25 feet away and spray for 6 seconds. Just don't spray yourself! Cost: $50 a can.*

After a 24 mile day, just a few miles short of the Damascathon, I camped after dark and laid in my hammock listening to NASCAR racing from Darlington, South Carolina, on my FM radio. I fell asleep looking forward to the next day when I would cross into Virginia and visit the most famous trail town of all... Damascus.

Chapter 7. Virginia Bluegrass

Wild ponies grazing in the Virginia Highlands.

New state - Virginia! The border between Tennessee and Virginia was outlined with small stones and is only 3 miles from Damascus. This official AT community has white blazes painted on telephone poles to lead us through town. You won't find any traffic lights here, but a full-size shelter sits on the greens (display only). I was very excited to reach "Trail Town, USA" but ended up walking back into the woods a few hours later, dejected.

Goal #1: Blitz to the post office to retrieve my drop box, with food and the Virginia section of my guidebook, on Saturday, before 11:30. That was really cutting it close, and I missed it by just 5 minutes! More frustrating, I could hear people still working in the back and knocked with no answer. So, I left a note asking if my boxes could please be forwarded to the next town. Otherwise, I would have to wait there until Monday.

Goal #2: Wash clothes. Easy, right? Wrong! The most "hiker friendly" town on earth didn't have a public laundry. The only way to get this necessary chore done is to stay a night in one of the hostels, or pay for an elaborate system where you fill a basket with clothes to be returned clean and folded the next day. I only have a few articles of clothing (13 total, including hats and individual socks); what was I supposed to do in the meantime? Walk around naked?

Goal #3: Get a hot shower. Shaggy from Indiana, a dead ringer for the character on Scooby Doo, and his pretty redhead girlfriend were in town and recommended "The Place," so I went over to visit and maybe stay the night. A big house, owned by a local Methodist Church, it has been a hostel since 1975. Most hikers had only praise for it, but right from the jump, Bayou, the big guy in charge, was leery of me. Surprisingly, this was becoming a recurring theme for me. Apparently, because of my tiny pack, he thought I was a homeless person looking to steal something. I did manage to look around a little during the interrogation: Inside were wood-planked bunks, no heat and very little lighting. I paid the $7 donation to stay the night, supposedly with full privileges, but like a criminal had to leave my backpack outside and was only allowed into a hall to take a disappointingly cold shower in a dirty bathroom, then basically asked to leave. Whatever dude.

"Happy Trail Days!" Since 1987, Damascus has been most famous for this annual festival. Population is normally less than 1,000 people, but each May, the weekend after Mother's Day, it swells to nearly 20,000, with partying hikers who form a giant tent city. Many thru-hikers walk into town; others take shuttles or hitchhike from miles away to join the celebration and former thru-hikers return for class reunions. Activities...

- **One Way Ministries:** Free haircuts (mohawks are popular).
- **Ride board:** Offer a ride/get a ride!
- **Free food** and speed eating contests.
- **Hiking pole javelin contest:** Held at Billville encampment.
- **Gear auction** benefiting "The Place."
- **Film screenings:** Squatch makes regular appearances.
- **Seminars and presentations** by Warren Doyle and others.

- **Manufacturers midway:** Fittings and free gear repair.
- **Author's tent:** Meet writers and preview AT books for sale.
- **AWOL:** All pages posted, and current hikers mark their progress.
- **Talent show:** It's not American Idol, but draws a huge crowd!
- **Hiker prom:** Complete with crowning of King and Queen.
- **Drum Circle:** Dance around the bonfire. Hosted by Miss Janet.
- **Hiker Parade:** Main event complete with Mardi Gras costumes!

Everyone loves a parade, and it is tradition for all the hikers to walk through town while being hosed-down by residents with garden hoses and oversized water guns! Oddly, harmless water balloons are now outlawed due to safety concerns. How lame - "no water balloons."

During the festivities of 2013, an elderly man had a medical incident and accidently drove his car into the crowd. Hikers jumped to the rescue and lifted the heavy Cadillac off people pinned underneath. Three were airlifted to a hospital, and up to 60 were injured. The scary event was updated on Good Morning America.

> FUN FACT: Mount Rogers Outfitter is well stocked, but more interesting, memorabilia on display includes Keds worn by Grandma Gatewood (1st woman to thru-hike the AT solo) and a model of Lost Mountain Shelter.

Damascus has more hostels and Bed & Breakfasts than any other town on the trail. Here are some hiker hangouts...

- **Hiker's Inn:** This beautiful, 2-story house on the main drag is operated by Skink, Class of 2010. Wi-Fi and AC, but no TV. Bunks/$25; privates/$50-$75.
- **Dave's Place:** Across the street from Mount Rogers Outfitter. Shower and Bed/$21 (no mattress.) Shuttle service within 100 miles.
- **Crazy Larry's Hostel:** A tiny home, right on the trail.
- **Woodchuck Hostel:** Continental breakfast. Pac-Man game and full-sized Indian teepee in the backyard! $25/bed; $10/tenting.

Bismarck. If you hiked on the AT between 2009 and 2015, you probably crossed paths with this bushy bearded, likable man. But this was no ordinary hiker. Accountant turned white-collar criminal, James T. Hammes, embezzled nearly $9 million over an 11-year period, from his employer Pepsi-Cola bottlers of Kentucky. When the scheme was finally uncovered, Hammes denied everything, then almost immediately abandoned his wife and daughter to fake his own death. But he wasn't as smart as he thought. FBI agents soon found forged birth and death certificates, boxes of documents proving he stole the money and computer searches on "how to disappear." He was also under investigation for a house fire that killed a previous wife, and 4 other blazes at properties he owned. For most of 6 years, Bismarck hid in plain sight on the AT. But another hiker happened to be watching a 3-year-old rerun of 'American Greed' when he recognized the profiled criminal as Bismarck.

Montgomery Homestead Inn's website suggests, "A place to forget life's stresses for a slower, simpler life." This is where Hammes was arrested when the FBI raided the home, during Trail Days, 2015. He stayed here often and frequented other B&B's along the trail. Authorities seized $3,000 worth of gift cards, $11,000 in cash, plus $70,000 more from a storage unit. Not shy about having his picture taken, he was photographed at the parade, laughing and blasting away with a Super Soaker. David Miller, author of the 'AWOL' guide, knew Bismarck and said sent him corrections and updates from time to time.

Facing 20 years, Hammes pleaded not guilty, but just before trial, agreed to cooperate. Seventy-four counts of wire fraud and money laundering were reduced to just one single count. A judge sentenced him to 8 years in prison and ordered him to pay $7.5 million restitution, though most had been lost in the stock market.

Yard sale day! The whole neighborhood participated, forming a maze of folding tables covered with anything and everything. Tons of people were walking around so it was hard to look while carrying my backpack and hiking poles. Some interesting things I saw: hand carved walking sticks, old backpacks and a few local arrowheads. My only purchases were a BBQ sandwich, a couple of sodas and homemade brownies from various stands run by Girl Scouts and church groups. I was looking forward to real food, but all the restaurants were full of bargain hunters, so I bought bread and baloney for lunch.

This whole town seemed geared more toward bicycle tourists. People pay to get shuttled in long passenger vans pulling trailers loaded with dozens of identical bikes. Then, with almost no peddling, they coast down the Virginia Creeper, a "rail-to-trail" bike path named after steam locomotives that once chugged up and down the mountain.

Riders return their rentals then hang out at ice cream shops. Rental packages start at $29.99. Blue blazers use maps here to shortcut elevation changes and AT miles.

Maybe I'm just paranoid, but besides being treated like a thief at "The Place," I also got very little cooperation, at a gas station while buying aspirin; from an impatient librarian when I tried using the painfully slow Internet; and from a Dollar General cashier where I bought lunch and resupply (maybe because 25 hikers inside at one time). Also, I had to go to 3 different "outfitters" before finding alcohol for my stove. While there, I considered buying new shoes and a replacement guidebook, but preppy employees gave me a bad vibe, so I taped up my shoes and would just wing-it until my mail caught up with me. *Update: In 2016, I returned to Damascus for Trail Days and can honestly say it was a wonderful experience.*

Maybe so, maybe no, maybe rain, maybe snow? Several of us were stationed in the trees near Beech Mountain Road. It stormed throughout the night and temps dropped. There was even some sleet. No need to fetch water; I simply set my cup out to collect rain.

By chance, I found a local station on my trusty FM radio and enjoyed an entire old-time bluegrass concert. Amazingly, it was recorded live during a festival on nearby Whitetop Mountain, the very one I was about to climb the next day! Sounds of the Whitetop Mountain Band have echoed through these hills since the 1930's, with songs and instruments passed down through generations. Today, they carry on the rich tradition of "claw-hammer" banjo picking - a style unique to this region. Mandolins, fiddles, acoustic guitars, stand-up bass, fast picking banjos and the heavenly voice of a young woman captivated me. Some tunes were slow, others lightning fast, starting and stopping on a dime. Most numbers had lyrics about the area and the Appalachians. Enthusiastic, the audience hooted, hollered, clapped along and even danced! Immersed into the local culture, it felt like I was right there in the crowd. In between songs, lead singer Martha Spencer had to change keys on her Great Uncle's banjo - "string stretchen," she called it - and joked in a sweet, southern accent, "Banjo players spend half their time tuning, and the other half... playing out of tune!"

Setting off again the next morning, the trail had turned into a stream. You couldn't go around because standing water was everywhere you looked. So, I just sloshed around in the puddles like a small child. I had lunch with some other hikers on Buzzard Rock. The AT doesn't go to the viewless summit of this mountain, or its sister and highest in Virginia, Mt. Rogers, 5,729', but both can be reached by side trails. I made a video, wishing my mother and sister a Happy Mother's Day. Another difficult thing about being away 5 - 6 months is not being there for family gatherings. I missed being home, but was reinvigorated by the mountain music that I could still hear in my head, a hint of sunshine, and the anticipation of entering Grayson Highlands.

> FUN FACT: Scattered on Mount Rogers are rocks formed by ancient volcanos. Look for light colored, fine grained stones with little round holes caused by bubbles of volcanic ash.

Passing Thomas Knob Shelter, one of the newest on the trail, I met a hiker named "Oak." From Missouri, he used a single wooden walking stick and wore a yellow T-shirt with the "recycle" symbol on the front. Once past the gates, you can start looking for wild ponies; you might also run into a longhorn or two. Herds of small horses were introduced in 1974 and numbering about 150, they graze on abundant grass, keeping meadows bald. I had seen this section in AT videos and was eager to experience it for myself, but walked and walked without seeing any ponies - only pony poop!

Ready to give up hope, in the distance I spotted a group of the furry creatures. Determined not to miss my chance, I went way off trail to hang out with them. Not exactly miniature horses, they were bigger than expected and adults stood up to my waist. A few foals were also running around. Beautiful animals, they had different colors, markings and personalities. Some walk up and lick your hands, looking for salt; others grunt if you get too close. They may seem tame as house cats and puppy dogs, but don't horse around too much. I've heard stories of people being bit, knocked down, kicked and one cowboy who sat on a pony to get his picture taken when it started bucking like a rodeo bull! Once a year, the Wilburn Ridge Pony Association rounds them up to do checkups. If the herd has grown too large, excess colts are sold at auction. A pony to take home would make a great souvenir!

In hindsight, my extra credit was unnecessary as ponies were everywhere I went - some directly on the AT! One blond pony with a long mane was especially fond of my buddies High Gear and Hot Shot.

From Georgia, Hot Shot was given his trail name by his daughter, and spent a lot of time searching for phone signal so he could call home.

After passing the 500-mile mark, I crawled through Fat Man's Squeeze, a cave-like tunnel formed by 2 large slabs of rock stacked together. Then, at Dickey Gap, a large gathering of hikers, maybe 2 dozen, were all waiting for shuttles back to Trail Days. One girl had the cutest gray tabby cat riding along on top of her backpack. Looking happy as could be, "Trail Mix" was popular at shelters, as she was an excellent mouser.

Looking along the way, I was disappointed not to find an old school bus that had become a popular landmark for hikers. Long abandoned, hunters had built bunks inside and fashioned a woodstove from a 55-gallon barrel, similar to "The Magic Bus" made famous in the movie 'Into the Wild' (highly recommended). Willing to go back and look for it, I checked Whiteblaze.com at the next town, but learned it had been removed the year before. The trail is constantly changing.

Camping a half mile short of Partnership Shelter, I could still hear crowd noise late into the night. The shelter itself was modern and impressive, with a flush toilet and propane heated shower, but neither worked. With the additional loft, there is room for 16 hikers to squeeze inside, but is almost always over capacity because of its close proximity to the road. Hikers, friends of hikers, anyone else and their brother can just drop in. Rangers visit on occasion and signs say: "No alcohol allowed," but that doesn't stop anybody and the parties are legendary. There is also a two night limit.

Another YouTuber, TNT Tom, couldn't stand a long night in Partnership Shelter with 28 other people packed in like sardines. Calling it "absolute squalor," he hiked through sleet in the middle of the night, and left the AT forever.

Only a few hundred feet away was Mount Rogers Visitor Center with a free phone outside to order pizza or Chinese food. The interpretive center had a stuffed black bear, local history and a scale for hikers to weigh themselves. I'd lost over 40 pounds already and was now an even 200! A sign on the bathroom door: "Do not bathe, wash your hair, or wash dishes in the sinks," but didn't specify not to wash dirty clothes! D-Tour and others were waiting for the transit bus to Marion, only 50¢ away. They do pick-ups 3 times a day if hikers are waiting.

I made a big mistake during my pre-hike planning and requested a mail drop and my PC be sent to the tiny village of Sugar Grove. It was listed as a shorter walk, but I didn't know about the shuttle bus to Marion. I had to walk down the very narrow mountain road, only feet away from speeding cars and tractor-trailer trucks. I couldn't get a hitch and even tried to "yogi" a ride at a gas station café.

Yogi. This term is, of course, named after the loveable cartoon bear who, although friendly, tried to trick Jellystone Park visitors out of their "Pic-a-nic baskets, treats and other snack type goodies!" In this case, I simply asked, "Is the post office nearby?" Patrons pointed me in the right direction but no one offered a ride, so I added, "Is it a long walk?" Basically, asking without begging and hoping my marks would get the hint. Most people jump at the chance to help and this technique can be used for all kinds of goods and services. It's considered rude to yogi other NOBOs (northbound thru-hikers), while townies, tourists, day-trippers and especially SOBOs are all fair game. I got pretty good at it, but had no luck with these hardnosed logging men. When I finally made it to the post office, the postmaster lady was shocked to see a hiker. Thankfully, a nice pregnant woman picked me up for the way back, saving me a 3-mile climb and bypassing an unfriendly dog I had to duel on my way down.

Marion is a large town with a movie theater, bowling alley, Greyhound and choice of hotels, but town was spread out and more walking was involved. I chose Virginia House Inn because it advertised good Wi-Fi and the hiker rate was just $40. In the end, I still had to hack the signal from another hotel. To save money, I washed my clothes in the hotel sink and dried them on the window sill. My room had a full-length mirror and I experienced the odd feeling of not recognizing my reflection. Growing feral, my trail beard was getting longer and I was much trimmer than I remembered. The swimming pool was half-full of the most disgusting black water I've ever seen -

or smelled - but if you want to take a dip, just ask, as the nicer establishment across the street is owned by the same family.

> *HIKER TIP: When checking into hotels, always ask for the "hiker rate." Most listed in the guidebooks are hiker friendly and may knock $5 to $10 off your bill. To keep goodwill, please don't get too loud or leave a mess.*

The AT makes for hungry hikers, and I pigged out at the first Taco Bell since Franklin, 400 miles ago. I ordered 13 tacos and a bottomless soda. Unfortunately, my mail didn't get forwarded, but a nice postmaster lady here called Damascus, so the boxes would be bumped up the trail. I was relieved, but still without my guidebook.

> *FUN FACT: Major League Baseball pitcher Nolan "The Ryan Express" Ryan played minor league ball for the Marion Mets in 1965. He was inducted into the MLB hall of fame in 1999.*

Like many old towns, Marion is named after an American Revolutionary War hero; this time, Francis Marion. I enjoyed looking around Main Street and its many historic buildings, antique shops and art houses. Most impressive was Lincoln Theater. This landmark opened in 1929 and was designed to resemble, of all cockamamie things, a

Mayan Temple. The Lincoln is also home to the popular bluegrass concert TV series, 'Songs of the Mountains.' The theater was closed, but a passer-by on the street saw me taking photos of the old-school box office, took me inside and introduced me to the manager. Busy setting up for the next show, he was kind enough to give me a quick tour. Giant hanging murals were almost 100 years old and very impressive, their restored colors vibrant with each cotton panel depicting local history, including one featuring Daniel Boone. My host told me the fascinating story of Lola Poston, who painted the masterpieces for only $50 each! Lola was something of a bohemian gypsy, who traveled across America in a homemade "house car."

Returning to the woods, the AT turned into a tunnel of rhododendrons, blooming purple flowers. Taking in the view from Glade Mountain, 4,120', rays of sunlight radiated from breaks in the clouds. I was also sporting new basketball shorts, hoping to avoid "monkey butt." If you don't know what monkey butt is - you don't want it!

> HIKER TIP: "Monkey butt" rashes are caused by dehydration or chafing and can make hiking almost impossible. Benadryl helps, but there are many creams, ointments and magic potions (Body Glide) for treatment.

Chatfield Memorial Shelter would be my unexpected abode for the night, and where I found my new friend, Half Speed. We had first met at a Marion grocery store, his backpack sitting in the shopping cart where an infant would ride. Half Speed liked to eat well, and bored of trail food, loaded up on gourmet snacks, deli ham and fancy tin foiled cheese balls. He even had wine coolers chilling in the nearby stream! He greeted me with a hardy hello, but I soon realized this poor man couldn't hold back grimacing and crying as he held his knee.

He had twisted it on a downhill and tumbled to the ground. It had now swollen to the size of a jumbo grapefruit. I'm no doctor, but we both knew his thru-hike was over. We wrapped the knee to apply pressure, kept it elevated and fed him Vitamin I, but distraught, he kept repeating to himself: "Oh yeah...It's all over," as he yelped with pain every time he moved. I suspected his heavy backpack caused the injury, but Half Speed insisted he needed his stuff. I had planned to hike on, but couldn't leave this injured man here alone. Hanging my hammock nearby, I reluctantly retreated to the shelter with a tangled ball of hammock and sleeping bags slung over my shoulder.

My first night ever sleeping in a shelter and I was not a happy camper. I don't carry a bulky sleeping pad because it's not needed with a hammock and the wood plank floor was, indeed, hard as a board. Wine coolers helped Half Speed sleep, but not soundly. With thunderstorms, mice scurrying in the rafters and my roommate's sad, ghost-like groaning, neither of us got much rest. In the morning, I tried to trade my much lighter 13-pound pack for his 50-pound behemoth, but he would only agree to offload some food weight, as he wouldn't be needing it anymore. The transfer was a solemn ceremony.

Hiking in silence, the trail was mostly flat, but muddy from the storms. Half Speed hobbled along all right and never complained, but any movement up-and-over the smallest obstacle sounded like torture. Later, we passed the time talking about his Army days and he taught me how to identify diverse types of edible plants and leaves: Ramps, wild onions, etc. I taste-tested each green leafy thing he pointed out and used this natural grocery store the rest of my hike.

HIKER TIP: Ramps are edible plants with two green leaves and taste like garlic or onion. Also called spring onion, wild leek and wild garlic, ramps have been used in traditional dishes in this area for generations.

An interesting landmark we passed on our way was Lindamood School. Always open, sometimes TM (trail magic) can be found here. Rows of old desks, an iron buck stove and an outhouse all looked like they did when the school opened in 1894. This school had seven grades, taught by one teacher who was paid about $30.00 a month. A portrait of George Washington even hung above the chalkboard where hikers had written their trail names. On a shelf was a pair of horseshoes and tin cans to play with during recess. Though injured, Half Speed demonstrated the stick and hoop toy, rolling the metal wheel down the aisle. This would have surely earned him a few lashes back in the day! His spirits improved, and I like to think he had some fun during the last few miles of his hike. Lindamood closed in 1937.

Finally making it to the road, he called his brother who would not be there to pick him up for another 4 hours. Atkins is a 5-building town with a garage (closed), Relax Inn (one star on Yelp), a couple of gas stations (limited resupply) and a crappy restaurant (very overhyped.) The one interesting feature was a faded red covered bridge, just big enough to walk through. If needed, modern facilities can be found to the west, 3-miles away.

The few hikers we met were looking forward to the Barn Restaurant, but this place wasn't hiker friendly in the least. Before we even got in the door, a waitress barked, "No packs allowed!" and pointed to a handwritten sign with spelling errors and bad punctuation...

"Attention Hikers, Due to state Regulations back packs Are <u>prohibited</u> from being Inside the Restaurant. thanks, mgt."

A "please" or a smile would have gone a long way. Equipment can cost hundreds, even thousands of dollars, and Half Speed, as you read, doesn't let his "baby" out of his sight. Compromising, he was allowed to leave his backpack in the foyer. Décor was basic folding chairs, plaid paper tablecloths, a dream catcher, and one 12-month calendar worth of farm tractor pictures fastened to the walls with Scotch tape. Just for fun, I looked at some official inspection reports online. Violations included... "Touching food or utensils after touching uncovered body parts or coughing," "Soiled counters, food thermometers not working" and listed as critical... "A direct connection exists between the drain line of the ice maker and the sewer system." Yuck! As of this writing, conditions have not improved.

Saying goodbye, Half Speed gifted me a sheet of gray plastic that I used the rest of my hike. So, in a way, part of him kept going. I made a few more miles that day, but my heart just wasn't in it and set up camp early and thought about all the wounded hikers that had been forced off the trail. When someone inevitably asks any AT thru-hiker, "What was the hardest part?" most may answer, "Being away from home," "The heat," "Bugs," "The cold," etc. While all those things are true, for me, the hardest part was the suffering of others.

Chapter 8. Spaceships and Lightning Strikes

Chestnut Knob Shelter. Mile marker 565.2.

As everyone else was partying in Damascus, I enjoyed the solitude of a nearly deserted trail, and on May 20th, after 6 weeks of steady hiking, I officially passed the 1/4 mark. After crossing fence stiles on both sides of 2 lane VA-610, I wound my way through several working farms. In one pasture, friendly cows seemed to be hiking along with me - just watch out for landmines! My favorite was #277, a playful calf with shaggy black fur and white spots. He kept running just alongside, then stopping to shake his head.

Climbing up to 4,409', I reached my favorite shelter on the entire AT, Chestnut Knob. Situated on a green bald, it had a commanding view of Burke's Garden, a huge, crater-like depression surrounded by endless ridgelines. Also known as "God's Thumb Print," in prehistoric times, this was the bottom of a sea. The small stone structure was orig-inally built as a fire warden's cabin for a tower, which is no longer there. Wooden bunks and a picnic table were squeezed inside, while Plexiglas windows let in some light. The fireplace would have been nice, but it was bricked in. On the mantel, an odd turtle shell, with a joke written on its side: "Welcome to the shell-ter." Get it? Someone had also jokingly drawn an arrow, pointing under one of the beds, and wrote: "AT&T service here." The only other people in the area were a couple from the UK, but I had already passed their tent and knew I'd have this shelter all to myself. The weather was perfect and I watched the white-hot ball of the sun, surrounded by burning reds and yellows, descend behind the mountains.

> HIKER TIP: I chose not to carry a phone, but others bragged about Verizon for cell service, at least in the south, with AT&T and Sprint reported as having some problems. Also, set on "airplane mode" to save battery life.

I hate aliens! Hanging in my hammock between bunk posts, I fell asleep with the radio on, and woke up to a strange program called 'Coast to Coast.' Everyone calling in was either a conspiracy theory schizophrenic or alleged alien abductee. I closed the door but still had nightmares! I mostly slept unafraid while on the trail, and if I was ever visited, abducted, lost time, scanned, or probed in any way by an extraterrestrial, I was too tired to notice.

With wide-open skies, away from the bright lights of town, the AT would be a good place to look for UFOs. During my hike I saw heat lightning, shooting stars and maybe a few satellites streaking by, but nothing, in the sky, that couldn't be explained. I was told about a group of hikers, who stayed up all night in a North Carolina shelter, watching glowing orbs floating up and down through the trees. There's a lot of UFO graffiti in shelters and registers, and I left my own logbook entry with childlike artwork of a spaceship flying over Chestnut Knob with a smiling alien at the controls.

The next day, weird rocks imbedded into the trail were fossils resembling giant grey pasta noodles. Nearby, a big wooden sign originally read, "WATER .5" with a blue arrow, now pointing into overgrown wilderness. Graffiti advice on the sign didn't sound too promising...

- "Take sign down!"
- "Uphill both ways!"
- "Bull S--T!"

- "Steep switchbacks and overgrown, bone dry, don't go!"
- "If you have some WATER - don't bother!" (My favorite, as it incorporated "water," which was already on the sign).

Thankfully, trail angels had left gallon jugs of water at the next trail intersection, Walker Gap. Later that day, I happened upon another TM - 2 semi-permanent coolers, one blue and one red, complete with fresh made (and dated) peanut butter sandwiches, pop and snacks. There was even a printout of the day's weather forecast, complements of Lab Rat and Lumbermack, AT Class of 2006. A register was provided, as was the religious tract, 'How to get to Heaven from the Appalachian Trail.' Years later, I sent an email, and Lumbermack told me the story of his trail name: "A hiker in Georgia gave me that because he knew my first name was Mack and I was dragging logs down to the campfire on a snowy night."

He added, "Our 8th season of trail magic, we do around 1,000 sandwiches a year, and at least that many, or more, little Debbie cakes and about 2,000 soft drinks. We aim to achieve Fellowship, Goodwill and Community Service."

> HIKER TIP: Avoid the pavilion at VA-623. Owned by Ceres Ruritan Club, with graffiti, trash cans full of hiker garbage and a kicked in outhouse door, it's no surprise we are no longer welcome there.

Next stop was Jenkins Shelter, where there was a sign in all caps:

BEAR WARNING! HANG ALL FOOD AND SMELLING ITEMS.

Numerous entries in the logbook told of a "harassing bear" that had torn claw marks into tents, knocked down another with a hiker inside, bounced still another person sleeping in a hammock and stole toilet paper. One entry was by Passion Flower, a sweet girl with pretty pigtails who I consider a friend. She wrote "...he didn't even try to get the food hanging low on a branch." No wonder the bear was sniffing around! Others at Jenkins that night: Aimster, Subway and Scooter.

Some hikers burn food packaging, plastic bags and other trash, in community fire pits. This may seem like a good idea but these items rarely burn completely, and bears are attracted to odors in the ashes. Please practice "Pack it in, Pack it out." Someone could get hurt, lose gear, or worse. This shelter may have to be temporarily closed and the poor bear will probably be tranquilized and moved to a more remote area. But like I said before, once he has a taste for human food, he'll be back. Eventually, this bear may have to be put down (i.e. killed!) by rangers to prevent human injury.

> HIKER TIP: Smart hikers know it's important to hang food bags. But it's also a good idea to hang anything with fragrance. Black bears also seem fond of soap, toothpaste, wet wipes, lip balm, etc.

Trying to get as far away from the problem area as possible, I crossed a walk bridge over beautiful Laurel Creek and its small cascades. But while getting water, I found two dirty diapers contaminating this precious water source. **START RANT:** What were these townies thinking? Why even come to a pristine place like this if you're just going to foul it up with stinky trash? Ever hear of the concept, "Other people?" It's your baby - be responsible for his or her poop! IT'S NOT THAT HARD! Just put the soiled diapers back in the Wally World bag from where they came and find a trashcan. Lots of folks put more effort into cleaning up after their dogs! **END RANT.**

Hiking until the edge of darkness, the trail through this section was cut out of steep mountainsides and when I was ready for bed, I set up my hammock directly on the AT itself. One tree even had a white blaze on it! Camping this close to the trail is not recommended. You could inconvenience other hikers and the path is also traveled by wild critters - big and small - especially at night.

The first thing I saw the next morning was a metal AT sign riddled with bullet holes. This whole area felt uncomfortable, with lots of road crossings. One segment followed high above highway I-77. Absent of trees, stone cairns were placed on guardrails to show us the way. Many hikers took the opportunity to resupply in the small town of Bland, Virginia, but I skipped this one. Just happy to be back in the woods, I passed the number 600 drawn in pinecone art. Trail Days was winding down and hikers were getting dropped back where they left off. Funny, one saw my makeshift hiking poles and yelled, "Ski pole twins!" We were both using the same brand. This fellow had started hiking from Georgia without sticks of any kind, but bought these from Ron Haven's wife in Franklin, North Carolina. Continuing, we walked up on a wild turkey. Trying to lead us away from her half-dozen chicks, she did the broken wing routine, making squawking noises while dragging one out-stretched wing on the ground. We stood still, but the scared turkey still flew off. I worried all day (and still feel bad) and hope their mother returned.

Next, a long suspension bridge bounced over the very wide Kimberling Creek, also a popular swimming hole. Here, I saw a glimpse of fox but didn't have time to get a picture. Trent's Grocery is only a half-mile road walk away and provides made-to-order food. Crowded and slow, the store's hotdogs and fries were worth the wait. Basically a hunting camp, they do accept mail drops but there was plenty of overpriced resupply stuff. I did pay a reasonable $3 to wash clothes while I visited resident horses. Dark brown with tan manes, these steeds were huge compared to the ponies I had met. One of their corrals had been converted into a camping area, and some friends paid to tent, but with storms coming in, they found an old, unlocked RV in which to spend the night instead, without asking. Pay showers (advertised as "warm") were absolutely the most disgusting on the entire AT, and that's really saying something! Used Band-Aids, sticky pieces of dirty duct-tape and something alive in the black, murky, clogged drain freaked me out. I felt dirtier when I came out than when I went in! Also, the commode was gross and definitely "Out of order."

From this point on, the forest closed in on us and felt more remote. Spotting a deer eating only a few feet off the path, I stopped to watch. Then a pretty, young woman I've never seen before, wearing dreads tied-up with a bandanna and a colorful hiking dress down to her feet, stopped as well. We just stood and watched the deer together for a few moments before she said, "Cool" and went on her way. I wouldn't see her again for several hundred miles and never learned her "real" trail name, so I just called her Rasta-Girl.

Wapiti Shelter was a classic Adirondack style structure in a peaceful setting. Inside, some stoner wrote "Smoke weed" on the wall with hiker chalk (campfire charcoal), starting an episodic chain of graffiti by a succession of hikers...

- "Smoke weed" - "go to jail."
- "Do coke - go to congress."
- "Do meth - live in a trailor park."
- "Spell trailer wrong and you are a burnout!"

Hanging from the rafters was an assortment of antique mouse trapezes, contraptions Macgyvered from rope and old tin cans that campers hang their food bags and packs on to discourage mice. Rodents like to hang out at shelters because there are always food scraps and hikers to harass. Most shelters are quiet during daylight hours, but once the sun goes down, they turn into a circus, complete with high-wire acts, acrobatic running jumps, near death free-falls, games of chase, rope-repels and squeaking and/or taunting. My personal favorite: mice walking across your face!

During lunch on Sugar Run Mountain, I watched two hawks flying together. I could have watched them all day, but ominous storms were rolling in. I desperately tried to get off the rocky ridgeline as echoing thunder crept closer until it was right on top of me. Rain, then razer-sharp marbles of ice, sliced green tree leaves into shreds that covered the forest floor with green and white (like snow) that crunched under my feet. Then, a lightning strike! Woods flashed yellow/white for a second, electric and buzzing. Ears ringing and the hair on my arms standing up, by instinct, I just took off running. Surrounded only by trees and rocks, I found the safest place I could, a low place near some smaller bushes and crouched down. There were several more strikes and for moments after, I could feel an electric charge lingering in the air, crackling. Uninjured, I can still recall that tense feeling, years later.

Lightning can be deadly and is one of the biggest dangers hikers face...

- **Auditory range** is 5 to 8 miles. Hiking expert Tuts says... "Don't be fooled: If you can hear thunder, you can be struck by lightning."
- **Find the lowest point possible.** Shrubs or small trees of uniform height, ditches, or trenches.
- **Stay away from water,** rocks, solitary trees and open spaces.
- **Don't stand close to others.** Spread out 15-20 feet apart.

- **Crouch down** in a baseball catcher's stance with hands on knees, or with hands over ears to prevent acoustic shock.
- **Canopies** (trail magic tents) and rock overhangs are NOT SAFE.
- **Metal objects,** including trekking poles and framed backpacks (or anything with metal inside), can be dangerous.
- **Apply first aid or CPR** to the injured immediately. Lightning victims don't carry an electrical charge and are safe to touch.

During another downpour, I stopped for an hour at Doc's Knob Shelter with some others also seeking refuge. Sunrise was comfy in his sleeping bag where he had been most of the day with the contents of his food bag spread out all over the floor. Very polite, this young religious fellow wanted to hike the whole trail, and then buy a small boat and sail home to Florida. He said a prayer for my safe travel.

When the rain finally let-up, the Appalachian Trail had turned into the Appalachian River. Temps dropped, and puddles were ankle deep in places. I was still having a blast even with the rain, flooding and cheap poncho torn and falling apart. If it was sunny and pleasant all the time, with no challenges to overcome, we wouldn't have as many exciting stories to tell. The experience reminded me of a saying by my Native American friend, Jumanji, during a bad hail storm in the Smokies: *"We needed some adventure - in our adventure!"*

Approaching Angel's Rest, nestled among huge rock formations, I heard a windchime that someone had left hanging in a tree, its eerie songs heard long before arriving. I'm told this is one of the best views in the area, but unfortunately, it was fogged in. Hikers can't just wait around for skies to clear. Some you see, some you don't. Also in the area, one of my biggest regrets from the trail was not visiting Woods Hole hostel. The 1880's chestnut log cabin has been a hiker rest stop since 1986, perfect for those looking for a communal, hands-on, back-country homestead experience complete with tending garden, bee-keeping and yoga classes.

Abruptly, the AT spit me out into a neighborhood, but finding Pearisburg wasn't as easy as you would think. Without a guidebook or blazes of any kind, I was lost, so I headed down the highway toward what looked like civilization. After a mile or so, a trooper buzzed his siren, pulled over and pointed me in the right direction - back up the mountain.

Before I tell you about town... have you heard the unbelievable story of Randall Lee Smith? Resident psychopath and AT serial killer? May 1981. Robert Mountford Jr. was thru-hiking to raise money for a school helping mentally retarded children. His friend, Laura Susan Ramsay, had joined him for a few weeks. They were both 27-years-old and from Maine. Putting faces to the names, grainy newspaper photos showed Bob, outside a shelter, wearing a thick jacket. With dark hair and mustache, he loosely resembled Tom Selleck from the TV show 'Magnum P.I.' Susan, wearing a hiking vest, had long braids and a huge, happy smile on her face; the biggest smile you've ever seen. Heartbreakingly, family members reported them missing when they didn't check in as expected.

Over 100 people joined the search. When blood was discovered on the wood floor of Wapiti Shelter (the one I passed with the old mouse trapezes), officials combed the surrounding area and made a shocking discovery. Partially covered by leaves, Susan's body was found inside her sleeping bag. Cadaver dogs were brought in and sniffed around until one sat down near a large tree stump, alerting his handlers. No one wanted to look, because they knew Robert's body was inside. Robert had been shot three times, Laura beaten and stabbed. For the first time, officials closed a section of the AT for safety reasons. A double-murderer was on the loose.

"Lyin' Randall," as he was known around town, was a person of interest from the start. Shortly after the murders, Smith himself left an odd handwritten note saying he'd been kidnapped! I'm not making this stuff up. Of course, no one had kidnapped this psycho and he was captured a month later, hiding in the swamps of South Carolina.

Smith was returned to Pearisburg to answer for his crimes, and mountains of evidence looked damning. Two murder weapons were recovered (a piece of angle iron and a fireplace poker), a cryptic confession note left in his truck and some of the victim's belongings that were found hidden in knot holes and under rocks, including a paperback book, belonging to Susan Ramsay, with a bloody fingerprint inside belonging to - Randall Lee Smith. But most importantly, eyewitnesses, including US Forestry workers finishing up at Wapiti Shelter, had taken photos of Susan on the day the murders were committed. Another man there didn't want his image taken. Eerily, when the film was developed, Randall Lee Smith could be seen lurking in the background! Case closed, right? Wrong! Out of nowhere, and without consulting the victim's families, a prosecution attorney negotiated a plea-bargain deal with defense. What? I know this was 1981 and still a long way from CSI and same day DNA results, but come on!

Pleading guilty to 2 counts of second-degree murder, Smith was sentenced to 30 years. Our justice system at work, he was released on parole after serving half that time - a measly 7.5 years for each precious, innocent life he senselessly erased with brutal violence. In 1996, the monster was returned to society and came home to Pearisburg. Appalled, victims' families and the hiking community, including Warren Doyle, picketed outside the courtroom. Tragically, their concerns would be realized 12 years later.

May 2008. Randall Lee Smith had taken to hiking deep into the mountains almost every day until he again went missing. Officials posted a missing person flyer throughout the area, including Trent's Grocery. Around the same time, hikers reported seeing skulls and crossbones painted on rocks and trees in the woods along the AT. Then, one fateful night, again for absolutely no reason and only a mile-and-a-half from the site of the original murders, reformed Randall Lee Smith shot 2 men. It's very possible he even used the same long barrel .22 pistol with which he killed Robert Mountford as it was not initially recovered.

Sharing their campfire and dinner with Smith, fishermen Sean Farmer and Scott Johnston said he told them his name was "Ricky Williams" (a professional baseball player) and that he had written papers for NASA, among other lies. Growing darker, Smith got up to leave, then, unprovoked, opened fire. Scott was shot in the neck and took another bullet in the back. Sean was shot in the head, but still attempted to charge the shooter and took a second round, point blank to the chest. The struggle only ended when Smith ran out of ammo. But the harrowing experience wasn't over. Not by a longshot.

Both friends critically wounded, they somehow made it to a Jeep and raced down the dark, dangerous mountain road. Sean, no longer able to see or talk, was sitting in the driver's seat and worked the pedals. Scott sat on the passenger side, turning the steering wheel with one hand, plugging a bullet hole in his neck with the other and yelling instructions when to press the gas and when to press the brakes. They nearly crashed twice before finding a house. Eventually medevacked to a hospital in Roanoke, they were rushed into emergency surgery. A state trooper tore a missing person poster off the wall and showed it to Scott who made a positive ID - Randall Lee Smith. It didn't take long until he was spotted driving Scott's pickup. The quick chase ended when he crashed a mile later. Arrested, Smith was transported to the same hospital where Scott and Sean were fighting for their lives.

Smith was released to police 2 days later. Up to his old tricks, knives and sunglasses belonging to the victims were found stashed in rabbit holes and underneath logs. Charges: 2 counts attempted capital murder, 2 counts using a firearm during the commission of a felony, 1 count possession of a firearm by a convicted felon and 1 count grand larceny (for stealing the truck). Smith's mug shots showed him still wearing a hospital gown and looking much older than his 54 years. Four days later, Smith was found dead inside his jail cell. An autopsy revealed he died from internal injuries sustained in the crash. Thankfully, this time, his victims would survive, but years later both still have unwanted souvenirs: scars and shrapnel. Their story was featured in Time Magazine, on Dateline and the 'Fatal Encounters' TV Series. The 1981 murders were the subject of a book, 'Murder on the Appalachian Trail,' by Jess Carr.

Now, back to our story... Pearisburg is a small town named after George Pearis, who lived in a fort, operated a ferry/tavern/store, donated the original 50 acres that became downtown and was its first Justice of the Peace (self-appointed). Buildings were being restored to original designs and inmates in orange jumpsuits were putting fresh, drab red paint on everything. An official Appalachian Trail Community, the town's website boasts that over 1,200 hikers visit each year.

A strip mall had a Food Lion, Goodwill, Mexican restaurant and a Chinese buffet. Very convenient, but if you need more services, like the PO, library, Wally World, or Pizza Hut, there's road walking involved. Hikers hate road walking. My choice was the Lucky Star Chinese buffet. Their storefront looked plain on the outside, but really nice inside, with impressive blue chandeliers. They had everything I craved and the food was awesome.

Next stop was the post office, where a total of 6 packages were waiting. Sometimes you can have too much of a good thing! Because of missed boxes in Damascus, these all ended up here at the same time. Another box was my computer. I picked out a couple to use and bounced the rest up the trail. The only thing missing was the guidebook I was depending on. Nope, still not here.

> HIKER TIP: The PO will forward (bounce) any package, with paid postage, anywhere else for free, so long as it has not been opened. Also, rubber bands the PO uses come in handy. Free if you ask politely.

Holiday Lodge is where all the hikers stay. However, a maid, wearing a purple uniform T-shirt, said they didn't have Internet, but I was happy to see High Gear and his buddies. Last time I saw him, he was petting a pony in the Grayson Highlands and trying to trade some gummy snacks. This time, he was all excited because his girlfriend was coming to visit. I never saw him again.

I tried to upload videos at the public library, but the connection is almost always terrible in these little towns, and I struggled for an hour. Then, I noticed a funky smell in the nice library. So bad, it reeked like a dead animal! First, I looked around at my fellow hikers, then turned my nose up at some local townspeople, before finally realizing the smell was me! My shoes were rancid. Dry, they weren't so bad, but rain reactivated the funk and my rotten, duct-taped shoes were stinking up the whole place! Mortified, I quickly packed up my stuff and left.

Time to retire my New Balance 101 Trail Runners after an amazing 630 miles. Completely blown-out, they should have been retired long ago, and admit I took it way too far. Looking around Dollar General, I found a pair of blue Vans knock-offs for $8. Cheap shoes like this are NOT recommended, but there was no other choice. Wally World was another 2-mile road walk - each way - and Pearisburg had no outfitter. There was a shoe repair shop there, but I don't even think trained professionals could have saved them! They probably stunk up the dumpster I put them in.

Back on the trail, I passed overgrown Pearis Cemetery. A sign counted 205 known graves entombed from 1810 to 1930, including 12 Civil War veterans. Town founder, George Pearis is buried in a brick enclosure at the far end. Here, I ran into Lt. Dan from Nashville, Tennessee. Smart fella, he suggested I take photos of his guidebook pages to get me to the next town. He had started the trail much earlier than me, but took a few weeks off to heal a sprained knee.

Finally climbing into the forest, I passed a box turtle going the opposite direction. I waved, as two cars do when they meet on a country road, but didn't break stride. Within a few hours, my new shoes were totally soaking wet from mountaintop balds of tall, wet grass. At dusk, I stood on a rock trying to film the sunset but my slick shoes slipped and I busted my butt! But there was still ground to cover if I wanted to find a place to sleep. It gets dark fast under the canopy of trees.

Chapter 9. The Trail Provides

Trail magic cooler with sodas and snacks.

The longest distance yet between resupply points, 90 miles of wilderness separates Pearisburg and Daleville. My dollar store shoes were really going to be put to the test and I hoped the food in my pack would be enough. A piece of paper nailed to a tree pointed to "The Captain's" across a stream. He's a longtime friend of the trail who built a zip-line so hikers can get to his property. The pulley is a slow moving, 3-person operation over water barely 2 feet deep, but looked like fun. Not a hostel per se, we're invited to camp in the backyard for free and there were tents and sleepy people milling about. Having a reputation for alcohol and wild parties, many look forward to the visit, but I quit drinking when I was 7 (dad let me sip his beer and I never drank again!). To be fair, my friends Sassafras & Kaboose, a father and his 13-year-old daughter, stayed with the Captain the next season and reported having a great time with no problems.

Baily's Gap Shelter. The big joke here is some wise guy installed a fake power outlet. I'm sure everyone who stops by posts a picture of it on his/her social media of choice, and I wonder how many people have actually tried it. Checking the register, which could also be considered a form of social media, folks made sarcastic remarks about the power box: "My phone was plugged in all night but never charged!"

"Someone didn't pay the electric bill!" etc. Instead, Tarzan drew a funny cartoon of the water sign we passed with all the graffiti on it (at least 2 hikers were called Tarzan that season).

There were also 3 fuel canisters left here for trash. Some hikers use these mini gas tanks to fire up their stoves. Offended, I videoed a pre-view of a rant I had later during a Pennsylvania meltdown. There was also fresh shelter graffiti, a drawing of a flower in black and red magic marker with an uplifting message: "Believe in yourself."

Finding a red and yellow Hacky sack laying on the side of the trail, I knew immediately to whom it belonged: Prophet & Canecutter. These two friends worked together in Alabama. They mentioned Jesus from time-to-time and prayed before meals, but were not overpowering with their message. I was always happy to see them and hear about their adventures. I packed that hacky sack for about 20 miles until I found Prophet at War Spur Shelter. Tossing it to him, without missing a beat he instinctively bounced it between his feet and knees, thanked me and put it safely into his pocket.

Prophet's trail name could have been "Bob Ross," because he looked like a stunt-double for the eccentric TV show landscape artist who painted "happy trees." Prophet even wore a Bob Ross T-shirt and sported the same white-dude afro that got bigger every time I saw him! Canecutter got his name from his father, who said rabbits back home were called "Canecutters," and the name stuck. His dad, David, even watched my videos to keep track of his son's progress. Nursing a sore ankle, Canecutter never gave up.

The AT then leads directly under massive Keffer Oak. Over 18 feet in circumference, and estimated to be at least 300-years-old, this White Oak was named after former landowner, Rex Wallace Keffer. Purple and yellow flowers dotted edges of the trail, and a fearless lizard, brown with prehistoric spikes down his back, was sitting on a log and instead of darting away, just looked up and smiled. Too brave for his own good, part of his tail was already lost escaping a predator.

Virginia and it's 544 miles would take over a month to complete. You may have heard rumors that Virginia is flat. Well, it's not. Maybe terrain here is a little more "even" relative to other mountainous areas, but there were still lots of tough climbs; some, straight up-and-over that made me miss endless switchbacks I cussed back in North Carolina. But at the top of one particularly steep ascent, Brushy Mountain, a handwritten sign offered a reward...

TRAIL MAGIC!!! Saturday 4 p.m. - Monday. Drinks, hamburgers, camping (Be ready to party!)!

Brier, and a half-dozen friends, had a sweet set-up. Unfortunately, a mutt running around loose stole my hotdog, but I enjoyed two of the best, icy cold Mountain Dews I've ever had! Ah! It was fun meeting other hikers, and our hosts all but insisted we make camp right there and stay for breakfast, but I left when the party got rowdy.

Only yards away, a sign pointed to the Audie Murphy Memorial. Audie was the most decorated hero of World War II. Lying about his age to join the military, he received the Medal of Honor at 19, after combating an entire company of Germans for over an hour - single-handedly. If that wasn't heroic enough, he then led a triumphant counter-attack, taking many prisoners, all while wounded and out of ammo! Audie would become a popular actor, and appeared in over 40 feature films. Tragically, he was killed, along with the pilot and four other passengers, in 1971 when their twin-engine plane crashed into this mountain. Valley residents still recall hearing the bomb-like sound made by the impact. Audie was 45-years-old. I added a small stone to towering cairns put here by visitors. Others left notes and tiny American flags.

Struggling up the next steep incline, a cute young woman I met at the cookout powered by me. Just over 5 feet tall, she was a very strong hiker. Gumby was her trail name, I assume because of the green shirts she wore - the same color as the toy action figure spoofed by Eddie Murphy on 'Saturday Night Live:' "I'm Gumby, dammit!" When I finally made it to the top of that mountain, Gumby had already set up her campsite, fire and all. I was impressed.

For several mornings, I passed another tent, but never saw anyone up-and-about, and couldn't help wondering: who was inside? Then one morning, I finally caught them getting packed. Pippy & Bojangles were friendly folks and we took a few breaks together over the next couple of days. One afternoon, we were hiking along a ridge when Pippy stopped, signaled me to come closer, and whispered, "Deer!" Slowly, I took my camera out and started filming as the doe, about 15 feet away, stood staring at us. Suddenly, it reared-up and charged poor Pippy! She called out, "Oh my God!" closed her eyes and turned away at the very last second! "Whoo! She came right at me!" That deer passed within a foot of Pippy, jumped across the trail and down the other side. Close call! It's rare for critters we meet to be aggressive. Most run the other direction, but any animal that feels threatened may charge. Last time I heard from Pippy, they were taking a zero in the next town.

Seen all along the AT, whitetail deer flash the white underside of their tails to warn their deer friends of danger. Sometimes they also breathe heavily, called "blowing." Average sized bucks usually weigh 200 lbs. The largest on record was claimed to have been over 500 lbs. A doe usually weighs between 100 and 200 lbs. Bucks shed and re-grow antlers every year, and fawns lose their spots during their first summer. Deer have unique, 4-chambered stomachs that allow them to eat things humans cannot, such as poisonous mushrooms and ivy. They've been recorded running at speeds up to 47 mph, and can jump almost 9 feet high!

Dramatically jutting out of the top of Cove Mountain were 2 huge monolith formations named "Dragon's Tooth." You can free climb 2 stories to the top for a better view at 3,020', but I didn't chance it with my dollar store sneakers. This was a heavily overused campsite and the earth between the stones was bare and littered with old cook pans and tin cans.

Doing this section in the rain is not recommended. Challenging, this mountain has rock scrambles, stone stairs and bouldering. Ladders and handholds made of rebar, helped in the steepest areas. Also, an overzealous volunteer empowered with some paint and a brush, got a little crazy with the white blazes. Some led straight up - nearly vertical shear rock walls! I took a less direct route, but no one makes it to the bottom without some bumps and bruises. Filming one particularly difficult example: First, I clambered down, set up my camera and started it recording. Second, scaled all the way back up to the top where I started. Third, descended back down to get the shot. I edited out the unneeded bits later. The things I do to make a (hopefully) interesting video!

My food was already running low, but a trailhead sign indicated a store 7 miles north, so I ate freely. Of course, when I got there the store had closed forever and I ran out a day early. I remember eating ramp leaves and rationing my last few Kool-Aid packets for nourishment. There was plenty of water, but a thru-hiker burns around 4,000 calories a day and must replenish that amount, also daily. There were other hikers in the area, but I was too embarrassed to ask for help.

Exhausted from climbing up a steep series of wooden steps, I stopped for a break. Sitting there - starving - I noticed that a previous hiker must have sat in this exact spot and, judging by the evidence, was eating trail mix. Apparently, he didn't like almonds, as dozens had been discarded to the ground. My favorite! Some had rodent teeth marks on them, but were delicious and just what I needed to make it up that mountain. You can call it, "guardian angels," "one mind," "3rd man factor," "God," or maybe it was somehow the trail itself? All this talk of finding food reminds me of a joke: ***What's the difference between a day hiker, a section hiker and a thru-hiker?***

• **A day hiker** (only walking a short distance and then going home) sees a colorful M&M on the ground and thinks, "Oh, that's a shame," and keeps going.
• **The section hiker** (camping for several days or weeks) spots an M&M on the ground, stops, looks around to make sure no one is watching, picks it up and eats it, then keeps going.
• **The thru-hiker** (hiking 4 to 6 months) sees an M&M on the ground, eats it...then digs for more!

I went to bed hungry, but in the morning cooked the last oatmeal packet (cinnamon flavor) I had been hoarding. Oatmeal is my absolute least favorite thing in my food bag, but I carry it because it packs small and is loaded with carbs.

AM showers ended by noon, making it very hot, very fast. The humid environment became rainforest-like, and zealous box turtles came out in droves. Perhaps it was Spring mating season, as I saw 5 in just a few miles - each with bright, colorful shells adorned yellow, red and orange. Some had black dragonfly markings lined-up on their backs. I didn't get any pics, as my camera batteries were as depleted as my food bag.

I found another pair together, one on top of the other either having sex, or trying to kill each other. Do you have any idea how hard it must be for a tortoise to even find another of its kind? They may crawl a little faster than you would think, but have huge forests to cover and can only see a few steps in front of them and no higher than a couple inches. No wonder they live to be 100 years old - it might take them that long to find a mate!

As a child, I collected dozens of these fascinating reptiles while exploring the vast woods behind my home. Turtles are also my token creature, as we both travel through lonely lives, slowly, with our homes on our backs. Box turtles are unique, with a hard shell that hinges on the bottom, front and back. When threatened, they can become totally enclosed by withdrawing their head and limbs. That is, if their bellies are not too full of snails, earthworms and berries. They will eat almost anything they can fit in their mouth. Males have red eyes; females, brown. These tortoises may seem common, but are listed as "vulnerable," with a population decline of 35% over 3 generations, mostly due to loss of habitat and fatal road crossings.

Miles later, I made it to a gravel parking lot with rows of cars on Catawba Mountain. Desperately needing a store to buy food, and without my guidebook, I was flying blind, but only waited a few moments before a group of day-hikers emerged from the woods. My Jedi mind tricks improving, I yogied a ride just by asking, "Which way is the closest store?" They said, "Get in!" and away we went! They asked questions all the way down the mountain, and I paid my fare happily.

Catawba Quick Mart offered made-to-order gas station food, but I had other plans... food haul! I grabbed a loaf of bread, a pack of baloney, mustard packets (from the grill), heaps of chips, Slim Jims, Combos, candy, cookies, Nutty Bars, Power bars and a couple of Gatorades. I even scored a map (a free tourist pamphlet of the area, vague, but better than nothing). Sitting in the parking lot, I made and devoured 3 sandwiches before a compact car pulled up and asked if I needed a ride. Roundtrip to the store and back was only a half hour. Not normal backpacking food, the bread got beat-up, and I learned Combos "sweat" in Ziploc bags. I also bought batteries, or would have missed memorializing an upcoming highlight of the trek...

McAfee Knob is the single most photographed landmark on the Appalachian Trail. Because of the vast numbers of tourist who visit, the Roanoke Appalachian Trail Club (RATC) took it upon themselves to form the militant-sounding group, "McAfee Knob Task Force," to help ATC ridgerunners keep watch. As predicted, 30 or more people were already here, taking pictures and gazing at the awesome view, each taking turns walking to the edge of the large, pointy rock that appears to be floating out and far away from the cliff, high above the valley below. Others seemed perfectly comfortable dangling their legs precariously over the edge.

> FUN FACT: 'A Walk in the Woods,' starring Robert Redford and Nick Nolte (based on the book by Bill Bryson), used imagines of McAfee Knob heavily for promotional advertising.

> FUN FACT: Over 100 years ago, the beautiful "Scarlet Woman" plunged off this cliff. Legend predicts she reappears every 23rd of July, luring men to join her on the other side. Women seldom see the apparition.

Once past the knob, the trail is empty again of all but thru-hikers. I enjoyed walking through a maze of monstrous, cube shaped boulders, each towering high as a house. Next was Tinker Cliffs, every bit as amazing as McAfee Knob but without the crowd. Continuing along this mile-long cliff walk, a mist hung 2,980' above Catawba valley, below. Jumping over deep cracks was exciting, but some white blazes were painted only inches from the edge of steep drop-offs - not very safe, especially for hikers navigating through thick fog. Fellow thru-hikers enjoying the day: Canecutter, Prophet, B1, and from Georgia - Garner brothers: Grady & Harrison. They told me all about visiting The Home Place Restaurant in Catawba, well known for home cooked food and southern hospitality. I could almost taste the chicken-fried steak and gravy.

The $8 specials held up okay, but didn't have the grip level serious hikers need. Comfort was the real disqualifier, as the cheap rubber soles became more pliable with every uneven rock I walked over. The last couple of days were almost like walking barefoot. Guess I just like to torture myself. I also got tired of day-hikers questioning if I had really walked all the way from Georgia, judging me by my small backpack and those ridiculous shoes.

> HIKER TIP: *Rockhounds, keep your eyes open for crumbling shale near streams that may hold a fossil or cast of an ancient trilobite or gastropod. Both are known to be found in the area.*

Getting dark, my encampment had a relaxing view of the Daleville nightlights, below. A previous camper had made a teeny-tiny fireplace out of stone slabs, and I enjoyed a half-hour of "hiker TV," watching flames dance and flicker. Campfires add to the adventure, but make you and your gear smell like smoke. I made very few fires on my trip, but am not at all opposed to it. I'm no Eagle Scout, and conjuring up a fire from scratch without dry, perfect conditions can be extremely frustrating. Plus, I always worry about fires getting out-of-hand.

> HIKER TIP: *If you make a campfire, keep it safe. Most of the following tips are from the 'Smokey the Bear' website. For fun, read the following instructions with a heavy 'Smokey the Bear' voice...*

• **Rules:** Some states don't allow fires of any kind. New Jersey (I would find) takes offenses very seriously.

• **Conditions:** Never make a fire if extremely dry or windy.

• **Location:** Use existing fire rings, or make a circle lined with stones at least 15 feet away from tents, shrubs, or flammable objects.

• **Tinder:** Loosely pile twigs, dry leaves, grass, or pine needles.

• **Kindling:** Add sticks less than 1" around, in a pyramid shape.

• **Ignite:** Blow lightly at the base of the fire.

• **Warning:** Don't stand over a smoking fire. You could inhale smoke, pass-out and fall into the flames.

• **Never leave a fire unattended.** There is no "OFF" button.

• **Be careful drying gear near a campfire.** Sleeping bags, shoes, or other items could shrink, melt, or deform.

• **Extinguish:** Pour water (or sand) onto the fire until cold to the touch. Never cover embers with ashes - they may fester and reignite.

• **Keep campfires small:** You don't need a pep-rally bonfire to cook. I saw some real monsters on the trail!

Cicadas! We'd been hearing insects for days, but suddenly, they were freaking everywhere! The constant, deafening sound resembled 50 car alarms going off all at once, but after a while you get used to the drone of a noise they make. "Jar Flies," as some people call them, were on every single leaf of every single tree. They fluttered erratically, and I dodged more than a few kamikazes. Spending most of their lives underground, these Cicadas only come out to mate - then die - every 17 years. Last seen in 1996, this brood was expected to be in the <u>billions</u> and their offspring won't emerge until 2029! Too many to avoid, bug carcasses crunched under my feet.

The last stretch took me under several large rock overhangs. Native Americans used these natural roofs for shelters and I could visualize a family of Indians sitting under them, cooking by a fire. Sadly, some of these sacred places were now covered in spray paint and graffiti.

Town days are rarely zeros for me and in fact, can be quite hectic. It takes time to get all my errands done. I try to check-in early - and always leave at checkout time, usually with a maid banging on the door. In Daleville, the AT crosses the road within sight of all the amenities: convenience stores, hotels and fast food joints. The larger city of Roanoke is only 15 miles away if you need more services.

First, I went to the HOJO (Howard Johnson Express). This location is famous for being hiker and pet friendly, with cheap rates and a big breakfast buffet. Balcony railings were draped with sleeping bags and pack covers of all colors, drying in the breeze. I waved hi to several buddies and planned to stay here, but the check-in girl was honest and said they were waiting for a tech guy to fix the Wi-Fi. Across the street, I checked into the more expensive, but much more modern, Super 8. An easy choice as they are always clean and have dependable Internet. Well worth the extra $20 bucks and you never have to worry about getting a TV without a remote or shower that doesn't get hot. Plus, you could stuff up to 4 hikers into a room for $60 total, that's about the same price as the HOJO, but with more creature comforts. The 8's owners have had some trouble with disorderly hikers so they can be a little stuffy, but were nice to me. My luxurious room was decorated with designer carpet and hand-painted, original artwork.

Washing all my clothes, I made several toga towel hallway runs to the laundry room. In my mail drop, Mom sent the book Appalachian Trials, by Zach Davis, aka Badger. A thru-hiker himself (Class of 2011), he wrote this book from a psychological perspective focusing on overcoming mental hurdles, setting goals and readjusting to the real world after you're done. I finished it in three nights. Badger gives back by sponsoring a handful of long distance hikers each year.

Just up the street was Botetourt Commons Shopping Center with a Kroger grocery store, BBQ joint, Wendy's, coffee shop and Outdoor Trails Outfitter. OTO is well known for helping hikers get defective gear replaced and will even do most of the communicating with vendors for you. You would be surprised how often high dollar boots, backpacks and trekking poles, fail. A nice girl assisting me was familiar with the AT and couldn't believe I hiked the previous 90 miles in dollar store shoes. She was happy to deposit them in the trashcan as I strutted out on new tires. I was stoked to find a nice pair of New Balance Nergy trail runners, $59.50, on clearance; a little heavier than what I was used to and a half-size larger, but no big deal. My sister Beth gifted me the cash and I still had walking around money left over. Thanks sis!

The store was sold out of the current guidebook, but I found a year-old Companion in the bargain bin for $6 and only noticed minor changes. In all, I hiked 255 miles from Damascus to Daleville with no instructions. I survived, but it sure would have made life easier.

> HIKER TIP: *Gear from established brands is usually guaranteed. Ask nicely, and most companies will repair or replace worn-out or broken items and send them to your next stop. Socks are replaced right off the shelf.*

Cooking with Loner! I'm no chef and cook very little - on the trail or at home. To give you an example, I can honestly say that I have never cooked a hamburger in my life! It's just not in my program. That being said, one of the staples I can make I call, "Hobo Wraps." I used a few items from my mail drop and bought other ingredients at the grocery store. If I can make them, anyone can! I ate 4 for lunch, 4 for dinner and had the last 2 for breakfast; 3 delicious meals for only $15 total. Don't forget a 2-liter pop and a bag of candy for dessert!

Ingredients: (Makes six servings):

- 10 soft tortilla wraps
- Pepperoni (Exchange or combine with bacon bits, etc.)
- 2 cups shredded cheddar cheese (or your favorite)
- Head of lettuce
- 1 onion, 1 green pepper, 2 tomatoes
- Jar of salsa
- Small bottle of ranch dressing

Directions:

- Sprinkle some cheese on a tortilla shell.
- Add pepperoni or protein of choice. Some prefer rice or beans.
- Add salsa and diced veggies.
- Heat in the microwave for about 1 minute, 45 seconds.
- Add lettuce, more cheese and ranch dressing. TA-DA!

Staying up late, I watched videos on YouTube posted by another subculture, arrowhead collectors. One was by a pretty, young woman named Cora Jean who did a cartwheel every time she found a nice point. I already had a crush on her for a while, but was sure we'd never meet. Still, I commented on her video with my Appalachian Trail Loner user name, hoping she'd catch on out of curiosity. I also got my fix of American Pickers and Storage Wars on TV. Just by luck, I picked a good night to stay in a hotel because it stormed very hard outside. With howling wind and rain coming down in sheets, I worried about all the hikers out there in the woods.

I still made a 15-mile day leaving town well after lunch. Following a lush greenway, I waved thanks to a volunteer with a loud lawnmower. Thru-hikers strolling along freshly cut green grass feel like movie stars walking the red carpet. At the top of the first hill, Fullhardt Knob Shelter had an interesting cistern system for collecting rainwater. Rain runs down the slanted roof into gutters, then down a pipe into a holding tank. Brackish liquid comes out of a spigot; however, it still needs to be boiled or treated. Not my first choice, but a novel idea for shelters without a water source.

Paralleling the Blue Ridge Parkway (BRP), some hikers hated the next section because we share our ridgeline with car tourists who stop at parking lot pull-offs to take in the view, and read information boards describing what they're viewing. Other than traffic noise, I found it to my liking because there were picnic tables and trashcans (the previous segment had a 70-mile stretch without a single can).

Called "America's Favorite Drive," The Blue Ridge Parkway was built to connect the Great Smoky Mountains with Shenandoah National Park and its famous Skyline Drive. Both roads join end-to-end, but are two separate entities. Work began on the BRP in 1935 but wasn't fully completed until 1987, 52 years later. Construction created many jobs, but also displaced longtime residents and brought strict new rules for those who remained, including the Eastern Band of Cherokee Indians.

B1 was a cool guy who got his trail name from an airplane baggage ticket still attached to his backpack, reading of course, "B1." Missing most of one hand, I honestly hadn't notice until he joked it got lots of attention while hitchhiking! He loved his AT experience so far, but was talking about going home to Portsmouth, New Hampshire, for a rock concert. Checking out the impressive Bryant Ridge Shelter, this clubhouse-looking mega shelter had a main floor and two loft platforms reached using built-in wooden ladders and sleeps 20.

It's tradition for hikers to take pictures at "The Guillotine," an immovable round rock wedged between 2 tall boulders with the AT's path passing precariously underneath. It looked ready to drop at any moment! Some pose under it as if they are about to get squished. Others pretend to be running in slow motion - like Indiana Jones escaping a booby trap! Nearby, I found a small, mossy looking ball that turned out to be a rolled-up fluffy caterpillar, well camouflaged to look like a twig and very convincing. Just one of many cool critters I would see for the first time during this expedition.

Sunrise walked up as I was taking a break. Like I had done recently, he had misjudged his food/mile ratio and ran out early. He yogied a couple of peanut butter packs and a box of raisins then thanked me for 5 full minutes. We agreed to hike together to the next shelter after local tornado warnings were broadcast over the radio. Walking along, Sunrise told me he was leaving the trail. He wasn't injured, nor run out of money. Only in his 30's, he had already survived multiple heart operations and had zipper scars as a reminder. There was some trouble getting necessary heart medications refilled in trail towns, but that wasn't what was bothering him.

Until recently, Sunrise had been part of a 3-piece group staying together for several hundred miles... then basically... ditched. I don't know the reasons why, or if it could have been handled in a better way, but he did tend to be over excited about every single little thing. Also deeply religious, he could be insistent about it at times. Now alone, he missed his buddies and was genuinely concerned about their wellbeing. Asking me if I had seen his friends, I had to awkwardly tell him "yes," and that they were fine. No one likes to feel abandoned, but their bond was broken. Once safely to the shelter, Matt's Creek, everyone there pitched in some food for Sunrise and his mood improved.

> HIKER TIP: Hiking with medications? Always carry photo ID, prescription papers, doctors' names (and number) and the original pill bottle they came in. You may need these items to get refills, or replacements if lost.

This was the first time I met Radio and Tyvek. Radio was a heavyset young man who started a month before me and was having fun just taking his time. Showing me his top of the line hammock system, pimped out with all the bells and whistles, he reminded me of "Badger," my favorite character from the TV show 'Breaking Bad.' His buddy Tyvek was a thin fellow from Georgia, known for drawing funny logbook caricatures of hikers he met (secretly, I hoped he would do one of me). Tyvek was named after waterproof material used by hikers making DIY camping gear.

> FUN FACT: Tyvek. You probably use this DuPont product every day: Priority Mail envelopes, waterproof maps, hospital bracelets you can't tear and coveralls worn at the Fukushima Nuclear site, are all made of Tyvek.

Intimidated by the imminent storms, this was one of those rare instances I made camp within sight of a shelter just in case I had to run for cover during the night. Thunderstorms rolled through, but everyone made it just fine, though I woke to find a large tree had fallen right across an empty tent site. I never heard a thing. Very scary. A beautiful morning, this would turn out to be the final time I saw my friend Sunrise. I'll remember him fast asleep and snoring, with his mummy-shaped sleeping bag zipped up over his head. To hike almost 800 miles, especially considering his health conditions, was a huge accomplishment.

Using my newly acquired, handy-dandy guidebook, I was surprised to learn James River was less than 700 feet above sea level. For comparison, "The Guillotine," a few pages ago was upwards of 4,000'. All hikers cross the 700-foot long James River Footbridge, longest on the AT. It appeared to be made of steel beams from an old train trestle with a newer wooden floor. Warren Doyle started a tradition that thru-hikers jump off the bridge and into the river. Sorry Warren - I can't swim and float like a brick - but crossing the bridge, a feeling came over me that I was making real progress. But then, on the north side of the bridge, a humbling mile marker brought me back to reality: Only 775 miles down and 1,403 to go! *Update: Jumping off the James River Footbridge is now "prohibited." Whatever.*

After a hard, 3,000-foot climb up the other side of the valley, on top of Bluff Mountain was a concrete memorial...

"This is the exact spot Little Ottie Cline Powell's body was found, April 5, 1891, after straying away from Tower Hill School house Nov. 9, A distance of 7 miles. Age 4 years, 11 months."

Visitors built little cairns and someone had left a turkey feather. I gifted an old blue marble I had picked up along the trail. The guidebook officially lists this area as "haunted."

Chapter 10. Peanut Butter Pie

"The Tribe," on top of Spy Rock. Left to right: Rainbow Eyes, Apache and Orion.

Taking a Pop Tart break on a gravel service road (USFS-38), I lay down, using my backpack as a pillow. Just then, a group of Boy Scouts emerged from the woods and thought I had been hit by a car! After assuring them I was just being lazy, they asked all kinds of AT questions while waiting for their leaders to catch up. Those kids had out-hiked the adults by at least 10 minutes!

> FUN FACT: Kellogg's Pop Tarts first hit the market in 1964 with four flavors. The name was a spin on the phrase "Pop-Art," made popular by Andy Warhol. Over 2 billion of the treats are sold each year!

B1 and I explored Brown Mountain Creek, a beautiful, wooded valley, former home to a community of freed slaves turned sharecroppers from the time of the Civil War to the early 1900's. As we hiked a mile or so along the creek we saw old stone walls, foundations and cemetery grave markers from the past. Weathered interpretive signs told the story of the area's rich history and former resident, Elie Taft Hughes, provided many of the reflections. He was born here in a log cabin where he lived with his mother, father and 8 brothers and sisters. One story that I will never forget was about Taft's mother making "ash cakes" for the children... After baking bread from scratch in the fireplace stove, she would sweep the hearth clean and put handmade cornmeal cakes onto the warm rocks, covering them with ashes and hot coals. Taft described these treats as the shape and size of a terrapin (small turtle). After a while, she would sweep the ash off with a hand broom made from a corn stalk, and wash them. He remembered, "They were much sweeter than if you baked them in a stove - much sweeter. I wished I had one now. It would be impossible to match that flavor."

This felt like a very special place, and I took a few moments to imagine what Taft's home may have looked like, smoke puffing out of the stone chimney as a horse-drawn wagon rolled up the dirt road heading to the creek's gristmill. I also thought it was interesting that Taft started smoking tobacco at only 9 years old, and used a corncob pipe to smoke it. Just don't let "Scare Rock" keep you from walking this part of the AT!

Something I saw at one of the shelters disturbed me: the name "Papa Smurf" written in black marker on the back wall among other graffiti. Smurfs? Those blue cartoon characters who live in mushroom-shaped houses in the forest? What could be disturbing about Smurfs?

> FUN FACT: Smurfs, elusive but friendly nature loving creatures, can sometimes be spotted dashing across the trail on foggy mornings. Standing "three apples high," they're bigger than you might have thought:)

Seemingly harmless, this tag caught my attention because a deadbeat hiker by that trail name - a man described as "a homeless military vet with mental problems" - was a person of interest connected to an unsolved murder on the AT just the year before. My mother had emailed me an article about it in case the killer was still hanging around. A young man from South Bend, Indiana, Scott "Stonewall" Lilly, had started his southbound section hike in Maryland, but never made it to Georgia. Passing hikers found him buried in a shallow grave off the blue-blazed trail leading to Cow Camp Gap Shelter, his body hastily hidden with loose brush.

A Civil War buff, he was only 30 years old. His mother spoke about her last conversation with her son, "He was just so excited and happy to be living on the trail."

Most of Stonewall's gear is still missing: "New 'Ozark Trail' shoes, a blue or purple backpack, Nintendo game and an AT handbook." Crimes committed on federal land, fall under the jurisdiction of the Federal Bureau of Investigation (FBI), so they took charge of the case, but in my opinion wasted precious time.

Lilly's last contact was a log entry dated July 31. His body was found August 12, but not identified until 4 days later. The FBI then waited months before releasing a frustratingly vague update, only calling the death "suspicious" with a murderer still on the loose. Autopsy results revealing Stonewall died from "asphyxia by suffocation," confirming the death a homicide, were not released until January of the following year. Six months? To be fair, they interviewed 83 people, collected more than 100 pieces of evidence and offered a $10,000 reward for info leading to an arrest and conviction. **Anyone with info should contact FBI's Richmond office: (804) 261-1044**.

Passing 800 miles, I was happy to get back on track for the goal I set for myself: 100 miles per week - average. I've never been one of those ultrahigh mile hikers, around 15 was the norm for me after getting my trail legs. There were lots of low 20s, with my personal best (later in the hike) being a 29-mile day. Like the children's fable, 'The Tortoise and the Hare,' again representing my token animal (or reptile), I would get up early and hike a steady pace till dark. Most others moved faster and had more free time to socialize. Everyone finds his/her own speed. Some (younger) hikers can do 30s on good days, with 40s being extremely rare. Trained runners may do more than that. But the most I heard of, by a thru-hiker walking the trail with a backpack and camping in the woods, was Bomber from Rochester, New York, with an insane 62.4 miles during a 24-hour period! He did all that with a rubber chicken named "Henry" hanging off his pack!

> *HIKER TIP: Big mile days? Once in hiker shape, it can be invigorating to see what the human body is capable of and how far you can push your endurance. Be proud of yourself no matter how far you traveled.*

• **Get started early!** This is the biggest secret to big mile days!

- **The lighter your backpack**, the faster you can hike.
- **Take breaks** - just keep them brief if the goal is to crunch miles.
- **Stay well fed, hydrated, and rested!** Food gives us energy, water gives us life and rest rebuilds our muscles and mind.
- **Snack all day.** Keep treats in your pockets so you don't have to dig through your pack. Eat a non-cook lunch high in carbs & protein.
- **Drink freely** and allow time to find and treat water.
- **Use your guidebook** to plan sections conducive to big days: long stretches without town stops, big elevation changes, etc.
- **Music**, audio books, whistling, or even singing can help rhythm.
- **Listen to your body** and don't over-do it. If you experience pain, faintness, or lameness - adjust your pace or shorten your day.
- **Have fun!** Experience the trail and don't just race across it.
- **Allow time to rest and recuperate**. Avoid back-to-back mega mile days. Eat well and drink lots of fluids that help your body rebuild.

A popup thunderstorm came out of nowhere, with heavy rain, hail and a single, frightening lightning strike. Afterward, I noticed my hands were shaking. At the Seely/Woodworth Memorial Shelter, a week-old logbook entry was obviously started during another rainstorm and had a funny rollcall with names of each of their party, condition and their favorite movie catch phrase! Some, if not all, were part of a hiking collective who called themselves the "Wolf Pack."

- **Walk and Eat** - Texas - Soaked - "Say hello to my little friend."
- **Hobo Joe** - Maryland - Soaked.
- **Atlas** - Florida - Soaked - "Feel lucky? Well do ya?"
- **Ragweed** - ? - Soaked - "Yippy Kai Yay."
- **Lobster** - Vermont - MIA.
- **Chickadee** - Maine - MIA.

Hanging on the shelter wall, a handwritten advertisement for the "Dutch Haus" offered free lunch - no strings attached! Going for it, I followed signs down a mile-long, steep private road to the meeting spot - a small parking area behind Montebello State Fish Hatchery. A couple of other hikers were already waiting: Loophole & Sleeping Beauty - both dudes from Georgia. Right on time, a blue 4x4 pickup showed up and I sat in an oversize beanbag chair as the driver raced down the rutted-out gravel road. Overgrown tree branches slapped both sides of the truck as I joked that the driver does shuttle runs and practices Baja racing at the same time! Loophole, sitting on an unsteady wooden stool, really got bounced around but said, "They could tie us to the top of this truck and we'd still be happy."

Dutch Haus Bed & Breakfast was a beautiful log cabin where owners Lois & Earl were over the top friendly. They offered private rooms in the house (a very reasonable $30 per person) and had a compact, but cozy, bunkroom out back. There were no "Budget Inn" - tourist trap tricks. I did buy resupply from a big suitcase of hiker grub organized into rows of different staples: Ramen, Pasta Sides, candy bars, etc. This is what it might look like if you were trying to smuggle trail food into a foreign country! For decoration, a stuffed Jack-a-lope hung on the wall (a rabbit with fake deer antlers) and a funny sign with skulls and crossbones read: "Many have eaten here, few have died." No worries; our lunch was wonderful: Mac & cheese, candy carrots, orange slices, brown sugar apples and to drink - cold lemonade & iced tea mixed together (it's a southern thing). The absolute best was dessert: peanut butter pie with whipped cream and chocolate chips on top! According to nutritional facts for a recipe I found on a cooking website, each slice is worth a whopping 745 calories and 16g of protein. That's what I call hiker fuel! I still reminisce about it, like Elie Taft talked about his mother's ash cakes.

Our free feast was made-up of leftovers from the previous night's home cooked dinner for the paying overnight guests, who also joined us for lunch. Each was freshly showered and squeaky clean wearing white robes and slippers, living it up like VIPs with only their trail beards giving them away as common hiker trash. To thank my hosts, I donated 'Appalachian Trails', by Zach Davis, to their small library of AT and local history books, hoping other thru-hikers would find it as helpful as I did. *Update: I would love to recommend the Dutch Haus to future hikers, but sadly, they have closed indefinitely.*

"The Rock of Eyes." On our way to Spy Rock, 3,680', we gained 1,000' elevation in just a mile. Day-hikers I met there were searching for a geocache, found using GPS coordinates on a list. Kind of like a primitive Pokémon GO. Truly gigantic, this boulder was big as a 6-story building laying on its side, like it was placed there by God. There is no marked trail to the top, but free climbing was a fun challenge and amazing 360° views were worth the effort. From here you also get a good look at the Religious Range of mountains including the Priest, Little Priest, the Friar, Little Friar and last, but not least, the Cardinal.

For me, being here was one of the highlights of Virginia. Native Americans visited this landmark, and soldiers on both sides of the Civil War used this natural vantage point to track opponent's movements. On top of the rock were dozens of tadpoles in several small pools of standing water. How do mama frogs even get up here!?

This is where I finally met Apache and his trail family. With Apache's camera phone, I took a picture of the trio having fun doing poses from 'The Matrix' movie. Apache started his thru-hike several weeks before me, and I think we were both surprised that I had caught up to him, even though he had taken time off to heal a bum ankle. His mother posted nice comments on my videos, keeping me informed where "The Tribe" was on the trail. I have a lot of respect for Apache, a laidback young man with a heavy North Carolina accent who, preceding his hike, documented making a hammock and much of his own gear, on YouTube. I watched and posted messages on his video blog before leaving for the AT.

At the top of Priest Mountain, 2 stones formed a monolith about 10 feet tall, standing in front of the shelter of the same name. If you squinted your eyes, it did indeed look like a praying, robed priest. A fun tradition: each hiker climbs to the top of the mountain and confesses to the Priest by signing the shelter's logbook. My confession: "I loved the peanut butter pie, with whipped cream and chocolate chips, at the Dutch Haus." Here are a few I'll leave unsigned...

- "I confess: I never dig a cat hole and just cover it with leaves."
- "I skipped a white blaze in Georgia."
- "I confess I hid a rock in my friend's backpack 400 miles ago, and he still hasn't found it!"
- "I stole a roll of toilet paper from the motel in Atkins."

Much later, I couldn't pass the chance to camp right on Tye River, so I stopped early. The water was cold, but soaking my tired dogs in the rapids was invigorating and cooking Ramen over an open fire warmed me up. Some nights were still chilly, even in June, and I'm glad I didn't send home my sleeping bag and warm clothes as others had done.

Another interesting design, the Paul C. Wolfe Shelter had a high roof and was situated on a creek with a scenic little waterfall nearby. Someone left Jules Verne's 'Around the World in Eighty Days,' and I carried it for almost a week without reading a single page before leaving it at another shelter. The Tribe walked up, had lunch, filled their water bottles and then got ready to take off again. Watching them organize, their leader Apache stood behind an invisible line directly at the spot they had left the trail, then his buddies fell in line behind him like baby ducks following their mother. Now that's what I call purists!

Next, I found a collapsible luggage buggy, like you would see at an airport, except this one was abandoned directly on the AT. Apparently, someone thought this would be useful and then just left it out in the middle of nature. LAZY! Then a few steps later, a rattlesnake! Thankfully, someone left a danger note, as the large reptile with lots of buttons on its tail was only inches off trail resting on a log. I tiptoed by safely.

Miles were coming easier and I knocked out a 22, but it had rained all day and by nightfall I just wanted to get into dry clothes, eat and go to bed. This was the only night of my entire hike that I slept with my food bag instead of hanging it in a tree. B1 told me the next morning he saw a medium sized bear sniffing around my tarp and scared it off. I didn't even know it was there! Of course, I was never too lazy to hang my food bag after that.

First thing in the morning, I was surprised to find an Indian arrowhead! After 2 months, and more than 800 miles, this nice grey quartz example was hidden amongst gravel of the same color, but to my trained eyes stuck out like a sore thumb. I rescued this point and will keep it forever, one of the few "Leave No Trace" principles I fudge on. Please try to imagine its maker walking along this same path centuries ago. He or she depended on this stone to feed their family. The feeling you get finding a gift like this is hard to describe. I took it out a half-dozen times that evening to stare at, using my headlamp, then kept it safely wrapped in tissue until I got a chance to mail it home.

Rockfish Gap. Before the first pyramids were built in Egypt, Native Americans - the Monacan - traveled here between ancient villages. Trails widened over time, and by the late 1700's, carriages of colonists crossed through this pass towards the west. Back then, this area was called Teasville after a tavern that served many intriguing, and sometimes infamous, guests including: George Washington, Thomas Jefferson and the Marquis de Chastellux, who described the tavern as

"One of the worst in America!" In 1797, John Wallace renamed the town after the famous war hero, Major General Anthony Wayne.

A friend of Benjamin Franklin, and handpicked by General George Washington, Wayne's military career could be described, at best, as "uneven." Besides fighting Brits, Indians and a brazen unsuccessful invasion of Canada, he also firmly settled no less than FOUR mutinies by his own men, one ending immediately after aiming his pistol at the uprising leader's head until he begged for his life. Even worse, Wayne once ordered <u>himself</u> court-martialed for evading injury and capture when comrades fell to bayonets.

Acquitted, Wayne rebounded by winning the important Battle of Stoney Point, 1779, personally leading his army on a daring nighttime attack. First, decoys fired muskets at the main entrance of the fort, creating a diversion as Wayne and his men climbed the steep rocky slopes of Stoney Point, its base only accessible during low tide. With only bayonets, axes and their own bare hands to use as weapons, the battle lasted less than 30 minutes. Even though Wayne himself survived a bloody musket shot to the head, he showed unexpected mercy to his prisoners. The victory is considered one of the most brilliant maneuvers of the Revolutionary War, earning Wayne a rare gold medal and the nickname "Mad Anthony."

Still, the Major General went on to negotiate peace treaties with Cherokee and Creek Native Americans, then led wars won and lost against "The Western Indian," including a victory over Shawnee War Chief Blue Jacket and his army in the Battle of Fallen Timbers. Wayne died a painful death in 1796 at the age of 51, not from battle, but rumors suggest rival General James Wilkinson, poisoned him. Nevertheless, a peaceful rest for the General was not to be had. As if his natural life was not sensational enough, the truly bizarre details leading to his supernatural afterlife are too ghastly for this book! Want to know what happened? You have some homework to do, but I'll give you a little hint, "Mad" also became known as "The Man with Two Graves."

Besides a ghost story or two, his most compelling distinction to history is his ancestral lineage to the (fictional?) comic book superhero, Batman! Batman's public persona, Bruce "Anthony" Wayne, is depicted as Major General Anthony Wayne's direct descendant! Even more thought provoking, Bruce Wayne's home (and Batman's underground base of superhero endeavors), Wayne Manor is said to have been built on land awarded to General Wayne for service to his country. In historical fact, the General was once awarded a large plantation as a prize. As I always pull for the underdog, sometimes to a fault, I've chosen "Mad" as my favorite General.

In addition to its cool name, Waynesboro was the most hiker friendly town I visited. There may even be a shuttle car waiting at the trailhead when you walk out of the woods! If not, check the trailhead kiosk for a list of trail angels, eager to pick up stinky hikers and deliver you to town (otherwise a dangerous 5-mile road walk.) No phone? Just follow signs a quarter mile to the Rockfish Gap Tourist Center. The small, nondescript building sits up on a hill, open 9 to 5. A volunteer called a ride for me. While here, pick up a booklet called, A Guide to Hospitality for Appalachian Trail Hikers. It contains info about the bus service, (13) hotels and (63) restaurants! Food choices vary from Mom 'n Pop places to Applebee's and Cracker Barrel.

At the info center, I met a thru-hiker from Maine: Johnnie Walker Red. He added the "Red" because someone else had already claimed the similar, Johnnie Walker Black. They had not met each other, but each modified their name to avoid confusion. Just a few minutes later, a nice fellow picked us up and into the back of a red truck I went. First, we stopped at the Shenandoah Valley Art Center, where our driver's wife was getting ready for an exhibit and gave us the exclusive, pre-opening tour! We even moved a few easels and helped hang some lights. Hey! They yogied us!

After picking up drop boxes and hitting a thrift store to buy a clean pair of town clothes for $6, I got dropped off at the YMCA, where they offer free camping and showers (with photo ID). But once inside, I was horrified to find the showers were "jailhouse movie style" - I don't like those. After waiting around for everyone to leave, I jumped into the darkest corner of the white-tiled shower room, splashed some soap and water around, then got the heck out! Dressed and safely outside, I realized my trusty, ultralight pocketknife that I had carried for over 800 miles was missing! I must have lost it in my haste to flee and I was NOT going back in to look for it.

Already feeling the pinch of low funds, I didn't want to spring for a hotel room. Then again, bad storms were forecast and I also didn't want to sleep outside. Thankfully, Grace Evangelical Lutheran Church graciously hosts a free hiker hostel in their large basement/evacuation shelter/fellowship hall, from middle May to late June. Doors open at 5:00 p.m. sharp, and there were at least 15 of us waiting outside. When they let us in, the rush was on like general admission to a Metallica concert. I was nearly knocked down the narrow stairs by an anxious man racing to the front of the line. Hey! No cutting! Posted on the walls were signs and rules that we were expected to follow in an orderly fashion. It's also required you have your photo taken, no big deal. The biggest drawback is they have a "lock-in" format, just like kids going to "All Night Skate" at the local roller rink.

Our happy hosts were a sweet, older couple who stayed in an RV in the parking lot and just made sure everything went smoothly. Also helping out, Santa's Helper, from Tennessee, was an older man with snow white hair and a long straggly beard, wearing glasses and a straw hat, but no backpack. He's been around the trail for years.

Just by pure luck, I was here on hiker feed night. Taco casserole! A pretty blond church woman was totally flirting with me the whole time - sat with me and even asked what I do for underwear! I answered her question honestly (commando), and we both blushed till our faces turned rosy red. There was a brief bible study upstairs for anyone willing, but only 3 of us went. The message was AT related and after, we got to watch choir practice. I was moved. The social room had a big fridge full of free fruit, snacks and leftovers. Not to mention shelves of books, a pair of computers for guests to check email and an impressive movie collection. Everyone watched 'Dances with Wolves' on a big screen TV. Memorable quote: "How many white-men are coming? As many as the stars." I also took another shower - 2 in one day!

Lights out! Rows of military-style folding cots along the walls reminded me of a refugee camp and B1, Sleeping Beauty, Loophole, Slim Pilgrim and the woman hiker I called Rasta Girl were just a few of my bunkmates. Thankful for a dry place to stay as storms raged outside, it was still a very long night. I'm just not used to ranks of people snoring, coughing, talking on the phone and even farting (taco night). Plus, the cot itself was very hard and not comfortable in the slightest. I gave up and retreated to the TV room, where I hung out with Pops and Rasta Girl, my fellow insomniacs. We had fun watching the AT documentary, 'Flip Flop Flippin,' while eating free ice cream.

Pops was a thin guy with a gray beard and long ponytail, a retired New York police officer who had the accent to prove it. He told story after story and had us both rolling in laughter. Sadly, he was icing a swollen knee and had already been there a couple days. It was not getting better. Through the trail gossip grapevine, I found out Rasta Girl had started the AT with a boyfriend, but they broke-up somewhere along the way. Both still hiking to Katahdin, things were awkward between them and their common friends.

The church kicks everyone out at 9:00 a.m. after a free breakfast of cereal and toast. Hikers fold cots, sweep floors and take out the trash. If you're staying a second night, they'll keep your backpack locked up so you can slackpack town. I didn't get much rest here, but really enjoyed the experience. I thanked my hosts and left a donation even though it's not required, then set out. This was also the last time I hung out with B1, but would see his name in logbooks from time to time.

Exploring town, my first stop was the Waynesboro Museum. Formally First National Bank, most interesting to me was a large room displaying Native American pottery and frames of arrowheads collected over many years by one local man. He kept careful, hand drawn records and maps in a stack of notebooks. Beautiful, the drawings were detailed with colored pencils. I also learned that during the Civil War, the 'Battle of Waynesboro' took place right here in 1865, along present day Main Street. Town was under Confederate control for 2 weeks and some older buildings still show scars from the battle.

Next stop: Little Caesar's Pizza. Just $5 for a large pepperoni! I added a 2-liter soda and order of breadsticks. Doing laundry, I met another hiking couple. The young woman, Bunny, was from Florida and earned her trail name when she placed Easter eggs in front of each tent and at the foot of every sleeping bag at Springer Mountain Shelter, back on Easter Sunday. Amazingly, we had started on the same exact day, but had never met till now. Also, she felt the need to explain that the friendship with her much older, male hiking partner was strictly platonic. I also saw Prophet and Canecutter at the grocery store, our unofficial meeting place in almost every trail town for hundreds of miles. You could almost set your watch to it. Other popular landmarks and food joints in town...

- **Ming Garden**. Trail famous AYCE Chinese buffet. $7.15 + drink.
- **Weasie's Kitchen.** AYCE pancakes and a food eating challenge.
- **Kline's Dairy Bar.** I loved these little ice cream shops.
- **Graham's Shoe Service.** Hiker friendly and does gear repairs.
- **National Soap Box Derby** races have been held on Main Street every May since 1962. I'd like to come back and see that one day.

> FUN FACT: National Soap Box Derby racing began in 1934. Boys and girls, ages 7 through 20, build their own gravity racer from kits and blueprints. The Waynesboro event is called the "Blue Ridge Classic."

Rockfish Gap Outfitters let me borrow a phone to call for a ride back to the trail, and by the time I bought water treatment and went outside, a running car was already waiting for me! Many thanks to this trail angel, but he dropped me off on the wrong side of the overpass. Taking a purist cue from Apache, I walked across to where I stepped off the AT the day before, then started hiking again without missing a single inch of the AT. Three other cars were already parked at the trail head, two waiting for random hikers to emerge from the forest so they could run them to Waynesboro, the other with trail magic pizza and pop. Having just ate, I only had a couple slices. It would have been rude to turn down trail magic!

Chapter 11. Playing Chase with the Bears

Billy the Bear gave me a scare, but let me go on my way.

Welcoming hikers to the Shenandoah National Park (SNP), a sign-in kiosk can be found as soon as you enter the woods. I filled out a carbon paper form (in triplicate) that hung off my backpack like a luggage tag. Similar to permits we carried in the Smokies, we listed exactly where we planned to stay each night, except here, things are a little more laidback, and I was never asked to show my made-up itinerary. Free for hikers walking into the park, cars and RVs are charged $15; motorcycles $10. Pets are allowed but must be kept on a leash.

Shenandoah has been a national park since 1926, and being only 75 miles from Washington, D.C., more than a million people visit each year. Encompassing almost 200,000 acres, the corridor's width varies from less than one-mile-wide to thirteen at its widest. Thru-hikers travel from one end to the other - over 103 well-graded AT miles and hiking here is what we dream about: flat trail - mostly free of rocks.

An interesting eco system, the SNP holds more plant types than all of Europe combined. Here, you can also count over a thousand varieties of flowering species, including 18 orchid types. Woolly adelgid beetles have destroyed nearly all the eastern hemlocks in the park, and another tree, the mighty American Chestnut, is all but extinct because of blight. Sometimes, you can still spot a doomed sprout trying desperately to grow out of an old stump, hanging on for a few days before withering away. Constantly evolving, this forest is now inhabited by over a hundred different tree species.

Also like the Smokies, wild animals within the park are protected and have never met a hunter. Almost immediately I saw a deer, the first of literally dozens I would interact with, in the park. After that, I almost stepped on a red anthill the size of a riding lawn mower. Looking around, several of these giant earthen mounds dotted the landscape. Watch out - they bite!

Nailed to a tree was a weathered diamond shaped marker. This rare survivor is how the AT was marked in the old days. Even earlier, brass markers were used. Tempting souvenirs, many were stolen, leaving the trail unmarked in places.

Emile Benton MacKaye, known as "Father of the trail," conceived the idea for the AT. The very first student to earn a Master's degree in Forestry from Harvard University, he remained at the school as an educator. In 1921, he wrote an article entitled: 'An Appalachian Trail: A Project in Regional Planning,' published in the 'Journal of the American Institute of Architects.' MacKaye believed it was most important to balance human needs with those of nature. A daydreamer and deep thinker, he visualized a wilderness utopia with a footpath connecting mountaintop farms, schools and communal camps, where people could escape the hustle and bustle of city life. His original concept was almost 1000 miles shorter, and the schools never materialized, but his positive effect on society was the same.

Four years after MacKaye's article, the ATC was formally organized, but the AT would still take another 15 years for volunteers to complete. MacKaye personally oversaw it's planning and construction until a proposal was made to relocate the trail, making way for an auto road running the length of Shenandoah National Park. MacKaye insisted the AT be left wild and urged ATC members to fight the road altogether, but fellow trail builder, Myron Avery, was more open to compromise, and argued to let CCC workers reroute the trail if that's what it took to keep the park open to hikers. The AT now runs parallel to famous Skyline Drive, crisscrossing the road 28 times. MacKaye left his project over the controversy and the two friends never spoke again.

I admire both men for following what they believed. MacKaye died in 1975 at the age of 96 and is buried in Massachusetts under a nondescript rock covered in New England moss.

FUN FACT: Benton MacKaye's father, a stage actor, was also a visionary, earning patents for over 100 theatrical inventions: flame-proof curtains, folding theater seats, cloud making machines, etc.

Myron Haliburton Avery, graduate of Harvard Law School, went on to oversee the completion of the AT. Although a very youthful-looking man with wild blond hair, he was a veteran of both world wars. Encouraged by his mentor and first ATC chair, Judge Arthur Perkins, Avery was enthusiastic about the AT's potential, and over many years, tirelessly flagged hundreds of miles for clearing. He also measured the overall distance himself, pushing along a surveyor's wheel, a contraption that looked like a bicycle wheel on a stick. In doing so he became the very first "2,000 Miler," or person to walk the entire length of the AT, although done in piecemeal fashion. A man of few words, when Avery and his men placed the original wooden terminus sign atop Mount Katahdin, he simply said: "Nail it up."

Aware that a living trail would need to be cared for continuously, he founded the Potomac Appalachian Trail Club (PATC) and numerous other clubs who maintain the AT to this day. Married, with two sons, he did all this as a volunteer, over 21 years while serving fulltime as a military admiralty lawyer. In 1952, Avery passed away at only 53 after a series of heart attacks. Colleagues said he died from overwork. "Avery Peak," a formidable mountaintop in his home state of Maine, was renamed in his honor.

Still tired from town, I barely walked off trail and went to bed early, then first thing in the morning, I spotted a Sasquatch; Scott "Squatch" Herriott, that is, former stand-up comic and lifelong Bigfoot believer. A tall, slender, bearded man, I recognized him immediately from his 'Flip Flop Flippin' movie I had just watched. What synchronicity! He had also made a series of movies while completing the Pacific Crest Trail (PCT). The AT, he found out, would take him 3 years to complete due to injury and illness.

My guidebook indicated the next 13 mile stretch, from Calf Mountain Hut to Blackrock Hut, had no water. For dry hikes like this I always camel-up, and fill both my water bottles before setting out. But this spring was barely a trickle.

> *HIKER TIP: To make a leaf funnel, pluck a thick green leaf and lay it in a shallow stream cascade. Then place a pebble on top to hold it down. You now have an easier way to quickly fill water bottles.*

The trail led through Black Rock Summit, an impressive pile of boulders, once a cliff or rock face, now rubble crumbling down the mountainside. Walking back into the woods, I spotted a black bear! This medium-sized fellow either didn't know I was there, or didn't care, as he just moseyed along. Moments later, a different bear on the other side of the trail was more skittish and ran off. To make this day even more exciting, near dusk, I was speed walking around a bend when I had to stop suddenly: a big bear ass blocked my path! I almost ran right into it! After a few moments, he sensed my presence, turned his head to look at me, and stormed into thick brush with a violent burst of energy. The largest black bear I've ever seen in the wild, he was every bit of 300 lbs. This park was crawling with bears!

This all happened only a few hundred feet from Loft Mountain Campground, one of several commercial camping areas in the SNP. Hikers are welcome to stay here too, for a fee and if there's room, but it can get very crowded, especially on weekends and holidays. Tent sites start at $16, but there's no need to pay because thru-hiker huts are stationed along the SNP. Here, shelters are called "huts," while the word "shelter" is reserved for picnic areas. Either way, I just stealth camped as I've done the whole hike, allowed so long as you stay at least 50 yards away from campgrounds, roads and water sources. Still, there were some late evenings walking further than I wanted to find a good spot. Hanging my hammock in a dense thicket of short, leafy trees, I had a visitor during the night, close enough I could hear it breathing. I would like to think it was just a deer but never got up to find out. The next morning, I was shocked to find both trees I was hanging from had old claw marks in the bark. Bears do this to mark their territory!

Some new hikers hear a noise and stand guard all night wielding sticks, building raging bonfires, or have nightmares straight off the TV show 'When Animals Attack!' But over time, I've learned not to jump every time I hear a twig break in the dark. In fact, it's kind of exciting.

Even packs of wild coyotes howling nearby don't bother me anymore and I sometimes wished I had packed some earplugs so I could just get some sleep! I never had any real problems with animals other than a few brazen mice trying my patience. Still, I usually took the following safety precautions...

- **Cooked meals** well away from camp to prevent lingering smells.
- **Hung my food bag every night**, also away from camp.
- **Avoided camping** at shelters (others sleep with their food).
- **Avoided camping** near wild berries, nuts, or fruit trees.

Black bears are usually docile, and there has never been an "unprovoked" attack on a human anywhere in Virginia. In fact, more people are killed in the US each year by common vending machines. That being said, bears are unpredictable and will protect themselves if they feel threatened. By the way, guns would just make them mad and are prohibited in the SNP anyway...

- **Never leave food unattended** and don't feed wild animals.
- **Keep dogs on a leash**, they could be seriously injured or killed.
- **Never corner a bear** and give extra room to bears with cubs.
- **Don't panic** as it may startle the bear.
- **Slowly back away** without turning your back.
- **DON'T RUN!** Bears may begin chase like a cat after a mouse.
- **If a bear seems friendly**, let him know he's not welcome.
- **Wave arms to appear larger.** Never charge or play dead.
- **Throw rocks or sticks**, but never throw food.
- **If attacked**, fight for your life with anything you can find.

Concrete posts mark side trails in Shenandoah, and I followed one 70 yards to Loft Mountain camp store. The grill was closed but they had a broad selection of resupply, first aid and hamburger/hotdog makings. High prices, but this is a good section to pack light and replenish food as you go. This location also offered laundry/$1 a load, and showers/$1 for 5 minutes. Bunny and her gentleman friend were getting snacks too.

Déjà vu. At Pinefield Hut I found an older man lying down in the middle of the day, his expedition-size, full frame backpack beside him. It was way too large for a week in the woods on an easy trail that passes stores every day. In pain with a swollen knee, he reminded me of Half

Speed back in Atkins, but this man was, in fact, an ATC ridgerunner. They can get injured just like anyone else. He didn't want any help, even though he was scheduled to hike to the next hut, 8 miles away.

Leaving the crippled man behind, I found a note for trail magic. Star Craft, named after the slide-in camper on her pickup truck, was doing vehicle support for her thru-hiker husband, Spot. She would drop him off at a trailhead, set up TM somewhere along his route, then pick him up where he finished. They would sleep in the RV and repeat their routine day after day, all the way up the trail. Star Craft would happily hand out sodas and do needlepoint while she waited. I saw them almost every day in the park and they even tried to give me the trail name "Slackpack," as my backpack was so small, they thought I was slackpacking the whole time!

Soon after, a doe leapt from the trail to protect her Bambi-looking fawn. Even for those who have seen many deer, being this close to these majestic creatures gives you a peaceful feeling that's hard to describe. The next stop, Bearfence Hut, had many posted warning signs about...bears. A tall metal pole looked like a hall tree turned upside down and had a long hook with which to hang food bags. Also provided was a big brown metal box for hikers to keep food locked up safely - with fresh claw marks in the paint! I did meet a singles group here who had arranged their outing through a local dating website. A very eclectic group, I saw no matches. A skinny Asian man was trying to impress the few females in the group, telling stories of wilderness survival as an attractive woman rolled her eyes as if she were on a bad date. Ah, trail love.

One morning I came upon a Hobbit house imbedded into a woodland hillside; the small door had ornate hinges surrounded by a stone foyer. I imagined myself in the Shire, where Bilbo Baggins would invite me in for hot tea, or maybe second breakfast. Glumly, this underground doorway only housed an annoying sounding electric pump. Blast! I also spotted a very colorful bird with black and orange feathers, one of 200 birds species that make their home here - at least part of the year. On my FM radio, I picked up an interesting program about two pioneering naturalists, both competing to be the first to catalog all the local varieties. One bird so rare it was sighted only twice, as each of the scientists shot and killed them for study. But, by doing so, they erased their unique species from the earth. Nice work guys. Not!

Near Hawksbill Mountain, the AT passes a very old cemetery. Many of the crude tombstones were just thin rocks stuck vertically into the earth. As you hike, pay attention to the landscape - you may find pits and heirloom tomatoes, remnants of ancient fruit sellers. Prior to being made into a park, much of this area was farmland and its apple orchards supported dozens of communities. To build the park, the right of way was purchased from landowners. Others resisted. Slowly, their land was acquired through eminent domain, or sadly, even taken by force. A few were allowed to stay with "life tenancy," living in their homes inside the park until nature eventually took its course. The last holdout was a 92-year-old woman who passed away in 1979. Another sad part of SNP's history that's not often talked about: Segregation. According to laws of the day, planners originally designed separate facilities for whites and blacks.

It was getting late when I came upon Skyland Stables, where tourists go on guided horseback rides. Closed for the night, a soda machine stood glowing outside. Quickly, I retrieved quarters that I had carried hundreds of miles for just such an occasion! But my coins kept being returned while the machine tormented me with weird humming noises. Finally, it accepted the credit, and looking over the selections carefully, I chose Mountain Dew, pressed the button, and a small blinking red light indicated it was sold out! Next, I tried Pepsi, then root beer, then Sierra Mist - all with no luck. At last, the machine gave up a...Diet Pepsi. This refreshing delicacy cost $1.75.

Emerging from the morning woods, I accidently stumbled upon a young couple frolicking outside their tent during a very intimate moment. Later, we met formally and had breakfast together on the patio of Skyland Lodge (built 1895). Butterfly Sports Bra & Clayton, now wearing matching black spandex uniforms, were not on a hiking trip, but rather a long-distance bicycle ride down the east coast from New York to Florida. Covering at  least 60 miles a day, they still took time to see the sights. Their top end bikes were customized to carry all their gear: camping equipment, food, spare tires and tools. Kind of like backpacking on bicycles!

These two befriended me immediately and were excited to learn all about my hike. I found their adventure just as interesting and they told several funny stories. Butterfly Sports Bra (BSB) got her "trail" name when a butterfly flew down her shirt as they were riding. Another time, one of their sponsors called to get an update when BSB answered her phone racing down a hill going 30 mph. Judging by the wind tunnel noise, their sponsor knew they were still going strong. They even hooked me up with a bunch of the Red Bull inspired energy bars and pointed out one flavor in particular to use during a really gnarly climb, promising it would have me running up the mountain yelling and screaming!

Tragically, in 1996, two section hikers were murdered near Skyland: Julianne "Julie" Williams of Minnesota, 24, and Laura "Lollie" Winans from Maine, age 26. Authorities began searching for the two after Williams' father called the park when his daughter failed to return home. Known to be hiking with Taj, a golden retriever, who was found running around loose, the rangers had an idea where to look. Their bodies were discovered just off the AT. A recurring theme, park rangers waited another 36 hours before alerting the public of the obvious double homicide. Downplaying any danger, park superintendents called the brutal murders "an isolated incident" without having any idea who did it, or why.

Working together, park officials and the FBI determined the last person to see the two girls alive was a Skyland Lodge waitress who had served them breakfast. America's Most Wanted featured the case on its TV series. 15,000 leads were collected and 75 possible suspects investigated. Eerily, FBI posters seeking info included photos developed from a camera found at the crime scene. It's not known who took the pictures showing both girls posing together, happy and smiling.

A media frenzy ensued when a church minister decided to disclose to reporters that the two women were a couple. Only concerned it would be in the best interest of the lesbian and gay community, the minister didn't bother talking to the deceased women's families and neither had any idea their daughters were even gay. The public outing made coping with the tragedy even more difficult.

Six years after the murders, Darrell David Rice was indicted for the crimes while already serving 11 years in prison for attempting to abduct another woman, also in the SNP. Even with videotape showing his truck entering the park twice during the time frame that Julie and Lollie were missing, Rice denied he was in the park at all. Then in 2003, the FBI's own labs determined a single hair found on duct tape used in the crime didn't match either women, or Rice. This didn't necessarily exonerate the suspect, but forced federal prosecutors to drop all charges. There is still a $50,000 reward.

Close call! Again, walking around a corner, I came upon a bear only eight feet away. Stopping me in my tracks, we faced off for about 30 seconds. My heart racing, I stood perfectly still. This one was only around 100 pounds. Not huge, but also not in a hurry to get out of my way. Reaching for my camera, the bear aggressively stomped both front paws on the ground, giving me a bluff charge to let me know not to get any closer. I didn't run, but flinched, then backed away slowly. Annoyed, the bear walked off the trail a few feet and resumed chowing down on his lunch of green leaves. This encounter gave me an adrenaline rush and afterward, I had to sit down for several minutes. I will never forget our brief meeting as long as I live. Out of respect and fondness, I nicknamed him "Billy the Bear."

The most beautiful hut in the SNP was Byrd's Nest #3, a former picnic shelter made of stonework. Close to the road, it shared a bathroom with a nearby parking lot, but had real running water and I was happy to take a hobo bath.

> *HIKER TIP: Super absorbent, fast drying, ShamWow towels really work! I carried two small, 6x6 inch swatches of the bright orange cloth advertised on late night TV infomercials. "You'll say WOW every time!"*

Looking in the logbook, there was a sad post by a thru-hiker couple who decided to hitch off trail and find a doctor. We had met a few days prior and the young man had cold-like symptoms and headaches, common indications of Lyme disease. Another telltale sign of infection is an expanding area of redness, or a bullseye on the skin, although 25% of those infected never get a rash. If not treated, Lyme can cause chronic fatigue and debilitating nervous system damage. Common Doxycycline antibiotics are the main treatment.

Lyme is another serious danger hikers face on the trail. As you probably already know, Lyme is caused by ticks. Ticks love tall grass, short grass, trees, weeds, reeds, branches and bushes. Some ticks are about the size of a dime and reasonably easy to spot and remove, but a more potent species called "deer ticks," are teeny-tiny and only the size of a pencil point (yeah, really). It's important to do "tick checks" every day you're in the woods. Here are a few more tips...

- **Wear light colored clothing** to make spotting ticks easy.
- **Use tweezers** to remove ticks from the skin immediately.
- **Be sure to remove** their tiny mouth parts as well.
- **Don't burn** or suffocate ticks. Dead ticks still transmit bacteria.
- **Do not crush** or rub ticks with your fingers.
- **Wash your hands** immediately after touching ticks.

Bug spray (hiker perfume) with DEET helps keep ticks away, but is not healthy to use long term. The toxic chemical should also not be used under clothing or on damaged skin. It's a trade-off: what's worse, getting Lyme from a tick, or exposing yourself to chemicals?

From the trail, you can see Elkwallow, the last store NOBOs pass before leaving the park. The gift shop had fun touristy items like butterfly nets, critter cages, plush bears (heck... bear anything), fake Big Foot feet kids wear to leave oversized tracks and even infant-sized ranger costumes. I was surprised at a modest selection of camping gear that included sleeping bags and hammocks. Not outfitter quality, but might get you out of a pinch. As usual, my only purchases were postcards and foodstuffs. This location had every snack and soda you could think of, but prices were expensive! This was also my last chance to get a giant salted pretzel and a traditional, delicious, blackberry milkshake. Outside, I hung out with some other hikers, one of whom said he spent the night in the bathroom here.

Up the trial, I met yet another wounded hiker; this time a heavyset, middle aged school teacher decked out in bright yellow plastic rain gear. Boots off, he was attempting to crudely administer first aid on multiple, painful looking blisters. Sorry to sound like a broken record, but his pack was enormous. Wet weather and cotton socks had made things worse. Suggesting the store a few miles away might be a good place to bailout, he said he had been looking forward to this hike for months and wanted to keep going. Barely after lunchtime, he decided to set up his tent right there. There was nothing else I could do.

For my last night in the Shenandoah, I set up camp near an old fireplace standing tall like a tree. Foggy and damp with thunder in the background, it was still fun listening to deer playing in the woods and reflecting on how much I enjoyed the SNP.

Aquablazing. Some hikers skip this beautiful section all together and prefer a different kind of adventure. Instead of walking they canoe or kayak, floating North along the Shenandoah River, usually with coolers full of beer. They pullover to camp at pay sites at night, and trips include several boat portages around dams (carrying your boat and all your stuff). The biggest thing to consider is that aquablazing disqualifies an official thru-hike. As a kayaker, I see its appeal if you're on a blue blaze kind of hike, but watching many video blogs, only about half make it to the end and none survive without getting dunked by rapids at least once. Upfront rental costs range between $350 solo/$550 for two people (not including extras). No refunds.

After leaving SNP, the next structure for thru-hikers to use wasn't called either a hut or shelter, but curiously, "Tom Floyd Wayside." A sign on the sprawling front porch read, "Stay off roof." I also thought it was funny someone left a credit card hotel passkey in the register and Tree Hugger, from New Hampshire, wrote in the logbook that masked thieves ran off with all his Honey Buns. Raccoons!

Beeping sounds from the emergency broadcast system interrupted music on my FM radio, only these were not a test. A powerful thunderstorm was moving in. Hiking as fast as possible, I scanned trees, scrambling for a safe place to hunker down. Unfortunately, this area was very rocky and I had to tie my tarp down with rocks instead of putting stakes into the ground. I got set up just in time, but with leaves blowing around in the wind, I still worried about falling branches, called "widow makers." Heavy rain and scary lightning followed, but I woke up unharmed.

The morning was cold enough to need my insulated vest and fleece beanie as I walked a long boardwalk that paralleled a tall fenced area described in the guidebook as "a sanctuary for exotic animals." Run by Smithsonian's National Zoo, this is a breeding and research facility with bison, endangered cranes and even wolves. I was hoping to see something exciting, but the place looked abandoned with chain link fences covered in green vines and even falling down in places.

"Headed to town?" Getting to Front Royal was easy, as a car had just pulled up to drop-off another hiker. It had been over 2 weeks since I had slept in a real bed. My hammock was nice, but it's not a real bed. I was delivered to the front door of another Super 8. The nicest this town had to offer, it resembled an apartment building and was not up to the same standard as other 8's I had enjoyed. Some other hikers stayed at the Pioneer Hotel but didn't have anything good to say about it either.

I jumped into the shower and after a few minutes, a deafening alarm startled me. Was my room on fire? The whole hotel? I jumped out and ran into the bedroom with shampoo in my eyes. Thankfully no flames, but the hot shower had filled my entire room with steam, setting off an alarm on the ceiling. Not wanting to evacuate the hotel, I leapt onto the bed and started removing the alarm's battery. At that very same moment, a maid heard the noise and used her master key to open my room's door...without knocking. Panicked, she rushed inside but froze when she saw me standing on the bed, soaking wet, and buck-naked! Both of us screamed at the same time as the poor woman retreated to the hallway, then slammed the door shut! I bet she'll knock next time!

After all the excitement, I hit Mickey D's. I rarely eat there in real life, but wolfed down 5 hamburgers, a large fry and 20 chicken nuggets. They don't sell 2-liter drinks there so I went to a gas station for a hiker-sized root beer.

When exploring any town, a good place to start is the visitor's center. This one was built in Main Street Station, a beautifully restored train depot. A sweet woman working there gave me a map of town, then marked various locations, with colored highlighters, that I may want to visit. They also have for thru-hikers a complementary, blue and polka dot fanny-pack filled with first aid supplies, toothpaste, "Virginia is for Lovers" bumper sticker, granola bar and other goodies. It feels good when a community genuinely embraces us like this.

Front Royal had a lively main street with a beautiful gazebo. Sitting down on a park bench, an older gentleman told me about the old town square clock and offered to take my picture with it. I couldn't believe how thin and svelte I looked! My confidence soared, as I must have lost at least 60 pounds by this point and was the strongest I've ever felt. I've always had big Popeye legs, but now my calf muscles were truly hiking machines!

Following a suggestion, I visited the Warren Riffles Confederate Museum with many items on display important to "the war against Northern aggression," including actual battle flags, firearms, uniforms and rare photographs. I'm not a Civil War enthusiast but found it very interesting. My favorite was a collection of little toys and jewelry hand-carved by soldiers out of buttons and other common items. Known in collector's circles as "trench art." $5 donation.

Of course, I saw Canecutter and Prophet, among others, at the grocery store. One hiker kept an eye on everyone's gear, while the others made food runs. Any and all outside outlets were clogged with phone chargers, and sometimes ride-on-toys and soda machines became unplugged. Oh yeah, if you happen to need a car part while in town, try the 'Little Red Fender' whose sign was…a little red fender.

It's always fun to visit trail towns, but after 1 night, I'm anxious to get back into the woods. I only had my thumb out for 2 minutes when a white import car screeched to a stop. Wing on the back and racing graphics down the sides, this guy thought he was Brian O'Conner from Fast and Furious, just not as outgoing. We rode 3 miles in silence. Thanking him when I got out, he nodded then sped off in a cloud of smoke. My lucky day, I found some delicious baby green apples just above a strategically placed wooden bench. I'm sure lots of hikers enjoyed this natural trail magic. Going deeper into the woods, an ominous hiker notice read in all caps:

"WARNING!! YOU ARE ABOUT TO ENTER THE ROLLER COASTER!! BUILT AND MAINTAINED BY THE TRAIL BOSS AND HIS MERRY VOLUNTEERS. HAVE A GREAT RIDE AND WE'LL SEE YOU AT THE BLACKBURN TRAIL CENTER. (IF YOU SURVIVE)."

Reading this, I imagined running up and down mini mountains with my arms raised above my head! Spoiler alert: This section was completely uneventful. The Trail Boss also needs to devise some less confusing blazes. A cluster of three small trees each had at least one white blaze, all pointing in different directions.

I did manage to make it to Sam Moore Shelter, where the logbook was stowed in a beaten-up mailbox, sans door. Checking the mail, someone had left a jar of peanut butter and half a bottle of cheap whisky - sounds like a party! Happy Birthday messages were posted for 3:10. Yoko, from Georgia, drew a cupcake, and Grundlehammer, a young man from Grand Rapids, Michigan, usually known for intricate ink pen artwork of axes and swords, drew a slice of spam.

Just before the road crossing at Route 7, there was more white blaze insanity by those "merry" volunteers. This time, a single telephone pole had no less than four white blazes, an arrow, the letter "N," "AT" and last, but not least, an orange line. With blazes like this, it's a wonder anyone makes it to Maine!

Here, hikers can take a blue blazed trail 150 yards to a beautiful stone mansion called The Bears Den. James Bond-like, there is a security keypad on the hostel door and a note requesting a secret code to let yourself in. A clue is provided: A certain landmark mile marker that can be found in either guidebook. It sounded like one of the more unusual hostels and wish I had visited but I was starting to not feel well, and just wanted to get the heck out of Virginia. At dusk, I finally found the VA/WV state line. For some, this is start of the "4-State Challenge," a non-stop, 43.3-mile race setting foot in Virginia, West Virginia, Maryland and Pennsylvania, all within a 24-hour period. I didn't attempt this, but have lots of respect for those who do!

Chapter 12. Mason-Dixon

Boy Scout Troop (BS 222 NC), hiking for a week on the AT.

West Virginia is the shortest state on the AT - only 4 miles long - but I would stay here for almost 2 full days. Harpers Ferry was a day's walk away, but the post office is only open 2 hours on Saturday and I gave up trying to make it (have your mail sent to the ATC). With a touch of dehydration, I was feeling lethargic and couldn't have walked faster if I wanted to. So, I just took extra-long breaks and even hung the hammock for a rare midday nap. Dizzy, a slight breeze turned shadows of leaves on my tarp into a kaleidoscope of hallucinations. Almost asleep, I could hear kids playing and chasing each other. Did I hastily set up my hammock next to an unseen playground? I got up and the sound of children had stopped. Was it a dream? Or imprinted echoes from the past?

Lifting my spirits, I saw a piece of 2' x 4' nailed to a tree with 4 characters carved into it: 1-0-0-0. A very big deal. That's the number of miles I had walked to get here! Taking a side trail to Blackburn Trail Center, I found the downhill 0.2 miles difficult in my condition. A big porch wrapped around the main house, which is owned by the ATC and managed by PATC. I was dying for a cold soda, but no one was home, so I settled for refilling my water bottles. Also disappointing: a solar shower on the lawn was closed for repair. A small cabin out back that originally housed the rich family's staff, was now a hostel with bunkbeds (less mattresses) arranged on either side of a buck stove.

What's this? Back on the trail, I found an odd, very heavy, black rectangular object...and it took me a few moments to figure it out. This was a cement brick wrapped in black electrical tape. Apparently, someone training was using this as a weight and either dropped it by accident, or jettisoned it from their backpack when it became too heavy. I left it for the next person to puzzle over.

At Keys Gap VA-9, "A Trail to Every Classroom" was the title of a kiosk displaying artwork by local school children. I chuckled at a crayon drawing showing a scared rabbit clutching an oversized carrot from an evil, human hand. Making breakfast, I saw a hiker emerge from the woods, obviously in a huff. I said hi, but he just stood staring at my backpack then snapped at me, rudely questioning if I was a day hiker. Telling him "I walked here from Georgia," he mumbled to himself that the AT was not the same anymore. Wanting to help, I asked what was wrong. He said, he had the time of his life thru-hiking the trail back in the 1980's when everyone had "real" hiking boots and "normal" backpacks. Ranting, he said everything was too high-tech now, and everybody was in a race, hiking as fast as they could. The seasoned hiker took off his large, external aluminum frame backpack covered with old trail patches, and chucked it to the ground. Pointing at the behemoth, he told me this was a "real" backpack, and scoffing, said mine looked like a toy. He was out of breath with disappointment.

Trying to calm him, I explained the simple concept of "Hike your own hike" - do your own thing, at your own pace, and let everyone else do whatever they want, however they want, without judgment. This philosophy is commonly embraced by the hiking community, but this unhappy man who I nicknamed "Old School," was having none of it and vowed never to set foot on the AT again.

Signs invited hikers to visit The Twelve Tribes, a working farm and store well known for homemade organic bread. A bunkhouse is offered for hikers doing work in exchange for a place to stay (hikers call this "work for stay"). Just don't expect to simply clean a few windows or take out the trash for your keep. Two hikers told me they spent an entire day out in the fields, but enjoyed the experience. There was no pressure to join, renounce citizenship, or commit hari-kari. Still, a few stories were going around, one about a 21-year old woman who worked at their deli who was never taught to read because she was cast only to work in the store. Also, members are not allowed to have or watch TV, while their leader had a huge flat screen in his own home.

Walking into Harpers Ferry, Quicksilver, from North Carolina, was indeed quick and passed me going under the massive US highway 340 bridge. It was fun walking across the wide river, but speeding cars scared me. I had been in the woods for so long, they looked like they were going a million miles an hour and sounded like Star Wars TIE fighters!

ATC headquarters. A stone stairway, up a blue blazed trail, led 0.4 miles to this modest white building, made of bricks and stone-work. Hikers are welcome to hang out, check email, or enjoy a cold drink from the stocked fridge. Dozens of photos on the walls showed smiling 2,000 milers. A gift shop sold hats, shirts, patches, stickers and socks with AT logos. They carry necessary items, such as books and guides, too. None of the staff gushed over me as they just went about their business filing papers and typing on keyboards. Member-ships are processed, volunteer activities coordinated and hundreds of other responsibilities, keeping the Appalachian Trail open, are all or-chestrated from this facility.

> FUN FACT: Jean "Trail Mom" Cashin started the tradition of taking hiker photographs in front of the ATC in 1979 when she was given a Polaroid camera as a gift.

Often called the AT's psychological halfway point, this visitor's center is 74-miles shy of the actual milestone. It's tradition for all hikers to have pho-tos taken. I arrived June 17th, 2012, and officially counted as thru-hiker #529 for the year. Couples take pics together; friends separate. Photos are kept in dozens of binders archived on shelves, always available for viewing. I'm proud to be on the same page as my buds Prophet & Canecutter. The ATC can also print out your photo as a

postcard for a couple of bucks a copy. A fun souvenir.

> **HIKER TIP:** As of this writing, hikers who visited ATC headquarters prior to 2009 have had their Polaroids scanned and uploaded to the World Wide Web. Hopefully, this ambitious project will include all years.

A table, 20 feet long, held an inclined 3D topographical relief map. An inch equaled about 9.5 miles, and put in perspective, the trail's enormous length. Also displayed, an original sign from the top of Mount Katahdin. Touching the weathered wood covered with carved initials really hit home that this trip is something epic. Flip-floppers who complete their hikes in Harpers Ferry take their "summit" picture with it. Also of note - the hiker box here was awesome! I scored a brand-new pair of expensive shoe insoles, but was more amazed someone had discarded a full collection of books and Nat Geo maps for every state on the trail. These cost around $30 a set!

Right on the trail you'll find Jefferson Rock, a naturally arranged, inclined ramp, balanced on top of another rock. Back in 1783, Thomas Jefferson stood here in awe of two massive rivers, the Potomac and Shenandoah, converging below, and called what he saw "...perhaps one of the most stupendous scenes in nature..." Today, four wooden braces hold up each corner like a table:

"DANGER! Jefferson Rock is unstable. Walking on, climbing, ascending, descending, or traversing Jefferson Rock, or its stabilizing base rock, is prohibited."

Because of its strategic location, the American Civil War took a huge toll on Harpers Ferry, which was fought over and changed hands often, being occupied by both North and South at different times. While stationed there, General Stonewall Jackson made his headquarters in a confiscated brick home near the ATC. One of the more remarkable ruins is on top of the hill overlooking town, St. John's Episcopal Church. Built in 1852, it served as hospital and barracks during the war, and suffered severe damage. All that's left are a few beautiful archways to explore. On the other hand, St. Peter's Roman Catholic Church, 1833, escaped relatively unscathed as Father Michael Costello flew the Union Jack, protecting it from both Union and Confederate bombardment. Mass is still open to the public every Sunday.

Continuing down flights of ancient stairs into historic lower town, white blazes painted on lampposts led hikers by the oldest standing structure in town, Harper House. This was originally the home of Quaker colonist Robert Harper, who started a busy ferry here in 1747, giving the town its name. Reenactment actors, wearing fancy hats and long dresses (convincing garments of the period), made the old boarding house come alive. George Washington, Thomas Jefferson and Captain Meriwether Lewis all stayed there.

Soon after the Louisiana Purchase was signed, July 4, 1803, Thomas Jefferson dispatched Capt. Lewis, who he admired as a frontiersman, to Harpers Ferry to obtain supplies and weapons for the Lewis and Clark Expedition. Here, Lewis oversaw construction of a collapsible "Ironboat" of his own design, and purchased knives and handsome tomahawk pipes to be given as gifts to Indian Tribal Chiefs.

Almost every old building has been repurposed into little shops, or free, self-guided museums hidden in alleyways or at the bottom of stairs. Here are a few I visited...

• **Cannonball Deli:** The ATC had a coupon for 10% off and I finally got the meatball sandwich I had been craving.
• **Scoops Ice Cream Café:** Hikers sit out back on a patio.
• **Goods Store Museum:** Stocked with items (display only) available in the 1800's: hats, fancy tea sets, spices, wooden toys, etc.
• **Civil War Museum:** Examples of canons, uniforms, a soldier's backpack and a display case full of artifacts dug up at the arsenal site across the street. The first factory in the world to use interchangeable parts, it produced more than 600,000 muskets, rifles and pistols.
• **Archaeological site:** This demonstration revealed the unearthing of a basement with foundations from previous homes.

The Baltimore & Ohio Railroad built Harpers Ferry Station in 1889. Partially restored in 2007 - at a cost of $2.2 million - it's still in operation. I say "partially" because you could see where the money ran out. While the main building was attractive and freshly painted, a covered platform on the other side of the tracks, accessed by underground stairs, was literally falling apart. Railroad enthusiasts bring lawn chairs and hangout here all afternoon. It was very exciting watching a long CSX train go by. The seemingly endless metal snake pulled dozens of flatbeds, carrying drab green ARMY trucks, tanks, and Hummers. For a fun side trip, many thru-hikers board the Amtrak to visit nearby Washington D.C. Prices start at $13 for the trip to Union Station, but trains don't stop every day. I had planned to visit Washington, too, but I was already way over budget.

Looking for a place to stay the night, I considered Harper Cemetery, final resting place of Robert Harper, and other residents, for many generations. Victorian wrought iron fences surrounded green grass and gray tombstones, but I never understood if fences around bone yards were to keep the living out, or to keep the dead in? Camping in town is prohibited by city ordinance, and I wasn't up for dodging both ghosts and cops, so I kept moving. Too bad there's not some inexpensive choices in town, or hikers would spend more time here.

• **Teahorse Hostel:** Classy compared to other hostels and includes a waffle breakfast. Bunks$33.
• **Town's Inn:** An old-timey, three-story building, circa. 1840. Hiker friendly. Shared room/$35. Privates/$120-$150 + $20 EAP.

Almost dark, I washed up in the Shenandoah River among ancient turbine tunnels. Intricately built, these masonry structures were fascinating to look at. The island between the river and town, reached by a footbridge, was teeming with life and I saw a white crane, a family of ducks and large, alligator-snapping turtles about the size of a basketball. Then, for about 10 minutes, a curious deer followed me around everywhere I went. Running out of daylight, I finally found a hidden spot out of sight among crumbling walls of a forgotten cotton mill that also served as a hospital during the Civil War. It felt eerie being there, but exciting to sleep in such historic surroundings. Emerging from my hiding place early the next day, three park rangers blocked my escape route. But they weren't waiting for me. Another hiker boldly hammock camped right on the greenway in clear view of the ranger's station!

Picking up my resupply box, I went to the post office, where the police station, courthouse and Olde Towne Liquors, were all located in the same building. How convenient! I also got a card from my niece, Kendell with crayon drawn sandwich, mountains and trees.

I made time to visit one more exhibit, the John Brown Museum, which tells the story of an important part of our country's history. Walking in, you can't help but see a life-size mural of John Brown screaming, while holding a rifle in one hand, bible in the other. I was struck by the man's ferocity and couldn't get this image out of my mind.

1859. John Brown, a religious fanatic against slavery, led a makeshift army of about 20 men including free and runaway slaves in seizing the Harpers Ferry arsenal. They hoped to capture weapons, and ultimately, start a slave uprising. Unfortunately, the first shot accidently killed a free black man working for the railroad. The group did manage to capture several buildings, and even George Washington's own great-great-nephew, Colonel Lewis Washington, as hostage.

Robert E. Lee, then a US Army Lt. Colonel, arrived on the scene in civilian clothes because of short notice, confronted Brown and his men barricaded in the armory's brick firehouse with no food, water or escape plan. Defiantly, "Old Brown" refused to surrender and Lee ordered his 86 marines to bash in the doors. The battle was over swiftly, with all inside killed or captured. Lee's men sustained one casualty themselves: Marine Private Luke Quinn.

John Brown was found guilty of treason and hanged in nearby Charles Town. Other members of his party including 2 sons, met the same fate. The acts of John Brown, and his death, escalated tensions between the North and South perhaps igniting The Civil War. Now known as "The John Brown Fort," the actual firehouse has been restored and is open to the public.

Thru-hikers cross into Maryland on the Goodloe E. Byron Memorial Footbridge and then follow the Chesapeake & Ohio Canal Tow Path for about 3 miles. Some neat stealth camping spots can be found there, not to mention lots of deer and more canal locks and aqueduct ruins.

I absolutely loved an ancient brick house, all its white masonry still standing strong but long-lost of doors, windows and roof.

Known as the "Grand Old Ditch," this waterway and path was conceived by George Washington and signed into bill by President James Monroe, 1825. Man-made bypass canals allowed specially made boats to avoid river rapids and channels parallel the Potomac for 184 miles, from Washington, D.C. all the way to Cumberland, Maryland. For almost 100 years, donkeys and horses walking along the path towed cargo boats up and down, carrying coal and other goods. One-way trips took 7 days.

The next morning was foggy, but down a short side trail there was still a pleasant view from Weverton Cliffs. At the trail intersection, a half dozen backpacks lay on the ground or leaned against trees, left by a group of day hikers checking out the view. Hikers don't carry heavy packs any further than we have to.

Ed Garvey Memorial Shelter was not just a shelter, it was a penthouse! This large log structure had an enclosed loft with a door, windows and roof insulation. Craftsmen even built an AT logo into an upper railing. There were 2 outhouses and I preferred the log cabin model, over the Army barracks style privy. In 2015, heavy winds pushed over a dead tree here, killing 36-year-old hiker, Jason Parish. Tragically, the tree was scheduled to be cut down.

Maryland, only 40 miles long, is short but full of interesting history. We tread across state parks, stringing the AT together in bits and pieces. First on the list, Gathland, the South Mountain estate of George Alfred Townsend, a chubby man with a handlebar mustache. He was a journalist during the Civil War writing under the pen name "Gath." Interpretive tablets describe buildings and landmarks, intact or in ruins, most designed by Gath himself and built using abundant, local stone. You can't miss the ginormous War Correspondents' Memorial Arch towering 50 feet into the sky. It's castle façade decorated with random crests, life-size statues of soldiers and horse heads. Built in 1896, it's dedicated to journalists killed reporting during combat.

Nearby, there's a soda machine and several of us hikers waited out a rain shower under a long picnic pavilion while locals held a kid's birthday party. They even gifted each of us a bag of candy!

Somberly, we strolled along Wise's Field at Fox's Gap, where an American Civil War Battle was fought on September 14th, 1862. A stately memorial for Union Major General Jesse Lee Reno (namesake of Reno, Nevada) had manicured green grass protected by a concrete barricade. Only a few feet away was a simple commemorative marker for a Confederate also mortally wounded here, Brigadier General Samuel L. Garland, Jr., great-grandnephew of James Madison. Fighting on opposite sides, both Generals were from Virginia and died the same evening.

Dahlgren Backpacker's Campground was basic, but free, and had hot showers. What many people don't know - on the other side of this forest lay Burkittsville, where the original 'Blair Witch Project' was filmed. Premise: A group of film students go on a camping trip in the rural Maryland woods to make a documentary about an urban legend. Spoiler alert: They never come back!

> FUN FACT: Blair Witch started as a 35-page outline with nearly all dialogue (and screaming) improvised. Made for $25,000, filming lasted only eight days, but earned $248 million at the box office!

South Mountain Inn and Restaurant, just out of the woods, is along Old National Pike. In operation for over 275 years, it's seen a lot of action: A 1700's stagecoach stop, captured overnight as a staging point for John Brown's Raid, used by Confederate Major General D.H. Hill's headquarters during the Battle of South Mountain, then returned to a tavern again in 1925. Today it offers, "fine dining with a Colonial atmosphere." Sleeves, please. Too fancy pants for me, the AT guidebook actually asks that hikers shower before visiting.

My ghost story... Beware the *"Snarly Yow!"* Across the road, an information board depicted the legend of a shadowy black dog that has roamed this area since the late 1700's. Then, just a quarter mile past the sign, movement caught my eye. Maybe it was the power of suggestion, heat exhaustion, or just my eyes playing tricks on me, but I did see a black dog-like creature running along the top of a decrepit stone wall. Thinking it was a large fox, I reached for my camera to snap a pic, but it quickly jumped down and disappeared, all without making a sound. I presumed it went into a hole in the ground. But when I reached the end of the wall where it had vanished, hairs stood up on the back of my neck - there wasn't any hole and the dog creature was gone. I wasn't scared, but rather felt an excitement I've only felt a few times in my life. And I'm not the only one to have seen it. Hundreds of people have reported being confronted by a demon dog over the years. This mischievous phantom has even been known to chase cars! Madeleine Vinton Dahlgren, once the owner of South Mountain Inn, and a nearby Dahlgren church, documented many sightings in her 1882 book, 'South Mountain Magic.'

The AT passes through Washington Monument State Park and right by the first tower built to honor George Washington. Local villagers constructed it to celebrate their independence on July 4th, 1827. Restored by CCC workers to its current configuration in 1936, it took the shape of a stubby milk bottle, 40 feet tall. A doorway accesses the dark, circular stairway where it was at least 15° cooler inside. On top, there was a sprawling, hazy view. Mid 2015, the tower was struck by lightning and closed for repairs.

Camping illegally within the park was not my first choice, but it had gotten dark. I did spot a beautiful Luna moth with a long sweeping tail. If you've never seen one, they have a wingspan of 4 or 5 inches! These sea-foam green and gray insects only live in this form, to mate, for about 1 week. Very efficient!

Come morning, I hiked between neighborhood houses then over I-70 by way of a chain-link footbridge covered in vines as cars sped by underneath. Honk if you love hiking! From 1,829', the cliffs of Annapolis Rocks had a very impressive view. Noticing ropes attached to trees and hooks imbedded into the stone with bolts, it was only a few moments before I heard someone making their way up the jagged rock face. Looking over the edge, a cute rock climber girl was carefully choosing her handholds. Making it to the uppermost point, she then repelled back down bouncing off the mountain as she went. Campsites can be found nearby, but this is one of the most overused and environmentally stressed areas on the entire AT. Bare places were fenced-off to let vegetation regenerate and a caretaker now stays on site. Sadly, in 2015 a day hiker fell 50 feet off the cliffs to his death while taking photos. Forty-four-year-old Alexei Likhtman was a British university physics professor.

Miles away, Raven Rock Shelter was well designed and looked new with stained logs, a green tin roof and a covered picnic table. Marking their spots, campers had already spread out empty sleeping bags inside where they wanted to sleep. Sipsey was named after the famous Sipsey Wilderness in his home state of Alabama. He actually started his hike there. Yup, he hiked over 100 miles just to get to the AT! Not to mention he recently conquered the PCT, and had already completed the AT twice. Easily recognizable with a Santa Claus beard and tennis visor, this tall man was welcoming to everyone he met. Mr. Breeze, the more laidback of the two, was a thin man from New Hampshire, who sported a floppy fishermen's hat.

Nice and flat, the next stretch was built on an old trolley line leading through, once-thriving, Pen Mar Village. Next to the trail, someone left an interesting collection of found artifacts, probably from a trash pit near the many overgrown house foundations. Displayed were an old hubcap, vintage glass bottles, a JIF peanut butter jar, part of a toy car, tin cans and broken plate shards.

In the 1870's, Pen Mar was a famous amusement park. Attractions included a roller coaster, carousel, pony track and penny arcade. During its heyday, daily attendance reached nearly 20,000 visitors. Closed in 1943, the property reopened as a county park in 1977. Looking for vending machines, I peeked into the dance hall and imagined couples spinning across the hardwood floor to live music. Playing that summer: Fancy Brass, Andy Angel Quartet and a lone accordionist. Also contained within Pen Mar: the Mason-Dixon Line, where NOBO thru-hikers leave the South to enter the North, also the finish line of the Four State Challenge.

My first night in Pennsylvania, I found a quiet area where I hung my hammock on a hillside. After an hour or so, an approaching sound and bright lights lit up the entire woods. As the noise grew closer, moving lights magnified by the darkness, made shadows of trees run around the forest. My first panicked thought was an airplane was about to crash, but at the moment of impact it passed right over me! I then realized my camp was set-up just below a neighborhood street where a car had simply driven by. It was a very strange and awkward place to sleep.

Shelters in the Keystone State were becoming more elaborate. Twin, Tumbling Run Shelters were designated as "snoring" and "non-snoring" respectively and featured a rare clothesline. H2O gets scarce in these parts and we have to fill-up when we can. As we passed by a monastery, monks were kind enough to provide fresh tap water (unblessed). Their modest but noble, Church of Old Forge Park was built of brown stained wood with a green roof.

Next was Caledonia State Park. During the Civil War, armies of both Reds and Greys marched through burned-out ruins here on their way to and from The Battle of Gettysburg. Green pastures and playgrounds today served as grim field hospitals for the wounded. I was walking with a happy hiker named Italian Guy (from Denmark), who always wore the same white trucker hat. We found that trail angels had set up a big spread. The grill wasn't hot yet, but we had all you can eat peanut butter sandwiches and chips. I even tried some dried kelp. Yuck! Camping here costs $23, or just walk into the woods and sleep for free.

Quarry Gap Shelter(s) was the most over-the-top on the trail - twin log-built structures were connected by a covered veranda with a spire on top. Colorful flower baskets hung from rafters, a sundial told the time, clever signs adorned the walls and tacky yard art was placed around the clearing. By the way, today was June 21st, Summer Solstice and "Hike Naked Day," but I didn't see anyone participating.

Weather had been near 100° for two days in row. Fighting fatigue, I was still humping 20-mile days when my luck ran out. Getting up before daylight, I felt bad from the start and my body was all out of whack with dehydration. Drinking 8 trail magic sodas the day before probably didn't help. I've lived with low blood sugar most of my life and knew the warning signs. I was in danger.

After resting for a while and eating some candy that I save for just this occasion, I got up to try again but didn't get very far. Feeling faint, my vision got dimmer until all went completely dark, like someone slowly pulled a blindfold over my eyes. Stumbling into a tree, the weight of my backpack overtook my balance and I crashed down with a thud. Vomiting, a cold sweat came over me and my body felt like pins and needles. I just lay there, in a blur, until I saw something in the distance. A plastic cooler!

Slipping out of my backpack, I stood up and was surprised to see I had wandered off trail at least 50 feet. Using trees for balance, I reached the oasis but found it full of no-name beer. Shucks! I couldn't think of anything less appealing at that moment. Desperate, I fished around in the ice and found a couple squeeze bottles of kid's "blue" flavored juice. I don't know what flavor "blue" is, but it perked me up immediately! I rested, drank as much cold water as possible and ate all my granola bars. Then, preparing for another go, I refilled my water bottles with ice water from the cooler.

> HIKER TIP: Feeling bad? Pinch the skin on the back of your hand and pull upwards. If it snaps back - you're good. If not - you're dehydrated. Also, if your hat or shirt turns white with salt, double your fluid intake.

Only managing a grand total of nine miles that day, I did find the first snowmobile sign of the trip, some sour blackberries and a dilapidated chimney still useful to hikers judging by fresh ashes. Two makeshift memorials were on this section: one hand drawn on a rock in memory of Sharon Parson; the other for "Bartleby the Trail Dog."

Posted on a tree, a sign informed us that timber rattlesnakes are protected in this section. Almost on cue, a snake was found right next to Birch Run Shelter. These cold-blooded reptiles often reside around shelters... looking for mice... that are looking for food... left by humans. Because of its markings, at first we thought this one looked like a copperhead. A hiker messing around picked up a stick saying, "This will really make it mad!" When it started rattling, we all realized it was a rattler. Socks (another common trail name) warned us, "Be careful!"

Socks and I had met briefly in Harpers Ferry, but I had noticed her personalized cartoon doodle of a dog in logbooks for hundreds of miles. She was a polite, tall woman from Koelm, Germany, who spoke good English. She has hiked all over the world and traveled around Europe competing in motorcycle rallies. She was very excited to be hiking in the US, but was nursing 2 sore knees. During this trip, I met dozens of hiking enthusiasts from Germany. Some talked about watching an AT documentary aired on German television, then came all the way to America to experience it. Now here, most said it was much more difficult than the program let-on.

Everyone I met that day was excited to be getting closer to the up-coming halfway point. I also quickened my pace seeing a tall, wooden marker ahead. Here, a mailbox held a logbook, but heavy red ink on every single page bled through making it impossible to read. A couple of people had even signed flat rocks and put them in the mailbox to prove they were here. Someone spent a lot of time making this fancy sign, but a note indicated the "real" halfway point was still a bit further up the trail. The total distance of the AT changes every year because of relocations, detours, flooding, etc. A few minutes later, I found the current and actual halfway point. This line, drawn in the dirt was a little anticlimactic, but was a huge relief reaching midway on this trip. Now, the promise of ice cream dangled in front of me like a carrot.

Chapter 13. Walking with Ghosts

Twin, Deer Lick Shelters. Mile marker: 1062.9.

I scream, you scream, we all scream for ice cream. Vibrant orange irises lined either side of PA-233, a short road walk to Pine Grove Furnace State Park. The first thing you see is the massive Iron-master's Mansion. This long English Tudor was built in 1829 and its rumored, earthen crawlspaces underneath were part of the Underground Railroad. I was looking forward to seeing that, checking out the hostel and even considered taking a zero, but it was temporarily closed because of a wedding. Two crowded bunkrooms can hold up to 28 hikers - women upstairs/men downstairs - $25 with waffle breakfast. Call ahead if you plan to stay: (717) 486-4108.

Pine Grove General Store is home of the "Half-Gallon Challenge" and thru-hikers look forward to the tradition almost as much as passing the halfway point! Goal: Consume a half-gallon of ice cream in one sitting. Your reward: a tiny wooden spoon. About 70% are successful. Early birds and SOBOs also partake in the ritual. I've seen videos of hikers outside in freezing weather struggling to finish a tub of ice cream with icicles hanging from their beards, snot running down their faces and hands (and spoons) shaking uncontrollably. That should be called the "Frostbite Challenge!" I can't think of anything more excruciating.

Loophole saw me and said, "Hey, Loner - quit taking photos and come eat some ice cream!" He and his friends had already started, with some yelling, "done!" while slamming their tubs down. Also here were friends Passion Flower and Voltron, both from Florida, and another couple who didn't seem to be talking to each other.

> FUN FACT: The AT's most popular tradition started in 1980, when a manager noticed thru-hikers consuming ice cream in mass quantities. Today, state contract requires the store keep tubs in stock.

Daydreaming of all the tasty flavors from which to choose, I decided beforehand on a smooth orange sorbet, with my second choice being cotton candy. Imagine my disappointment when I found the store sold out of both and I had to settle for plain chocolate. And apparently, a tub of ice cream isn't technically a half-gallon these days. Some do-gooders in politics decided to save us from ourselves and force companies to package processed foods in smaller portions (of course prices stayed the same). All this to say, as a purist, I bought an extra pint (not required). Total price: $8.50.

> FUN FACT: When I made my attempt, the fastest known time was 24 minutes, 40 seconds, set by Samsquatch. Sound easy? Try it at home! By the way, a half-gallon of ice cream packs 1,360 calories!

Eager to break the world record, I knocked out my tub in short order, but the pint of green mint was just too rich and I gave up after 45 minutes. A cashier girl still awarded me a "half-gallon club" commemorative wooden spoon that I still have to this day. To celebrate, I ordered a couple of hot dogs - all the way.

> HIKER TIP: Want bragging rights? Stall a few minutes to let your frozen treat thaw. I recommend bringing your own steel spoon. Plastic sporks can break and wooden ones are useless (except as souvenirs!)

A few steps away, the Appalachian Trail Museum had a sign out front bribing visitors with cold A/C. The museum is housed in a beautiful stone gristmill built over 200 years ago and inside you'll see another barely legible Katahdin sign and an actual trail shelter built in 1959. Dismantled piece by piece, it was set-up inside the museum, complete with an old mouse trapeze, carved initials and vintage graffiti. Like Harpers Ferry, they take your photo here, too, but seemed redundant. Free admission 12 p.m. - 4 p.m., 7 days a week.

The AT Hall of Fame was added in 2011 and introduces visitors to pioneers responsible for the Appalachian Trail: Benton MacKaye, Myron Avery, Earl Shaffer and Arthur Perkins. Some other inductees...

• **Emma "Grandma" Gatewood,** at 67-years young, became the first woman to solo hike the AT in a single season (1955) and the first person to complete this feat 3 times. The original ultralight hiker, she carried a laundry bag over her shoulder containing only an ARMY blanket, raincoat and shower curtain. Mother to 11 kids and 23 grandkids, upon leaving for a hike she would tell her family, "No one have any babies, and no one die, till I get back!"
• **Gene Espy.** This Eagle Scout and Air Force aerospace engineer was the 2nd person to thru-hike the AT (1951).
• **Edward B. "Ed" Garvey,** one of only 10 people to complete a thru-hike in 1970, he served as president of the PATC and ATC. Also instrumental in passing the National Trails System Act of 1968, protecting the AT forever.

The state park is centered on the towering, triangle shaped Pine Grove Furnace, which was in production from 1764 until 1895, and where charcoal was burned to produce cast iron. We pass several of these furnaces along the AT and this one looked in good enough condition to fire up. The most popular spot in the park was Fuller Lake, a 1.7-acre abandoned quarry filled with water. Many hikers took advantage and some even played Frisbee with local girls.

"All your lives, and all you've seen, is in your heads, and in your dreams." James H Fry/Tagg Run Shelter is haunted! The cryptic verse above was written on a wall with blood (probably just nail polish). Looking at the structure, you could see it was built on top of a much older stone foundation. Shelters are almost always situated near water sources that are safe from flooding. These same sites would have also been the best choices for generations of settlers, and before them, Native Americans.

This shelter had a complex outhouse with 2 thrones (but no divider). Someone engineered the wooden door to stay closed by incorporating a system of ropes, pulleys and large stone counterweights. You had to pull the door toward you really hard just to open it. Then, when you let it go, the weights would slam the door shut. It got pretty dark inside, too.

The following ghost story was told to me by my buddy Roboticus, a friendly, pretty girl in her early 20's, and a very strong thru-hiker who usually wore a bandana to hold back pigtails. I assumed she got her trail name because of the bulky knee braces she always wore. When Roboticus arrived at the shelter, she already felt uneasy being by herself and sensed someone watching her. She went inside the privy and a few moments later, heard footsteps on the wooden walkway. Before she could say anything, the heavy door flew wide open - then slammed shut with a loud crash! Startled, Roboticus called out, "Who's there?" with no answer. Cautiously, she peered outside but didn't see anyone. The experience spooked her at the time, but when she told me this story, 100's of miles up the trail, she was no longer afraid.

Along Appalachian Trail Road, I couldn't just walk by a permanent yard sale. The big-ticket items here were a pair of colorful talking parrots. Up the street was Green Mountain General Store. Besides snacks, shelves just out of reach were stocked with vintage tin toys, Indian artifacts, and old advertising signs. Display only. Cooks made me an awesome grilled chicken sandwich, to which I added an orange Sunkist, Bar-B-Q chips and Zagnut bar.

The trail then scrambles its way over random rock mazes in the middle of the woods. One rectangular stone, with a spray painted black cross on it, was just the right height and size for a person to lay down on and could've been used as a ceremonial blood alter. This whole area was kind of spooky, but I enjoyed seeing rocks jutting out of the ground like giant shards of broken glass and exploring lots of little overhangs and hiding places.

Center Point Knob, the original halfway point of the AT, was marked by another bronze plaque like the one found on top of Springer Mountain. Next, Cumberland Valley was a welcome change. Here, we popped out of the woods and entered Pennsylvania Dutch farmers' fields and pastures. Our rocky, dirt trail turns to flat green paths surrounded by golden grasses and old farmhouses. Barns and silos stood like giant mileposts in the distance.

> *HIKER TIP: This fun section was very hot and it would be good to wear a hat, sunglasses, sunscreen and bring along an extra bottle of water. Also, be sure to check for ticks.*

At this point in the trip, I knew there was only a couple weeks' worth of money left, if that, and I lay awake every night, thinking about what to do. My camera was also acting funny. Sometimes the lens wouldn't open, causing me to miss some important shots. I wasn't even sure I wanted to keep going without being able to document it.

Picturesque as a postcard, hikers are welcomed to Boiling Springs, Pennsylvania, by a stately, gentle tree at the foot of "Children's Lake." Here, I shared the last of my cereal with fish, baby ducks and a graceful white swan. Seven acres in size, this manmade lake is fed by 30 natural springs, producing 22 million gallons of water a day. That's a lot of H2O! Following white blazes along 'Lovers Walk,' you'll see a 1700's Georgian mansion, positioned on a terraced hill overlooking the water. It's been empty for years.

> *FUN FACT: Each summer, "Anything Floats" features teams racing homemade vessels, built from foam and blue plastic barrels, around Children's Lake. All members of your crew must be on the "boat" at the finish line.*

You can't miss the ATC/Mid-Atlantic office inside a restored train depot. Hiker box heaven! I reloaded my mini bottles of DEET and sunscreen, plus snaked rice sides and even a Rice Crispy Treat. There was plenty to go around. Sipsey suggested we split a room at a place he knew. Having already completed several thru-hikes, this guy knew all the tricks. I had no intention of staying in town and wasn't thrilled about sharing a room with a dude, but my PC and a drop box of food with a $20 bill from Mom was at the post office, so I went for it.

The Allenberry Resort & Playhouse first opened in the 1940's and it was immaculate, hiker friendly and right on the river. The hostess hooked us up with a room (normally $154!) to share for just $20 per person. Hiker priced rooms have tiny TVs and no cable, but you can upgrade. We were more than comfortable, our room had a pair of big soft beds, cold A/C and a hot shower. Situated in Meadow Lodge, several community nooks had comfy, deep leather couches. There was even a telescope for stargazing. You'll also find a huge swimming pool (loaner swim trunks available) and Jacuzzi next to the game room, replete with pool tables, foosball, air hockey and ping-pong.

Saving money, Sipsey and I both made dinner in our rooms, but there are formal dining halls and a first-class restaurant open on dinner theatre nights. This resort is famous for its 400 seat playhouse where they present Broadway plays, musicals, and murder/mystery weekends. Some hikers enjoy shows during their stay. I did see some pretty ballerinas rehearsing while washing my clothes in the laundry room of the theatre's basement. $4.00/load.

Staying up late, I got all caught up on making videos and couldn't believe how many people were subscribed. Now over a thousand! Tired, I fell fast asleep but was woken up when I felt someone sit down on my bed! I sat bolt upright and furious with my fist tightly clenched and ready to knock someone out for trying any funny stuff. But looking over at my roommate, he was 6 feet away, facing the other direction and snoring. Was it a ghost? I have no idea, but throughout the night I heard sounds in the dark. In the morning, my camera batteries were on the carpet a foot away from the nightstand where I put them! Someone, or something, was in the room with us that night.

Hiker guests were invited to breakfast at the snazzy Undershoot Lounge. Healthy portions of bacon, eggs, toast and juice really hit the spot and very reasonable. Just $6! A waitress was nice enough to take our photo showing Canecutter, Slow Foot, Sipsey, Prophet and myself. I really like this picture a lot, but it was the last time I saw Canecutter & Prophet together.

This hidden gem was the best value on the AT! Ask at the Boiling Springs ATC for directions. *Update: In 2016, the property was up for sale. Asking price: $6 million. Since purchased by a local businessman, hopefully it will be reopened by the time you read this.*

Amazing, the random things you find along the trail. Out in the middle of nowhere, an old, rusting-away car had trees growing through a tangled mess of iron and axles. No telling how it got there. I also found several possible Civil War relics in this area: part of an old belt buckle and a deformed lead Minié ball.

Darlington Shelter is where Sipsey and I met Jerry & Bazinga. They were a cute couple, and Jerry could have been a stunt double for Jerry Seinfeld and sounded exactly like the sitcom star when he spoke. Bazinga was a pretty girl with a bun of blond hair. I bet you can guess her favorite TV show? Sipsey didn't get it and kept telling her, "But you don't look like a Bazinga!" For several days, he made up new names for her, each rejected in turn.

Hiking together a lot, Sipsey and I had a loose arrangement. He slept at a shelter, and as always I'd camp off by myself in the woods a mile or so up the trail. We would then meet up the next morning. But one day, he didn't show as expected. Getting worried, I backtracked and found him sitting in the middle of the trail with a boot off. Freak accident. He had stepped on a broken beer bottle somehow imbedded into the dirt. It had penetrated his sole, and the jagged glass poked out the top of his pinkie toe. Ouch! Carefully, he removed the brown glass and after wrapping it with tape, we slowly walked toward Duncannon.

> HIKER TIP: Another trick Sipsey showed me was a tiny brown vial of vanilla perfume he carried. Two drops in his boots each night kept them smelling fresh. He let me try and it really worked!

The next water break was Cove Mountain Shelter. This one was built with wooden beams from an old barn. A "critter alert" asked hikers to cook and eat their food away from the structure, because hungry porcupines had been chewing on the building. Salt from perspiration also attracts these quilled creatures, so sacrificial plywood was nailed down over heavy use areas. Another shelter once stood in this same, beautiful clearing, Thelma Marks Shelter.

September 1990, a young thru-hiking couple, 25-year-old Molly LaRue of Ohio, and her fiancé Geoffrey Hood, from Tennessee, 26, had been making their way southbound from Katahdin and looking forward to reaching halfway. Both worked with a church helping troubled children gain confidence through outdoor activities. Geoff was called "Clevis," and Molly's trail name was "Nalgene," after a brand of water bottle. An artist, Molly had even designed a US postage stamp. For good luck, she hung a blue-haired troll keychain from her backpack. Resting for a night in room #33 at the Doyle Hotel, they took turns calling home. The next day they made their way up Cove Mountain, where they unfortunately came upon drifter Paul David Crews, or rather, he came upon them.

Crews was already hiding on the AT from murder charges in Florida. Without a backpack, he carried a red gym bag in each hand with Marlboro logos printed on them. It's assumed the couple shared Thelma Marks Shelter with him that night. Later the next day, another couple found a gruesome scene and quickly walked back to town and notified police. All uphill, it took authorities another three hours to reach the shelter and begin their investigation. In back of the shelter, they found Geoff covered with his sleeping bag as if he were sleeping, but he had been shot several times. In the other corner, Molly had been stabbed to death. Scattered around the area was trash and 2 empty red gym bags.

News of the crime spread up and down the trail and 8 days later, an alert hiker recognized a man wearing Geoff's distinctive green backpack. Arrested by park rangers while crossing the bridge into Harpers Ferry, Crews was caught red handed with Geoff's hiking boots, watch and AT guidebook. Not to mention he was still carrying both murder weapons: a .22-caliber revolver and double-edged knife, almost 9 inches long. Staring blankly in his mugshot, the average looking Joe was dirty, wearing a torn blue jean jacket. He was first sentenced to death by lethal injection; reduced to two life sentences. Crews has never talked about what triggered him to violence. The story was featured on TV's *'Top Cops.'* Ten years later, Thelma Marks Shelter was dismantled and burned.

Sipsey and I stopped at Hawk Rock with a view of Duncannon and the Susquehanna River below. Unfortunately, the rocks were all defaced with graffiti. Working our way down, the collapsed cliffs made the trail look like a gravel driveway - except every piece of gravel was the size of a basketball and sharp as shovels. This made for a precarious walk, especially when poor Sipsey's toe was falling off!

After a confusing trailhead junction, we walked up on the Road Hawg BBQ joint, "Food so good, sometimes we run out!" Motorcycles were lined up in rows as jovial people mixed in the parking lot. All this was particularly interesting to Sipsey, as he owns a bustling BBQ restaurant back home in Alabama. Oh, yeah, it's not a party until a mid-life crisis band plays ZZ Top...

♪ I hear it's fine, if you got the time
And the Ten to get yourself in
A hmm, hmm, hmm, hmm ♫

Hotel Doyle. Finally, we arrived at the most infamous hiker hangout on the AT. You might be surprised this was on my top 5 list of places to visit, as it has a reputation as a party stop. But I wanted to experience it for myself. This was one of several luxury hotels originally built by beer company Anheuser-Busch. Four stories high, the large red brick building has a white wrap-around porch with tall columns and a dome sitting atop a castle-like drum tower. Now over  107 years old, the hotel has become rundown and some sections were even cordoned off with yellow caution tape. Vicky & Pat took over the hotel in 2001 and have big plans to fix it up.

Once grand, the winding central staircase showed signs of water damage, with plaster crumbling around the skylight. For the sake of space, 2 Victorian dressers were stored on each landing, obviously removed from tiny rooms to make way for extra beds. The cramped pool table room had a wall covered with pictures of hikers who have stopped by. I only got a peek, but a "secret room" held a ping-pong table for private parties.

Kind of an off the wall place, inside the pub, shelves were lined with liquor bottles, toy space ships and alien heads. Sipsey had to loan me money for my half of the room and dinner (I paid him back the next day by over drafting my bank account), but the chicken fingers, hush puppies, and fries were off the hook! When checking in, half-jokingly,

I asked for the "haunted" room. Vicky winked and said she never tells which ones have ghosts. After drinking two tall Yuenglings, my buddy was out like a light. Room/$17 each ($25 a night + $7.50 EAP).

"We're known for our food, not our lodging." A far cry from the luxurious Allenberry, where we were pampered like VIPs a week ago, hiker worn rooms here were tiny and bare bones. Squeezed inside were 2 single mattresses (no frames or backboards) with flat pillows and dubious sheets. That's about all, so bring your sleeping bag. Also, be sure to check hiker boxes. There's one on every floor and I scored a nearly new poncho and other freebees.

> FUN FACT: While on a reading tour, Charles Dickens once enjoyed a night in a previous incarnation of the Doyle. His works include: David Copperfield, A Christmas Carol, Oliver Twist and A Tale of Two Cities.

My friend Socks had already been here for days. Both her knees were still swollen, but she was determined to do whatever it took to keep hiking. Imagine being from another country and having to go to the doctor, answer questions and fill out forms in a foreign language. Thankfully, she had befriended another German thru-hiker, Slow Foot, who located a good German doctor for her to see.

It was a full house with no AC, and the evening was very humid, even with a fan in the window, but uneventful. That is, until a loud siren atop the nearby fire station woke everybody up. I still have no idea why it went off at 3:00 a.m.; there was no sign of fire, flood, or air raid. Still, I had a wonderful time at the Doyle. If you understand, going in, that this place is on the rough side, this landmark will win you over with its charms. Plus, you'll have a story to tell! Vicky & Pat have been very loyal to AT hikers and the Doyle is a part of our subculture, so even if you don't stay the night, stop by for a burger and feel the ambiance.

Mail magic! The GA Gang was a family I knew from the arrowhead collecting community, but had never met. Also interested in hiking, they followed along with my AT videos and sent a care package with Jolly Ranchers, M&M's, Cliff bars, beef jerky and an encouraging letter. Thanks Rob, Terrie, Ty, Katie and Zack! I didn't know it at the time, but posting this unboxing video online would really start something! Even though I never mentioned a word about being broke, more people started writing, eager to help. Still, because of pride I held off letting more people send stuff.

Squished coins make cheap souvenirs. While waiting for a train to go by, I saw a majestic bald eagle swoop down and catch a fish right out of the river. Sadly, a drunken hiker was hit and killed on these same tracks a year later. Duncannon had really fallen on hard times and some buildings were abandoned or dilapidated. There were no fast food joints or grocery stores, only a small convenience store and a seedy strip club built into a rundown gas station. Harrisburg, Pennsylvania, is a 14-mile hitch away with more amenities - just be sure to ask if there's a charge for this. Tuts accepted what he assumed was a free ride, but when he arrived, the townie demanded money and left poor Tuts stranded miles from the trail. Stories like this are rare, but can happen. Other places around Duncannon...

- **Goodies** is known for a big breakfast and pancake challenge.
- **Sorrento's Pizza** was lit up with red and yellow neon lights.
- **Riverfront Campground** tent sites + shower, $5/hiker rate.

Crossing the long Clark's Ferry Bridge, I filmed Squatch...filming me...while he was filming Sipsey! These guys already knew each other from the PCT. Poor Sipsey tried to hike, but the next climb caused him too much pain. With diabetes, he didn't want to take any chances, so we wished each other well and he limped back to town.

At the next shelter, also called Clark's Ferry, Tyvek penned a logbook art tribute to the Doyle. He was upset, as was I, that so many people had left negative comments about the historic hotel. Basically, he said anyone who had a problem with it "...could kiss his ass." A shelter pet lived under the building: a friendly gray tabby cat. It looked a little thin in the skin so I shared a few bites of my tuna wrap.

The next few days, stretches of woods were broken up by road crossings. In one spot, a chain-link pedestrian bridge was built high above a busy curve in the road. Before the walkway, a continuous stream of traffic on PA-225 was dangerous for hikers. Stopping at Peter's Mountain Shelter, the spring was a quarter mile down 300 rock steps. I skipped it. This huge, 2 story loft is listed as being able to sleep 16 hikers. Hanging out: Radio, Late 4 Dinner and The Georgia Boys.

As I walked along, I found a notebook page held down with a stone, and which warned: "SNAKES under rocks 10 feet ahead." I could just see the serpent's beaded black tail sticking out from under a bush. I tried to get him off the trail using my hiking pole, but he told me to "stay away" with his rattling. Not far away, I found a colorful eastern box turtle. Turtle patrol! I was able to move this docile reptile to safety. That day, I also saw frogs and lizards. It felt like being on a reptile and amphibian nature walk!

I caught a trail angel reloading his Styrofoam cooler. Enjoying the crackers and bottled water, I called him "All Star" because of his old-school Converse sneakers. He grinned, happy that I thanked him with a trail name. I also met another troop of Boy Scouts. Unlucky for me, I accidently surprised an adult chaperone in the group, bent over with his pants down! Everyone has to make like a bear in the woods, but find a more secluded tree - especially when there are thousands to choose from! I rushed by with my head turned.

It was much more fun walking through Yellow Springs, a vanished village circa 1850. Jumbled rocks were former foundations of cabins housing coal miners. Picking up off the trail a golf-ball sized piece of raw, black coal, I looked up and noticed this was just a drop in the bucket. Piles of coal, each tall as a 2-story house, stood like pyramids in the woods. An unseen shelter nearby was "Closed for Repairs" with very short notice and judging by the language on the sign, they want hikers to keep moving: "Overnight camping permitted for thru hikers walking the Appalachian Trail from point of beginning to an exit, which is not the place of beginning." Try saying that 10 times fast!

Dewey & The Georgia Boys were three purists who never skipped a single white blaze all the way from Springer to Katahdin. Dewey had made friends with Brad & Bill, who, with matching trail beards, looked like twins. One afternoon, I waited by a stream to film them crossing a creek using a large downed tree as a bridge. Without missing a stride, the trio marched over the obstacle like a single hiking machine.

Cautiously, I crossed the same tree, holding my hiking poles to each side like a high wire act walking between two skyscrapers.

First thing the next morning, I peeked inside 501 Shelter, a detached garage behind a private house. You can follow either the PA-501 or a blue blazed trail to find it. At 6:00 a.m., most everyone was asleep and I was surprised when Bazinga came out wearing a blue windbreaker over her cute nightgown. It had been well over a week since I last saw her, so it was nice to catch up. She also brought me the logbook to sign and read. Sipsey had been there the day before, and sadly, left a note saying he was going home. Bazinga and Jerry were going home, too. Almost done with their section hike, they had to get back to work.

Missing signs. Three out of 4 trail junction signs in these sections were either vandalized or gone altogether. Navigating was not a problem, as the painted white blazes were still there, but hikers could get turned around or run out of water. Springs in the summer can be undependable, so if you miss any one of them, you're out of luck. Temps of 100°+ can make it uncomfortable and even dangerous.

Next, I'll rant about misbehaved dogs. I've always been scared of scary dogs and they can sense it. In this instance, I startled a brown German shepherd. A beautiful animal, but he started barking aggressively. Calling out, "Do you have it?" I saw three college boys staring at me like I was stupid. Getting angry, I asked, "Can you please at least hold onto the dog?" Reluctantly, one of them did so but said annoyed, "He's not going to bite." I don't like being barked at and had to skirt the narrow trail as the beast dodged back and forth, raring to get at me. I yelled: "If your dog doesn't like hikers, don't take him hiking!" This overlook was known for hang glider watching, but I couldn't even stop with this demon dog trying to rip out my throat.

This was the third dog I met on the AT who was hostile toward me. I blame it on their owners, as I never had any trouble with trail dogs thru-hiking with their masters (yet). Some people feel entitled to let their dogs run wild, and like proud parents, think their "kids" are always little angels. One video series I watched featured a loveable puppy who would shoot into the brush every time he heard a sound. That ankle-biter killed at least 4 birds and his owners just laughed. They even filmed him leaving stinky landmines directly on the trail.

- **Leash your dog around cliff edges.** People have died trying to protect their fury friends from falling.
- **Doggie backpacks** (to carry their own food) should be properly fitted. Too tight may restrict breathing; too loose can cause chaffing.
- **Inspect paws daily** for cuts and check for ticks as well.
- **Dog collars** need ID tags with contact info and proof of vaccines.
- **Have a picture** of your pup. I saw several notes about lost dogs.
- **Take extra breaks.** Your puppy can't say, "Hey, can we slow down?" Many hikers are heartbroken sending their buddies home.

> FUN FACT: In 1990, Bill Irwin, with help from his faithful dog, Orient, became the first blind person to hike the entire Appalachian Trail. Bill said, "God led the dog, and the dog led me."

> HIKER TIP: Man's best friend, dogs offer unconditional companionship while doubling as guard dogs, but takes special consideration, as leading a house pet on a 2200-mile journey is a huge responsibility...

Everyone talks about the Virginia Blues, but Pennsylvania and its 230 miles, better known as Rocksylvania... "Where boots (and trail runners) go to die," really wore me down. The joke was that trail maintainers stay up all night sharpening rocks with files and chisels. Both my hiking sticks had holes worn into the ends, letting dirt pack inside. I missed my family, friends, kayaking, skateboarding, my home (an old RV), and even my j-o-b. Being broke and living out of hiker boxes sucked too, but decided if I had enough food to get to the next town, I would just keep walking.

Chapter 14. Rocksylvania

Loner hanging out with "Wilson the Propane Cylinder."

Walking into Port Clinton, I had $2 to my name and no food. A blue blazed trail leads along neighborhood streets to the Hiker's Pavilion. This large, covered rec center has been provided by a local church for many years and who, understandably, posted several signs reading: "No alcohol allowed." If that's all our hosts ask in return for a free night stay, I guess that's asking too much as trash cans were overfilled with empty beer bottles.

With a total area of 0.5 square miles, this whole town would fit into the parking lot of your average Wally World. Little shops and churches had charm, but like Duncannon, this township had become blighted. The post office was in the basement of a random building and had odd hours. Still, the postmaster was cool and played KISS full blast in a backroom. I could imagine him singing along as he sorted letters and packages...

♪ *You keep on shouting, you keep on shouting*
I... wanna rock and roll all night
and party every day ♫

No library, I had my PC sent here in case it would have to be sold for bus ticket money, but bounced it ahead. Mom had sent a drop box with just enough to keep going: food, batteries, a small bag of quarters to do laundry, plus another $20 bill. Still cutting all my resources really close, I was almost out of water treatment, and the stove alcohol had run out a few days back. Oh yeah...and the section of guidebook pages I was using ended at the next town. Thinking for sure I was going home, I never requested the next section be put in the mail.

Port Clinton Peanut/Candy Shop was the best thing going for this town. They had anything fun and tasty you can imagine: fudge, roasted peanuts, candy buttons on long strips of paper, marshmallow ice cream cones and so on. Dozens of oversized PEZ candy dispensers were on display, but not for sale. My score: orange circus peanuts, 'Round Up' bubblegum cigarettes (I prefer white chalky ones), little gummy hotdogs (candy pizzas were sold out), chocolate raisins and blueberry mothballs (my favorite). And, of course, a root beer to wash it all down (I'm getting a sugar rush just typing this!).

Spending most of my meager budget, I didn't consider this splurging, as there was nowhere else to eat here, anyway. The lone hotel/restaurant was closed, because the owner was on vacation during peak season, but there were enough bad comments in logbooks about this establishment to avoid it anyway. Leaving town, I walked up on a bunch of purple butterflies. My mother, who knew better than anyone how tight my finances were, saw this in a video and thought it was a sign things would somehow work out.

How much does it cost to hike the AT? This is the most common question people ask - and the reason many hikers drop out. Don't underestimate what it costs to live out here. Too many hopefuls try to hike up or down the whole side of the country for the very least amount of money possible, like I did. The point of all this shouldn't be to deprive oneself, but rather, to live life to the fullest. Naively, I attempted to hike the entire 2,200-mile AT for $1 a mile, or $2,200, but failed terribly. And believe me (or ask any of my ex-girlfriends), I'm cheap as they come. $1 a mile would basically mean living like a homeless person. Now, I suggest $2 a mile, or a minimum of $4000 for thrifty people. A buffer would also be advisable. No one ever plans for unexpected shuttle rides, gear replacements or repairs, sick days and doctor visits. Ideally, a starting budget of $5000 should fund a hiker from one terminus to the other with no worries. Of course, none of these estimates include the gear you start with, or transportation to and from the trail. Depending on your current lifestyle, I'll bet the cost of living on the AT, 4 - 6 months, is less than in the "real world" for that same period of time. Think about it - $4,000 for the adventure of a lifetime is a bargain.

> HIKER TIP: Don't forget to leave enough cash leftover for return travel. Depending on how far you are away from home, it could cost hundreds of dollars. Many a hiker has run out and had to hitch his/her way home.

When finances were less stressful, I liked to Zen out and hike with the sounds of nature, and even meditate. I've always had a vivid imagination and would walk along all day, daydreaming. "In my mind!" I built my dream log cabin piece-by-piece, wrote songs with matching music videos, and ran a NASCAR race team spending hours choosing drivers and running races in my head. Kind of like Dungeons & Dragons meets Fantasy Football! I've read about people held in solitary confinement doing the same thing, such as playing 18 holes of golf in their heads each day to keep from going crazy.

After a tuff climb, I reached Pulpit Rock. Through the trees, and only a few hundred feet off the AT, were 5 big observatory domes. Lehigh Valley Amateur Astronomical Society (LVAAS) was founded in 1957. A secret green outhouse can be found here, as well, but most hikers just walk by never knowing anything's here. Stars and celestial bodies are not the only things spotted here. Members have reported almost daily black bear sightings.

Giant telescopes or not, the view from Pulpit Rock, 1,582', was the best I'd seen for hundreds of miles. McAfee Knob-esque, I hung my legs over the edge of the protruding cliff. Very exciting! Getting late, I made camp here, with 2 perfectly spaced trees. Woken up in the middle of the night, head-lamped hikers stopped to take in the full moon view. The Dayglow Crew, easy to spot wearing bright neon orange and green shirts. Back in Duncannon, I snapped a pic of 4 of them walking over a crosswalk, very loosely reminiscent of the Beatles famous 1969 'Abbey Road' album cover. Tonight, they had a goal to walk 40 miles.

Before daylight, chirping birds woke me up, just in time to experience another example of synchronicity. Here, I was within sight of the only astronomy observatory on the trail when my radio broadcast a 60 second radio show with instructions for viewing Venus and Saturn, two bright shiny dots on the horizon. It's moments like this when the trail, or unified field knows you're here and give you a little boost. I was very close to going home the day before, and would have if not for a well-stocked drop box.

> **FUN FACT: 'StarDate,' A public education outreach based from McDonald Observatory, University of Texas, began in 1978 and is the longest-running science radio series in the country.**

Speaking of my FM radio, it gave me many hours of pleasure, and sometimes I would spin the dial for a variety of music. Some of the bubble gum hits that season...

• **'Call Me Maybe'** - Carly Rae Jepsen. This catchy ditty played dozens of times each day and I couldn't get it out of my head!

> ♪ *Hey, I just met you, and this is crazy*
> *but here's my number, so call me maybe?* ♫

• **'Somebody that I Used to Know'** - Gotye.

> ♪ *Now and then I think of when we were together*
> *Like when you said you felt so happy you could die*
> *Told myself that you were right for me*
> *But felt so lonely in your company* ♫

• **'Good Feeling'** - Flo Rida. Also, used on 'Storage Wars,' TV ads.

> ♪ *Oh, oh, sometimes I get a good feeling, yeah*
> *I get a feeling that I never never never never had before,*
> *I get a good feeling, yeah* ♫

My radio also brought sad news. The terrible massacre at a Colorado movie theater showing 'Batman: The Dark Night Rises,' happened while I was out on the trail and I listened daily for updates.

The next morning, I found Dayglow Crew tented directly atop The Pinnacle, another rocky overlook with panoramic views (no camping allowed, but who am I to talk). I guess the rocks were just too difficult, at night, to make it 40 miles. Boulder fields for miles and miles were hard enough to navigate in broad daylight. Filming an action sequence of myself traversing this terrain, I made sure to get a white blaze in the shot to prove it was really part of the AT! I jumped from boulder-to-boulder, clicking away, using my walking sticks for balance and going faster than I should have. It took lots of concentration not to fall. I think my many years on a skateboard helped me stay agile as a cat!

If needed, a secret blue-blazed trail, starting back near the last shelter, bypasses this mountain. But I would have missed Star Craft, handing out cupcakes with one hand, her trusty knitting loop in the other. Her husband Spot had caught Lyme disease, but knowing the warning signs, sought treatment in time and was still trucking. The next stop was modern Allentown Shelter, with a checkerboard painted on the floor with game pieces fashioned from small stones and acorn tops.

Rub a dub dub, thanks for the grub! Hiker picnic! Many thanks to our hosts, Tony and Mountain Goat. Nothing is more patriotic than hotdogs on the 4th of July. A succession of hikers threw their backpacks into a pile and chowed down. One of them was D-Tour. We last saw each other in Marion, Virginia. Like me, he always wore the same exact green shirt. Xamot & Tomax said hi, identical twin brothers that I had never met before, or since. MMRF (pronounced "Murph") from Charlotte, North Carolina, was hiking in memory of his dad, David. They were supposed to do the AT together, but David passed away of Multiple Myeloma, an incurable blood cancer. MMRF had business cards with a website where people could donate - a good idea for those walking for charity. He collected $8,114.00 of the $10,000 goal.

Knife Edge was a rocky ridgeline with a great view. On top, I met some day trippers who asked all kinds of questions and gifted me chilled grapefruit and strawberries. Sometimes I felt like a trophy dog at a judged show, answering questions instead of doing tricks for snacks. After the Q&A, I still yogied a couple of peanut butter sandwiches and power bars, with each of their group pitching in. Sadly, when they asked me: "You going all the way to Maine?" I had to reply, "Going as far as I can."

An overlook at the former site of Bake Oven Knob Fire Tower had a view even nicer than the last. Too bad the entire vicinity was ruined by loser graffiti that looked like some three-year-old kids got ahold of some rattle cans. Go tag a falling apart building or rusty train and leave wilderness alone! I did get a chuckle from a quote written on a rock: "You had me at hell," a play on the famous tag line: "You had me at hello" from 'Jerry Maguire.'

An old cookpot wired to a tree marked the side trail to Bake Oven Knob Shelter. Built in 1937, this chinked log cabin is one of several original shelters remaining in Pennsylvania. First thing a hiker does when arriving at any shelter is check the logbook, but in this case, the register was completely full! There was not one single blank space left on any page to even write your name. Judging by the dates, this shelter hadn't been visited by a ridgerunner or maintainer in at least a month.

> HIKER TIP: Avoid Bake Oven Knob Shelter. Parking lots in close proximity make easy access for party people. New Tripoli Campsite, four miles back, would be a better option. Next shelter north is 6.8 miles away.

Temps nearing 100° and I was dry on water. Trudging through jungles of briers and relentless rocks makes hikers very thirsty. Of course, the spring was bone dry. The best thing to do when this happens is to follow the empty streambed downhill. Sure enough, a quarter mile down was a nice spring, flowing with ice chilly water.

Trying to take a nap in the shelter, it felt like a sauna under the old tin roof. So, I just lay there sweating, swatting at black wasps and getting angrier by the second, staring at four green propane tanks, each about the size of a two-liter soda bottle.

START RANT: Litter bugs! Why would anyone leave these here? Every single person has a responsibility, when we set foot in the woods, to carry out everything we bring in. No one is so privileged they are forgiven for pollution. Why in the hell would anyone even carry these monstrosities into the woods? Are they so lazy they can't build a fire in the existing fire pit? People like this don't deserve the privilege of visiting the backcountry. Have you never heard of "Give a hoot, don't pollute?" Local trash service is not going to come in here and clean up after you. If you had the energy to carry it in full, the very least you can do is carry it out empty after cooking your $8 dollar, prepackaged Mountain House meals (I actually love these). And don't rationalize this offense by leaving a tiny little bit for others to use - thru-hikers don't bring the biggest, heaviest hunk of junk they can find. If you don't want to carry it...don't bring it! It's not that hard of a concept! I'm not yelling at everyone. I'm yelling at the LAZY BASTARDS who left these here, or anyone who ever left a propane cylinder in the woods. **END RANT.**

Reading the long warning label on the back of a canister, I became even more incensed...

- **DANGER** - Extremely flammable.
- **DANGER** - Fire explosion hazard.
- **DANGER** - Carbon monoxide hazard.
- **NEVER** use around people that are sleeping.
- **WARNING:** "This container and the combustion of its contents contains chemicals known to the state of California to cause cancer, birth defects and other reproductive harm."

Sounds like fun, let me carry one! As a protest, and to do something about the situation besides complain, I put one of these bulky cylinders into my ultralight backpack and carried it to the nearest dumpster - eight miles away.

More fun with garbage! Someone also left an empty beef jerky packet. This really pissed me off! The only excuse for not carrying this out...is the LAZY BASTARD blew-off both their arms trying to ignite their stupid Colman stove. I also put this rubbish into my backpack.

NEXT RANT: Privies. Two of the last three shelter privies have been full. When I say full - I mean FULL. One to the point the lid wouldn't close. Just to give you some idea how large these underground reservoirs are, imagine one of those plastic porta potties found at construction sites, buried under the ground, with a seat on top. That's a lot of crap. Please believe me, the very last thing I want to do is crack on maintainers and volunteers, but this can be a toxic waste hazard. These toilets are very remote and you can't just drive a honey wagon up the trail to pump them out. I can't even envision a process to begin cleaning up these years of neglect besides moving the outhouse altogether and burying the holes forever. It's a shitty job, but someone has to do it. **END RANT.**

During a Pop Tart break, I decorated my new propane cylinder with pieces of duct tape - making a smiley face expression. I named him "Wilson," after the volleyball that was Tom Hanks' lone companion while stranded on a deserted island in the movie 'Castaway.' Together, we watched a white sports car race up and down a gravel road. Sometimes, the wannabe stunt driver pulled the emergency break and did a slide maneuver. I just shook my head, amazed at the intelligence of the local wildlife. Making camp on a bluff, Wilson sat quietly keeping an eye on dinner as 4th of July fireworks exploded in the distance. It was kind of exciting and lonesome at the same time, even with Wilson there to keep me company.

The next morning, the AT spilled me out near an abandoned NAPA store where I used a hosepipe and bottle of Greased Lightning to take a cold hobo bath and wash clothes. I got clean "In a flash!" as cars honked their horns. All clean and smelling fresh of degreaser, and I come across a skunk! Spotting him moving in the brush, terrified of getting sprayed, I dropped my poles and retreated. I was more frightened than when I came face-to-face with Billy the Bear! But tiptoeing within 5 feet of Pepé Le Pew, I learned that wild beasts don't care about humans if they have something to eat.

The blue blazed maze to Palmerton was an adventure-in-itself. A mile and a half side trail with twists and turns, an abandoned road, loose boulders high overhead held in place with nets of chain-link fence, active guardhouse and then through a poor neighborhood.

Native Americans first lived along these riverbanks when this area was a thriving green forest. After that, settlers raised generations of families. Then the mines came, and Palmerton grew around it. But careless profits were all that mattered, without a moment's remorse for the future. A hundred years of Zinc smelting eradicated almost all surrounding vegetation and the devastation was complete. Mars red, this barren landscape now resembles another planet.

The EPA describes this area as an "uncontrolled or abandoned place where hazardous waste is located, possibly affecting local ecosystems or people." Added to the National Priority List in 1983, it's still an active US Government "Superfund" site. Clean, outside soil is brought in by a constant convoy of huge dump trucks, then helicopters drop thousands of pounds of seed. But political infighting has further delayed cleanup. The citizens' group, 'Palmerton Citizens for a Clean Environment' (PCCE), believes a cleanup of the town's soil and water are necessary for human health. In stark opposition, the Pro-Palmerton Coalition (PPC) argue that any health risks are exaggerated, and the Superfund status stigmatizes Palmerton's reputation. Why would anyone NOT want to fix this obvious mess? Speaking of contamination, I finally said goodbye to Wilson. I hated putting him into that dumpster, not because we had bonded, but because I was afraid the garbage truck might blow-up! All jokes aside, these canisters are horrible for the environment.

> NOT SO FUN FACT: Coleman invented a "Green Key" tool to completely empty a tank by releasing raw propane into the atmosphere. Great idea! NOT! There is no way to safely refill, recycle, or dispose of these cylinders.

Walking onto Main Street, I got the distinct feeling that I was, indeed, in the north. Corner fruit stands and city busses felt like they did when I was growing up in Massachusetts. But this whole area had a faint smell of ammonia and I wasn't the only one who noticed some of the townspeople were a little... off. Some turned their nose up at me, while others saw my backpack and went out of their way, even crossing the street, to ask about my hike. Town itself was nice, with colorful life-size donkeys, jackasses and burrows placed all over town.

Visiting Palmerton Historical Society, the friendly lady seemed very excited to have a visitor, and gave me the deluxe tour. Of course, she taught me all about Zinc, but I was fascinated by a B&W photo of a scary looking house I had seen walking into town. Known as "House on Marshall's Hill," this Victorian mansion has been a landmark since it was built in 1881, and was rumored to be haunted...Reclusive owners who never came to town, barking guard dogs and iron bars bolted across windows all added to the mystery. Then, Mr. Marshall suddenly "left." Some say Mrs. Marshall murdered her wayward husband and buried him in beneath the mansion. Over a hundred years old, the home has been renovated and is not so scary looking anymore. After all, haunted houses don't have baby blue vinyl siding.

> FUN FACT: Zinc, (Zn) was named Zinke, by German alchemist Paracelsus. Today, it's used as a corrosion resistant coating for galvanized gutters, mail boxes, fences, etc.

No bounce box this time, so there wasn't any food or money to keep going. Was this the end of the line? All I had left in the world was $6 in quarters and will never forget having to choose between much-needed socks, or food. Deciding socks wouldn't matter if I had to go home, I enjoyed my chips, salsa and soda in Borough Park. Like the old days kids played on swing sets, couples walked their dogs and girls giggled while braiding each other's hair, all while the Palmerton Community Band played patriotic songs in the park's bandstand, as they have since 1911. It might sound cliché, but the experience reminded me of a Norman Rockwell painting.

The Palmerton Area Library was a beautiful marble building, but librarians had strict time limits for using their computers. You can connect to their Wi-Fi but must pay first even when using your own device. Oh yeah, they don't take cash, only credit cards. I had my PC here but couldn't afford to use it.

Needing a place to stay I went to Borough Hall, called the "Jail House Hostel," in the guidebook. I envisioned each hiker being assigned a separate cell, but the truth was less exciting. Construction of a jail below the borough had begun, but was left unfinished and never actually housed inmates. Signing in, an imposing detective in a suit and tie checked my ID as he interrogated me: "Are you alone?" "Did you walk here?" "Where are you from?" "Do you expect anyone else tonight?" He then informed me of the rules: no cars, no drinking, no drugs, 10:00 p.m. curfew, one night only, etc. My favorite suggestion was written on a chalkboard: "This is not a flop house!" Cool place - there were shelves of paperback books, high-power cooling fan and a ping-pong table - but no ping-pong balls. Hikers used a white tile shower room in the gym with very intense water pressure - strong enough to wash deer ticks off your back!

Doughnuts make me go nuts! Someone left a half dozen, day-old, cream-filled doughnuts, and the hiker "box" was a table covered with gear including a pair of hiking boots, shirts of assorted sizes, shorts, sleeping pad and a decent red backpack. Almost everything you need to start hiking! Another box had first aid and food. I snagged a pouch of precooked beef taco mix (a $6 value!) and made taco-nachos in the microwave with my leftover chips and salsa. Surprisingly, my PC picked up great Wi-Fi here and I got all my videos downloaded in short order.

Checking my email, Mom sent a reply to a message I sent weeks ago, telling her I might be coming home. She said to wait - there was important news! My grandmother, who we affectionately call Babchie (Polish word for grandmother), was coming to my rescue! I had no idea she was watching my videos, or if she even knew I was hiking, but she had been following along the whole time. Grandmas are cool! Wanting to help, she called my sister every night for a week to see if I had checked in, and asked how much I needed to finish. My sister guessed at $1,000 and Babchie was sending a check. What a relief! It would still take 2 weeks for my sister to get the check in the mail, deposit it into her bank and then transfer it to my account. Thankfully, Mom also put $100 onto my debit card to keep me going until then. Yes! I couldn't go crazy, but it should be enough if I was careful. I was jumping around and over the top happy!

Then, I opened the next email. It was from my father. I love my dad, but we just hadn't talked much since my parents divorced when I was 12, and had only seen each other twice in 30 years. Very upset, he made me feel guilty for accepting grandma's offer, saying she was on a fixed income and didn't have extra money. Mostly, he was hurt I didn't come to him for help. All my excitement instantly deflated and I was ready to return the money and just quit.

No one else showed and I had the jail all to myself. The basement was a real mess, so I stayed awake, cleaning up while listening to music. I made beds, organized the gear table, folded towels, swept up a gallon bucket worth of dirt and took out the garbage. It took my mind off things. I picked a bunk in a dark corner that had bare metal springs for a mattress but made a nest using a flattened cardboard box and my sleeping bags. During the night, I heard footsteps upstairs and boiler room pipes creak, but no ghost stories to report.

> *NOT SO FUN FACT: Palmerton Borough Hall has served AT thru-hikers for over 40 years. Sadly, this service is no longer provided because of bad hiker behavior. Shocking, as this was a special part of many journeys.*

> *HIKER TIP: Now, the only choice for lodging is Sunny Rest Nudist Resort - yes NUDE. It's not required you go "au-natural" but other (mostly retired) guests will be! There are several "clothing optional" stops on the AT.*

Worrying all night, I decided by morning that Babchie and her husband Sam were grown adults who could make their own decisions. Besides, they were hardly in the poor house (they have residences in both Las Vegas and Maine). So, I wrote a nice letter, thanking them for their help. I thanked my mother, too. Because of her, I was able to get new socks, lunch at a deli and trail food. I also left cookies and goodies at the jail for arriving hikers, including a pack of ping-pong balls I found at an oddball dollar store in town - kind of repayment for what I used, when I needed it most.

Waiting out the hottest part of the day, I wasn't feeling well and all the recent stress and swings of emotion didn't help. Mom, seeing the latest set of videos, sent several panicky emails begging me to go see a doctor. Moms are worriers, and she was concerned about my weight loss, black spots beneath my eyes and that I called out litter bugs and trail maintainers. She had never seen me so mad in her life! I could only try and assure her that I would be fine. When I headed out at 3:00 p.m., it was still 103°.

Lots of mountains are named "Blue," but this one, also known as "Dante's Inferno," was very intimidating because it's considered the most challenging climb on the AT until we get to Maine. Starting at 380' elevation, we climb straight up to 1,251'. I just took my time, boulder by boulder, and finally made it to the graffiti American flag at the summit. This test was very satisfying with a grand view as payoff. Almost like starting over, thanks to Grandma a huge weight had been lifted off my shoulders.

Walking along the top of the mountain, white blazes were painted on old fence posts because there were no trees. I took in a sweeping overlook of town; row houses dwarfed by the enormous Zinc factory. Once modern and teaming with activity, the decrepit building was rusting away, turning back to earth as all things do. They must be treating this area with Miracle Grow, because some freakishly large dandelion wishes I found were big as grapefruits! I also devoured lots of plump blackberries. Not sure how safe these were to eat - growing directly on a contaminated Superfund site - but I didn't grow a third eye. The drought was hard on hikers and wildlife alike, as I saw a lone coyote in the distance; a rare sighting as they are usually only heard, not seen. I felt bad for him, looking mangy and gaunt as he ambled away, peering over his shoulder to see if I was following.

Delaware Water Gap, once a town I dreaded would be the end of the line, was now a place I looked forward to. It was hard not to feel better passing ponds covered with Lily pads and floating purple flowers. With the calm that came after the Civil War, stylish health resorts sprung up here, attracting wealthy tourists. Each built to outdo the last, they boasted the latest high-tech amenities: phone service, hydraulic elevators, steam heat and even electrical lights!

> *FUN FACT: Kittatinny Resort offered moonlit excursions aboard their own steamboat. The hotel burnt to the ground in 1931, but a rock garden, once surrounding an elegant fountain at the grand entrance, remains.*

Enjoying myself, I totally missed the white blazes when they started into town. Backtracking to find my way, I followed sounds from Church of the Mountain's tolling bell tower. This red brick church basement has been a hiker hostel since 1973, the longest running on the entire AT! A big help, because the 17-mile stretch between the last shelter in Pennsylvania and the first one in New Jersey, is more of a hop than some shelter dwellers care to make.

Their clubhouse was awesome. I strummed on an acoustic guitar and played Mario Brothers on a Nintendo Game Boy. A bulletin board had pizza and Chinese menus and ads for upcoming hiker feeds. A nice touch, wooden bunk beds were lined with a thin layer of carpet. The only thing missing was a computer. There's also a wooden shelter out back called "Matt's Place" and plenty of tenting space. After a hot shower, I sat down for a moment in a deep Lazy Boy recliner and, more tired than I realized, ended up falling asleep. All this works on the honor system. First night free; second just a $3 donation.

Walking inside Village Farmer & Bakery was a hiker's dream. Tables covered with dozens of fresh made pies! I was eating better these days: (2) hotdogs, a Stewart's cream soda, Doritos, and of course a big slice of homemade apple pie! During the feast, Chameleon from Wyoming, & Roboticus from Pennsylvania, sat down with me and brought 2 college friends hiking with them for a few days. One was from England. We had a great time catching up, but I regret being too shy to ask someone to take a group photo of us. Other attractions around town...

- **Water Gap Trolley:** Bus tours. $8/includes Putt-Putt!
- **Deer Head Inn:** "Oldest jazz club in the country." Rooms $120.
- **Edge of the Woods Outfitters** mostly rent bikes and canoes.
- **Castle Inn:** A grand resort, featuring mosaic floor tiles, bowling alleys, and billiards. Now a Victorian ice cream parlor an antique mall.
- **Water Gap Adventures** specialized in fishing gear but carried the water treatment I needed. A repurposed vending machine had an exciting picture of a big bass on the front. Nightcrawlers/12 for $2.50.

Same old story, neither outfitter carried guidebooks so I would just wing it like I've done before. No grocery stores either, and made do resupplying at a mini mart: candy, jerky and a whole box of Cheerios, plus GORP (good ole raisins and peanut butter). After retrieving my backpack, I continued over Delaware River on the Route 80 bridge, bouncing up and down like a trampoline every time an 18-wheeler went by.

Chapter 15. Boardwalkin'

The mile and a half long, New Jersey Boardwalk.

In New Jersey, I stopped for a moment at the Delaware Water Gap National Park Visitor Center. There, I bought postcards and had them canceled with the special ink stamps they use for those little AT passports some thru-hikers carry.

> HIKER TIP: AT Passports. Document your journey by collecting personalized ink stamps from hostels, outfitters, trail angels, post offices (with purchase of a one cent stamp), hiker famous restaurants, etc. $7 / 1 oz.

Sunfish Pond, with white clouds reflecting in the water like a mirror, was too beautiful to walk by without stopping. This 41-acre oasis was left here by the Wisconsin Glacier during the last ice age, and is one of the Seven Natural Wonders of New Jersey. Adding baby blueberries to my Cheerios, I soaked my dogs in the cool, clear water. I even dozed off a little as deer played in the shallows. Threatened in 1965 by a proposed reservoir, protest hikes involving hundreds of people overwhelmed the owners, a power company, who donated it to the state. Sunfish Pond was declared a National Natural Landmark in 1970.

These shores were once covered with stone cairn sculptures that protruded out into the lake, but vandals have knocked them over and only a few small rock piles remain. It was over 80° and some tried to

take a swim, but could only stand the chilly water for a few moments before shrieking and running out. Signs informed us of many rules. #4... "No Swimming." It's unfortunate there are so many rules on a wilderness trail.

Also against the rules and strictly prohibited in New Jersey: fires of any kind. Local law enforcement takes this offense very seriously! I know, because two armed police officers walked up, deep in the woods, and interviewed me for several minutes. Apparently, someone had reported an unresponsive hiker sleeping next to a smoldering campfire, and I fit the description: "A white male in black shorts, with a beard." Well then, that narrows it down to about 90% of hikers on the trail! I even showed them time-dated pics I took at Sunfish Pond, proving I was miles away during the time in question.

Meandering along Kittatinny Range, there were remarkable views of the New Jersey valley below. Far from the rundown stereotype I expected, treetops spread far as the eye could see without a skyscraper in sight. Even after reading books and watching videos about the AT, I still worried the trail here would follow alongside subway tracks and down back alleyways. Nothing could be further from the truth. New Jersey was beautiful, scenic and alive with wildlife. In fact, this state has more black bears per square mile than any other on the AT.

I climbed Catfish Fire Tower, continuing a ritual of scaling each one I came to. This 60-foot monstrosity was built in 1922, of iron beams painted red and white. The cab was locked, but the view from on top of the stairs was nice. Later, I had lunch with Chameleon and Roboticus while trading ghost stories. Also, they asked if I had seen the thru-hiker named "Animal." His family was asking about his whereabouts on Whiteblaze.com, worried because he hadn't checked in recently.

A troop of Boy Scouts at a trail intersection were waiting for the rest of their group, who trickled by a few at a time. A couple of scouts took turns pumping water for me and the girls, from a rusty, iron hand-pump. This was a two-person operation, as a brass knob must be lifted for the contraption to work. With one hand holding the knob, and the other pumping the handle, how are you supposed to hold your bottle?

> HIKER TIP: I found that water bottle caps are the perfect size to wedge under the brass knob, holding it up while pumping. Handpumps of this style were frequent in the North, and I used this trick several times.

Hiking with the Scouts for a few miles reminded me of my childhood in the Cub Scouts - the little league of Boy Scouts. These young explorers had a ragtag assortment of thrift store backpacks, walking sticks picked-up off the ground and dull green military style sleeping bags rolled-up and towering above their heads, completely exposed to the elements. One boy even carried an oversized iron frying pan, tied to his back with twine, while another struggled to tote an awkward wooden box with rope handles. Still, they were loving every second.

The troublemaker of the group was a robust young man with a crew cut. Being disciplined for cursing and throwing rocks, he unwillingly had to stay within sight of the Scoutmaster, even though he looked strong enough to out hike anyone in the group, including me. There was also a straggler in their ranks, who I never saw, as he was having a very hard time just keeping up. Another scout was assigned to wait for him. Leaders invited me to camp with them and share supper, but it was still early so I kept trucking.

Next, I walked for a while with 5 thru-hikers I hadn't met before. One of the men took a tumble on a rocky downhill section, badly wrenching his knee. Luckily, another member of his group happened to be a US ARMY medic and stabilized the injury. US-206 wasn't far away and they phoned for help from the top of the mountain. Two of his buddies carried the injured man down the mountain, another lugged his backpack and I his trekking poles. It shook me up seeing another thru-hike end right in front of me. Each time I was reminded that anything can happen to anyone, at any time.

Later, I arrived at Sunrise Mountain Scenic Overlook, 1,653'. A long stone pavilion, built by the CCC in the late 1930's, this flat mountaintop was a shoeing station for pack mules and horses during the building of the AT. A weird homeless dude was holed up here who kept asking for cigarettes, so I didn't hang around.

Surprised, I found several gallon jugs of water and a whole bag of Lucky Charms in the metal bear box at Mashipacong Shelter. They were "magically delicious!" Scanning old pages in the register, Fatherman, from Tennessee, reported he filmed a fun night video here. FM edition #59 featured his buddy DK (short for Donna Karan), and some other girls, playing with hula-hoops that had battery powered, flashing lights. I could also hear people in the background ordering Chinese take-out. That does sound like a party!

I felt a kinship with FM. The preceding winter, he announced on YouTube his intentions to thru-hike and we traded messages about start dates, gear, etc. We had completely different documentary styles. Mine focused on trail towns and showed a solitary view of AT life, while his were all about the people he met, often doing mini interviews with every single person staying at a shelter on any given night. I hoped to meet him, but it seemed like he was always 2 weeks ahead.

This shelter was only a half mile from Stokes Forest Correctional Facility, a minimum-security youth prison. The word "youth" is very misleading as it only houses inmates aged 18-29. Built within Stokes State Forest in 1965, it was designed to hold 48 prisoners in a single dormitory, but business was good and the average daily population was double that. A satellite unit to the state's much larger Mountainview Youth Prison in Allendale, holding an additional 1,000+ offenders. With 747 acres of rolling foothills, a dairy farm, greenhouses and apple orchards, it sounded nice as far as hoosegows go.

For safety reasons, a sign asked motorists not to pick up hitchhikers - and asked hikers not to hitch. It was very odd to learn prisons are built on park lands at all, but apparently this is common practice. The organization, 'Citizens Opposed to Prisons in Parks,' protests the arrangement as there have been multiple escapes. In several instances, officials tried to keep things quiet and never alerted residents.

• **Christopher Miller**, 23, walked away from a work detail, caught a hitch and then stole a car. He was captured the next day.

- **Charles VanTassel**, 22, ran for the hills, hotwired a farmer's pickup truck and then was arrested in a neighboring town 2 days later - for driving the stolen truck. Police there didn't even know about the escape until they noticed numbers on his prison issued boots.
- **Shawn Boisvert**, 21, and **William Richards**, 22, were doing 4 years for burglary when they ran away, 6 months before parole.
- **Keith Garcia**, 27, sentenced for weapons, drugs and assault crimes, failed to show for roll call. He was busted 2 days later, standing on a street corner in Newark.

I always take it too far. Rocksylvania had really done a number on the New Balance trail runners I bought 600 miles ago back in Virginia, to the point a sole came loose and was flapping. I had to take giant steps like I was wearing clown shoes so they wouldn't drag the ground. But I fixed them up with a plastic cable tie. Things were looking up because this section of AT was maintained by the NY/NJ Trail Conference, and the path's condition was pleasant to walk.

> *HIKER TIP: Plastic cable ties can come in handy for all kinds of repair projects. I kept a couple in the bottom of my backpack. Also, wrap a few rounds of Duct tape around trekking poles instead of carrying a bulky roll.*

> *FUN FACT: The NY/NJTC began maintaining trails in 1920. They are now responsible for 2,000 miles, from Delaware Water Gap to beyond the Catskill Mountains, including all of the AT in New York and New Jersey.*

High Point State Park was very hiker friendly and hikers walk right by several recreational opportunities. Bathrooms here even had hot water! Most do not. You can send maildrops to the visitor center and they offer a free soda just for saying hi. Inside was a large tombstone-looking tablet with hand chiseled numbers and a mile marker from an early stagecoach road. Also on display, an impressive collection of Indian artifacts found on the property.

Directly on the trail was an impressive wooden observation deck, 2 stories high, with views of nearby Veterans Monument. Made of timber beams and flights of stairs, the platform reminded me of the Swiss Family Robinson treehouse and would make a fun stealth camping spot. The Bonkman had obviously been here, judging by his scribble strategically placed in line-of-sight of photo tourists like me. Some people write on stuff and others take it too far, to the point of vandalism. This individual tagged every sign, shelter, fence, rock and privy he passed, among other things. I was not a fan. ATC ridgerunners had been actively looking for him since Virginia and I was questioned at least twice. Getting wind of this, he slightly modified his tag but didn't stop defacing the trail. In later states, he became bolder and just used his actual trail name.

A sign welcomed thru-hikers to visit Lake Marcia (open Memorial Day to Labor Day). Snacks & showers? Count me in! However, the side trail seemed to go away from the beach, so I bush wacked my way down - not the brightest idea in the world. I had been craving cotton candy flavor ice cream since halfway but the busy concession stand was sold-out. I still got washed up and twisted my clothes clean while taking a free hot shower. My visit was on a weekend and there were TONS of people. Lots of beautiful, bikini clad women too! But none seemed interested in a bearded, ruggedly handsome hiker?

High Point Monument was built to honor veterans of war. This was a little ways (0.3 miles) off trail and when I got there, was surprised to find the marble tower's door boarded up with a sheet of plywood like a ghetto crack house. Resembling the Washington Monument in D.C., 220 feet tall and constructed in 1930, this also marks the highest point in New Jersey, 1,803'. I tallied 19 miles that day, even with the side trips.

Waking up the next morning, I found myself smiling for no apparent reason. Things just seemed to be clicking along. Landscape in the valley on this 13-mile stretch had freshly cut fields and old limestone walls crisscrossing the wooded areas. The weather was perfect and I would run into an old friend.

The address of the "Secret Shelter" is not listed in either guidebook so I won't reveal it here, but it's hard to miss. These 2 heated cabins are on private property along with acres of green grass for tents. There's also an outdoor shower (with no walls). I met Jim Murray (AT Class of 1989), and he's a super nice fella who provides all this out of the kindness of his heart. At least 10 other hikers were hanging out, all excited after just seeing a huge, 400-pound black bear a mile away while on a food run. One of them was Sipsey!

I was surprised and happy to see my buddy again and he told me all about finding a doctor who fixed his foot. The two became friends and the doc even let Sipsey stay at his house for a week while driving him around so he could slackpack as he recovered. I had planned to keep hiking and said goodbye to my friend, but would see him again.

Night hiking. I don't do much real night hiking, at least not on purpose. I do enjoy hiking at dusk, the best time to spot wildlife and often set up camp with only my headlamp for illumination. To beat the heat, some hikers do it on a regular basis and at least once a week I'll hear someone trotting by in the middle of the night.

Just for the fun of it, I set a goal of hiking another 8 miles after the sun went down and wearing the headlamp, I looked like a coal miner. White blazes reflect brightly at night and I could see the trail and immediate trees on either side very clearly, but that's about it. Hundreds of fireflies flashed in the dark, and I heard critters moving in the brush but couldn't make out what, or where they were. Hiking in pitch black was a little unsettling with a recent bear sighting, but I was more worried about barking dogs I heard at houses near the trail.

Patches of woods were intersected by numerous road crossings and marked with red and yellow arrows spray painted on the asphalt. One section, poorly blazed, led up and down narrow streets busy with traffic. I also came upon a parked car with drinking teenagers sitting all over it, even on the roof. I waved hello but didn't stop to socialize.

Hopefully in the future the ATC can negotiate with landowners to get the trail here off the streets and back into the forest. Four miles in, the headlamp's strap broke while I was trying to tighten it. It still worked as a flashlight until I found a spot to set-up camp on the edge of a farmer's field as cows shuffled a few feet away. My headlamp only cost $5 at a Big Lots store and used 2 quarter-sized watch batteries. I would suggest one of the many, higher quality headlamps on the market for serious night hiking.

I awoke to a foggy morning and got moving. An abandoned house along the way looked like it had been empty a long time. Fixed up, this would make an awesome hostel, an endeavor some thru-hikers think about taking on after the trail. In the front yard were 2 pickup trucks from the 1940's rotting away in knee high grass. One of them was a

Chevy that may have been a hotrod judging by racing stickers on its

rusty hood. The house where the trucks sat Nearby, on Oil Road, someone left an un-used maildrop as trail magic, with funny car-toon artwork of a hiker on the box. I claimed a bag of granola cereal and left the rest for others.

Our next section traveled 2 miles through Wallkill National Wildlife Refuge, established 1990. Tiny toads smaller than a quarter, grey with black spots, were hopping around everywhere so you had to really watch your step! Native Americans called this valley, "The land where plums abound." I didn't see any plums, but these 5,100-acres of vast wetlands provided an important habitat for 200 species of birds. I saw ducks, Canadian geese and short herons. Federally threatened bog turtles are also protected here after decades of illegal poaching to sup-ply the pet trade. Several duck blinds were set up for wildlife photog-raphers and an older gentleman I met carried a huge pair of binocu-lars, 2 feet long, hoping to spot a rare Cooper's hawk.

Another AT landmark, Pochuck Boardwalk (more commonly known as the "Jersey Boardwalk") was a mile and a half long and winds its way over a marsh floodplain with tall green grasses, wildflowers and cattails dancing with the wind. Depending on the season you could be walking over dry land or across a vast, shallow lake. A 110-foot long suspension bridge in the middle was fun to walk across. Lizards were getting suntans as kids played in the quagmire, making bucket sandcastles out of... mud. Opened in 1995, before this boardwalk was built hikers had another 2 miles of traffic dodging.

Coming out of the woods at NJ-94, I found a small trailhead parking lot with a couple of cars. I usually scope these out before walking to town in case a hitch presents itself. Just then a tall, thin man in a green uniform emerged from the woods wearing a custom frame backpack designed to carry tree clippers and power tools. One of the craziest packs I've ever seen, it held a gas-powered weed-eater and chainsaw! This man's trail name was Alf, after everyone's favorite alien from a

1980's TV show of the same name. This Alf was a three time AT thru-hiker and now a trail maintainer. A real asset of the AT, he's also the helpful person who left jugs of water at dry, Mashipacong Shelter. I gratefully accepted a ride when he offered - a dangerous, 2½ mile road walk otherwise.

After being dropped off at the post office, I picked up my PC then immediately got another ride to the Appalachian Motel. I hadn't relaxed in a motel room by myself for over a month, so I splurged. Located near the trail, this was a nice, basic place with comfortable rooms. Hotels up north were more expensive than the south and this one set me back almost $80! But the Internet worked great and I got right to work processing videos and watching TV. I even treated myself to delivery from Anthony's Pizza. New Jersey is famous for its pizza pies and gooey with cheese, didn't disappoint! "Breadsticks" were a single 12-inch sub bun cut down the middle, toasted and smothered with melted butter. Not what I expected, but delicious!

I used Whiteblaze.com to lookup upcoming food stops and wrote directions down on the back of a colorful pizza coupon that came with my pie. I also made plans for my remaining guidebook pages to be waiting at the next post office. It sounds like I almost had my act together, but now I was also without a light. I usually wore the headlamp around my neck, even in the daytime, but after the strap broke I kept it in a pocket and somehow lost it.

Vernon looked like a nice little town, but I didn't have time to explore much. A grocery store, Burger King and post office were all close together. You can also find a vet, urgent care center and library here. Most hikers stay at the church hostel in Vernon, Saint Thomas Episcopal Church, where you can sleep on the floor, one night only, for a $10 donation paid with credit card. Hikers are asked to keep their stuff tidy as the rec room is also used for AA meetings Tuesdays and Saturdays. Opened in 1998, the hostel has provided shelter and rest to over 500 "pilgrims" each season. "Traveling mercies to you." *Update: While doing research for this book, I was shocked to learn St. Thomas has closed forever.*

While dropping off my PC at the post office, a man saw me wearing my backpack in line and offered me a ride without me even trying to yogi! But before walking back into the woods I visited Heaven Hill Farmers Market, just up the road from the trailhead. Folks were hiker friendly and had fresh fruit and tons of ice cream flavors. Yup, I finally got the cotton candy ice cream I had been yearning for and it went great with bananas and plums. After lunch, I walked around a small petting zoo. Hippity Hop Village had bunny-sized farmhouses and cabins. I put a quarter into a machine dispensing food pellets, and all the rabbits came running out after hearing the sound - about 10 in all. It was funny how the population count had to be changed on a sign several times - you know how bunnies do.

A brown llama in the exhibit next door showed off by rolling around in the dirt, taking a dust bath while his mate and I just watched and laughed. Long greenhouses held colorful flowers, the gem mine slew had a western goldmine theme and yellowjackets swarmed around a glass beehive. There was a wood planked outhouse, but it was occupied - by a skeleton! "Hey, don't die in there!" This was obviously part of a seasonal Halloween display, as Heaven Hill is well known for hayrides and pumpkin picking.

Continuing back up into the mountains, "Stairway to Heaven" had dozens of stone steps and must have taken months to build. I found the tree blow-over that ALF had worked so hard to clear from the trail the day before. It would have been impossible to climb over otherwise. There were also some defaced white blazes. An artist saw natural features in the bark and added eyes and mouths to several markers without rendering the blazes undistinguishable. I don't condone this, but thought they were fun (one greets you on the cover of this book).

Later in the afternoon, I found King Author's sword! The random things we find in the woods, huh? Someone with a sense of humor had stuck a plastic toy sword into a cracked rock. I was not its true owner; therefore, was unable to remove it, but like to think whoever claimed Excalibur earned a new trial name.

Chapter 16. Rembrandt & the Pizza King

Left: Rembrandt on Bear Mountain Bridge. Right: The Pizza King.

Territories were going by faster now, and on July 14th, walking along the top of the massively huge boulders of Prospect Rock, I couldn't believe I was hiking in New York. The 72 miles in New Jersey were awesome, but I looked forward to what our 9th state and its 88 miles had to offer. There sure are a lot of rocks in the world. Parts of the trail here were so rocky, it almost reminded me of Pennsylvania, then became unexpectedly technical with deep crevasses carved by glaciers. It felt like being in a 'Tomb Raider' video game!

Best thing about the Empire state? Deli blazing! First day in, I followed an advertisement to Hotdogs Plus. This mobile concession was made from an old camping trailer, but chips, root beer and New York hotdogs were a bargain at only $5. Just up the street, atop Mount Peter, was another treat, Bellvale Farms Creamery. World famous since 1819, through 7 generations, they offer 50 flavors of homemade ice cream. Local = good. I enjoyed a small cup of green sherbet, delicious but expensive. A nice couple wearing shirts with AT logos could tell I was a thru-hiker (probably from the smell) and asked about my trip. I mentioned not having a guidebook and this gentleman went to his car, dug around for a bit, then returned with 3 maps of the area.

Also here enjoying ice cream: The entire Suffern, NY, little league baseball team decked out in blue and white jerseys with matching caps, celebrating a big win.

A dry section because of the drought, what was once a cascading waterfall was now reduced to a trickle. Stagnant pondwater with a strange smell and brown tint was sometimes our only source of drinking water for many miles. Treating it with Aquamira, I felt no ill effects. Thankfully, water jugs had also been stashed at several road crossings, complements of the Tuxedo Trail Angels.

> HIKER TIP: Everyone loves TM, but there are responsibilities as well. If not there in person, leave a trash bag and come back to retrieve empty containers, garbage and your notebook full of "Thank You" notes.

A notice on a telephone pole brought bad news. The post office in Arden, New York, had permanently closed and all hiker mail was redirected to another location. I wasn't about to walk 4 extra miles so I skipped Arden altogether and hiked on, still without directions. Crossing over a bridge, I found a cool bug with markings on its back that looked like huge eyes. I learned this was an "eyed elater click beetle," its colorations meant to deter predators.

On the shore of Lake Greenwood, trail angels Wizzy Wig & Matty hooked me up with pop and homemade cookies. They saw my pathetic shoes and slipped me a $20 bill! I was humbled by their generosity but it would come in handy up the road. Wizzy Wig, from New Jersey, started a thru-hike from Georgia in the spring but injured his knee and had to come home early. He hoped to see hiker friends he made as they reached his neck of the woods.

Also in the area was Late 4 Dinner. Quick with a smile, we first met back in Gatlinburg, Tennessee. Call him anything you want, just don't call him "Late 4 Dinner!" He was hiking with 3D, a Boy Scout leader who hoped to thru-hike one day. He watched lots of AT blogs and when Late 4 Dinner reached New York, 3D hosted him at his house for a few nights. 3D also followed along with my YouTube videos and recognized me immediately. I was surprised how he could recall my AT experiences in detail.

Easy peasy lemon squeezy. Late 4 Dinner and I climbed through the very narrow "Lemon Squeezer" as 3D filmed. A tight fit, my cook cup scraped against the rock walls sounding like a cowbell. Good thing I had lost a lot of weight! Coming upon a trail intersection with signs pointing in all directions, if you take a wrong turn here, 52 miles later you'll end up in Manhattan! Milestones start counting down after halfway and we now had 800 to go. Piles of loose stones littered the ground and 3D explained how workers drilled iron veins using hand drills and hammers. Slackpacking and pushing for 20 miles, these guys were going faster than I could, so we signed the logbook at Fingerboard Shelter together and said goodbye.

Next, massive 4-story tall boulders towered around me with the cave-like William Brien Shelter nestled between. Made of local stone, the inside was dark and damp. Setting up camp outside, I spotted 3 deer grazing nearby and felt a peacefulness come over me, in sharp contrast to the violence of a nearby coyote kill with tuffs of fur and bones strewn about. A thunderstorm shot several bolts of lightning uncomfortably close. Peaceful feelings turning uneasy, all I could do was lay there, pitch black flashing bright as daylight with each strike.

Palisades Parkway. Hikers cross this famous 4-lane highway, awkwardly carrying backpacks while dodging traffic racing 60 mph to-and-from the Big Apple, 34 miles away. Like playing 'Frogger' in real life, it was scary and exciting at the same time. Between highways was a narrow, wooded buffer with an unexpected trail register. The adrenaline rush I felt crossing the road dissolved immediately as I scanned old pages for a name, and found it... **Parkside.**

Mother had sent an email that, sadly, said this fellow thru-hiker had recently passed away. He had left this entry... "Name: Parkside. Group name: Monty Parkside's Merry Circus. City: Queens, Baby!" Only 20 years old, he was one of the very first thru-hikers to start that season, #11 to sign in at Amicalola. He set out February 17th and 4 months later, June 15th, he died only 150 miles shy of his goal. After a 20-mile day in Maine, Parkside dove into Pierce Pond to cool off. But the water was deceptively chilly and he developed leg cramps. Hearing his screams, buddies tried to find him until rescue workers arrived. His body was recovered that evening and his parents notified the next day. How heartbreaking. Friends later carried his ashes to the summit of Mt. Katahdin, completing his hike. An athlete, he was always up for a baseball game and worked as a caddy to save for his hike. We never met, but both of us were on this same journey. We walked past the same trees, climbed the same rocks, maybe talked to the same trail angels and surely stared from the same overlooks. He has been in my thoughts every day since I learned of the tragedy.

Stopping at a vantage point later that afternoon, I could see the Hudson River and Perkins Tower far away atop Bear Mountain, named so because in profile it resembles a bear lying down. I also found a gold colored motorcycle necklace hanging from a tree branch, probably a kid's toy from a supermarket vending machine.

Carelessly, I dropped my camera while putting it away and it never worked again. Already surviving several months of rain, dust, humidity and similar tumbles, I couldn't complain when there was no choice but to check out Perkins Tower, walk by the famous Trailside Zoo and cross Bear Mountain Bridge over the Hudson River - all without taking a single picture or video for documentation. Without a guidebook, I didn't even have an idea which way to try and hitch to a store. Hitchhiking is illegal in New York, anyway.

Then, on the north side of the bridge I found a man wearing a wide-brim hat, painting with small tubes of colors lined up along the railing. Another interesting photo opportunity missed, I thought, but we got to talking. Clay, an art teacher at a local high school knew about the AT, having met several hikers over the years. Simply asking how far the nearest store was, without a moment's hesitation, he packed up all his stuff and drove me to Wally World, 10 miles away, where I bought a ninja replacement for my camera. $100+ for a new camera wasn't in the budget, but there was no other choice.

Clay paints a lot, so his car's trunk was overflowing with canvas and supplies. His easel had a trick design that folded up and could be carried over his shoulder. There was still some daylight, so he set-up his equipment and finished working. By chance, a tall ship sailing toward us was incorporated into the painting, his artwork changed by helping me out. Very talented, he made the water appear moving and green trees swayed with a breeze that gently pushed the sailboat. Mom, an artist herself, told me this was a specific landscape style called "Hudson River School." This movement romanticized pastoral views of the Hudson River Valley, Catskill, Adirondack and White Mountains. Frederic Edwin Church is the most well-known painter of the style. Clay is the real deal and paints in a variety of styles. He worked previously as assistant to Willem de Kooning, an abstract artist from the Netherlands. In 2015, David Geffen sold a painting by de Kooning, called 'Interchange,' for $300 million, as of this writing, the highest price EVER paid for a painting.

Months later, after returning home from the trail and other adventures, I found a special parcel waiting for me from New York. Clay had sent the very painting I watched him create that day! Wow! Every time I look at it, memories of the AT come rushing back. Respectfully, since our meeting, I have referred to my friend as "Rembrandt."

With the sun going down, there was still time to hike 3 miles back to the tower. I really wanted to document this and Trailside Zoo for everyone following along. I also met Swiss Toni for the 1st time. This smiling gent was a thru-hiker from the UK who got his trail name from an English TV character who had the same puffy white hair.

Trying to hurry, I was out of breath after hundreds of steps, but the tower had closed. On the bright side, cars had emptied the parking lot and I had this amazing mountaintop all to myself! Taking advantage of candy and caffeine vending machines, and the resulting sugar rush, I explored until well after dark. Without a headlamp, my human eyes adjusted to the night like a racoon. Mazes of car-sized boulders were fun to climb and I jumped from one to another like a small child at a playground. Even a family of whitetail deer came out and we played chase and hide-n-seek between the rocks and trees.

Stealth camping on a cliff out of sight, I watched fireworks exploding above New York's skyline (possibly Wrigley Field?). It was mind-boggling to imagine throngs of people mucking about the noisy city while I relaxed all by myself within eyesight, in near total silence except for the wind. Early the next day, a sunrise with rolling waves of orange, red and white clouds blended into the blue morning sky, almost close enough to touch. It's a hiker's instinct to get moving, so it was excruciating waiting for someone to come unlock the tower's door.

Perkins Tower, a unique structure built of granite stones by the CCC in 1934, is 5 stories high with pairs of perpendicular, rectangular windows on all 4 sides of each floor. This purpose-built observation tower was named after George Walbridge Perkins Sr., founder and first president of Palisades Interstate Park Commission.

B&W images, printed on wall tiles, depicted antique buses, huge steamboats and massive troops of Boy Scouts. The top floor had a commanding view and at 1,305', on a clear day you can see into 4 states: NY, NJ, PA and CT - or with help of those silver colored, coin-operated machines called "tower viewers."

FUN FACT: Tower Optical, founded in 1932, only manufactures about 35 tower viewers each year, but thousands more are maintained by the company. Viewers can hold up to $500 in quarters.

I finally resumed heading north, and more snack machines were stationed at Hessian Lake, including a bright yellow, full-size M&M's dispenser also offering Skittles and the like. Another machine vended 20 various kinds of popsicles. This was my kind of place! Visiting a snack bar, I had been craving a mouthwatering pepper steak sub, but prices were sky high so I only bought a small order of french-fries. Sneaking up in slow-motion, a tame grey squirrel leapt onto the picnic table across from me, laid down like a dog and started eyeballing my fries! Tossing him one, a couple of southbound section hikers and I laughed as he fetched it. College girls from New York, these 2 were looking to meet up with thru-hiker friends in the area. One chick with punk rock hair gave me a green apple. In some primitive countries, that means we're engaged! Too bad she wasn't hiking north.

Bear Mountain Carousel had wooden chariots and hand carved critters to ride on including black bear, deer, fox and so on. Even a skunk! Hares appeared to be hopping and bobcats pouncing. Sadly, no joyful merry-go-round music was playing because the pavilion is closed Mondays and Tuesdays. Fun should never close! Rides $1.

The pool was open, but empty of swimmers this early in the morning. Come afternoon, the blue sparkling water would be full of screaming kids and smelly hikers. I ran into Late 4 Dinner who should have been way ahead of me by now. Somehow, he missed a fork in the road (trail) and ended up on top of the wrong mountain. After a few calls to his buddy 3D, he figured out where he was and bushwhacked his way down a dry streambed to a road. Hot, thirsty and frustrated, he accidently bypassed 9 miles of the AT. As a purist, he was now making it up going SOBO. 3D would then drive him back where he started. Late 4 Dinner joked he should change his trail name to "Extra Credit" for all the additional hiking he was putting in! Respect to him for doing those missed miles, and to 3D for coming to his rescue.

> FUN FACT: In 1982, the popular children's TV show 'Sesame Street' taped a week's worth of episodes at Bear Mountain, in which Big Bird went to "Camp Echo Rock" and got into several adventures.

Trailside Museums & Zoo. This paved path was the very first part of the original AT to be built. Opened October 7, 1923, every thru-hiker, over the years, has walked this hallowed ground - most of the rest of the trail has been relocated at some time or another. This spot also marks the lowest point on the entire AT, only 124 feet above sea level. The path meanders through various wildlife exhibits...

• **Black bear:** Two very large examples live here, about 400 lbs. each. One paced back-and-forth, only deviating from his OCD pattern to scare off dozens of buzzards waiting for leftovers. The second bear, standing up with his arms sticking through the bars, appeared to be trying to undo an oversized padlock and escape.

• **Red fox:** Strikingly beautiful, inquisitive and agile. Our eyes locked and he could smell the woods on me.

• **Eastern coyote:** Leery, she hid from view and let out a single howling sound at low volume. You could tell she was still wild. I find coyotes to be the most secretive animals we share the wilderness with.

• **Busy beaver:** Zookeepers had just given this fury fellow a fresh branch of green leaves. He looked happy as could be.

• **Porcupines:** Hanging out in an artificial tree, they slept with all four legs dangling down. Boy, do they stink.

• **Owls:** Nocturnal, they had hollow trees into which to retreat.

• **American bald eagle:** Posing like his ancestor on the dollar bill, many hikers' blogs have pictures showing him always sitting on the same branch, in the middle of his cage, looking toward the sky.

My favorite was a turtle pond outside the Herpetology House of Reptiles and Amphibians, but seemed way too tiny for the dozens of water turtles sharing a space smaller than your kitchen table. Inside the building, rows of aquariums contained spotted salamanders, lizards of different colors, timber rattlesnakes and spring peepers suction-cupped to the glass. A larger tank held a 15-pound alligator snapping turtle, small considering adults are about the size of a car tire. In the next container, a vigorous tortoise with bright markings, had been hit by a car. Over time, a turtle's damaged shell can regenerate, but this guy's dome was cracked and repaired with epoxy. His girlfriend was hiding under a hollow log, embarrassed because her pretty shell was covered in spray paint. Probably a teenager's prank, but now she can't grow or absorb sunlight, both vital for coldblooded reptiles.

All inhabitants of this zoo are native to this area, and were either injured, rescued, or orphaned and can no longer survive in the wild. The zoo also brings awareness to the importance of conserving natural habitats. Still, there are mixed emotions within the hiker community. Personally, I found it educational to observe the wildlife's size and mannerisms safely and felt closer to them than ever before. On the contrary, some hikers blue blaze around the zoo altogether because they can't stand to see wild animals locked up. I understand this point of view, also, and worried about the small size of their enclosures. Especially the concrete floors these forest dwelling creatures were forced to walk on. I know how much walking on cement hurts my feet, and these wild animals had no choice.

> HIKER TIP: Trailside Zoo is the only section of the AT that is ever "closed," but a blue blazed trail around a perimeter fence counts as the official AT, 4:30 p.m.-10:00 a.m. Pets are not allowed inside zoo.

Many historic sites and museums are also within the zoo...

• **Geology Museum:** Dioramas of a mining rig and very impressive, the Gordon Mastodon exhibit with a huge pair of ivory tusks found nearby in 1902. It's astonishing to think that these giant, hairy, prehistoric beasts roamed current day New York!

• **Historical Museum:** Native American artifacts were on display representing many cultures. Even Clovis hunters, the earliest humans on our continent, lived right here 12,000+ years ago.

• **Fort Clinton:** This star-shaped Revolutionary War era fort (now in ruins) was built to defend a giant metal chain, each link about the size of a suitcase, that stretched across the Hudson River to prevent enemy ships from advancing. Fort Montgomery protected the North side, but British soldiers overran both redoubts, with garrisons of 300 men each, within the same hour.

Just outside the zoo's back gate is a beautiful bridge tollhouse. East-bound cars pay $1.50 to cross US-6/US-202, even 2 girls in a bright red Ferrari F430 Spider. There's no toll to walk across, but the very first thru-hiker, Earl Shaffer, had to pay a nickel! True déjà vu, I crossed this very claustrophobic pedestrian walkway 3 times in 24 hours. Talk about extra credit!

Another potential danger: Dive-bombing peregrine falcons, the fastest birds on the planet (recorded up to 242 mph). The threat of being attacked by screeching raptors with razor-sharp talons made things more exciting, but I didn't see any. Signs on 24-hour suicide prevention lifeline telephones had a pleading message: "Life is worth living." Tragically, there have been several jumpers here. How many I'm not sure, as statistics about suicide bridges are not released to the public.

NOT SO FUN FACT: Benton MacKaye's own wife, 45-year old Jessie "Belle" Stubbs MacKay, plagued by mental illness, plummeted to her death off a New York bridge into the East River.

Making new ground, the seemingly wild trail dropped right off onto an unseen street, creating a dangerous optical illusion where cars looked like they're driving right through the woods. I got back into the mountains for only a few miles when the trail passed a 24-hour gas station called Appalachian Market where a bunch of hikers had converged for lunch. I bought some hotdogs and Rice Crispy Treats.

Also of note in this area, Graymoor Spiritual Life Center. Several hikers I knew, including Late 4 Dinner, had only nice things to say about the Franciscan Order of Monks. Their Monastery rehabilitates homeless men addicted to drugs. Hikers have been welcome to camp in the monastery's ballfield picnic shelter for free since 1972 and robed monks often invite hikers to share communal dinner with them.

While eating handfuls of juicy blackberries, I explored a beautiful building covered with green vines. Masonry work was of the highest quality, as were built-in fireplaces and archways - just no roof or windows. Next, it was fun walking along old mining territory on long forgotten, elevated railroad beds with narrow trestles. The air was super humid, so I drank lots of water and took my time. Some days miles come easy, others you just get what you can.

A blue-blazed trail led around beautiful Canopus Lake in Fahnestock State Park, where winter signs referred to snowshoe trails and thin ice. At the beach, Acorn Concession Stand had a cook-to-order grill and camp store where you could buy toy sailboats and inflatable waterwings. Best of all, free showers, although "community style" - I showered with my clothes on. Very refreshing and I washed my clothes at the same time! I had lunch with a couple I met back in the Virginia Highlands. I had to laugh when the husband fetched both their backpacks, wearing one on his back and the other across his chest, while carrying a set of hiking poles in each hand and joking he was "going ultralight!"

Slim Pilgrim, from Maine, was also at the beach and slim indeed. I found it most exciting that he had walked within several feet of a mountain lion laying on a rock and had an amazing picture to prove it. Eastern puma as they're called, were deemed extinct by the US Fish and Wildlife Service in 2011, but have still been caught on trail cams or sighted in NC, TN, VA, CT, NH and ME. There have been other scary reports of lions, even black panthers, stalking hikers for miles.

Comparable in size to an adult human, mountain lions can grow 9 feet long, nose to tail, and weigh up to 220 lbs. They'll prey on anything from insects and snakes to deer - even coyotes and bull moose. They hide larger kills with brush to feed on for several days. Cougars can't roar, but are known for their bloodcurdling night screams. Keep your distance, because they can run up to 50 mph and leap 18 feet in a single bound! Not a pet.

Although unlikely, should you see any ferocious felines use the same precautions as if meeting a black bear: DO NOT RUN, don't climb and make yourself appear as large as possible without showing aggression. Oh yeah - don't try to swim for it. Eastern Cougars are unique as the only feline not to fear water.

That afternoon, I heard a disturbing news report on my radio. A trail maintainer in upcoming Salisbury, Connecticut, had somehow struck his head on his own pickaxe. Ouch! He had to be carried out, then airlifted to a hospital. The 3-hour rescue involved ATVs, chainsaws and 22 rescue personnel. I hope he made a full recovery.

Miles away, Ralph's Peak Hikers' Cabin (RPH) was a fully enclosed, yellow cinderblock building, and I was amazed how clean it was. Someone even left a basket of red tomatoes, and I ate mine like an apple. All the double-decker bunks were taken and a few tents overflowed onto the lawn, although tenting is discouraged. Two thru-hikers here were old school skateboarders like me, so we had other stuff to talk about. One, from New York, was trail named Cheese Water because he always added too much water to his Mac & Cheese.

> HIKER TIP: Near the road, you can order pizza takeout from Ralph's Peak Hikers' Cabin. Gian Bruno's Restaurant Pizzeria is open Tuesday-Sunday. Phone: (845) 227-9276.

Serious weather was predicted, so I camped near the shelter in case things got bad. Wind blew and lightning flashed, but heavy rains somehow missed me. Still, my trees were a little too close together, and a carabiner rubbed a hole in my tarp. At least the damage was on a far end and didn't leak very much.

Directions inviting hikers to a free breakfast were stuffed into a plastic bag pinned to a wooden walk bridge. The skater hikers joined me and we were all treated to OJ and waffles! I Yankeed mine up with lots of maple syrup. Preschool girls danced in circles and sang along with cartoons on TV, then gave each of us a little note with a quarter so we could do laundry next time we found a washing machine. I was humbled that this mother of two young children would allow, even advertise, for complete strangers to come into her home. Thank you to our hosts: Amy, Claire and Ella.

Back on the trail, switchbacks zig-zagged up a hill with an overabundance of white blazes painted on every other tree. Probably washed out by rains the night before, I spotted another arrowhead! Almost two inches long, this projectile was fashioned from blueish flint and notched at the base. Kismet, today was my 40th birthday and I felt it was meant for me - a gift from the Indians and the trail. It's my hope that everyone who sees this book will admire its handcrafted quality.

Two simple words written directly on a white blaze, "Deli 0.4," and an arrow pointing down NY-52 was all it took for me to take a side trip to Danny's Pizzeria. From the moment I walked in, I knew this pie was going to be good because the cook was watching chef Gordon Ramsay's 'Hell's Kitchen' on TV! Also on the menu was a sandwich called the "Appalachian Trail Blazer." Mountain Top Market in an adjoining storefront was also hiker friendly.

The woods came to an end, and hikers navigated another tricky road walk while looking for white blazes on unfamiliar objects like guardrails and stop signs. A note with directions asked, "Please do not bother the neighbors." I took a picture of the map to review, if needed. A trick I learned from Lt. Dan.

Next stop, Morgan Stewart Memorial Shelter. IBM donated $2,500 toward materials, and volunteers carried it into the forest one board at a time and assembled it here using hand tools. The structure itself was well built, but not a place I would like to spend the night. A warning advised we boil water because the well was a 100 years old and had an alarming bacteria count. I passed. Also, a tattered blue tarp lay on the ground and a moldy tent, flattened by rain, lay in the woods, abandoned. Worse, a big black trash bag hung from the rafters. Do people not realize this attracts mice, flies, wild animals and at the very least, is unsightly and the stench horrible? Who wants to sleep with bear bait hanging over their head? I carried that bag a mile to the next road crossing while holding it as far away from my person as possible.

A short road walk in Pawling, New York, passed Dover Oak. This monstrous, 300-year old tree had numerus branches spiraling toward the sky like many arms, each as big as a tree itself. You can't miss it. Twenty feet in girth, this is the largest tree on the entire AT!

Catching up with Tree Hugger and D-Tour, we had fun hiking around Nuclear Lake. Because of its remoteness, a well-guarded experimental nuclear research lab was built here in 1958. Then in 1972, a chemical explosion blew-out the windows, spewing bomb-grade plutonium across the formally pristine lake and woods. A cover-up followed, but a local nurse leaked info that at least one person died, his watch melted to the bone. After a 2-year, $3,000,000 clean-up, the

REMBRANDT & THE PIZZA KING

area was declared safe and sold to the National Park Service, even though floating booms remain in the lake like those used to contain oil spills. It's also rumored a contaminated ambulance was buried somewhere on these grounds, and is still here. I forgot my ultralight Geiger counter but don't think I suffered radiation poisoning, although ginormous mosquitos here were obviously mutated.

> HIKER TIP: *Several Bigfoot sightings have been reported in the dense woods surrounding Nuclear Lake. Try taking a stick and banging on a tree or log three times - you might hear a sasquatch answer back!*

Hikers are not supposed to camp in this section, but I couldn't resist the view. Birds and frogs sang me happy birthday as a pack of coyotes howled in a frenzy. It was a little lonely today, but I was happy to spend it on the AT. Besides, I did receive a few unexpected gifts: a section hiker gave me a Mountain House breakfast, I enjoyed free waffles and juice, I found a sweet arrowhead and I slept by a beautiful lake. What could be better?

Waking up to rain, I found my water cup was full for cooking and I enjoyed the gift of reconstituted eggs and bacon very much. Worried about sleeping late, I passed several tents before reaching the Great Swamp Boardwalk where I saw a large crane fly overhead. At the end of the walkway is the AT's very own railroad station. A blue and yellow wooden platform built in 1991, it's serviced by Metro-North's Harlem Line and will take you to Grand Central Station, two hours away for $15 cash. Trains stop Saturdays, Sundays and holidays.

Then, I found... The Pizza King. Of course, I couldn't pass up my last chance to enjoy real New York pizza! This bright yellow, custom-made trailer had loud logos and was decked out with a real wood-fired oven! Tony knows where the business is at, but tried to talk me out of a large pie, saying in his thick Italian accent, "It's just too much!" Still, he baked me an awesome 19-inch pizza pie! And for $17, even threw in a free pop and candy bars for including his business in my video series.

The next part of trail was obstructed by a GIANT cow on the other side of a fence stile. Black with white spots, she weighed at least 700 lbs. Doing trail maintenance, she continued munching on tall grass, wagging her tail and staring at me defiantly. Only after pleading, "I've got 7 miles to go. Do you mind moving?" did she let me pass.

At dusk, I caught Mac & Cheese (no relation to Cheese Water) refilling her "Magic Coolers." An attractive, older woman with a quirky personality, she started doing this in 2005 when a hiker in distress, Still Walking, knocked on her door for help. One cooler had cold sodas and water, the second was filled with first aid, stove alcohol and homemade cookies! She had even set up a whole wrought iron patio set for hikers to sit on. This sweet trail angel left a funny post in her own logbook: "Caught in the act! Oh, no!"

Finally, I reached my goal for the day, the New York/Connecticut border! This milestone was a little anticlimactic, as it was simply a logbook box nailed to a tree, but I still celebrated with 2 leftover slices of pizza.

"Bear Mountain Magic," by Clay, aka, Rembrandt.

Chapter 17. Hanging Over Rivers

My hammock hanging eight feet above the beautiful Housatonic River.

Officially in New England, nights were getting noticeably cooler and my Yankee accent was coming out more and more the further north I ventured. The trail was mostly empty because everyone else was in a big hurry getting to Kent. Instead, I took a lazy day at Ten Mile River, making breakfast and just laying around. This shelter is one of the best kept on the AT and located on a former farmstead surrounded by rusting equipment and beautiful pastures of purple, sweet smelling flowers. Well-water is retrieved using another squeaky handpump and felt like being on 'Little House on the Prairie.'

Ned Anderson Memorial Bridge was a concrete, iron-railed apparatus named after Nestell Kipp "Ned" Anderson, a local farmer who took on the challenge of clearing the original section of the AT in Connecticut, often recruiting Boy Scout Troop #48, first in the state, which he also organized. The Ten Mile and Housatonic rivers meet here and their convergence was impressive, but don't eat the fish. These sacred waters are contaminated with PCBS from General Electric's factory upriver.

Hearing rock music playing from boom boxes, just for the heck of it, I went off to explore a blue blazed side trail hoping to stumble upon a soda machine. There were little beach inlets where locals spend after-noons swimming and having BBQs. I was just thinking to myself how beautiful Connecticut was when I found something that broke my heart: A huge, disgusting pile of trash. Enough to fill a dumpster and right next to a trailhead kiosk! I guess visitors can't read, either English or Spanish, as a pair of signs read, "Carry out what you carry in." "Llevar a cabo, lo que llevas en." Townies addicted to government trash pick-up, see this and think: "This must be where we put all our garbage! Someone else will just come and get it!" But no one does. Lazy bastards, but it wasn't even funny this time. A refuse heap this size must have taken weeks - even months - to accumulate.

Included in this monument to self-entitled laziness were broken camp chairs, busted up Styrofoam coolers, a BIG blue tarp, bags full of hotdog wrappers, tin foil, fast food containers and empty cans. All now a huge mess made worse by rain, rats, dogs and wild animals. The stench made me want to puke. I can't even comprehend how anyone could stroll by, let alone want to hang out here and party. Still without a guidebook at the time, I didn't know this trail led to Bull's Bridge, a one-lane covered bridge built in 1842. I would have liked to see that. Disgusted, I just turned around and walked back into the woods. Even a cold soda didn't interest me anymore.

After a few miles, I calmed down a bit, intrigued by a hand-lettered sign: "Native Indian Village." Imagining a mock-up of teepees and dugout canoes, I walked up the road for an hour only to find an abandoned farm stand. Luckily, I hitched a ride most of the way back. Just then, a huge barred owl landed on a tree branch right above me! At least 2 feet tall, I've never seen an owl this large before, although we've all heard them hooting, "Who cooks for you? Who cooks for you-all?" My mom had a similar owl living in her backyard. It had taken over a large squirrel's nest and even shared it with a hawk. The owl slept in it during the day while the hawk was out hunting, and vise-versa. Owls know all our secrets.

"Indian Rocks," is the only section of the AT that passes through a Native American Indian reservation. Hikers are granted permission from the Schaghticoke Nation to cross near their historical snake den, also known as "Rattlesnake Mountain." Consisting of 300 members from several remnant tribes banded together, this reservation was granted to them in 1736 by the Colony of Connecticut. Once 2,100 acres, now only 400 remain. After finally winning federal recognition in 2004, it was rescinded a year later due to red tape and influence from wealthy land owners.

Mt. Algo Shelter is where I met the first true southbound thru-hikers of the season. One chubby guy, thinking I was also headed south, immediately started criticizing my ultralight backpack, "You'll never make it all the way with that!" But the look on his face changed when I told him I was NOBO and had already hiked 1,400 miles. Another SOBO, wearing round John Lennon glasses, and tapping drunkenly on a small bongo drum, smirked but was only interested in the number of bears I'd seen. Making camp on a hillside between the shelter and a visible road, I heard obnoxious people laughing late into the night, as car's headlights strobed by, some picking-up or dropping-off hikers, pizza and beer. Sleep did not come easy.

> FUN FACT: SOBOs start their thru-hikes at Katahdin, the Northern terminus of the AT, beginning May or June. Backwards, they hike south toward Georgia, finishing between Halloween and Christmas.

A mile away, a large sign welcomed hikers to the one stoplight town of Kent. Hikers walk by several old homes and buildings, now foodie bakery boutiques and book stores. All well taken care of and very "New England." We also pass Kent School, which hosts jazz festivals that can be heard from the preceding shelter. The main drag was very lively on the weekend with an odd assortment of bikers, vintage car enthusiasts, hiker trash and trendy music people. The latter, formally dressed and having coffee or hot tea before that evening's concert, but everyone got along fine. There was no organized car show, but vintage motorcycles and classic cars, including a black Ford woody station wagon and a yellow Porsche, lined both sides of the street. A sidewalk book sale was popular, with people browsing rows of fold-up tables covered in paperbacks. A raffle ticket might have won a little red corvette. That would have been a fun way to get home after the hike!

> FUN FACTS: Seth MacFarlane, creator of 'Family Guy' and 'The Cleveland Show,' was born here. Ted Danson, from 'Cheers,' graduated from Kent School here. Henry Kissinger, former U.S. Secretary of State, lives here.

Next, I checked out Backcountry Outfitters, an ice cream shop/outfitter. Asking for the 'Companion' Guidebook, the nice lady offered to order me a copy... to be picked up next week. I didn't think she quite understood the concept of hiking the AT and I had to explain why I couldn't come back. Instead, I bought the 'AWOL' and after a little getting used to, found it helpful. Trail runners were too expensive.

> *HIKER TIP: Which guidebook should you use? 'AWOL' has elevation maps and straightforward text, while the Thru-hikers 'Companion' has more notes about interesting history. Both had a few mistakes, but either will do the trick. My buddy Sipsey carried full editions of both books.*

Self-conscious walking around town, I found some new kicks on sale for $40 in a backroom of trendy Sundog Shoe & Leather. Etonics (fake Reeboks) with bright white and blue graphics straight out of a Jane Fonda workout video.

Doing laundry, I used the two quarters Ella and Claire had given me. There were stories going around about Kent Green Laundromat, but I felt like I could get along with anyone. Wrong! After reading a lengthy list of rules posted on the front door, I felt unwelcome from the start. The owner, who had a striking resemblance to "Mama Fratelli" from the 80's movie, 'The Goonies,' went into a small room with no windows, closing the door behind her like I was going to loot the place.

After putting my clothes in the washer, I noticed there was no coin machine. So, I simply knocked and asked her to please change a $10 bill. Barely cracking the door, she stood there red faced and furious, "You should have asked when I was up!" Reluctantly, she made change but snapped, "I won't get up again!" Hearing a parrot in the room with her, I tried to diffuse the tension by asking meekly, "Does he speak any words?" She balked, "He doesn't like strangers!" and slammed the door shut! Jeez! Some people you just can't be nice to.

Then I realized Mama Fratelli had given me all $1 gold coins - not quarters. They fit into the washers, but these dryers only took quarters. I felt baited, but didn't dare knock on that door again and walked to the grocery store to get more change.

> *HIKER TIP: Future hikers found this sign on the door: "Due to the inconsiderate hikers that have come before you, hikers are no longer allowed in this laundromat for any reason."*

In a story from The News-Times, the laundry lady called said ban: "The most stress-reducing thing I've done in years." Jim O'Neill, legislative liaison with the state Commission on Human Rights and Opportunities, when asked if this was legal, replied it was not against the law, nor was the ban discrimination. The paper actually quoted him as saying: "Stinky people are not a protected class."

A local man, driving a vintage safari Land Rover, recommended I visit the Machinery & Mining Museum and gave me easy directions. It's only a mile road walk north of Main Street; just be careful on the narrow shoulders. When you see an old Train Engine, you're at the right place. Connecticut Antique Machinery Association (CAMA) members obviously spend a lot of time and money rebuilding these important machines from the past (donations appreciated). Hawaii Railway #5 was the centerpiece of the collection. This 1925 Baldwin steam locomotive has been lovingly restored and powered by a coal engine with brass gauges. It even had its own garage. Partly outdoors/partly enclosed, the museums and buildings have lots to see...

• **Straight out of the old west,** a wooden passenger train car with shutter windows awaited restoration.

• **Tractors of different makes and models:** John Deere, Caterpillar, International and others. Not to mention a dozen steam-powered rollers and tractors. One even had tracks like a tank!

• **The Hubbard Steamcycle.** This motorcycle looked like a dirt bike with a pair of copper cylinders instead of a gas tank.

• **Mining Museum:** Outside, examples of local ore. The vintage train engines and coal cars used to transport it were the size of shopping carts. Inside exhibits helped me better visualize abandoned mining villages hikers see along the trail.

• **A darkroom** was filled with rocks and minerals glowing neon blue, green and yellow under ultraviolet illumination. They absorb light and then release it on a different wavelength.

• **Mine shaft replica.** Inside gave me an idea of the cramped, dimly lit spaces in which miners worked. There was even a TNT blasting rig to play with, like a Roadrunner and Wiley Coyote cartoon!

• **A green locomotive,** about the size of a minivan, was fun for a short jaunt down the tracks running the length of the property.

Jim our host, with white hair and beard looked like piano rocker Michael McDonald. Very knowledgeable, he enjoyed showing visitors around and answering questions. Jim asked about my backpack and next thing you know, I yogied a choice camping spot down by the river. There were plenty of trees behind crumbling Mine Hill Furnace, but I hung my hammock directly above a steep riverbank. Relaxing, I waded around the shallow water and found some emerald blue slag from the furnace, a byproduct of iron smelting from 100 years ago. I even watched a deer fording the river. On the AT, you never know where you'll sleep each night.

> HIKER TIP: During your hike, you'll be offered all kinds of new and unexpected opportunities. Before instinctively saying "No," try saying "Yes!" These different experiences are what makes every thru-hike unique.

"Choo-Choo!" Come dawn, I walked to town along railroad tracks. Not recommended, as a train killed a girl hiker here in 2016. I picked up my PC at the post office, but the library Wi-Fi was hopeless. At least I was able to read a message from Fatherman, who said he was here in Kent! It was ironic we finally met at the laundromat, and it felt like hanging out with an old friend. His red beard was impressive and his personality was exactly like his videos. Camera twins, we both used the same exact model and color camera. FM did a short interview with me as part of his walking talk show and many viewers got a big kick out of it. Hanging out later, FM said he thought it was odd a "loner" would share his hike with the world through videos, as I did. FM appeared to be hiking by himself, a big surprise as he had traveled hundreds of miles up the trail with a crew: DK, The Big "E" and Bubble Foot. I asked about them, and he acknowledged they went their separate ways. I met the others over the next couple of months. Mentioning I recognized them from FM's videos, they only had nice things to say about him.

It had been several weeks since I uploaded any videos, so I stayed at Fife 'N Drum Inn at the wallet busting cost of $140! My room, #5 "The

Garden Room," was plush with vaulted ceiling, micro fridge (hidden in a closet for aesthetics), designer soaps and oak queen bed with Ralph Lauren quilts (per their website). The repeating pattern of Colonial green and white wall-to wall wallpaper made me cross-eyed, but otherwise I was embarrassed to have it all to myself. FM, Socks and Slug all split the rent, squeezing into one room next door. For supper, I bought salad fixings at the grocery store: lettuce, cheese, bacon bits, tomatoes, peppers, an onion and croutons. I like to use salsa instead of dressing. These ingredients made several meals. I met Medicine Man while at the IGA grocery in town. He always wore a kilt.

> FUN FACT: Owner of the Fife, Dolph Traymon is known as the "Man of 10,000 Songs." He graduated Juilliard, conducted the U.S. Army Band and toured with Frank Sinatra. Dolph still entertains patrons six nights a week.

Checking messages, I was surprised when a pretty, young woman I've mentioned before, Cora Jean, had just started watching my AT videos from the beginning and posting nice comments. I wrote her back explaining we already knew each other (a little) from the artifact hunting community on the Internet. I was happy to have made a new friend.

Mail magic! Like a mail drop, mail magic provides needed food and supplies, but sent by a fan or friend instead of a designated support person. From the very beginning, complete strangers wrote messages asking if they could send anything. For the longest time, I would just reply "Thanks, but I can handle it on my own." Then, after a video showing a care package sent by The GA Gang, more offers came in, some from people who were shocked when I hinted in a later video that I probably wouldn't be able to complete the whole trail in a single season. One viewer said he almost fell out of his chair! New money from Grandmother was a huge relief, but finances were still going to be tight. Still, I was reluctant to take what I considered handouts.

During my time with Sipsey, we talked about accepting gifts. He eloquently explained that I should just think of it as trail magic. Some may have been watching, because they've hiked in the past or hoped to in the future. Others may never be able to hike the AT themselves and may have lived vicariously through me. Thinking about it that way, accepting generosity was good for everyone involved.

I was very excited to receive goodies, and among three boxes waiting in Kent, there was more than enough to get me to the next town: Pop Tarts, Ramen, tortillas, power bars, candy, jerky, a Mountain House meal, summer sausage, pasta sides, powdered milk, tuna and much more! Other helpful items included Ziploc bags, batteries and a black and yellow headlamp. It was nice to have hands-free light again. Thanks Wesley, Kacie, & Parker from SC, Mark, aka Tick Bait, from KY, One Foot & Should be Good & kids, of CT.

This unboxing video would again produce more folks wanting to help, and so on. Also, I chose not to mention it, but some gifts also included cold hard cash! I absolutely couldn't have kept going without everyone's support, and hope my angels got something out of it as well. I sent everyone postcards to let them know I appreciated their help. Encouraging letters also touched me - I still have them.

Finally, I got back on the trail after staying 3 days and 2 nights in Kent. Many miles later, you could see one corner of a large racetrack from the trail. I had read journals mentioning the sounds of racecars, so I did a little research on Whiteblaze.com to make sure I found it.

Lime Rock Park is a winding road course opened in 1957. Legendary sports car drivers have won here: Mario Andretti, Sterling Moss, Dan Gurney, David Hobbs and many more. It's also home to the Skip Barber Racing School, where driving instructors give paying novices a crash course in souped-up Mustangs or full-blown race cars. A woman in a little gray house/office was very cooperative and just asked me to sign a waiver. She even kept an eye on my backpack, but gave specific instructions not to go past the fence. But when I got there, I asked some landscape workers where the nearest soda machine was and they pointed toward the infield. Well, that's good as permission, so I barged it and walked across a metal pedestrian bridge right into the pit area!

Today wasn't an official race but rather, "Porsche track day," with drivers adjusting their cars, except for a menacing blue Viper that must have snuck in, like I did. Even with my hiking clothes and homeless man's beard, no one questioned what I was doing. Walking freely through the paddock, I took pictures and even tried to yogi a ride around the track. I used to race Pure Stock V8 cars on dirt tracks around the south, so smelling race fuel and burning rubber really got my adrenaline flowing!

Larger teams had expensive transporters, multiple cars, rolling toolboxes and uniformed crewmembers. Weekend warriors had just as much fun, on a much smaller budget. Driver of car #40, wearing blue jeans and a T-shirt, got all excited hearing the track marshal calling his division over the P.A. His car still had license plates and he even drove it to the track! Another racer, #249, a baby blue 1969 Porsche Carrera 911, looked stock but the owner was quick to point out modifications he'd made. Of course, I couldn't resist a Lime Rock Burger at the infield concession stand. It was fun listening to drivers trade wild stories, but my sandwich and pop cost $9.

Then, I got really brave and went right into the timing room and started filming from the skybox, best view in the house. When an official asked where I was from, I honestly told him I walked here from the Appalachian Trail. He had heard of the AT, but had no idea it was only a mile away and certainly never had a hiker in his scoring tower before. Just then, he picked up a walkie-talkie and asked someone to come up to the booth. Getting paranoid, I decided this was pushing my luck and made my way out.

Back on the trail, I found myself leapfrogging with a new crew: Cherokee, LJ, and Achilles. This mother, son and his friend were in the middle of a 100 mile section hike. Entering Falls Village, we were definitely in the North, judging by a clam/lobster bake ad printed onto a paper plate. It must seem like I'm in town a lot, but hikers have to resupply, so I might as well look around. Please keep in mind there are usually 50 to 70 miles of beautiful wooded trails between stops. A small town, there was no fast food or hotel chains here, but adding to the cozy atmosphere...

• **Falls River Inn:** Built in 1834, their website hints it was once a brothel and that a ghostly presence resides. Cherokee told me this was the most luxurious place she had ever stayed and included a lavish dinner, but the bill for 3 people was over $400!

• **Toymakers Café:** This eclectic restaurant, catering to British motorcycle clubs, was marked by the Union Jack. Coolest thing on the menu? The two-pound "Wheelie Burger" of course! Hiker friendly, they let hiker trash tent, or crash in a barn out back, gratis.

• **David M. Hunt Library:** Parked out front, "The DOT Car," was a 1959 Fiat - turned summer art project, designed by Japanese avant-garde pop artist, Yayoi Kusama. Covered with red, blue, yellow and green polka dots, I thought it looked more like the Wonder Bread car. The nice librarian even gave me some stickers to leave my mark.

While reading my email, a very nice viewer offered to express-mail fresh baked cookies! Very sweet, but I didn't want her to spend so much money. Instead, this online trail angel, who I later called my "secret sponsor," deposited cash directly into my PayPal account and I couldn't believe her generosity. This really helped because between the camera, fancy hotel room and general higher cost of everything up north, Grandma's money was almost down to half - already. Thru-hiker Johnnie Walker Black was hanging out at the library, too. I had already met Johnnie Walker Red (no relation) back in Waynesboro, but these two still hadn't met and I'm not sure if they ever did.

My buddy Chameleon heard I was in town and came looking for me. She'd been worried about my shoes falling apart and was happy to see me sporting new ones. Chameleon had hiked together with Roboticus for over a thousand miles. But Chameleon's hike changed when she injured her knee. Now, her boyfriend who she met on the AT, stopped his own hike to do car support. She'd slackpack all day, he'd pick her up to stay in a hotel and then do it again the next morning. Starting to rain, they gave me a lift to the post office.

As a greeting, the postmaster gave me a soda pop just for coming in. YouTube buddy Bob had been planning to thru-hike the same season as me, but for some reason, didn't get to go, so he gifted me some of the food and freeze-dried meals he had already prepared. Another clever idea for mail drops, he included a travel-size pouch of Tide.

Leaving town, hikers walk by Falls Village Station Hydro Power Plant, put in operation 1914. A smaller red brick utility building, covered with green ivy, had an outdoor showerhead sticking out of a wall

- cold water only, and again no privacy in full view of the street. Next, hikers cross over an arched truss bridge, closed to cars.

On the other side, I found a grey-headed gent making his supper right in the middle of the trail as if he suddenly got hungry and stopped to eat. Coach was a teacher and wrestling coach from Indiana, known for his American flag bandanna and positive attitude. We would meet several times over the next week and his is a friendship that continues to this day. He was super excited, closing in on finishing his hike of the whole AT.

Finish here? With a family and full time job, Coach didn't have time to take 6 months off. Instead, he'd use weekends and summer vacations to hike what he could, in sections. A state here, a couple hundred miles there, and in any order or direction. Keeping track of starting and stopping points, he strung the bits together over 4 years. Even though not a "thru-hike," when he passes all the white blazes, he'll officially become a "2,000 Miler." Thru-hikers and section-hikers walking the entire trail, both receive equal recognition by the ATC.

Nearby, I stopped at Great Falls, another summer swimming hole which the village was named after, and enjoyed seeing the powerful plunge of water coming over the dam. I also stumbled upon an old bottle dump with vintage soda containers and broken pottery. But there wasn't time to look around as I was in a hurry to make it to a safe place as dire weather warnings called for damaging winds, lightning, hail and even tornados.

Limestone Shelter was deep down at the bottom of a rocky gorge and I couldn't believe how difficult it was to get to. I hate staying in shelters, but everyone else was holed up back in town so I hung my hammock inside. Expecting Coach, I left plenty of room and didn't think he'd mind, but he never showed. Scary lightning creeped closer. Trying to judge how far away it was, I counted the seconds between flashes and thunder: FLASH... one Mississippi... two Mississippi... three Missis... BOOM! I even made an overdramatic "goodbye" video in case I didn't survive, which I erased when I woke up the next day, completely unharmed. I would make 2 such recordings during my hike. Relieved, I also found Coach safe and sound. He had made it to the start of the shelter trail and wisely set-up his tent right there instead of climbing down the gorge after dark. Rain also brought out lots of little orange salamanders. Red Efts. You see these all along the trail, but not usually a dozen in one place!

In the next part of Connecticut, hikers walk by a cemetery complete with gothic statues, where we can refill our water bottles at a caretaker's shed. Creepy. This is where I met Big Bird and his trail dog, a collie named "Fresh." The next trailhead went between two nice houses and a sign featured a large Smokey Bear. Of course, someone had drawn a Cheech and Chong-sized joint hanging out of his mouth. I got a chuckle out of it. Even Smokey must like to party sometimes.

> FUN FACT: *Early fire prevention ads featured cartoon characters on loan from Disney. Then Smokey the Bear was created in 1943. The current voice actor is Sam Elliott. "Woodsy Owl" and "Mark Trail" were less popular.*

The trail became more remote walking along Sages Ravine. Little waterfalls emptied into pools carved into the rocks. A dry creek bed and a small wooden sign marked the state line, completing 55 miles. This point also marked 1,500 total miles hiked!

Chapter 18. Lighthouse in the Mountains

Mount Greylock, Adams, Massachusetts. Mile marker 1,581.3.

Hiking in Massachusetts brought back lots of memories.
I was born in Lowell, a small lakeside amusement park town outside Boston and remember playing among dilapidated carnival rides. Every year, green marshes and swamps froze over becoming winter wonderlands. All the neighborhood kids bundled up in coats and scarves, ice skated, played hockey and raced toboggans while I was rambling deeper into the forest, exploring areas that could only be reached during hard freeze. My family moved to South Carolina when I was very young and I've only been back to visit twice.

While I was riding a big boost hiking in my home state, others were getting bored and even going home. Union Jill was a tall, muscular woman who blew by me several times like I was standing still! Back home in her native UK, she was a competitive power lifter and trail runner. With her conditioning and stamina, she could have finished the AT easily but just wasn't having fun anymore. In a nice gesture, she gifted her expensive trekking poles to her younger hiking buddy, Count Chocula, from Georgia. He was surprised she had quit so suddenly and missed his friend. Maybe the thrill of adventure had worn off? After all, the learning curve was over as we all had our gear sorted. The trail had flattened out and felt less wild with numerous road crossings, and sweeping vistas that had taken our breath away down south were much less dramatic here. Effort and exhaustion were the same, but without the payoffs. Other problems: water was often questionable or scarce, and biting insects could be intolerable. Protecting themselves, some hikers took to wearing bug nets over their heads, making them look like beekeepers.

Up here, sometimes it was hard NOT to sleep near an official campsite or shelter, as some were positioned barely a mile apart. Setting up just outside Glen Brook Shelter's perimeter, I ran into my German friend Socks outside her tent, cooking. She yelled my name and gave me a big hug even though it visibly hurt her to stand. Fighting severe knee problems for several months, she was now hiking with a staph infection. A good German doctor had eased her pain immensely, but still, Socks said every step was "very heavy." Although she had lots of friends on the trail, she was homesick and missed her husband. Crying, she said hearing planes fly overhead in New York broke her heart - she wanted to follow them to the airport and go home. I cared about Socks and hated to see anyone suffer.

Radio was camping here too. Awhile back, he was sick with what he thought was dehydration, but kept going until he just couldn't walk anymore. Finally, he went to a doctor and was diagnosed with Lyme disease. That could have been a hike-ender, but he was doing better now. Even with a week off trail - he had still leapfrogged ahead of me again. Yellow blazing can do that for ya.

That next morning found me walking through soaking wet cornfields, over bridges and across boardwalks. Shoulder high, a hand-carved marble tablet on the side of a road read: "Last Battle of Shays Rebellion was here: Feb. 27, 1787." This was an unsuccessful, armed attempt to overthrow the government. Citizens wanted change because they were tired of bad economic policy, escalating taxes and corruption in politics. Sounds like today's headlines!

Egremont Road led to Great Barrington, where lots of backpackers were staying to get out of the constant rain. Later, I heard from Socks that some hikers started "big trouble" when the manager found 10 people squeezed into one room, with only one paying. The manager complained and the hikers cussed him out. Then the cops came. A lot of people think this is something fun or cool to do, and even rationalize it by saying rooms are too expensive. Call it whatever you want, it's illegal and the same as stealing. These little motels aren't getting rich and usually offer cheaper hiker rates just for asking. Immature junk like this gives all hikers a bad name.

This was where I said goodbye to my friend Coach. He was beaming, waiting for his wife and family so they could hike the last few miles together, completing his section hike of the entire AT. Almost 2,200 miles, it took him 138 days over 4 years at an average 16.2 miles a day (including one day over 30 miles). Soaking wet, he and his loved ones celebrated by toasting Dr. Pepper, his favorite, and praising God for a safe journey.

Rain and thunderstorms followed me again the next day and the cheap blue poncho I found in a hiker box at the Doyle was nearly useless. It may have kept some rain out, but the humidity soaked all my clothes underneath and turned my fingers pruney. My brand-new sneakers were also completely water-logged. I did find refuge under a rock overhang so I could at least open my food bag in the dry.

Walking again, the resonance of a dozen cowbells welcomed hikers with haunting sounds as black and white spotted bulls stuck their heads and stubby horns through barbed wire fences to reach greener grass on the other side. I then walked across wooded hillsides completely covered in green ferns except for the brown ribbon of trail, followed by a narrow boardwalk with few railings. Lopsided with overgrown weeds trying to reclaim it, the structure was still indispensable.

That afternoon, Chameleon walked up and laughed when she caught me during a failed, tragic, comic attempt at making Jell-O. I had received a few boxes in a maildrop but didn't know it helps to have boiling water (told you I don't know how to cook!). The thick green water still made a refreshing snack. Unfortunately, my translucent blue spoon got lost and I had to slurp soup and eat with my fingers for a day or so until I snaked a spork from Mickey D's. All to find my lost blue spoon at the bottom of my backpack 100 miles later.

Rambling along the shores of sparkling Upper Goose Pond, affluent Mohhekennuck Club Lodge was built here in 1909, entertaining members for 73 years. All that's left is part of a massive stone chimney. Soaking my dogs in the chilly water during lunch, I watched rowboats go by as minnows tickled my toes.

With my nose to the ground (as always), I stumbled upon a souvenir-squished penny from Cape Cod ZooQuarium, 200 miles away. Opened in 1969, this petting zoo/aquarium featured an albino alligator called "Creole," 2 ponies named "Calvin & Pumpkin" and a pig known as "Pickles." Hunter, a California sea lion was a 10-year US Navy vet, recruited to wear video cameras and tie ropes underwater. The ZooQuarium closed in 2013 after almost 45 years and all residents have been relocated.

Already having eaten most of my food willy-nilly, I loitered around a small trailhead parking lot hoping to catch a ride to town. Giving up, only 10 feet along the trail I found another unused mail drop filled with hiker staples: cereal, Ramen, summer sausage, etc. I sat down right there and ate a whole package of precooked bacon!

Count Chocula and I hiked together for an hour or so. Scenery included beaver dens in a New England pond and monster blackberries. We also went to visit the Cookie Lady. Since 1988, Marilyn Wiley and her husband Ron have handed out fresh cookies and let thru-hikers tent in their yard in exchange for a little yardwork. You can also pay to pick buckets of the plumpest blueberries you'll ever see. We were looking forward to the tradition, but no one was home.

Out in the middle of the woods, a green plastic newspaper box sat on its pole, awaiting delivery of the 'Berkshire Eagle', eerily, in front of a house no longer there. Back in civilization, sidewalks led us through Dalton, an old textile center right on the Housatonic River. Here, a big house along the sidewalk is a welcome site to many thru-hikers: Tom Levardi's. I was hoping to stop in for a hot shower but some pals out front, said it was broken. Tom also helps people slack-pack: stay the night, he drops you off 20 miles up the trail, you hike back to his house without a pack, stay another night, then he drops you off where you started the day before to continue north with gear.

Five more mail drops were waiting at the post office. In a hurry, I carried them outside to the bus stop and was shocked who was sitting there: Sipsey and Swiss Toni! These two made friends and had hiked together for several weeks. Frantic to condense my load, I tore into a box and emptied the contents into my backpack. One drop was from Lacey in Connecticut, filled with Slim Jims, batteries, crackers, etc. Sipsey snatched up all the coffee packets (I'm too young to drink coffee) and Swiss Toni claimed the Spam. It was fun catching up until their bus arrived. Sipsey was yellow blazing up to Katahdin so he could summit with his wife on their anniversary. The plan was to flip-flop and resume walking south but I never saw him again.

Climbing onto the next bus with the rest of my boxes, I took a very uneasy ride to Great Barrington, where there were modern motels and another food drop. Berkshire Bus Service travels through these shires: Lee, Dalton, Cheshire, Adams, North Adams and Williamstown. My bus driver may have looked like a senior citizen that should have been playing bingo somewhere, but she had a lead foot and jammed on the gas every chance she got. Used to walking 2 or 3 miles an hour for several months - racing 50 mph over bumpy streets about shook my teeth out and made me carsick. The one-way trip from one end to the other (with 3 transfers) covered 26 miles in about an hour and only cost $5. This bus route is also a famous yellow blaze shortcut.

> *HIKER TIP: Always carry a couple bucks worth of quarters. You never know when you'll come across a random soda machine or need coins for the bus. In town, they can be flagged down anywhere but don't make change.*

Like most cities in the north, Great Barrington is named after a township in England. Settled in 1726 and ranked #1 on "The 20 Best Small Towns in America" list by Smithsonian Magazine, it's also an official Appalachian Trail Community, although you won't find a word about it on the town's website. Most important to hungry hikers, the town boasts (55) restaurants!

This region even has its own local currency with over 7 million Berk-Share Notes in circulation. The attractive bills can be purchased for 95¢ per BerkShare and 400 participating businesses accept them at full dollar value, creating a 5% incentive. I never got a reply trying to get my hands on a few BerkShares for mementos. In a world of state quarters and limited edition potato chip flavors, I think they're missing the boat not making these available to collectors. Each denomination features images of local historical figures. There is no $100 bill.

- **$1: Mahican Native Americans:** First inhabitants of the area.
- **$5: W.E.B. Du Bois:** Local civil rights leader.
- **$10: Robyn Van En:** Supporter of community agriculture.
- **$20: Herman Melville:** Author of Moby Dick.
- **$50: Norman Rockwell:** Renowned painter, Stockbridge, MA.

> *FUN FACT: Crane & Co, in Dalton, made paper for engraver Paul Revere to print America's first paper currency. They are still the only maker in the world of a special linen/cotton blend used by America and other countries.*

My last transport wasn't Greyhound-style, but rather a glorified school bus covered in advertising graphics of ginormous chicken nuggets. This subliminal suggestion got the best of me, and my microwave supper consisted of a family-size bag of chicken tenders and chips - with salsa, BBQ sauce, French onion for dipping and a two-liter orange soda. Amused, I watched another hiker in the grocery store "grazing" the produce section, sneaking grapes and other loose fruit and veggies while waiting for the cracker lady to prepare another tray of free samples. Next door was The Travelodge, where I stayed up all night listening to music. $72.61.

Repackaging drop box stuff, Tracy from Pennsylvania had sent a big box that included "Hike your own Hike" stickers that I put on my laptop, duct tape with leopard skin print, Goldfish and canned chicken. Mother sent a mail drop containing Twizzlers and Boston Baked Beans candy - perfect to snack on while in Massachusetts. Thanks: Mom, Lacey, Tracy, Chris, Todd, and Mike & Tyler & Carter (from SD). Another week I didn't have to buy any supplies. Todd's box was sent all the way from Canada! Fun because common items were marked with Canadian labels such as: Mr. Noodles (Ramen), Toasties (Pop Tarts), Pal O Mine Fudge and Aero Bars filled with air bubbles. The note inside read...

"Hope you enjoy this stuff I sent you. Your journey is inspirational to those of us who have yet to do it. All the best, can't wait to see you on Katahdin. Stay strong and take care. Todd, aka Dragonfly Hiker."

I also need to give a big thanks to Garry, an active US soldier/DoD firefighter in Iraq, who saw a whiney video I posted and offered to buy me a new set of trekking poles. I was deeply honored, but my sticks had sentimental value as friends had given them to me. Not to mention I felt bad this man was in Iraq, risking his life protecting our country, while I was goofing off. Garry understood and very graciously still sent $200 to help me out! He bought FM new poles, too.

Main Street was not too big and not too small, with marble buildings and impressive churches. Trashcans were repurposed from recycled street signs. How creative! It's too bad Barrington Outfitter here was lame and basically just sells running shoes and Eddie Bauer jackets to rich folks. I needed a new rain jacket and looked at hats (the hotel washing machine ate mine), but everything was too expensive. I refused on principle, to pay $40 for a cheap painter's cap only worth $5 just because it had a name brand printed on it. Worst of all, they didn't even know what a hiker box was?! Also, my backpack had developed a tear where the straps attached. I did find a sewing shop and the repair would have taken 60 seconds, but the spinster declined.

FUN FACT: *Iconic 60's song, 'Alice's Restaurant,' is based on folk singer Arlo Guthrie's true-life events here. He now owns the former home of Alice Brock, Old Trinity Church, in Great Barrington.*

♪ *You can get anything you want at Alice's Restaurant*
Walk right in it's around the back
Just a half a mile from the railroad track
You can get anything you want at Alice's Restaurant ♫

Waiting for the bus back to Dalton, I met Weezy and Aisha (best trail dog ever), here all the way from California. Weezy wore camo shorts, a goatee and lots of tattoos. His entire backpack had been stolen after leaving it under a bridge while in a bar, but nice folks along the way helped him replace lost gear.

His ID had also been taken and he couldn't get money out of Western Union, so I gave him the $20 bill Wizzy Wig & Mattie gifted me back in New York. I was saving it for a rainy day, but seemed fitting to use it to help someone else. Weezy went into Mickey D's and bought burgers for himself and his puppy, telling the manager Aisha was a service dog so she could come inside and cool off. I would see them many times, and even though we were polar opposites, consider Weezy one of the best friends I made on the AT. He liked to party and was doing his hike, his way. Yellow blazing when he felt like it, and finding odd jobs to keep going. I respected him for that. Amusing, Weezy's dog absolutely refused to hike in the rain, but was otherwise famous for running WAY ahead up the trail. Sometimes a mile or more.

> HIKER TIP: *You'll need cash for hostels, Ma 'N' Pa places, and the unexpected. Post offices allow $50 cash back with purchase (even a stamp) and grocery stores grant up to $100 with no fees. Avoid ATMs.*

Back on the trail, I was looking a little disheveled, not from the jarring bus ride, or because I lost my hat, or anything to do with the AT. It was because my new pen pal, Cora Jean, had emailed her phone number and asked me to call. I was happy when she sent several long emails, but I was too shy to pick up the phone. Obviously, I'm not too smooth with the ladies. I do like to flirt and have my moments. It's just that I get my heart broken every time.

Free as bees in the trees. Before this hike started, I promised myself NOT to get involved with anyone out of a fierce determination to finish. It took the fortitude of a monk, at times, and had already passed up a couple chances to hook-up. We've all seen it before: hiker boy meets girl - hiker boy leaves trail (happens the other way, too). But this one was hooked, and I really liked her too. I've been prone to serious, sometimes debilitating depressions, but can honestly say this was the first time I felt this way on the AT. Yes, I felt sad for hikers who were suffering, and there was stress because of money, but those things are different.

I camped next to a beaver pond where the mosquitos were relentless. You've probably seen those joke T-shirts that depict the state bird (name any state) as a mosquito? Well, shirts sold here read: "Our state bird was the bat, but mosquitos ate them all!" I refused to bring a bug net for my hammock because of weight. The extra ounce or two wouldn't have hurt and my life would have been much more comfortable. Instead, I burrowed inside my sleeping bag and suffered in sweat. I could actually feel beasties bouncing on the thin material of the sleeping bag. Some still got in, or stung me from the underside. Ouch! I have bad memories of several miserable nights like this.

> HIKER TIP: *Taking garlic pills to keep mosquitos away is just an old wise tale. That may protect you against vampires (and humans), but not insects. For a natural remedy, try Vitamin B.*

In Cheshire, I enjoyed visiting old timey, H.D. Reynolds General Store. Hardwood floors squeaked and old shelves were stocked with modern things: folk art, local history books and snow shovels. I replaced my poncho and bought a Coca-Cola, a frozen fudge bar and postcards. One showed Reynolds in the 1930s with a Ford Model T parked out front where orange riding lawnmowers sat now. I wasn't the first hiker to stop here, as several summit photos hung inside.

The climb up Mount Greylock was one of the biggest we've had in a while, and led by a picturesque mountain pond surrounded by tall trees and a Walden-esqe cabin. Nearing the summit were several rocks inscribed with quotes from famous authors inspired by this mountain... My favorite...

"It were as well to be educated in the shadow of a mountain, as in more classical shades. Some will remember, no doubt, not only that they went to the college, but that they went to the mountain.' Henry David Thoreau. 1844."

• **Henry David Thoreau** was, of course, the noted transcendentalist who spoke of simple living in natural surroundings in his book 'Walden' after spending 2 years, 2 months, and 2 days in a wilderness cabin. Thoreau's name and influence comes up often when researching the AT: besides summiting and spending the night on this mountain, he also explored the (upcoming) Whites, visited Katahdin 100 years before the first thru-hiker, and composed the speech, 'A Plea for Captain John Brown,' strongly defending Brown's actions in Harpers Ferry. At age 44, bedridden with tuberculosis, when asked if he had made his peace with God, Thoreau quipped: "I did not know we had ever quarreled." Thoreau is buried on "Authors' Ridge" in Sleepy Hollow Cemetery, Concord, Massachusetts.

> FUN FACT: Thoreau accidentally burned 300 acres of his beloved Walden Woods when he set fire to a tree stump to warm fish chowder, earning the nickname "Woodsburner," perhaps sparking his passion to write.

• **Herman Melville.** It's widely said Melville, looking out the window of his study, 20 miles away in Pittsfield, Massachusetts, first imagined the white whale in 'Moby Dick' after seeing Mount Greylock covered in snow. He would also dedicate his gothic fiction novel, 'Pierre,' to "Greylock's Most Excellent Majesty."

• **Nathaniel Hawthorne** climbed Greylock several times and wrote his short story, 'Ethan Brand,' after seeing a lime kiln glowing in the dark while hiking here at night.

• **J. K. Rowling.** Fitting a land once notorious for magical spells, supposed covens and witch trials would be home to Harry Potter's world in North America. The book and movie 'Fantastic Beasts and Where to Find Them' depicts Ilvermorny, a stateside Hogworts hidden from non-magical muggles by fog atop Mount Greylock.

In real life, Bascom Lodge on top of the mountain was handsome in architectural design and beautifully built by the CCC in 1937 from local materials procured here after the original summit house, built circa. 1900, burned to the ground. Not necessarily here to cater to thru-hikers, it was full of college kids so call ahead: dorm room bunks cost $35 a night, or you can get lunch and a shower.

Marking the highest natural point in Massachusetts, 3,491', Veterans War Memorial Tower is topped with a large, perpetually lighted green globe that can be seen up to 70 miles away. The 93-foot tall beacon was originally intended for Boston's Charles River Basin, but plans changed and in 1932, was erected here instead. Striking even as lighthouses go, it honors fallen Massachusetts's soldiers of war. The inscription reads: "They were faithful even unto death." Visitors between 2013 and 2016 found the tower surrounded by scaffolding, undergoing a $2.6 million-dollar restoration.

Deep blue skies had puffy, white clouds wandering about, projecting long shadows onto the landscape and valleys below. An 8-mile auto road leads to the top, so there were lots of people about including a large Asian family celebrating...something. With their camera, I took a picture for them and then relaxed on the soft, cool grass. Camping is not allowed on the summit, but Thunderbolt Warming Hut can be used in an emergency. Well designed, a central stone chimney connects 4 buck stoves heating 4 single bunks laid out in a "star" pattern. Even though there was chalk and chalkboard, our ol' buddy still chose to tag a wooden door, "Don't write on wall, stupid!" It would be a fun place to crash and catch a sunset/sunrise, but please be respectful and don't leave poop in plain sight. Rangers hate that.

Strolling 3 miles into Williamstown on a beautiful day, I tried to hitch but enjoyed the urban walk with plenty to see. This quintessential New England community, had old churches that seemed to be getting more elaborate with tall steeples and colorful stained glass windows. The post office was a large building with marble features and even had a hiker box underneath a counter designated for hikers to sort packages. It was fun to get correspondence from Cora Jean, who sent postcards while visiting her family. The mailman chuckled reading a novelty card with a goofy cartoon horse on the front: "Kentucky - Where the women are fast, and the horses are pretty!" Another parcel was sent by Gustav, from New Jersey, a Hammock Forums member. His box was enough to last me another full week - filled with Slim Jims, rice sides, TP, a tiny lighter, batteries for my camera and other necessary items. Thanks!

> HIKER TIP: Hammock Forums is a spinoff of Whiteblaze.com that became an independent website in 2006. I learned lots of info from both communities and found some good deals on used gear in their "For Sale" threads.

I found this village and its occupants very charming, yet got very few chores done. The library incorporated a small museum, although once again, the Internet was so painfully slow I gave up before my allotted time had expired. More importantly, Mountain Goat Outfitter which I was depending on, had closed with no clue about its demise in the guidebook. Frustrated, I didn't even bother getting town food. On the return road walk, I saw an old timey mechanic shop with a VW bug rusting out front and parts of a vintage British green sports car hung on a wall like a puzzle: 2 wire wheels and tires, front and rear fenders and a door. I also found a pair of daredevils putting finishing touches on demolition derby cars they were building - one painted as the Beatles' "Yellow Submarine," the other named "The Tank," camouflage with a big white star on each door. I've been in a half-dozen demo derbies and it's like grown-up bumper cars!

Stopping at a little thrift store outside town I found a black trucker's hat to replace the one I lost. It had the name "MUNCHIE" airbrushed on it, but only cost $1. You can't turn down a deal like that! I was happy with my purchase, that is, until everyone asked if I had changed my trail name. Eventually, I let SOBOs think Munchie was my name so I could just move on. I even answered to it a few times. Still others took the name for slang, thinking I could supply them with marijuana and I endured several speeches about legalization.

Touchy subject. If you're reading this book because you're interested in hiking the AT, I think it's important you're informed about it. I don't know where people get it, or how, but there is a lot of pot smoking on the trail. You probably think you can tell who the potheads are, but you'll be surprised when you find the person you least expect, glassy-eyed and puffing on a bong. I don't smoke pot and admit that I have never even tried it. Just the smell gives me a terrible headache, so I avoid being around it. At the same time, I really don't care who does and even admire the "Zen" culture of it. It also has medicinal uses and relaxes sore muscles and joints. The top of a difficult climb, bottom of a long decent, landmarks, fire towers, or stream crossings all seem to be good occasions for a "safety meeting," but are just as popular behind restaurants and dumpsters.

Most partakers were cool about it and offered a hit. When I replied, "No thanks," they just said, "More for me!" Others became so paranoid they tried to hide it, like I was a narc or something. Who am I going to tell? The trees? Admittedly, even though I never said so, I resented others for firing up at public overlooks but learned to just ignore it so I could enjoy the scenery. I will note, except for a few suspicious pill bottles, I never saw anything heavier.

Reaching the big brown sign marking our entry into Vermont, I let out a rebel yell - "Yee-Haw!"

Chapter 19. Night of Owls

A crane standing on top of a beaver dam in my favorite state, Vermont.

Weather turning cooler, I was invigorated with new energy. Hiking through Pioneer Valley, split-log boardwalks, numerous ponds, and tremendous views added to my enthusiasm. The pinnacle of the hike seemed to be drawing nearer, almost in sight.

The MA/VT state line also marked the beginning of the Long Trail (LT), started 1910 and completed 1930, making it the oldest long distance hiking trail in the nation, it spans the state all the way to Canada. Total distance: 272 miles. The AT and LT share the same path and white blazes for about 105 of those and I would meet many "LTs."

My first night in Vermont turned out to be an eventful one. Stopping early to make camp, I boiled brownish pondwater to cook a Ramen bomb noodle soup, adding summer sausage and a pinch of stuffing mix gifted in a drop box. These fancy ingredients made a thicker soup and really added some flavor.

> HIKER TIP: Ramen Bombs are a trail staple. Try mixing noodles and instant potatoes together. Add ramps, hot sauce…heck…anything! P.S. - I once saw a hiker eat a cube of uncooked Ramen dipped in peanut butter.

It was a very relaxing evening... until about 4:30 a.m., when I was awakened by one of God's larger creatures stomping through the woods. In the dark, I listened closely trying to figure out what it was and if I was in any danger. Convincing myself it was just a black bear visiting the lower part of the pond, I tried to go back to sleep. Then, I heard the creature sloshing around and seemingly lapping up water by the gallon. Quietly, I snuck down to the shore, and after the sun began to rise could barely make out a shape through the fog. It was a big-ass moose! A few moments later, I realized there were also two baby moose! I watched quietly for a half hour, frogs chirping trying to give away my location, until "Mama Moose" led her brood back into the forest. I wasn't expecting to see moose this far south, but checked another "must see" off my list.

North American moose, largest of the deer family, can weigh between 600 - 800 lbs., with an unofficial record of 2,601 lbs. They eat up to 70 lbs. of food daily, and half their nourishment consists of underwater vegetation - roots and all. At other times, they stand on their hind legs to reach tall branches. Hikers may hear moose crashing their horns together as females make eerie wailing sounds. Antlers are shed after mating season, but are regrown, covered with "velvet" in the spring. The widest spread recorded was 7 ft. across.

> HIKER TIP: Adult moose can stand over 7 feet tall, so don't just glance at a lake and think, "no moose here." What you assumed was a rock or log may actually be a full-grown moose underwater!

A moose's lifespan is about 15 - 25 years, and they were once found as far south as Pennsylvania. Today, Maine has a population of approximately 76,000 moose, New Hampshire; 4,000 and Vermont; 2,200, about half their numbers from just a few years ago. Besides human hunters, adult moose have few predators. Their biggest threat is winter ticks, responsible for 70% of calf deaths. Usually, moose are only dangerous if harassed, or if you get too close. They also feel threatened by dogs. Be careful - moose can kick in all directions, including to the side. When a moose roars, or the hair on their neck stands up, watch out: They're preparing to charge! Run or hide behind a tree. Moose are not the brightest animals in the forest, and will simply think you disappeared. "Huh?"

Already awake, I packed up and started moving. Early birds are burdened with the task of walking through or knocking down spider webs spun overnight. They say, you're never more than 3 feet from a spider, better make that 1 foot on the AT. After a half hour of this, I came upon a hiker I'd never seen before, just lying limp in the middle of the trail. I was alarmed, but his sleeping bag was kind of on top of him, so guessed he was alive, but he didn't look comfortable in any way. The contents of his backpack were scattered about, blocking my path completely, but I tiptoed around and made sure he was breathing without waking him up. It would have made a funny photo, but out of respect, I never take pictures of people when they're sleeping.

Reaching Congdon Shelter, you can't miss this tiny 3-sided cabin as the AT leads us across an imaginary welcome mat where the shelter's front door would be. A cute little chipmunk terrorizes hikers every night and had gotten into several food bags. Brazen, he kept darting towards me, trying to make me flinch and drop my crackers. Ranger Bill from New Hampshire had a thick red beard and wore a blue floppy hat. He showed everyone a sign his kids made from Tyvek material that doubled as a sitting pad with colorful "Hiker-to-town" graphics on one side, "Hiker-to-trail" on the reverse - a fun idea for children to help their hitchhiking parent. I asked those who slept here, if they knew the hiker that I saw passed out. They all laughed and said they were wondering where he was. Fittingly, his trail name: Thirtypack.

Hurricane Irene. The previous season, this category 3, with sustained winds up to 125 mph and rainfall amounts of 22 inches battered the east coast for 10 days, from the Caribbean to Puerto Rico. A state of emergency was declared in 14 states and 56 people lost their lives. When Irene hit Vermont, it stayed inland for 12 hours straight, causing massive flooding. Many roads were damaged, or washed away completely, including several historical, covered bridges. Some towns were completely isolated for up to 2 weeks. Even a year later, several detours slowed us down along the upcoming sections.

Most of my day was uneventful until a pop-up thundershower required an emergency tarp setup. High in elevation, I didn't want to go any further until it was safe. So, I just put up my tarp and lay on the grey plastic sheet given to me by Half Speed. This storm lasted longer than usual, so I went ahead and strung my hammock up for the night. Of course, a few minutes later the sun came back out.

With an hour of daylight left, I hiked up the mountain to Melville Neuheim Shelter to cook dinner and hung out with a half-dozen, college-aged Long Trail hikers camping there. They were all very excited beginning their adventure and seemed to be faring well for their 2nd night. I thought it was funny how they were discussing gear choices, pack weights and so-on - just like me and every AT hiker had done back in Georgia. They asked lots of questions and were amazed how far I had walked. As of now: my 1,617 miles to their 15.

One hefty young man noticed the airbrush work on my hat and proclaimed loudly: "Your trail name must be Munchie!" Half-jokingly, I replied "Your name must be Psychic?!" And with that, he had his trail name! Quite pleased, he grinned the rest of the evening and practiced saying out loud funny ways to introduce himself: "Hi, I knew we'd meet today, I'm Psychic!" Thinking of that night, I admit it was pretty cool to give someone his trail name. Plus, on this occasion, it happened very spontaneously.

"Ver-mud!" Hell Holler was an unlikely name for the beautiful valley I trod through the next day. Steps and stonework added allure, although the trail was noticeably muddier, and nightly showers didn't help. You can try to walk around, but that just makes it worse with hundreds of hikers expanding mud holes even wider. Leave No Trace policy recommends walking right through the middle. I also had to avoid piles of what looked like brown charcoal biscuits - moose poop!

Known as the "Bennington Triangle," this 16-mile portion of the LT/AT is more than a folktale. Five people lost - in 5 years. The first, in 1945, was a hunting guide who knew this area like the back of his hand, but still went missing while leading a group. Second was an 18-year old college student. She had spoken with an elderly couple only moments before rounding a corner of the trail, never to be seen again. Three years later to the day, a man traveling by bus on Route 9 evaporated into thin air between stops, leaving his luggage above his empty seat. Most tragic, an 8-year-old boy was nowhere to be found when his mother returned after leaving him playing in a truck for a few moments. And finally, just 2 weeks later, in 1950, a woman on a camping trip simply disappeared. The only body to be recovered, she was found the following spring after winter snows had melted, in an open area that had already been cleared by searchers.

Search parties included local police, bloodhounds, aircraft, help from the FBI and in one case - the National Guard. No trace of the others has ever been found or the disappearances explained. Mountain maniacs, killer bears, Big Foot, extraterrestrials? The most unusual explanation could be what the Algonquian Indians called, "The Man-Eating Stone." Only exposed in the Fall, this living, mysterious boulder can change locations and when someone stands on it to see a view, it swallows them up like quicksand.

Miles later, Stratton Mountain is where both our long-distance trails were conceived: The Long Trail, by James P. Taylor, in 1909, and the AT, by Benton MacKaye in 1921. Even on an overcast day, it was easy to see how MacKaye, here while the LT was being built, found inspiration gazing among some of the oldest mountains in America. Vermont gets its nickname, The Green Mountain State, from this majestic mountain range.

Cresting this summit, we walked a path that was restored to the original route in 1987 after being relocated for many years. A one room cabin, about the size of your average lawnmower shed, has been here since 1928. White, with a single shutter window, it had a new door because the old one had been ripped-off by a bear only days before. Caretakers, employed by Green Mountain Club (GMC) occupy the cabin to make sure no one camps illegally or BASE jumps.

> FUN FACT: BASE is an acronym for "Buildings, antennas, spans and earth" that jumpers, without airplanes, parachute from. The extreme sport is illegal in US national parks (and most everywhere else).

The CCC assembled Stratton Mountain Lookout Tower, 55' tall, in 1934. If smoke or flames were spotted, a "lookout" would alert ranger stations, by carrier pigeon or Morse code, to help firefighters quickly locate trouble. Some have small boxes on top called "cabs." Others have larger tower-top "cabins," just big enough to live in. This tower looked like a massive grey erector set made of alarmingly thin, galvanized steel angle iron, and the entire structure was simply fastened to exposed granite with giant bolts.

Grasping onto the handrail, I climbed 60 wooden steps, arranged at a steep 45° angle, ascending an internal stairway up 5 flights of risers that ran back and forth like switchbacks. At the top, I was rewarded with spectacular 360° views at 3,940'. Towering over a dense forest of evergreen treetops, I could see Killington Peak over 60 miles ahead. Wind howled and battered the metal cab I was encapsulated in, causing blurry panes of old window glass to rattle.

> FUN FACT: Want a tower of your own? There's usually a few for sale on the Forest Fire Lookout Association's website. Price range: $14,000 to $37,000 - not including shipping, permits, and re-erection costs.

A fun, hand-drawn map welcomed us to Stratton Pond. The illustrations featured a pair of cartoon Loch Ness monsters with big, smiling faces. Legend says most nights a spirit woman can be heard singing from the other side of the water. The campground was very sparse and supposedly manned by caretakers I never saw. Passing their semi-permanent encampment, I found it a pigsty, complete with tattered blue tarps and rakes just strewn about.

> HIKER TIP: A high traffic area, there is a $5 fee to sleep at the shelter or surrounding campsites. Keep your receipt to redeem for a free night's stay at either Griffith Lake or Little Rock Pond.

Here, I met a talkative section hiker from India, part of a 2-man team, working together for over 10 years to complete the AT in sections. Hiking 50 to 100 miles at a time, these two didn't walk together but used a hopscotch approach where one would start hiking south and the other would drive a day's walk away, park the car and begin hiking north toward his friend. On overnight sections, they would meet in the middle to camp, cook and hand-off car keys. The next morning, the southbound hiker kept heading toward the car and would then drive to the trailhead where he started, to pick-up his waiting buddy. Sounds complicated but hey, whatever works. Both carried small backpacks with each carrying half their gear. One packed the tent and the other lugged the cooking stuff. Sounded dangerous, with each man carrying an essential piece of equipment, but they trusted that the other would make it to the planned meeting place.

The faster of the two already had a trail name, "Halftime," because he always had to wait and the hike took him... half the time. So, I named his partner "Overtime" because he was always the late one. At first, I thought this was clever, but now regret I've doomed this poor man to having to explain his derogatory handle to everyone he meets.

Walking down a rutted Jeep road, a sign on a tree instructed us to: "LOOK UP." Way up higher in the tree was another sign pointing to "Prospect Rock." Maybe they've had trouble with souvenir collectors, so they placed it out of reach? Boomer, from Grand Rapids, Michigan, and I arrived at the same time. He wore an average-sized green backpack, orange shirt and grey shorts. We were both looking forward to catching the sunset at this well-known viewing area, and a rocky outcrop made for makeshift stadium seating at 2,008 feet.

For me, the experience became mind-altering. During the sun's slow descent, I had a trance, Zen-like experience and saw some pleasant hallucinations; kind of like looking through a child's kaleidoscope. Maybe it had something to do with the sun setting behind the mountains at a sharp angle? Maybe it was dehydration, exhaustion, or just dirt on my glasses? The camera even caught some of it, with red prisms in the photos appearing stationary. My eyes saw these dizzying, radiating light effects color morphing, spinning around and pulsating!

As soon as the sun hid behind the mountains, I took off again, making it another 2 miles closer to town. That evening was clear, so there was no need for the tarp and I stared at the sky as I went to sleep. I made a wish, seeing a shooting star framed perfectly within a small opening in the trees. During the night, an owl let out a loud screech. This scares you at first because you're not sure what it is. Then I heard the owl fly over and land in the very tree I was hanging from, then another and another! Eventually, there were at least 4 or 5, all calling and screeching. I figured out what they were after when I heard a scratching behind me - a mouse had climbed into my backpack! Later that night, I heard several animals running through the woods. I couldn't see them as it was completely dark, except for a flicker of starlight, but it sounded like they were having fun. I went back to sleep, all cozy, and felt like a part of nature.

VT-11 & 30. Like many trailheads at road crossings, this dirt parking lot was barely big enough for more than a couple of cars, and was cluttered with warning signs. Comically altered, one featured an ambulance running over a poor hiker - "CAUTION, DON'T BECOME ROADKILL!" With nowhere to pullover safely, I didn't even bother trying to hitch. Instead, I just walked downhill to Manchester Center, 5 steep miles away. Shoulders were very narrow and littered with broken beer bottles, tire carcasses and debris from car accidents, including an errant license plate. I tried to stay out of harm's way by walking on the outside of rusty metal guardrails, but tore a hole in my vest. I was still having fun giving truckers the "blow your horn" sign like kids do on long car rides and laughed every time one patronized me.

Closer to town, there were several little motels from which to choose, but I stopped at the first one I saw, The Red Sled, a nice dated place and very "Vermont." Amenities included indoor/outdoor swimming pools, fire pit and gazebo overlooking a manmade fishing pond loaded with trout. Each room was painted a different pastel color. Mine was pink, complete with matching pink wallpaper, drapes and carpet. I took a little ribbing for it but the proprietor, good salesman that he was, suggested it had the best Wi-Fi. My new buddy Psychic was staying here too, and wish I had taken more time to hang out.

This was all very nice, but the hotel owner wasn't willing to do a simple shuttle run to town, so I emptied my backpack, took my dirty laundry and continued walking into Manchester Center. After washing my clothes, I picked up another trio of mail magic boxes and my PC from the post office and started back up the mountain.

After trudging for over a mile, a piece of junk compact car stopped and the slightly foreign driver asked if I wanted a ride. But he was headed the wrong way. Thanking him, I told him my motel was the other direction and I needed to go UP the mountain. He said, "That's fine, just get in." I wish I had never gotten into that car.

My first warning sign should have been having to shuffle empty beer cans out of the way, just to sit down. The driver also had one in his hand. But my boxes were heavy, the weather was hot and I just wanted to get to the motel. He took off down the mountain, but never turned around. I got worried when he started crying, telling me his "partner" had passed away, how much he hated his job as a cook and that he wanted to kill himself. I felt bad for the dude but wanted out. He stopped at his duplex and invited me inside...several times. I told him no, I'm a hiker and smell too bad. He waved me in, saying "It's fine," and goes on to make the creepy statement "I like the smell." Now I'm really uncomfortable! He goes inside and comes back out with a tiny white poodle and more beer. He also offers me the joint he is now smoking, then suggests I stay the night. At this point, it's obvious he wants me to be his boyfriend or something. I don't roll that way and tell him firmly, "I already paid for a motel room and that's where I'm going," and started grabbing my boxes. Franticly, he waved his hands and said, "Ok! Ok! I'll drive you!"

Noticeably upset, he started the car up in a huff, put it in reverse and floored the gas pedal! I had just enough time to look behind us and yell "Whoa! Whoa!" before we plowed right into a bright yellow car, now parked behind us. Even worse, that car then rolled forward and slammed into a black Hummer, setting off its alarm. Neighbors heard the commotion and came running out. Crazy dude jumps up and started cursing at them for blocking his driveway. Of course, one of the ladies called the police. I was kind of in shock all this had happened, but not injured, so I got my stuff and left. For a brief moment, I considered telling crazy dude to hide his beer cans before the cops arrived, but he was still raving. Great! Now I had to walk all that distance - again! It could have ended much worse, and I was still scared crazy dude would come looking for me, so I hid in the bushes every time a car approached.

> FUN FACT: Jake Burton began making snowboards in his Manchester garage in 1977. Now a multimillion dollar business, Burton was instrumental in growing snowboarding into a world-class sport.

Directly across from the motel, busy Dutton Farm Stand had a wooden garden horse with flowerpots for feet and a mane of vines. An electrical fenced-in pen held little goats and I had fun looking around the greenhouses before buying fresh veggies to make salads.

The next afternoon, I explored town and asked a kid carrying a skateboard for directions to the skate park. Only two kids were skating, and understandably, were a little leery of me at first, but let me borrow a board so I could get in a few tricks. By the end of the session, we were all buddies - they even asked me to smoke a joint with them - little 12-year-old kids! Sometimes I feel like the only person in the world who doesn't get high.

More mail magic! I stayed 2 nights in Manchester Center, resting and waiting for a couple of mail drops. I was in the post office so much the postmasters knew me by name! Opening a couple of boxes in their parking lot, I was very thankful for all the help, and filmed unboxing each one. I would later email a special link to the senders so they could watch privately. Otherwise, my YouTube channel would have been nothing but non-stop videos of me opening boxes! When possible, I added some "behind the scenes" footage, or notes about the trip. Some people also sent gifts; I wasn't expecting this at all, and still felt a little weird about it, but was touched by their generosity...

• **Mikey & Lucas,** buddies from Georgia, sent a "Tech Deck" skateboard about the size of a Hot Wheels car. A "Snake Session" sticker on bottom was from a company another friend and I started. We sponsored skaters in the US, UK and even a girl in Australia. Two have since turned pro, making me feel like a proud papa. I missed skating a lot, but was another thing I gave up to hike the AT.

• **Kath, my "secret sponsor,"** sent several boxes, this one express-mailed at a cost of $100! She kind of adopted me and included food, cash, candy and a card showing Snoopy dressed up like a Boy Scout leader, teaching his Woodstock flock. She also gifted me a compass imbedded into beautiful wood to hang off my backpack.

• **Mike, Tyler, & Carter.** New trail runners! Mike, from South Dakota, first wrote saying he had an extra pair of shoes, but they were a size too small. So, what does he do? Goes online and ordered my size! INOV-8 ROClit 295s, black with silver trim. I even wore them around the hotel room. I also got a big kick out of a note with my face photoshopped onto Presidents Mountain.

• **Cora Jean.** For lunch, she sent cuties, Grippo's BBQ chips (some are hot - some are not), Nutter Butters and applesauce packets. Besides a long letter (on Victoria's Secret stationary, no less), she sent a T-shirt with the Tolkien quote: "Not all who wander are lost." Made of cotton (a hiker no-no), I wore it in town or at night. She also sent 3 pairs of EcoSox that felt like heaven compared to the thin Dollar Store socks I was used to. Most special was a necklace handmade by her brother Tojo and his wife Michelle. Cora carved and painted a turquoise AT logo on one side of the brown pendent; the reverse had the symbol for water. It seemed to always rain when the water sign was facing forward, and stopped when I turned it around... true story.

> *HIKER TIP: Made from bamboo fibers, EcoSox can absorb 3-4 times more moisture than cotton, but dry quickly and regulate skin temperature. Just check labels as some styles have cotton woven-in.*

Main Street had coffee shops and foodie boutiques. Most were too fancy-pants for me, but I found a cool place: Wood Fired Pizza Co, with a fire pit dome covered in rock n' roll graffiti of Jim Morrison, Led Zeppelin, Jimi Hendrix, etc. Sam was a master at his craft and a couple slices and a grape soda hit the spot for $5. They had a Lethal Weapon pinball game and the biggest takeout boxes I've ever seen!

Northshire Bookstore had a decent selection of AT souvenirs and I bought one of those 4-foot tall maps of the AT and sent it to Cora Jean so she could follow along. I still hadn't called, but we had traded bunches of emails. Most people won't understand me for not calling, but to this day I don't own or carry a phone, even in "real life." In fact, I never even called my poor, worrying mother, the whole trip thus far.

Still traumatized, no way I was going to hitch again after being in a car wreck, so I walked 5.4 miles uphill back to the trail. Attacking Bromley Mountain by way of a ski slope, I found it tough in the misty rain, but I had a new spring in my step wearing mail magic shoes. As I neared the summit, I saw a huge, white spaceship, with black windows, rise out of the fog. No need to call the 'X-Files' - it was just a ski lift terminal I wasn't expecting, sleek and modern looking.

Also known as "Sun Mountain," this summit is 3,263'. Bromley Ski Patrol warming hut, a small brown cabin with a red roof, was another secret shelter not listed in my guidebook. No water available, but hikers are welcome to sleep inside on the floor, and I know of at least one person, who slept in a stationary ski lift gondola.

Rain delay at Peru Peak Shelter. NOBOs, SOBOs, HOBOs, LTs and day trippers had gathered to wait out a rain shower. Maybe 15 in all! The sitting area along the front was full, so I climbed into a back corner. Even with the wet weather, there was lots of kidding around and laughing. DK, The Big "E" and Bubba Foot were here. I always thought DK was cute in FM's videos - and even more so in person. She joked to her friends that she wanted to spend the entire day pretending to be from another country (who would know?) and had fun chatting in a convincing British accent. Another young woman was frustrated having a Tom Petty song stuck in her head...

♪ *Don't do me like that*
Don't do me like that

What if I love you baby?
Don't do me like that ♩

But that's all she could remember, and it was driving her, and her hiking partner, crazy! He joked, "Oh my God. All she keeps doing is singing...those lines...ALL DAY." Then, with the press of a button, Papa Wolf found the tune on his iPhone and played it aloud. On cue, everyone started singing along...

♪ *Listen honey, can you see? Baby, you would bury me*
If you were in the public eye givin' someone else a try
Someone's gonna tell you lies, hurt you down inside ♩

Garden of Cairns. The next day, I came upon White Rock Cliffs. I thought I knew what to expect, but the scale and creepiness of seeing hundreds of piles and columns of stacked stones still surprised me. A result of social ceremony, this expansive monument probably started as a simple pile of stones marking a side trail to the overlook. Now a tradition, every hiker leaves their creative mark, and over time, it has evolved into this amazing sight. My buddy Fixer says:

"If you stack a rock on someone's rock, you send them luck. When someone stacks a rock on your rock, they send luck to you."

Some of the stone formations were very imaginative: stone slabs arranged like shelves and bookends, towers bridged by oblong stones or sticks and stones placed in awkward balancing acts. Overwhelmed, I simply found my rock and placed it on top of a larger rock, topped with a smaller one. A couple of mounds were in the shape of animals (called petroforms), and wish I had taken the time to summon up a turtle. Other hikers left notes, mementos, written quotes and artwork. One small stone had a black sharpie outline drawing of a rhino by...Rhyno (that's how he spelled it). He was from Virginia.

> FUN FACT: Native Americans used cairns to mark hunting paths and as a primitive form of communication, like leaving a trail of breadcrumbs. Another practice was to bend a sapling, with a rock holding the top to the ground. Sprouts grew into full-size trees, called "Indian marker trees," with their trunks making a huge ark toward the ground.

Next was Claredon Gorge, with a suspension bridge high over Mill River - very bouncy, especially on a windy day but that made it more fun. Looking down, I saw the river had been made more powerful by recent rains. Near VT-103, a large natural camping area can be found, completely flat, shaded, and lined with pine needles.

Hurricane Irene caused lots of havoc here, too, destroying vital bridges and forcing a trail relocation, including a 2½ mile road walk with a brook ford and multiple twists and turns. None of this was in the guidebook, but was well marked with signs. A happy accident, we were now led right by a hand painted sign for Tangled Roots, an organic farm stand in Shrewbury. This small board and battered shed was self-serve with a pricelist and basket in which to put money, but I saw the owners working nearby, waved and waited to meet them.

Running up first, Penny, their Australian Shepherd, was friendly as could be. So were owners Lucas and Maeve, who rolled up on a red four-wheeler and looked much too young to be farmers. They were excited to meet a hiker and had lots of questions. I bought a small bag of shiitake mushrooms (grown here on managed logs), a small chunk of white goat cheese and an ice-cold quart mason jar of goat milk. As I've never had raw goat milk before, Lucas suggested cutting it with Hersey's chocolate syrup. With or without flavoring, it was the best milk I've ever had, and I gulped down the whole jar in short order. My hosts were kind enough to walk out to their personal garden and pick a variety of fresh veggies. It doesn't get any fresher than that! Sitting in the shade, I nibbled away like a rabbit, as colorful, free range roosters strutted by.

My brown bag salad, complete with broccoli and cherry tomatoes, was a delight. Another green leafy thing I ate (no idea what it was) gave me an intense sinus reaction that literally took my breath away! Maeve even brought me homemade cookies and wild blackberries for dessert! Everything was delicious and only cost $12 with lots of leftovers. I still remember the warm welcome I felt at Tangled Roots - like it was yesterday - and it felt good supporting local people. Maeve later wrote...

"We loved the trail detour and are grateful for the 5 years we spent running Tangled Roots. Hikers often came up in groups in the evenings, since we were so close to the next shelter -- I have some great memories of sitting around the picnic table, having a beer and listening to their stories."

Chapter 20. Blame it on the Blackberries

Clockwise from left: Loner, Radio, Cool Girl, Masshole, and Daffy Duck...

Hiking in Vermont continued to impress the feeling of peacefulness upon me. Recent rains had reinvigorated the forest to try and reclaim lost ground. As I walked along, wet fern leaves reached out, soaking my legs and feet. There was also the excitement of looking for moose around every corner. Continuing down the temporary AT along snowmobile trails and gravel roads, hikers bypass more washed-out bridges cordoned off with huge concrete blocks (called icebergs), eventually returning to an actual white blazed trail.

Finding a nice little stream, I decided it was a good place to film a quick video about how I treat water and make it safe to drink. Everything was all set up when Mojo & Sky, two golden retrievers, walked up, took a drink and then laid down right in the water I was trying to show how I keep clean! These two took turns wearing a specially made doggie backpack. After chatting with their owners, Crockadily & Papa Wolf, for a moment, I simply moved upstream away from the contaminated area and started filming again, even demonstrating how I take my bottles and do "the magic shake."

Papa Wolf was the leader of a larger group that bonded like a family and looked out for one another. This fraternity had spread out over time, while keeping in touch through trail journals, private notes (for Wolfpack eyes only) and festive get-togethers. Members received an additional "wolf" name besides their traditional trail names. For example, my buddy Thirtypack from Virginia, was also known as "Fire Wolf" to his tramily (trail family).

Each mountain we encountered was bigger than the last and seemed to be preparing us, and our hiker legs, for upcoming challenges. One of those warmups was Mount Killington. Now that's a climb that just kept on comin'! Closer to the top, Cooper Lodge was built by the Vermont Forest Service in 1939. Amusing, one of the few shelters to actually have a door - had all the windows busted out. We use it in the summer and share it with skiers and snowboarders in the winter as evidenced by ski shop stickers and related graffiti. Inside, a heavily initialed oak table and obvious rodent activity.

> HIKER TIP: Known as "Beast of the East," Killington Ski Area is the largest ski resort in the Eastern US. Gondola rides are free for thru-hikers, accessed from a side trail atop Killington, or from basecamp down below.

The final push to the summit was steep, and at 4,235', was also the highest I'd been since Virginia (insert Beavis & Butt-Head laugh here, "Huh, huh... cool"). Giving me the sensation of being afraid of heights, this dome of bare rock overlooks a vast landscape of lower mountains. A little red squirrel and I shared a granola bar. This was a bold little guy, undoubtedly used to gobbling up tasty morsels dropped by hikers enjoying the view. Cora Jean informed me in an email that the Perseids Meteor Shower peak would be on this very night, and I adjusted my pace to have a chance to see it from this vantage point. There were still a few hours until dark, so I spent the extra time exploring. The fire tower's stairs were locked, and sadly, at least 5 memorials here were dedicated to people who had lost their lives to this mountain. I can only assume they died in skiing or snowboarding accidents.

Scouting a place to hang my hammock out of the wind, I found a cluster of smaller trees right near the summit already had a pair of tents underneath. No worries, I hung my hammock diagonally across a side trail, but had to get creative with my tarp tie-downs as the uneven ground was mostly solid rock. One side of the tarp was tied to pine tree branches, the other held down by my walking sticks embedded at odd angles into scarce soil.

Cooking dinner, I had to make a wind-break of loose rocks to keep my stove lit, but after a little work, enjoyed a Mountain House beef stew livened up with leftover broccoli and mushrooms from the farm stand. I shared the rest with my new neighbors. Proving it's a "small trail after all," Space Train was from my hometown of Lowell, Massachusetts. Relaxing, he drew pencil sketches of the mountain range.

Weirder & 1up (Kurt & Karen) were a cute hippie couple who planned to bring a dog, but carried a plush green frog with them instead. Weirder got his name because he packed a small guitar - not a common sight, and his girlfriend was "1up" because she fell a lot, sometimes near mushrooms that grew along the trail - like Super Mario. From New York, they were thinking about moving to Vermont, and said, "What better way to get to know a state than to walk the entire thing?" 1up always smiled and made the perfect flower child. Very pretty, even when wearing a bandana and oversized headlamp over her long brown hair. I felt completely safe with these new friends that were strangers just a few hours before.

> *HIKER TIP: Compact "Martin Backpacker" guitars are perfect for the trail. Professional models cost $200+, but knockoffs can be found on eBay for much less. Other hikers carrying instruments: Garner Brothers packed a full-sized guitar, Chatty Cathy played the ukulele and DK carried a flute. A harmonica would also be a lightweight way to make music.*

It was cold and breezy out in the open, and everyone hung out all bundled up in sleeping bags. Setting the mood for the evening, Weirder strummed upbeat cords on his mini guitar and sang 'Ya Mar' by Phish as 1up hummed along...

♪ *Remember all them times... in the pond*
Catching wild trout... till the break of dawn
Now that you've become a man... You're looking very mean... ♫

After the opening act, nature's glowing yellow sun slowly morphed into deep orange, illuminating different layers of clouds as evening fog filled the chasms. Clouds followed the sun, clearing the sky that became pitch black, dotted with stars. Nothing else seemed important, no deadlines or concerns crossed my mind, and any soreness I felt drifted away. I also felt compassion for all those who went home early. If they could have just made it through the tuff states of Virginia and Pennsylvania, the trail gets amazingly better. Intense heat was waning and everything also seemed more laidback and relaxed.

Time for the main event! Tonight, we (the Earth and everyone on it) were flying through an alien comet's debris tail. Astronomers Lewis A. Swift and Horace Tuttle discovered Comet 109P/Swift-Tuttle in 1862, though cave drawings predate them by thousands of years. A very large comet, its nucleus is twice the size of the one thought to have caused extinction to the dinosaurs. Taking 133 Earth years to orbit the Sun, its debris is drawn toward us by gravity, and burns up in our atmosphere about 50 miles over Earth, creating showers of falling stars.

Away from the lights of town, our eyes gradually adjusted to the dark, and stars began appearing in waves. Some lit up the entire Northeastern sky with long, fiery tails; others only flashed and faded away like the end of a fireworks display. In all, I saw at least 50 good ones, but whipping winds made the cold intolerable, forcing me to the warmth of my hammock.

First to break camp, I said goodbye to everyone and headed out. I often wonder if any of them think about that magical night. Weather was getting cooler and I found myself wearing an extra layer of clothing, at least until lunchtime. My trail beard had turned silver-grey and bushy, but kept me warm like a bear's fluffy winter coat.

Maine Junction, a big trail intersection where the AT and LT split, was very confusing, with signs pointing in all directions. One sign even tried to convince us that the obvious footpath behind it was "Not a Trail." Only 167 miles from Canada, NOBOs still had 469 left to Katahdin. Zachery Green of Boy Scout Troop 100 walked this way and lost his military style dog tags. I left them hanging on a signpost. Just up the road, the Inn at the Long Trail has hosted hikers since 1938. I hear the hot tub is popular, as is McGrath's Irish pub. Pet friendly rooms and fireplace suites extra.

Hikers then wind their way through Gifford Woods State Park. A restroom area, surrounded by Winnebagos and pop-up campers, has a pay shower - 50 cents buys 5 minutes. I put in plenty of quarters but the water never got hot all the way. You can buy pop and Popsicles at the beautiful CCC parkitecture office with adjoining ranger's quarters. Outside was landscaped with pink and purple flowers, each one hosting an orange and black monarch butterfly.

FUN FACT: Monarchs, on a long-distance journey of their own, originate from Canada and cover thousands of miles migrating to Mexico. Only to fly back when it gets warmer. Rare "whites" have been seen in the area.

This was the only time - on my entire hike - that I paid to camp in the woods, but $8 bought me a safe place, among giant trees, to leave my gear while exploring Rutland, third largest city in Vermont. Commuter buses stop at a convenience store near the campground every other hour and cost $2 for the trip to civilization, one way. On the ride down, I met a friendly thru-hiker from Italy who had gotten the flu and was headed for the bus terminal, then home.

Double the size of most trail towns, Rutland counts 16,495 people. Tall buildings and storefronts stood on both sides of Merchant's Row. My favorite was Vermont Country Toymaker, with wooden airplanes, rocking horses and a ride-on Choo-Choo hanging from the façade. A shaggy street performer playing acoustic guitar on a street corner wouldn't take my dollar bill. Laughing, he said, "Man, I don't play for the money!" I think he may have been one of the Allman Brothers.

First stop: Rutland "Free" Library. This handsome, 3-story brick building was the former courthouse. Once inside, hikers must show ID and register for a legit library card. Free, but it seems every single library has their own policies. There needs to be a uniform plan and common rules for trail towns along the AT. Here, guests only get 30 minutes to use the computers. That's just not enough time.

A teenage boy sitting next to me obviously had a learning disability, but wouldn't stop talking and showing me pictures of scantily-clad girls on his Facebook. He would tap me on the shoulder, click on a picture and ask, "Do you think she would go out with me?" Tap, click, repeat...I tried to encourage him, "Just go for it," but found it impossible to concentrate on what I was doing. Cora Jean had sent several long emails, at least one a day since the last time I checked. I replied to one and took pictures of the rest (off the computer screen) to read later. I had written her a poem, reciting verse to myself while hiking. Finally writing it on the back cover of my guidebook. Nervous, I transferred it to a greeting card and dropped it in a mailbox.

The 12 Tribes religious cult runs another hiker hostel and organic restaurant here, this one called "The Yellow Deli." One of the men working here was on a thru-hike years ago when he stopped for a rest, and liked it so much he never left! There are men's and women's bunkrooms, separating couples even if they're married, and shirts must be worn at all times. If you can live with that, I think you'll have an enjoyable stay. $20/suggested donation. They also own the shop next door, Simon the Tanner - Your Family Outfitter.

That's where I found Radio washing windows while doing work for stay as his buddy Masshole joked, "You missed a spot!" Masshole was, of course, from Massachusetts. Except for tattoo sleeves and red hair, he was a dead ringer for actor Zach Galifianakis, who plays in those dreadful 'Hangover' movies. They invited me to join them for a ski lift ride. Daffy Duck...and his cute friend came too. We all caught a bus and the driver took pictures with each of our cameras.

The Pro Shop at Killington K-1 ski area specializes in skis and snowboards, but also sells drinks and snacks. The cable ride stretches 6,453' with a 1,642' rise in elevation. You could guess from Atari style graphics on all the cars, that this lift was probably built in the 1980's.

Waiting our turn, we scanned a dozen different warning signs. To name a few: "Poisonous plants;" "No dogs allowed;" "Do not swing or bounce cabin;" and another that read: "Maximum cabin capacity 1,400 pounds/or 8 people." We joked Radio's backpack would put us over the limit. His elaborate system of straps alone probably weighed more than my pack and making it even heavier, a pair of crocs dangled from a string, a blue foam sleeping pad hung off the bottom and trekking poles stuck out the top. A 1-liter bottle of Coke in his left pocket, a full bag of Chex Mix in the right!

We climbed through the narrow doorway of our gondola, which rocked back and forth and never really stopped all the way, making it  a little tricky getting all of us in and situated. Not for folks afraid of heights, it got very creaky swinging over support towers. Otherwise, it was fun gliding over streams as mountain bikers raced down the mountainside below. Getting out on top, I took pictures as Radio stood scratching his beard trying to decipher a cluster of maps looking for the correct blue blaze back to the AT. He had already beaten Lyme disease, but was now diagnosed with vitamin B_{12} deficiency. Symptoms include confusion, weakness, depression and psychosis. The most common cause is decreased food intake. Radio had lost a lot of weight, but not the dramatic transformation I experienced.

After saying goodbye to everyone, I rode down the mountain, took a shuttle bus back to town and enjoyed an awesome AYCE Hibachi Buffet with a big plate of chocolate pudding for dessert. But at the bus station, I learned the hard way that AWOL had printed a fatal error. Shocked, the last bus back up the mountain stopped running at 5:00 p.m., not 7:00 p.m. as listed. Huge problem! My warm hammock was calling my name from the campground 14 miles away (uphill), and it was already getting dark.

Refusing to hitch after nearly being kidnaped last time, I reluctantly asked a Texaco attendant if he could please call a taxi. A half hour later, a blue minivan pulled up, no taxi sign or nothing. The gruff lady then charged me $80 for the 10-minute ride. I could have stayed in a nice hotel, took the bus home in the morning for $2 and still had some money left over. Disgusted with my carelessness with money, this episode ruined an otherwise fun NERO day.

Around beautiful Kent Pond, Hurricane Irene had washed out creek beds and left footbridges tipped over. Next stop was Lookout Farm, a rustic A-frame cabin on private land. Hikers are welcome to visit or stay the night, so long as they don't leave a mess or make fires. Of course, the fireplace had been recently used; Bonkman had vandalized a sign asking us to respect private property (changing his scribble to

Bonkadad), and lazy bastards left 3 empty liquor bottles and three empty fuel canisters (sounds like a bad country song). Thankfully, this was the only trash I saw in all of Vermont. My pack was full so I didn't volunteer to tote any garbage this time.

Run down, the front porch had holes, shingles on the roof were gone or falling off and outside stairs with a single handrail to a lookout platform on the roof were very rickety. For safety reasons, I doubted this cabin would be open to visitors much longer but my view from 2,384'

was worth the risk. Way off in the distance, one tall mountain stood above the rest. I knew whatever mountain it was, we would probably be climbing it. Checking the guidebook, this was Mount Moosilauke, the first mountain in The Whites, still 68 miles away. *Update: Lookout cabin now has a new roof and stairs!*

Even a loner likes to see fresh faces, and the hiker bubble I was in now included Otto, Perch, Apollo, Rampage and his dog, Sandy. A tall, thin man in his 50's, Otto had a thin white beard, wore a blue bandana and pair of knee braces. A no-nonsense retired teacher from Tennessee, he was a former ALDHA board member. Also on his résumé: two AT thru-hikes, two PCT thru-hikes, 14 years of "Hard Core" trail maintenance and an additional 700 volunteer hours. Otto had a self-confidence about him that I admired, but even though he never said so, I always felt he disapproved of my ultralight gear. His best buddy, Perch, was from Florida. Much younger, with dark hair under a green Marine style hat, he was a friendly guy, but kind of reserved. He did explain that he got his name because he liked to crouch on top of stuff. Apollo was a cool dude, with short blond hair and a blazing red beard. He had previously hiked with Apache.

With several sunny days, I couldn't believe how every afternoon was nicer than the last. Some of the trail was along old wagon roads lined with stonewalls. What was the most random thing I found on the trail? How about the rusty white roof of a VW bus, planted right next to the trail? It must have been a heck of a project (or fraternity joke) to get something this awkward so deep into the woods. I also kept seeing plastic hoses strung from tree to tree, seemingly for miles. After a while, I figured out they were for collecting maple syrup.

I crossed White River over Patriots' Bridge, built in 2006, and dedicated to soldiers of Desert Storm. Down in the river, a School Zone sign stood eerily knee deep in water, washed there by Irene. Entering the one road village of West Hartford, I was again disappointed to find the post office had been shuttered and my drop box redirected 4 miles from nowhere. At this point, I became frustrated with my guidebook and found it useless in these matters. I do understand most discrepancies were due to Irene, or government incompetence, but this was getting old! If I hadn't had some cash to top-off my food bag, I would have been up a creek.

West Hartford Village Store was the only place to eat. Hiker friendly, a covered pack rack custom built especially for us, hung outside. Inside was regular resupply, and the Full Belly Deli (great name!). I recommend the Western Burger with melted mozzarella cheese, jalapenos and onion rings on top! Hikers were welcome to use a faucet outside, but the water was bright white and cloudy.

> HIKER TIP: Foamy white water is usually caused by harmless, dissolved air. Play Mr. Wizard and watch it for a moment - bubbles should clear from the bottom to the top and be safe to consume. DO NOT DRINK if it has an unpleasant odor or taste. This may be caused by a faulty septic tank. Yuck! (The only other time I saw this was at Fontana Dam.)

I checked the community message board; anyone need a Nigerian Dwarf goat for $100, OBO? "He is shy at first with new people, but will come around fast." The road walk out of town was fun, with brown horses playfully biting each other and creative yard art to admire: an upside-down toilet plunger doubled as a redneck birdfeeder and a lazy junkyard dog was crafted from an old well bucket, iron plant stand and bent fan blade.

Back in the woods, an unusual shelter, "Happy Hill," reminded me of a gingerbread house with oversized green metal roof, tiny windows and long gables. Unfortunately, the brook had run dry. For a privy, there was your classic quarter moon design, with green paint missing along the bottom of the door, chewed off by porcupines. The register had an illustration called, "Happy Hill vs. Evil Hill," depicting the shelter as heaven with dancing angels, hikers holding hands and a rainbow. While Evil Hill was being struck by lightning and all the hikers were on fire, being attacked by demons with pitchforks. Artist unknown. I also read entries by Prophet, Canecutter and ezNOMAD.

Looking over another forgotten home place junk pile, this time from the 1930's or 40's, I found an old pickup truck door, old stove parts including a fold-up bread box, cook pans with rust holes and lots of bottles - broken and unbroken. There was also a set of brass bedposts that could still be used if you wanted to pack them out several miles to the nearest road.

I had planned to camp directly on the outskirts of the next town, but didn't make it so far as that. A clearing under some power lines was bursting with plump and juicy berries! Picking and eating, I stepped deeper into thorns until I found myself surrounded, knee deep, in prickly bushes. Tired and stuffed, I only walked a few paces into the trees when a couple of men on 4-wheelers noisily bounced up the service road. They stopped for a moment, but left when they found their honey hole picked clean.

In the middle of the night, I was awakened by something walking in the leaves coming right towards me. My headlamp was no help, so when it got too close for comfort, I snapped a pic with my camera and flash. Startled, it immediately turned tail and waddled away. Looking at the photo, eyes appeared to glow bright yellow and it was an intimidating dark black color with silver spiked quills along his back. A porcupine! Porcupines are famous for stealing shoes, so I hung mine from my hammock lines after that. Good thing I'm a light sleeper or I may have been hiking with one shoe!

> FUN FACT: A member of the rodent family, porcupines are nocturnal. They can have up to 30,000 quills, but it's only a myth they can project them. Spines are only released by contact or by shaking its body.

Cooking breakfast, some nice people walked up, all smiles except their leader - Mr. Serious. He was indeed serious as a heart attack and wouldn't even dare crack a smile for a group picture. Heide, a woman wearing all black with gaiters up to her knees, was a section-hiker from Germany. *Update: I've traded emails with Mr. Serious a few times since and he's a really nice guy. His actual trail name is Zenith.*

HIKER TIP: Some hikers wear "gaiters" to keep rocks and mud from getting into their boots. Resembling chaps worn by cowboys, they also offer protection from snakes bites and low branches.

Walking into a neighborhood cul-de-sac, we were greeted by a trail-head kiosk with handwritten notes: A lost dog "medium sized, mostly white with spots seen walking by himself, but staying on the path headed south." Another was posted by thru-hiker Jeronimo, about money he found on the trail. He left it at a police station.

Norwich really rolls out the red carpet for thru-hikers! Several houses along Elm Street had trail magic totes out front with lids to keep snacks dry. Short & Sweet came running out with gifts of fresh fruit and sandwiches, then invited us to sleep in her garage! She was also looking for "a strong young man to help her in the garden," with pay. I quickly scarfed down the watermelon, said thank you, and kept moving. I couldn't help but wonder how long she watched out the window, waiting for random hikers to come by. She also gave us booklets called 'A.T. Hiker FAQs,' similar to ones used in Waynesboro. This booklet had maps, bus schedules and a list of trail angels willing to shuttle or host hikers for the night. Other pages had directions to libraries, hospitals, etc. More so-called "trail towns" should make these available.

Everything in Norwich is situated around Main Street. The post office resembled a horse stable, complete with faux gas lanterns hanging outside. The helpful postmaster here called around for 10 minutes, finding my misplaced mail drops sent to "ghost offices" that had closed unexpectedly, and had them forwarded again.

Dan & Whit's General Store is a gas station/deli/hardware/grocery store serving the community since 1891. Their motto is "If we don't have it - you don't need it." They offer free, day old sandwiches to thru-hikers - just show your backpack. Out front was an old piano painted white, with red and blue hippy designs, for a community art project called, 'Hands on Pianos.' Spreading the gift of music, 50 used pianos were cleaned, tuned, decorated and placed in 10 towns throughout the area. Each looked after by a "piano angel," who covered up their assigned instrument with a tarp in rainy weather. Other designs included: "Freaked Out Zebra," "Disco Piano" and "Blue Moon." The latter had blue whales and skyscrapers painted all over it. Mine was #29: "Paisley Piano," created by artist Sandra Williams. I couldn't help having a little fun making a video pretending to hit the keys while the Charlie Brown and Snoopy theme played in the background! It fooled lots of viewers, but I revealed at the end it was a joke.

By now, you know I love message boards, and Dan & Whit's had the longest one I've ever seen! The whole front of the building was entirely covered in post it notes and Xeroxed ads of all kinds: cats and dogs lost or found, Tai chi and guitar lessons, call to musicians, religious tracts, tree pruning, horses and houses.

> FUN FACT: Bob Keeshan, television's "Captain Kangaroo" lived in Norwich. Also, the Norwich Inn, was inspiration for the 'Bob Newhart' TV show, set here in Norwich, but to me, looked more like Norman Bates' house.

A 2-mile road walk near the turnpike connects Norwich and Hanover. There was a perfectly good sidewalk, but a narrow, well-worn footpath in the soft manicured grass paralleled it. After 1,800 miles of walking in the woods, hikers instinctively take to the turf because concrete hurts our feet. Finally, I came to a bridge crossing the beautiful Connecticut River marking the Vermont/New Hampshire state line. Done were the 150 miles of VT. I was having a great time, but needed to get my act together, as SOBOs kept reminding me... *"The Whites are coming."*

Chapter 21. Into the White

Baker Library Bell Tower, Dartmouth College. Center of their 269-acre campus.

New Hampshire, Live Free or Die! It was a beautiful day, and I looked forward to the spoils of town. A cairn of rocks marked the front of Robinson Hall, Dartmouth Outing Club headquarters. Founded in 1909, this is home to ski and rowing teams, but membership is open to anyone interested in the outdoors. Thru-hikers can leave their packs in the basement while exploring town (no camping please). Oddly, the hiker box was filled with "Out of date" meds.

NOBOs and SOBOs intermix here. You'd think we'd all be one big happy family, but there's hazing that goes both ways. SOBOs feel superior for doing the hardest part first, starting at Katahdin. We NOBOs joke back that they're doing the whole trail going downhill! One SOBO even told me I was "too clean" to be a thru-hiker. I took that as a compliment, but wasn't meant to be. All of this to say, members of either group would still help the other if needed.

Ivy League Dartmouth College (DC) was established 1769, in the name of King George III:

"For the education and instruction of Youth of the Indian Tribes in this Land in reading, writing & all parts of Learning."

Today, schools are open to everyone and teach Medicine, Engineering, Liberal Arts (problem solving, communication) and Business. The Dartmouth campus encompasses 9 libraries and the Hood Museum of Art, one of the oldest in North America. Many athletic collectives challenge athletes who compete in impressive stadiums. Large dorms, halls and Baker Library Clock Tower line 3 sides of manicured "Dartmouth Green," where a few remaining hemlock trees have survived blight and are cared for by groundskeepers. It was beautiful, not to mention all the cute coeds jogging around! Besides the traditional campus, Dartmouth owns 4,500-acres around approaching Mt. Moosilauke, and an additional 27,000-acres elsewhere. DOC also maintains the next 50 miles of the AT heading north. Blazes are still white, but trail signs are black/bright orange, Dartmouth colors.

> FUN FACT: Famous Dartmouth alumni: Theodor Geisel (aka Dr. Seuss), Fred Rogers of 'Mister Rogers' Neighborhood,' and Mindy Kaling from 'The Office' and 'The Mindy Project.'

> FUN FACT: Cult classic 'National Lampoon's Animal House,' 1978, starring John "Bluto" Belushi and his misfit group of fraternity brothers, was based on writer Chris Miller's fraternity days at Dartmouth.

Another fun thing about Hanover is that all the shops and restaurants have special offers for thru-hikers. I had fun bumming with Daffy Duck...who already knew all the stops. Cool kid, but sure dropped F-bombs a lot (this 4-letter word was even part of his trail name!). Try to patronize hiker friendly shops if their products or services are useful to you...

- **Ramunto's Pizzeria:** Free slice (I bought a few extras).
- **Metro Bakery and Café:** Free bagel (after lunchtime).
- **Mountain Goat Outfitter:** Free Snickers.
- **Dr. Sam's Eye Care:** Free eyeglass cleaning and repair.
- **Lou's Bakery:** Free donut or cruller.
- **Bagel Basement:** Free bagel.

Richard W. Black Senior Center wasn't handing out free senior citizens, but I got a hot shower and laundry for $5. Both amenities were in one small room, so I took a shower and washed all my clothes at the same time. A treasure trove, the hiker box/lost & found held a pair of boots, climbing rope and a decent daypack. I scored some lightly used socks (put in with my wash) and considered a blue soccer jersey, #69, but decided against it, not wanting to change my trail name. Other hikers who also enjoyed the facilities left amusing post-its. One read:

"I have not felt this clean in a long time. Thanks!" Signed, "A formally stinky hiker from Holland, Jiffy Pop." Additional notes were left by...

- **Johnny Rocket**, TX, NOBO. (Always drew a cartoon rocket.)
- **P2 (p-squared)**, PA, NOBO.
- **Voltron**, FL, NOBO. (Friendly, smiling man with a mustache.)
- **Split & Two Step**, CA, SOBOs.
- **Jukebox Lion Killer**, MA, Flip-flop.

Howe Public Library would make a good model for other AT trail communities to follow. No library cards, no fees, no time limits, shelves of free (discard) books and magazines and no waiting, as there was a dedicated bank of computers just for us. Summit pictures of past thru-hikers adorned a blow-up map of the AT on the wall. I had my personal PC here, but as nice as this library was, the Wi-Fi connection still didn't work well. So, I hung out with Weezy, who showed me an article on Whiteblaze.com about volunteers discovering Indian artifacts while building an AT shelter in North Carolina. This library also had a variety of framed artwork that patrons could check out and take home to display. Very nice!

I finally received a couple of drop boxes that had been delayed, and it was nice to get birthday cards and letters from home, even if they were over a month late because of misdirection. Hanover is compact, but efficient, with no vacant buildings. Strolling down sidewalks of Main Street, the AT passes sorority houses and telephone poles with flyers for local punk bands. Lots of students use bicycles for transportation, and rows of them were chained to bike racks all over town. I was here on a weekend and making me uncomfortable, this was the largest crowd I mingled with while on the AT. With few hotels, rooms here cost $100+ a night, but hikers are welcome to camp for free on the far side of town behind some soccer fields. A trio of tents were already set-up, and I made camp a few hundred feet into the woods.

Returning to town the next morning to finish my chores, I found a hiker in his sleeping bag, out in the open, between the fields. His wooden walking stick lay beside him, just like last time I found some-one passed out in the middle of the trail. Funny, it turned out to be the same dude both times! Thirtypack. I heard the story from him later - his original idea was to cowboy camp in the middle of a soccer field because it sounded like fun...until automatic sprinklers went off in the middle of the night! He had also been bitten on the behind by a black widow. What an eventful thru-hike!

My AM/FM radio had died again, so this time I bought an RCA MP3 player and loaded it with my favorite music. The tiny red device only cost $20 and used a single AAA battery.

Boogying along back on the trail, it wasn't until 6 miles later that I realized my blue bowl was missing. I had attached it to the top of my backpack with rubber bands, where it usually stayed secure. But this time, it fell off somewhere with no way to know how far back. Walking as fast as possible, I made backwards ground until dark. My water treatment was in the bowl, forcing me to drink untreated water. My lighter was also MIA, so I couldn't cook the Knorr's pasta Alfredo I was looking forward to. Not that I had my bowl to cook it in. Instead, I made tortillas covered in peanut butter with raisins on top. Not bad, but the loss of a 99¢ Bic lighter made a big difference, and from then on, I carried it in my pack's hip pocket. I wouldn't take it for granted again.

That night I heard a creature from the woods trotting up the trail, then stop for a moment, probably sniffing around. It let out a series of squeaky barks, then ran off. No, it wasn't a porcupine this time, or the Snarly Yow, but a curious fox saying: "What the heck are you doing in my woods?"

Come morning, a man and a young woman walked up. Castaway was from Arizona and very knowledgeable about tree species, as he had worked in the lumber industry. His friend, Kleenex, hailed from South Dakota and cursed with bad allergies, was fighting a cold worthy of her trail name. We had never met, but she had seen my name in log-books and wondered why I was going the wrong way. After explaining my situation, she said they saw something blue in the woods. 10 minutes later, I found my bowl right where Kleenex said it was, contents unharmed.

On the South peak of Moose Mountain, 2,290', was another somber airplane crash site, the 4th one I came across on this trip. Disintegrated upon impact, parts of twisted wreckage lay in a small pile. Northeast Airlines Flight 946 went down 10/25/1968, killing 32 of 42 passengers. Rescue workers struggled to reach the crash site as a bulldozer cleared a wider path. In town, cars formed a circle around Dartmouth Greens, using their headlights to illuminate an emergency helicopter-landing pad that airlifted doctors in, and the injured out. Two passengers escaped certain death. One survived after switching seats with another who died in the crash; the second made a last-minute cancellation.

Moose Mountain Shelter was classic Adirondack-style, built by the Dartmouth Outing Club (DOC). Reunited with my cook bowl, I cooked instant potatoes and made pepperoni hobo wraps, adding a couple of hot sauce packets for flavor. Deadeye and Castaway were having lunch, too. Then Weezy's dog Aisha showed up, and 15 minutes later, Weezy. He immediately climbed into the shelter and started searching the cracks between the rafters, looking for hidden contraband (Weezy said the best joint he ever smoked was found in a shelter). He was sporting a new blackeye, given to him by fellow thru-hiker, Otto, during a bar fight in Hanover. With no luck on the Easter egg hunt, Weezy collected spent cigarette butts from the ground around the fire pit, carefully tore them apart making a small pile of leftover tobacco, rolled it into a pitiful looking blunt, then lit up with a sigh of relief. I got the feeling all this was a ritual he performed at every shelter he visited.

This whole area was dry, but I passed on the water source consisting of a few mud puddles. At a previous spring, I had to follow a damp streambed until finding the top half of a rusty 55-gallon drum placed into the ground. With only a couple inches of standing water, I used my cook cup to fill my bowl. I filtered the yellowish liquid with a bandanna and treated it, but this was the most questionable water I drank the whole trip.

You never know where conversations might go. Making miles with Talloaf the Trail Ent (from Charlotte, North Carolina), Weezy and Aisha, somehow we got talking about survival reality TV shows. Weezy was a fan of a corny program called 'Mantracker' and wanted to be a contestant. He planned to call its producers, telling them "I can kick Mantrackers ass!" Premise: Terry "Mantracker" Grant is described as a full-blooded cowboy and search and rescue veteran of 25 years. On horseback, he uses his experience and grit following clues to catch 2 worthy adversaries. "The prey," as they're called, only have a map, compass and 36 hours to travel 25 miles through unknown wilderness. Their prize if they reach the finish line? Good ole bragging rights! Catch phrase: "Know your land, know your prey."

Just up the road, a hand painted sign pointed toward Bill Ackerly's house. Better known as "The Ice Cream Man," he's another longtime friend of the AT. Out of town, he still left a cooler filled with sodas and a note inviting hikers to camp in the backyard or take a swing at croquet. Everyone visits the Ice Cream Man and a tattered notebook on his porch is perhaps the most accurate record on the trail. It had been signed over 600 times this season so far: Trail name, age, town/state and starting dates (thru-hikers know their start date like they know their birthday). For comparison, here's mine and some NOBOs I haven't mentioned before...

- **Loner**, 40, Greenville, South Carolina, 4-7.
- **John Wayne**, 25, Ashland, Wisconsin, 4-21.
- **Mr. Fabulous**, 40, New York, New York, 3-19.
- **Seminole**, 23, Killington, Vermont, 4-8.
- **King of the Hill**, 40, Wichita, Kansas, 4-9.
- **Spirit**, 63, Chattanooga, Tennessee, 3-11.
- **EZ & Gravity**, 50, Clarkston, Michigan, 3-30.

Smarts Mountain was challenging, even with assistance of rebar steps imbedded into bare stone, some of which had beautiful white quartz inclusions with shiny, gold specks. From the cab of a fire tower on top of Smarts Mountain, 3,230', you even could see the arch of the horizon in the distance. A big crowd of people here were having lunch and telling stories, one about a hiker who was named "Mosey" for a reason. He had hiked only 3 miles and took 3 zeros!

Only a few feet away was an old fire warden's cabin. Used as a shelter for years, wooden doorframes were covered from top to bottom with carved initials. The only furniture was a handsome stool made from a tree trunk, with roots for feet. Hikers are just happy to have a roof over their heads and real glass windows separating themselves from the elements. Abandoned items: novel 'Panther in the Sky' (by James Alexander Thorn, about Shawnee leader Tecumseh), a broken mirror, used AA batteries, aluminum foil, one black glove, trial size 'OFF' bug repellant wipes and a single section torn from another book (check future shelters for subsequent episodes).

Someone had spelled out "400" with fern leaves, marking how few miles we had to go. An unfair comparison: A NASCAR race car running 150 miles an hour, making a couple of pit stops for gas and tires, could cover that distance in around 3 hours! Walking, I figured it would take me another month and a half. That evening, I found the bubble all camped out on the other side of Mount Mist. Everyone was buzzing about The Whites - the closer we got to the legendary span of mountains, the more intimidating they became. I finally made the Knorr's Pasta side I'd been craving. I don't know why they call these "sides," they do just fine by themselves.

Emerging at a gravel parking area on NH-25, this must be a rough neck of the woods as a flyer read:

"CAR BROKEN INTO AND PACKS STOLEN. REWARD OFFERED. Grey REI 'Flash' backpack, tent, sleeping pad, purple sleeping bag, glasses, medications, NY driver's license, journal, etc."

A setback like this could be a hike-ending event. Besides the aggravation of fixing a broken car window and the invasion of privacy, replacing all that gear could cost hundreds of dollars that might not be available near the end of a thru-hike. The driver's license could be impossible to obtain without returning home and would make it difficult to replenish prescriptions. I hope Coconut was able to continue, but his name is not included on the seasons list of 2,000 milers.

After a short road walk into Glencliff, New Hampshire, there's a rundown house known as Hikers Welcome Hiker Hostel (that's how it's written). After picking up a drop box from the post office in another home across the street (town is so small, PO box numbers didn't reach triple digits), my plan was to do laundry and take a shower. But there was already a line for the washing machine and the shower was a moldy contraption with blue tarps for walls. Like a shantytown, the backyard was inundated with hikers and hobos, metal pole tarpaulin shelters and rent-a-tents. That said, Welcome Hostel had a unique charm and was a magnet for hiking legends telling tales while hanging out around a fire pit surrounded by a handsome sofa made of stones.

An impromptu thrift shop in the kitchen had jackets hanging from a rack, priced as marked. The messy hiker box was a set of woven fruit baskets overflowing with odds-and-ends and who-knows-what. The clubhouse had a '70s refrigerator, '80s microwave and a '90s computer. Everything still worked and I read an email from Cora Jean saying she liked the poem I sent. An entire wall was lined with hundreds of DVDs, but disappointingly, just an old square TV to watch them on. Hikers sat in plastic beach chairs around a large table, loosely reminding me of club meetings on the 'Sons of Anarchy' motorcycle gang TV show. Except on top of this table were miscellaneous remote controls and condiments, instead of guns and gavel.

Using a checklist and envelope honor system, you can pay for the night or pig-out on frozen dinners and microwave corndogs. My haul: (1) frozen pizza, (2) candy bars, (4) Pop Tarts, (1) ice cream sandwich and (3) Ramen (for later). Total: $10.50. Just for fun, I tried a Moxie soft drink. It had a thick consistency like cough syrup with a bittersweet taste. Accommodations offered: Overnight bunk with shower - $20, or, tent site and shower - $15. *Update: A beautiful, 2-story bunk house has been added to accommodate 24 additional hikers.*

> FUN FACT: Moxie was first marketed in 1876 as a medicinal tonic called "Moxie Nerve Food." Advertised heavily, "moxie" became an actual word in the English language meaning, "courage, daring, or spirit."

I never got to meet Packrat, owner and a triple crowner (AT '94, PCT '99, CDT '06), but a stocky man with round glasses and ballcap on backwards walked in and started digging through the fridge. I recognized him immediately from watching AT documentaries - Baltimore Jack. After graduating college with a degree in history, he became disenchanted with the "real world" and started hiking - a lot. He thru-hiked the AT 8 times. Winters, he worked at outfitters to save up for the following season. Maybe it was in his blood; after all, his father helped build original sections of the AT. Larger than life, Baltimore

Jack asked our trail names and, holding court, gave us tips and secret stealth camping sites for The Whites we were about to enter. This chance meeting would be like Michael Jordan showing up at a high school basketball team's locker room just before a big game and giving them pointers.

Gumby from Tennessee, liked the atmosphere and was staying the night. I can't say we were best buddies, but we crossed paths several times and think she felt comfortable around me. I admired her because she started with her brother and continued alone after he bailed out. She had a wry sense of humor and I remember her rolling her eyes when a smitten hiker introduced himself, using his "real name." Another time, Gumby and I were gathering water at a stream where she was using her high tech Steripen to treat water. The device looks like a mini Star Wars lightsaber. Joking, I told her it only works if you make sound effects. On cue, she started humming "ZZZZZRRRR."

> HIKER TIP: Steripen water purifiers use UV light to destroy 99.9% of bacteria, viruses and protozoa (Giardia). Weight 3.6 oz. Prices range from $50-$100. Requires 2 (oddball) CR123 batteries.

The next big challenge: The Whites - 120 miles of high peaks and rugged terrain. The first mountain is Mount Moosilauke, affectionately known as "The Gentle Giant," and has been climbed by locals for nearly 300 years. Like a stairway, the incline rose ten miles up-and-over on a path composed entirely of stones, and was fenced-in by tall trees on either side. A sign warned...

"This trail is extremely tough. If you lack experience, please use another trail. Take special care to avoid tragic results."

Here, we enter the alpine zone. We've been on balds and bare spots before, but this was our first time above the true "tree line," defined by trees less than 8 feet tall. Gradually, mere hikers seem to grow taller than the forest around us and full-grown, adult trees become short as bushes, allowing unobstructed views in all directions. Then, there are no trees at all - just large expanses of rocks, pebbles and yellow groundcover struggling with all its might to stay adhered to the dirt to which it was still able to cling. In treeless alpine zones, trails are usually lined on each side with stones and the path is worn bare by erosion and hiking boots. Cairns of stacked stones are also used for navigation, especially helpful in snowy or foggy conditions when painted blazes on rocks become invisible. Cairns here were especially tall - some taller than myself.

> **HIKER TIP: DO NOT** *enter this section without a guidebook. The Whites are no joke and my AWOL was essential. I also recommend carrying all your cold-weather gear as conditions can be very unpredictable.*

Mount Moosilauke is 4,802' and has 360° views. Brother and sister mountains rose out of the horizon like a pod of whales in an ocean of blue sky. As majestic as this was, exposed to elements and without protection from trees, harsh winds made it uncomfortable to stay very long. The only refuge, the cobbled foundation of Prospect House, opened in 1860 and burned down in 1942, I huddled within the remains of its remains. Here, I met 2 former Dartmouth graduates who have hiked together to the top of this peak, every year, for over 2 decades. It's the only time they get to see each other. Unwisely, they placed their camera on a rock and it was blown off and destroyed. They settled for a picture I took with their cellphone, and returned the favor as I struggled against the wind to stand next to the summit sign.

With the sun setting, I had to get down this mountain, but the grade was the steepest we had encountered on this trip thus far. There was no hiking, only rocks to walk on, one step at a time, each a foot lower than the last, with no way to make time. Beaver Brook Shelter is the only legal camping site on this mountain, but long before arriving, I heard a blaring radio and dozens of people talking loudly, the first of many such groups I would encounter. College orientation kids. Freshmen getting to know each other before starting the new school year. Tents were crammed - almost on top of each other - resembling a Spring break party in the woods. Amused, I watched a group of boys and girls trying hopelessly to hang a food bag. Standing in a semi-circle, one member would attempt to throw a rock tied to a string over a branch much too high. Kids on the other side of the circle either tried to catch it, or scrambled for cover, laughing and screaming. The amusing part - they would then reform the circle with someone else taking a turn pitching the deadly projectile - again and again.

> HIKER TIP: To hang a food bag, tie your string to a rock (I prefer a stick)
> and arch it over a branch just out of reach. You'll be tempted to throw the
> whole bag, food and all, but it could get stuck in the tree or damage food.

No way was I going to stay the night with all these obnoxious people, so after a quick visit to the "Privy of Illusion," I precariously found my way down the trail of jagged rocks using my headlamp. Halfway down, I found a tiny nook literally a step off trail. These trees were still on the thin side, and when I climbed into my hammock, they bowed toward each other at the top and my butt dragged the ground. Rest still came easy, as only feet away were some of the prettiest waterfalls on the AT, cascades creating soothing sounds.

At daybreak, rocks were slick with dew and the steepest section had steps made of wooden railroad ties embedded into granite with rebar spikes. A blue blazed bypass is available in bad weather. At the bottom, I was very surprised to find Miss Janet at Kinsman Notch parking area, here all the way from Erwin, Tennessee. She's the one who hosted the AT film festival I went to months ago. Sadly, her iconic, burgundy four-door had given up the ghost. She now sported a white minivan. "Bounce Box" was written on a back window, and her mini disco ball transferred from one rearview mirror to the other. Ranger Bill, Roboticus and Croc Hunter  were about to go up the mountain I just came down. Miss Janet suggested it would be easier to do this one going south.

Miss Janet then drove me to North Woodstock, New Hampshire, where 2 small hotels were situated across the street from each other. For some reason, Miss Janet was very persistent I go to one and not the other. I tried to explain that my motel had Wi-Fi, but she gave me a lecture about needing to rest in town and not "play" on the computer. However, she still dropped me off where I asked. I know she meant well and everyone on the trail is lucky she's a part of it.

France & Dennis, owners of Carriage Motel, were friendly and asked all about my trip. My $74.12 room was a time capsule, with authentic 1960's wallpaper and paneling, lamps and linens. Curious, a self-explanatory sign posted just above the thermostat gave me a chuckle: "The heat will not work with the window open." The hot shower was one of the best on the trail and I was impressed to find a complimentary, blue, see-through plastic comb with the hotel's logo printed on it. This 10¢ novelty matched my spoon and became part of my kit. I wigged out every time I misplaced either one. But upon further inspection, I noticed a common item was missing from the room. There was a bible, micro-fridge, microwave and phonebook. I had finally gotten up the nerve to call Cora Jean, but there was no freaking phone! Don't all motel rooms have phones?

I retrieved my PC from the post office, but the Internet wouldn't connect and I got extremely frustrated. After an hour of clicking useless buttons, I was ready to throw the stupid thing out the window! No phone or working Internet, but my room did have a vintage "Magic Fingers Relaxation Service." I dropped a couple of quarters into the metal box on the wall...and...nothing happened. So I gave it a good rap with my fist and it started making a faint buzzing sound, just no action. To be fair, a short time later the bed vibrated mildly and felt pretty good. But by the end of the cycle, the whole mattress was bouncing up and down wildly to the point I left the room, embarrassed. There's no "stop" button on those things! During the night, I heard beds going off in adjacent rooms. "Try it, you'll feel great!"

After starting to nuke a couple of dogs in the microwave, I went to the office and asked my hosts to please reset the Internet router. When I came back, smoke was billowing out of my windows! The hotdogs were burnt to a crusty crisp and the whole room now stunk like... burnt hotdogs. I had accidently set the antique microwave dial timer to 20 minutes - instead of 2! By the way, the router reset fixed my connection problem, and I found a working pay phone at the gas station across the street. Spending a handful of quarters, Cora Jean and I really hit it off.

It was fun exploring the hotel's huge man cave for guests, with a central fireplace, working jukebox, pool table, air hockey, piano, etc. There was also a picture of a car that crashed into the swimming pool. Vintage pinball games included Water World (with Kevin Costner), Bad Girls and another Lethal Weapon III. That makes at least (4) of this exact model I've seen along the AT! A thru-hiker could get lots of practice on this title, visiting convenience stores, pizza joints and laundromats (another reason to carry quarters).

> FUN FACT: Twin Galaxies Intergalactic Scoreboard lists the official world record high score, on Lethal Weapon III, at a whopping 575,338,379 points, set by pinball wizard "Daz66" on a private machine in his home.

I finally got to open a food box haul from SmackNC. Besides meals and candy, he included HEET and even a Dr. Pepper. He sent it weeks before, but I had to bounce it up the trail several times. That's ok, because it came in handy here. Joe has been watching, encouraging and supporting YouTube hikers for years. Thanks!

The towns of North Woodstock and Lincoln sit side-by-side, with the AT circling 16 miles around the mountain ridge from one to the other. Stopping at Eliza Brook Shelter, I found that the metal bear box had a dozen empty Gatorade bottles inside, probably well-intentioned trail magic that will now have to be packed out by some poor ridge runner. Leaving trash is not always intentional. I lost my new bottle of HEET on this section and decided not to go back for it. Ramen is a hundred times better cooked, but room temperature soup isn't as bad as it sounds. Sometimes I added a little coco-mix to give it a little kick.

Already back in town, I needed to check the mail, but mostly wanted to call Cora Jean (I was hooked, too). I even invited her to come visit me and she said yes! Not a light decision, as she was living in Ohio. Weezy was in town and appeared to have a new girlfriend, too. He was staying at Chet's One Step at a Time Hostel. A few years ago, Chet was preparing for a thru-hike when he almost died testing a camp stove that blew up in his face. He survived in a coma for 9 months but is almost blind and now uses a wheelchair. He still has a great attitude and transformed his home into a hostel. Under the radar and not listed in guidebooks, there is space for a few hikers on a work-for-stay basis. If interested, Chet's is near the library with a flagpole and AT flag in his front yard.

Lincoln has several outfitters but Lahout's, opened in 1899, is the oldest ski shop in America. Look for the antique ski lift gondola out front. They also sell mountain climbing equipment, kayaks, bikes and any outdoor contraption you could think of. Moose tours are popular

- not guaranteed, but boast 99% sightings from a safari-style Land Rover with seats in the back. A chalkboard counted 6 moose seen last trip, and a record 25 in one night! Walking back up to Franconia Notch, I passed landmarks, roadside attractions and full-on tourist traps along Daniel Webster Highway...

- **Clark's Trading Post:** Opened 1928, features bear that climb vertical poles and sit on high platforms. I remember visiting as a child.
- **Historical marker** for the first reported UFO abduction. In 1961, a cigar-shaped spaceship chased Betty and Barney Hill before being taken aboard. Official reports filed with the US Air Force and NICAP were leaked to the public years later. Barney described the beings as "somehow not human."
- **Whale's Tale Water Park:** Wave pool, waterslides and a quarter mile lazy river. $49 after 2:00 p.m. "A splashing good time."
- **Indian Head Resort:** 100-foot observation tower, totem pole and Indian tepee, perfect for stealth camping (someone do this!).
- **The Flume:** A narrow canyon stream 10 feet wide, with walls of granite rising 90 feet overhead. $16. Restaurant and good hitching.
- **Indian Head:** Exposed by forest fire in the early 1900's, granite forming the top of Mt. Pemigewasset appeared in the shape of - you guessed it - an Indian head!

> *FUN FACT: Old Man of the Mountain, a rock profile similar to Indian Head, collapsed in 2003 despite years of mending fissures with steel rods and 20 tons of cement. He remains the state symbol of New Hampshire.*

Chapter 22. Worst Weather in the World

Lakes of the Clouds Hut, with Mount Washington looming over it.

Surprisingly, despite their difficulty and danger, The Whites are some of the most heavily traveled sections of the entire AT. I had already passed 3 large parties of Harvard College preps going the opposite direction. Each time, I had to step off into the woods and wait for them all to go by, awkwardly saying hi or nodding to each one as school girls giggled. "Peak baggers" also use these trails with goals of summiting all 48 peaks over 4,000' in New Hampshire. Camping in The Whites works a little differently. Maintained by the Appalachian Mountain Club (AMC), there are several options...

- **AMC high huts:** A series of 8 lodges based on similar systems in the Swiss Alps. Most were built before the AT came into existence and situated about a day's walk apart; hiking clubs and gold blazers reserve bunks. Rates hover around $100 a night, but include dinner and breakfast prepared in well equipped kitchens. Huts have no road access, showers, available power outlets, or heat. No pets allowed.
- **AMC tent sites, shelters, and campsites:** (Campsites have both tent space and a shelter.) These are the most common choices for thru-hikers. $8 cash, first-come, first-serve.

• **Backcountry camping:** Camp at least 200 feet off the trail and water sources. Never camp near huts, campgrounds, shelters, road crossings, above tree line, or anywhere marked "no camping."

Lonesome Lake Hut, 2,760', is the first one NOBOs pass. This key-hole-shaped building sleeps 40 and has spectacular views of its 12-acre lake. Cabins were first built here in 1876 by W.C. Prime, author of several books about world travel. AMC took over in 1929, with the current structure erected in 1965. Noisy, I didn't stop for a look.

Fogged in, Thirtypack tented on top of Little Haystack Mountain, 4,800', displaying a full-sized Redskins flag he packed the whole trip. That night was the only time I had no choice but to sleep on the ground because of no trees ("going to ground" in hammock speak). Making a nest, I slept in a hole partially cloaked by baby bonsai Christmas trees barely 2 feet tall. Clear skies woke me the next morning and sitting up, my head poked up above tiny treetops like Gulliver.

In the Presidential Range, most (not all) of the mountains are named after U.S. presidents and separated by peaks and valleys at least a mile apart. Up and down I went: Lincoln 5,089'; Lafayette 5,260'; Garfield 4,500'; - each an accomplishment in itself. At one of the official campsites, spring water coming out of the ground was so clear and icy cold, I drank it without treatment.

Zealand Falls Hut, 2,630', was built in 1932 and boasts 36 bunks. It's been a long tradition for thru-hikers to do "work-for-stay" in ex-

change for eating leftovers and sleeping on the floor. Just be one of the first 3 or so to arrive and ask the manager. Some huts take less, some take more, but be prepared to wait around and earn your keep mopping floors, cleaning windows - stuff like that. Motley crew for the night: Otto, Rambling Man, Perch & Apollo.

> HIKER TIP: Work for stay slots are coveted and hikers can be competitive. Don't arrive before 3:30 p.m. and be aware that if they've already picked helpers, you'll have to keep going, regardless of darkness or weather.

Drastic changes in elevation were slowing me down bigtime, and I was getting worried about making it to Katahdin before it closed for the season. I had been averaging around 100 miles a week, but here, it was impossible to do the 20's that seemed easy before. I was looking forward to the end, but started paying attention to each passing moment. Making things more fun, a curious black and white bird almost landed on my shoulder, then followed me for several minutes. Using a trick Baltimore Jack taught me, I camped just off the trail where a drainage spillway had been cut at the end of a switchback. During the night, a white owl small as a soda can, landed on a branch a few feet above me, and bobbed back-and-forth, checking me out.

Willey House Snack Bar is within walking distance of the Crawford Notch trailhead. If you read the restaurant sign when you're hungry, it appears to read, "Chili Pizza" & "Fudge Soup." I ordered an ice cream and a giant pretzel. I'll try the fudge soup next time. It can't be worse than coco Ramen bomb! They also have a gift shop and creepy bathrooms with lurkers. Payphones didn't work, so I sent postcards to communicate. This was the former site of Willey House Inn. In 1826, a whole family and 2 employees felt the ground shake and ran outside, only to be swept away to their deaths by a landslide. Amazingly, the house stood unharmed because a large boulder deflected the debris.

> FUN FACT: Walter White (Bryan Cranston) hid out in The Whites during the final episodes of the TV series, 'Breaking Bad.' Fictional Crawford County, perhaps referring to real-life Crawford Notch.

At the top of Mount Webster, 3,910', I could see Mighty Mount Washington, still 12.5 miles away. It always had ominous dark clouds looming around it like Castle Grayskull in the He-Man universe. Keeping an uneasy eye on the skies, I went up and over Mt. Jackson, 4,052'. Then, I walked by the scariest sign on the trail:

"STOP. The area ahead has the worst weather in America. Many have died here from exposure - even in the summer. Turn back NOW if the weather is bad."

Passing Mizpah Hut, 3,800', a different work-for-stay crew waited outside. The Hut, constructed in 1964, has an unusual architectural design - an A-frame, 2 stories tall, with slanted roofs designed to withstand 200 mph winds.

I didn't want to go much further or I'd be headed upwards of 5,000', the last place you want to be in severe weather. Finally, somewhere between Pierce, 4,312', and Franklin, 5,004', I found a tiny opening in a thicket and took my time setting up camp, making everything weather-tight as possible. One of my outrigger stakes was stuck through a decaying log and branches brushed against my tarp. I didn't know it at the time, but I wouldn't get to advance my position...for almost 2 full days.

I did make a failed attempt. The next morning, I completely broke down camp and hiked at least 2 miles in thick fog and freezing cold. Out in the open, wind was so violent that my cheap poncho kept blowing up over my head. Making matters worse, my glasses fogged up and taking them off made me dizzy, so I couldn't see. Mist turned to sleet, and then it started raining. All my clothes got completely soaked. Otto, the only other hiker I saw that day, found me going in the wrong direction. Much more prepared than I, he was wearing a balaclava and was all bundled up like a mountain climber ascending Mount Everest. We had to shout just to hear each other over the wind, but he encouraged me to come with him to the next hut. Almost in sight, Lakes of the Clouds Hut holds 100 hikers, and I just couldn't bring myself to go in there with all those people. He suggested "The Dungeon," a breezy concrete crawlspace underneath the hut which thru-hikers (it holds 6) can pay $10 to use in emergencies. I thanked Otto (maybe he did like me), but put my tail between my legs and retreated to the spot where I hid out the night before.

Demoralized and chilled to the bone, I rehung my hammock on the same exact trees, being very careful to keep my down sleeping bags dry. Hard to do when every single thing around you is dripping wet.

Passing time, I spent the long day studying the guidebook and listening to my MP3 player, at least until the batteries died. Then, all I could do was lay there. I had plenty of food and water, but no fuel to heat it with. Wind battered the mountainside, and the thin trees from which I was hanging shook in a circular motion, bouncing my hammock - and me in it. I used every trick I knew of to stay warm: wearing all my (dry) clothes, poncho draped over me and putting my feet into my empty backpack; distressing, I was still cold. Soaked thermal pants and 2 pairs of socks hung on branches, useless. Had I made a mistake? Worried about hypothermia, I recorded another "goodbye" video in case I froze to death.

> HIKER TIP: If gear made of down (goose feathers) gets wet - you're screwed. It takes forever to dry and can't insulate when damp. Synthetic (poly) items are usually slightly heavier, but insulate even when wet.

Overnight temps dipped below freezing and there was frost on both the outside and inside of my tarp, but I woke up relieved to see the sun shining. I was so well hidden, at least 2 parties hiked by without ever knowing I was there. First, a whole family complete with mom, dad and 4 tiny little kids, followed by a women's seniors group (I call these clusters "Golden Girls," after the 1980's TV show). Feeling like a wimp, I decided right then and there to get over this mountain and quit whining about it! Sun or no sun, it was still brutally cold. I usually wear my extra pair of socks for gloves, but they were hanging off my backpack to dry. Instead, I put plastic Ziploc bags over my hands, held on with rubber bands.

"Welcome and come in." Beautiful as its majestic name, Lakes of the Clouds Hut sits at 5,012', and is surrounded by barren tundra. It looked dwarfed as Mighty Mt. Washington rose up behind it. It's the largest and highest of all AMC huts, and there has been a shelter on this site since 1901, after 2 experienced hikers perished here in a snowstorm. This current building, was erected in 1914. Like all huts, the dining hall is open for anyone to warm up or use the (waterless) restroom. It was nice to get out of the wind, but best of all was a simple lunch - the first hot food I'd had in days - tomato soup with onions. Fair prices and I bought 2 Snickers for dessert, impressed they sold candy bars for only a buck with this captive audience.

A mini weather station of gauges hung on a wall, and someone interpreted them, posting the forecast on a board: Conditions at 10:30 a.m.: 39°, 40 mph winds, chill factor of 19° (all while temps in the valley were mid 70's!). Collecting rainfall, a device outside consisted of a funnel emptying into a tin can. About as simple as you can get besides wetting your finger to see which way the wind blows.

I desperately wanted to get over and way down the other side of Mt. Washington before nightfall, because the next 7 miles were still above 5,000 feet. As I left, a couple "croo" passed me packing wooden frame racks loaded top heavy with boxes tied on with twine. One girl in a hiking dress was carrying more than half her body weight. AMC hut crew call themselves "croo" (that's how they spell it). Each croo is required to make 4 of these resupply runs up and down the mountain during their 11 day stints. Other provisions are airlifted in by helicopter and water is sourced by springs, wells, and in this case from twin from twin, reddish, Lakes of the Clouds, the highest body of water in the Eastern US.

> FUN FACT: Croo entertain guests with evening history lessons, comedy skits and wild theatrics. I've also heard of thru-hikers performing a presentation to the paid crowd as their work for stay duties.

Mount Washington, European eyes first saw her from a tall ship

sailing the Atlantic Ocean, 1524. Over 100 years later, explorer Darby Field became the first man to climb to the top. Two Indian guides accompanying him were perhaps also the first of their race to reach this summit, as their stories told of gods living within the clouds, who they did not dare challenge.

I climbed Mt. Washington on August 29th. The final push was strenuous, but I think the excitement made me forget how cold it was. At 6,288', this crowns the highest point in New Hampshire and is the second highest peak on the entire AT. Only Clingmans Dome back in North Carolina is taller. But wait! Before taking a triumphant picture with the old wooden summit sign atop a pile of boulders, thru-hikers stand in line here with common tourists who "drove" to the top, some wearing sandals or holding Starbucks cups. Sorry to sound like an elitist, but this made all my effort and risk seem anticlimactic. Other ways to reach this summit...

- **Hiking:** Numerous trails converge here from all directions.
- **Mt. Washington Auto Road:** America's first manmade attraction was opened as a carriage road in 1861. Starting at an altitude of 1,527', with an average grade of 11.6%, 45,000 vehicles climb to the top each year. Total length: 7.6 miles. Narrow, and there are no guardrails. Cars $29, motorcycles $17, EAP $9. Obnoxious bumper sticker included: "THIS CAR CLIMBED MT. WASHINGTON."
- **All aboard!** The 1869 Cog is a National Historic Engineering marvel that took 3 years to complete. The first engine each day is a vintage locomotive burning one ton of coal and 1,000 gallons of water. They spew thick black clouds and whistle like a giant teakettle. Modern biodiesels only burn 18 gallons of fuel up and down the mountain. Round trip $62. The Cog might even be made into a Lego set! I hope it includes a thru-hiker mini-figure.
- **SnowCoach:** During wintertime, ride about 2/3 of the way up in heated vans that have tank tracks instead of tires. $49.

> *FUN FACT: Washington Hill Climb is the oldest auto race in the US. Harry Harkness won the first in 1904, driving a Mercedes: 24 min. 37 sec. 1956, Carroll Shelby did it in 10 min, 21 sec. driving an open wheel Ferrari. In 2010, Travis Pastrana drove a Subaru Impreza to the top in 6 min. 20 sec.*

A large visitor center on top of the mountain was designed to withstand 300 mph winds and has a fancy restaurant (or cafeteria), museum and its own post office with unique zip code (no mail drops). Stamps are canceled with a special seal. Morbid, a plaque listed the names of all those who have passed away in the Presidential Range. Since 1849, nearly 150 deaths have been recorded. Also of note, a weather counter with real time computer forecasts and staff meteorologist to answer questions. A colorful train had just unloaded and the hall was packed with people, so I retreated to a small room downstairs designated for hikers.

A weather observatory and tower were added in 1932. Heavy chains strung over their roofs anchored down other structures. The summit is fogged in over 50% of the time, you gain 20 extra minutes of daylight and the ground is permanently frozen. More proof Mt. Washington has "The Worst Weather in the World."

- **World record highest wind speed** measured on the surface of the Earth: 231 mph, 1934. (Only Tropical Cyclone Olivia, off the coast of Western Australia, had greater wind gusts, 254 mph, 1996.)
  - **Hurricane force winds:** 74 mph+, 110 days a year on average.
  - **Record high:** 72°, 2003. Annual number of days over 60°: 13.5.
  - **Record low:** -50°, 1885. Temps below zero 65+ days a year.
  - **Record wind chill:** -102°, 2004. Average velocity: 37 mph.
  - **Record rainfall:** 130 in., 1969. Average per year: 96 in.
  - **Average annual snowfall:** 280 inches (23+ feet).

I didn't stay on the summit more than an hour and crossed the cog railway tracks moments before another train passed. It used to be a thru-hiker tradition to "moon" passengers, but engineers started carrying pellet rifles and several jokesters have been arrested for indecent exposure. I just waved. Following rocks with confusing white blazes painted on top of yellow ones - this part kicked my butt and I took a tumble. Falling forward then rolling on my back, I somehow landed on my feet 5 paces below the trail, unhurt. Near dark, I hiked downhill until I found trees and a place to camp out of the wind. Joe Fore had the same idea and set his tent up in another little clearing. Back home, near Hot Springs, North Carolina, he's an artist specializing in traditional Native American jewelry. Always smiling from behind a beard, he had a jolly spirit and I enjoyed the times we hung out together.

> HIKER TIP: Hammocking in The Whites? There are trees - you just have to look a little harder. Most times I followed blue blazed trails downhill to below tree line, a half mile or so, where trees are larger.

Madison Spring Hut, 4,800', first built in 1888, accidently burnt down in 1940, then rebuilt using as much of the original materials as possible. You can still see the stone cabin incorporated into the T-shaped layout. In 1906, 6 weary travelers paid 50¢ per night; now it holds 50 and at a cost of $100 each! Joe Fore and I arrived just as paying guests were leaving. It was his suggestion that we ask for left-overs and this was a great way to score free grub! Up here there are no dumpsters, trash burning, or any other way to dispose of unused food. The 5 croo would rather we take the scraps than them have to pack it out. We did do a little work to earn our keep. I was assigned the task of organizing a shelf of green and red logbooks, while Joe Fore wiped down tables. I enjoyed the experience, and the pancakes!

Wind whipped around the building, making foreboding screeching sounds. Weather reports predicted gusts up to 70 mph. For reference, the National Weather Service issues hurricane warnings when sustained winds of 74 mph or greater are predicted. Those setting out the same time us: Roboticus, Ranger Bill (hung his hammock inside the hut), Thirtypack, Apollo, Otto, Perch and Rambling Man.

For me, getting up and over Mount Madison, 5,366', was the most difficult part of The Whites. 3 miles of bare, exposed ridgeline, bumps protruding from the earth like giant steps, each a mountain taller than a skyscraper. There was no trail, just random white blazes generally guiding us, but honestly, wind gusts determined our paths. Joe Fore and I, both large men (him tall and me wide), were each blown off our feet several times.

It was difficult trying to place each footstep safely and stepping down onto a lower rock, I would catch air against the wind and feel weightless for an instant. Released by gravity, I got the scary sensation of falling, just as my foot landed on the next unsteady rock. The worst part was when wind blew from behind and pushed me downhill, forcing me to run faster than my stubby legs could go! A pair of women section hikers, climbing UP the mountain, were fighting with all their energy just to stay upright. Judging by bloody scratches on their knees and legs, they had taken a few falls themselves.

Another strange feeling that I have never felt before or since, is when a strong gust of wind would fill the inside of my mouth and nose with cold air. It happened 10 times and literally took my breath away for a few moments. All that being said, this was by far the most exciting part of my journey, and I couldn't help but hoot and holler.

Once we made it safely to the stillness of tree line, everyone gathered in a little nook of small trees to lick our wounds. Animated, we couldn't stop talking about the adventure we just had. It was fun sharing this important part of the hike with these guys and girls, each celebrating in their own way. I marked the joyous occasion with a Twix candy bar. Soon, I was back up and at 'em, in a race against time to reach Gorham before the post office closed. I hate to always be in a rush, but my secret sponsor had mailed money to get a hotel room.

Miss Janet had warned, "The AT is very insignificant in The Whites," and she was right! White blazes are spread much further apart than usual, and at one point, I hiked almost 2 miles without seeing a single one. Like a maze, multiple trails crisscross in every direction, with only vague signs at intersections. They may say, "Appalachian Trail," but don't always point in a specific direction. Adding to the confusion, most were defaced by past hikers trying to help, carving AT logos and unofficial directional arrows (check backs of signs for more clues). Often, there was nothing to do but pick one and see where it took me, kind of like those 'Choose your own Adventure' books I read as a child. I just hoped my chosen path wouldn't be a wrong turn.

This time, the trail came out at the auto road where it was supposed to, and then it was smooth sailing all the way to Pinkham Notch Visitor Center/AMC NH Headquarters. Opened in 1921, this large complex was originally a logging camp. Today you'll find an outfitter, impressive bookstore, 24-hour pay showers and a $10 AYCE breakfast buffet in the cafeteria. Joe Dodge Lodge next door has shared dormitory style accommodations between $70 and $125 a night.

> FUN FACT: Joe Dodge, "father of the AMC hut system" was huts manager, 1928-1959. He supervised rebuilding projects and personally oversaw 100+ rescue missions. He also broadcast weather forecasts for WMTW.

Planning to return the next day, I hid my trekking poles behind a log and made a beeline for the parking lot. Immediately, I saw Thirtypack with 2 pretty women. Thanks to him, I had a ride to town! Girls in front, Apollo and Thirtypack in the middle and me and Perch in the back. My backpack, compared to everyone else's, looked toyish and rag-tag.

Gorham, New Hampshire, also known as "The Village," is a touristy town with most services. Making it to the post office, I found three hikers already waiting in line! I picked up my PC, a letter containing a $100 bill from Kwartz Krazy in North Carolina (Thanks Ken!) and correspondence from Cora Jean. Unexpectedly, there was also a suggestive fan mail type letter from a young woman. I didn't pursue this and have never mentioned it until now.

Another mail magic drop box was waiting at the rundown, Hiker's Paradise, on the far edge of town. Ready to pay for the night, I asked if there was a password for the Wi-Fi. The office lady was honest and said their connection was "spotty," so I explained that my reason for staying was to use the Internet and apologized for leaving. I even offered $5 for the mail pickup, but she was still put off. Taking my things, I scanned both sides of the main drag. Too many screaming kids in the pool at that motel, trashcans filled with beer cans at another...Finally, I settled into Gorham Motor Inn, $69.99/night, x2.

Basic and dated, it had a hot shower, good Wi-Fi and a phone. Yes, I asked this time. Getting to work editing videos, I had no idea this would be my last chance to upload for over a month. I spent lots of time on the phone with Cora Jean, planning her visit. I also called my mother for the first time on this trip. It was nice to talk to her and I think it calmed some worries. I regret not calling sooner.

Promising my "secret sponsor" a personalized video, understandably, she sent an email telling me she was waiting and even called me, "a rock star who had gotten too big for his britches!" She was right. Without her support, I would never have made it this far and I admitted being overwhelmed. Opening the package, I couldn't believe her generosity. A giant box of Slim Jims, vegan meals, loads of candy, batteries, bug spray, a roll of quarters and gift cards (Wally World, fast food and iTunes). There was even a travel size Simon game to hang off my backpack. She was more than kind and by the end of the unboxing, I was embarrassed at all the loot. Thanks Kath!

> *HIKER TIP: Backpack friendly games: A pack of cards, marbles, or Rubik's Cube. Going ultralight? How about a pair of dice (or even a single die) for betting games. I also saw hikers playing Jacks and tic-tac-toe.*

Getting to Gorham was easy. Getting back - not so much. I was 12 miles out, and as you know, had sworn off hitchhiking. So, after studying the guidebook, I found that the AT crosses NH Route 2, 4 road miles away. Not wanting to skip, I would then hike south, back to Pinkham Notch where I left off and figure out the rest from there. With very rugged terrain, lots of slippery rocks and contorted climbs, this section turned out to be a very demanding. I'm not sure if it was because I was going backwards or because I didn't have my trekking poles, but it would take almost 3 days to do these 20 miles. Out of control, I fell twice. One could have ended my hike for sure, but again, luck was on my side.

Still struggling with knee problems, Socks left a telling entry in the free, Rattle River Shelter's logbook, "No dope, no hope!" A longer entry by Voltron, also battling, said he was taking a zero to soak in the river: "...my body deserves it after all it's been through." I took a breather above the clouds and watched white fog floating between the mountains. Hearing a steam locomotive cutting loose, I looked up and saw Mount Washington in front of me again. It felt like I had been circling this landmark for weeks.

Miles away, Carter Notch Hut, 3,450', was deep inside a gorge. A cabin has been here since 1904, and again, older sections were fashioned from stone with newer add-ons made of wood. This was my favorite hut. The main hall was small, but had flags hanging from rafters, snowshoes on a wall and worn pack-racks lined up in the mud room. Croo here were laidback and let me raid the kitchen of leftover eggs, grits and peach slices covered in brown sugar. I mixed it all together. The last hut in The Whites, this was also my last chance for homemade cornbread and hot potato soup (my favorite), so I waited around to buy lunch. In a separate bunkhouse, small rooms held 4 or 6 bunks with fresh blue blankets and pillows, about as rich as it gets and still called primitive. Twin ponds and a beach here were peaceful, but rock faces towering high above were my next intimidating task.

This would be where I decided on Cora Jean's trail name, "Wildcat." She wanted me to name her, and as I wrestled up Wildcat Mountain, brainstorming took my mind off rocks and roots. She was born and raised in Kentucky and a longtime UK basketball fan. So, you could say she's named after her home and also this mountain, with the basketball link a bonus.

Wildcat Mountain Range actually has 5 summits with the highest being 4,422'. On top was another ski lift terminal, rotating sightseers up and down. For $12 round-trip, you can ride to the bottom where a gift shop sells snacks and bag lunches. A man saw my backpack and kept drilling me with the same question: "How long did it take to climb up here?" I briefly explained, "Well, I didn't start at the bottom where you parked your car, I started from Georgia."

One good thing about doing this section SOBO was meeting trail celebrity, Animal. Very strong, this tall man wore a straw cowboy hat and was well known for carrying a 10-gallon plastic drywall bucket in one hand and walking stick in the other. Not only that, he was hiking on a budget of only 50¢ a mile when most struggle with $2! His super low figure sounded impossible, but he had a game plan. The bucket was filled with food so he could avoid going into towns. He also foraged for plants, nuts and berries. Back in Pennsylvania, he "went missing" (didn't check in) for a while. Worried family members posted messages on Whiteblaze.com looking for him. He had taken time off because the rubber crocs in which he hiked caused a nasty case of "croc rot," bruising his feet with purple rashes. After getting proper hiking boots, he was on his way again. He also carried basic equipment to pan for gold.

Again finding myself at Pinkham Notch Visitor Center, I quickly retrieved my hiking poles from their hiding place. In town, I had bought a cheap, pay-as-you-go cellphone. It worked fine listening to messages, but I only got to make two calls before the battery died. Dead weight. In the end, it was necessary because I didn't want Cora Jean, aka Wildcat, to arrive in Maine while I was still out in the middle of nowhere.

Charging my battery in the hiker lounge, I found I'll Try. He didn't remember me, but last time we met was at the NOC. He had hiked NOBO to Harpers Ferry, flip-flopped up to Katahdin and started hiking SOBO back towards Harpers Ferry. A big guy, he predicted his thru-hike would take him 9 months total. That's commitment!

Pinkham Notch parking lot was teeming with a different hiker bubble. A young man with spiked hair from Dambeck, Germany, introduced himself slowly, "I'm... Lost," grinning ear to ear that his clever trail name had a built-in joke. There were also lots of day trippers, and I yogied a ride in no time. These nice folks had to rearrange luggage and car seats, but were happy to help and even took my picture! Maybe I was a rock star? Dropping me off at a convenience store, I celebrated completing The Whites with an 85¢ superhero Slushie and my Cotton Candy Commander was delish! Other flavors: Mad Cola, Sour Apple Shock, Nick Kick and so on.

Déjà vu all over again, I walked up the same road toward the same trailhead that I had days before but this time, headed north. Gentian Pond Shelter. This one had a magnificent view and solar privy to help decompose waste. I found Apollo, Perch, Otto and Ranger Bill, playing cards. Bill had also taken to wearing a do-rag and hiking kilt. They were all talking about Tropical Storm Ivan and the rain it would bring. Taking heed, I camped near the shelter and with nothing else to do, ate most of my food. That night proved rainy but otherwise uneventful.

Passing 1,900 miles and the Maine state line, I was sporting new duds I found while investigating an abandoned campsite just off the trail. From the looks of it, a storm ran off unprepared section hikers the season before. They left a collapsed tent, moldy blue jean shorts and other rubbish. I scored a purple poncho and blue rain pants hanging on a tree and used them the rest of my hike. Finders keepers!

Chapter 23. As the Crow Flies

Just one of many river fords in Maine. Notice white blazes on other side.

No pain, no rain, no Maine. 282 miles to go. Hikers familiar with the Pine Tree State warned me it would be difficult. Trail builders seemed to lead us up-and-over the most rugged terrain they could find and like to "keep it wild." There are no footbridges on the AT here, so hikers must ford streams and rivers. I respect this, but being unable to swim, found this the most intimidating challenge I would have to overcome to reach my goal.

> FUN FACT: Maine has an estimated 30,000 black bears, but are rarely seen along the AT here. Instead look for deer, eagles and big kitty cats. Also, moose are often seen on roads, licking salt used to melt snow.

Walking across another alpine bald, winds swirled grey fog around me and I felt like I could walk right off the edge of the mountain. There would be many windy, cloudy days ahead that some hikers found gloomy. I felt excitement and saw the landscape as beautiful. Board-walks zigzagged back and forth and went on and on. Downhill, some had cleats like the ramp of a chicken coop. These helped, but the wood can still be slippery when wet. On top of another clearing I found the muddiest mud hole on the entire AT. No walk boards here - heavy rains made this mountain bog even more treacherous. Testing the depth of its soupy black muck with my hiking pole, I couldn't find the bottom so I tried to go around. Both feet sank under the surface and I felt like there were suction-cups on my shoes. Twice, I had to reach - elbow deep - into the cold mire and feel around for a lost shoe.

Mahoosuc Notch, another "must see" on my top 5 list, is an insane rock jumble at the bottom of a deep gorge formed by retreating glaciers. Videos I watched from previous thru-hikers were interesting, but didn't portray how daunting this can be. Taking the difficulty level up a degree, it had rained the night before so rocks were slick. Putting on my backpack before starting the attempt, my adrenaline ramped up like a Hobbit preparing to enter Smaug's dragon lair!

> HIKER TIP: Before entering the Notch, make a note of your start time. Using my camera as a stopwatch, I took a pic at the beginning, another at the end, with date and time recorded on files.

Every hiker's transverse through these car-sized boulders is different. White blazes, arrows and "X" markings suggest a defined route, but there are plenty of opportunities to get creative. Some SOBOs I talked to said it took about an hour to reach the other side. BS, I thought, but as a point of pride I endeavored to complete the task in under 45 minutes. There were rocks to climb over, crawl under, tiptoe across, tests of balance, overhangs, small caves to go through and vines to be climbed like Tarzan! All while a bubbling creek runs underfoot between the rocks, if it's not frozen. Also in the back of my mind, all these giant rocks had broken off from cliffs high above at some point or another.

With a big smile on my face, my useless hiking poles clanked on either side as I grunted over each obstruction. About halfway in, I had already taken a few slips and spills but nothing to slow me down. Then, on a particularly awkward gap I leaped down from one rock to another, about 4 feet away. During my airtime, view obstructed by the bill of my trucker's cap, my head hit an overhanging rock with a thud. Surprised, the crash threw me backwards, falling to the bottom of the narrow 5-foot-deep crevice that I was attempting to clear.

My backpack broke the fall, but my eyeglasses, hat and trekking poles all went flying. Stunned, the impact knocked the breath out of me. I just laid there gasping for air like a tortoise that couldn't flip over. Realizing how cold the ground was, I wiggled around till I could at least sit up. Damage: wrist scrape, elbow raspberry, glasses bent, headache, and a swollen egg on my forehead like the elephant man. I began getting out of this mousetrap by tossing my backpack out of the hole, then pulling myself out. The mishap broke my spirit.

Muddy, sore, and cold, I took a long break and let sunshine warm me. Instead of charging ahead, now I took my time and analyzed the safest way to conquer each encumbrance I came to. Getting frustrated, even dirt between the rocks was muddy! At least once I had to crawl on my belly and there were several tight squeezes that required removing my tiny backpack. I have no idea how "real" hikers with "normal" size backpacks make it through without dragging their gear behind them on a rope.

Demolishing my self-esteem, it took 2 hours and 18 minutes to cover this 1 mile. So much for my goal of 45 minutes! From this point on, "How long did it take to get through the Notch?" became a topic of conversation with other hikes. Most did it faster, a few did it slower, but all had vivid memories of the experience. I'd love to have another shot at it. As a more realistic point of reference, Class of 2015 hiking machine, Gator, took an hour and a half... "See ya later. Bye." I heard of another man that made it to the end, only to discover he somehow got turned around in the maze and came out where he started! He had to do it all over again. There were also reports of a moose that got stuck in the rocks and died here. I don't want to know how they got it out.

Beat, I went to bed early but ended up on the ground. Hammock failure! One moment I'm getting dressed; the next, I'm rolling down a hill. At least fluffy green moss made for a soft landing. I'm also lucky it didn't happen while hanging off a cliff or riverbank. I can't complain; today marked 5 months on the trail and this hammock had over 150 nights on it. I think a sleeping bag zipper snagged it. First rule of hammock hanging - NO ZIPPERS! Now what was I going to do? There's not exactly an outfitter in the middle of the forest.

At Grafton Notch, Clock Tower & Violet both wore bright colors. Him orange and she, of course, violet. They were concerned how gaunt I looked. No matter how big you start, after a thru-hike men look like Ethiopian famine victims and women look like anorexic fashion models.

Because of my slow pace I was just about out of food, but like real trail magic, a former thru-hiker named Finch, pulled up. He was here on a bird watching trip, but brought sodas and granola bars to leave for thru-hikers. He read my mind and offered to drive me to a store. Bear River Trading Post, 12 miles away, was an old gas station with a gravel driveway and moose horns over the door. Signs on gas pumps read, "NO GAS" and food selection was limited so I grabbed a box of Fruit Loops, chips, candy, Honey Buns and a big Grandma's Cookie. Thanks for the ride Finch!

Back on trial, ascending back to the tops of mountains, I'm not sure how "wild" rebar handholds and wooden ladders are, but was happy they were here. I stopped for supper at Frye Notch Lean-to, where I met a slim fellow who wore bulky kneepads like a skateboarder. He signed logbooks like this... "BOB spelled backward is still BOB." Only 56, he retired from teaching at a Christian college in Atlanta, Georgia, and aligned his hike to raise money for a village in Cambodia. I left the Grandma's cookie where he would find it and he thanked me the next day. It's amazing what a simple cookie can do to lift someone's spirits.

> *FUN FACT: Shelters in Maine are called "lean-tos" and some have uncomfortable looking "Baseball bat" floors made of, split, same-sized saplings nailed down in a row. Sleeping pads recommended.*

At dusk, I tarp camped at Dunn Notch, right next to a raging waterfall. I built a nest between 2 trees, plastic and ponchos on top of pine needles, sleeping bags on top. Hanging the tarp lower than normal helped keep wind out. I really missed my hammock but slept OK.

Resupply towns in the north are further away from the trail than in the south, and months ago, I fell into this unfortunate pattern of arriving at trail towns on Saturdays, with resupply boxes to pick up before noon. On a quiet road with no traffic, BOB and I walked 6 miles (really) down a road before a pickup truck finally stopped. The driver said, "Hold on tight," and away we went! The bouncy 60 mph ride was fun and we laughed all the way. A duplex had the post office on one side; postmaster's dwelling on the other. Come to find out, there were 2 drop boxes here with plenty of goodies to make it to the next stop. Thanks Fixer and Bob!

Andover, Maine, is a small town but a necessary stop for thru-hikers. Miss Janet was here with Baltimore Jack as co-pilot. Backpacks (and tiki lamps) were strapped to the van's back door. Andover's first residents, Ezekiel Merrill with his wife and 7 children, settled here in 1789. The handsome Merrill house still sits on a hill east of town. This community is also home to Andover Earth Ground Station, the first place on Earth to transmit info with satellites in space. Built by AT&T in 1961, a huge Epcot Center-like dome protected a giant antenna, 7 stories high, that amplified signals 10 billion times. The largest dome was removed in 1995, but smaller ones can still be seen from the trail.

> FUN FACT: 'Myth of Fingerprints' (named after a Paul Simon song), starring Julianne Moore and Noah Wyle, was shot in Andover, 1997. It featured the General Store, a church, and extensive filming at Merrill House.

Andover Public Library was an unusual white octagon shaped building with cathedral ceilings and stained glass windows, but very dark inside. A librarian insisted I bring my backpack into the foyer. I did as she asked, but then a crabby old lady started complaining about how smelly it was and how all hikers are inconsiderate. I left after getting online long enough to read that Wildcat had bought her plane ticket.

> HIKER TIP: Taking a shower is great, washing clothes is even better, but you still stink! Don't forget to throw your backpack into the wash occasionally. A hiker's backpack can stink up a room or car in short order!

Pine Ellis Lodge has been hosting hikers for 24 years. $25 per person includes laundry & coffee. SOBOs encouraged me to stay because of pending storms, but I paid $10 for the shuttle woman to drive me back to the trail, 10 minutes by car. A real bargain! Owners also operate a campground ($25 a site) near Lovejoy Covered Bridge (1868).

Daylight was getting noticeably shorter, and I made camp at Surplus Pond in full "storm mode" with my tarp closed off on either end. I also put several small logs inside, so I could sleep off the ground. The things I do, to avoid sleep in a crowded hostel! It rained hard with lots of flashes, but... I lived.

The trail had lots of PUDs (pointless ups and downs), but few peaks above 3,000'. Sabbath Day Pond Lean-to had several entries in the logbook about a large moose that tromped through the camping area the night before. Left here was a worn copy of 'The Firm,' by John Grisham and a Lego helicopter complete with pilot - probably a Happy Meal prize. I was taken by the beauty of this New England pond and its gentle waves reminded me how much I missed kayaking.

Approaching Little Swift River Pond, I could smell campfire smoke a mile before I found tents there. Three old canoes were left for anyone to use, a common sight in the north, but 2 had holes, there was only one paddle and only one life vest. A SOBO had Macgyvered a fishing pole from a tree branch, using line and lures he packed in. He slowly trolled around the lake that he said was "...loaded with brook trout." Other hikers in the area: Yukon and Hobo.

Making camp by myself a couple miles away along the shore of stunning South Pond, I found it hard to sleep. I even used some giant, 2-foot-long fern leaves as insulation, but woke up to an amazing sunrise, with the sun's reflection in the glassy water. It was a magical sight and my girl was on an airplane, headed my way. A countdown to town was spray painted on rocks... 3 miles... 2 miles... 1 mile...

"Real" trail magic. I got a ride to Rangeley within 30 seconds of walking out of the woods, without even trying to hitch. The nice lady was even going to the same exact place, the laundry. Village Scrub Board was owned by a former thru-hiker and had vending machines and a weathered Saddleback summit sign. There was also a box with "loaner" clothes to wear while washing clothes. Sporting a black T-shirt with Harley Davidson logo, I walked to the post office and picked up a drop box from Mom. I had asked her to send my backup ham-mock from home. Innocently she wrote, "Oh no! You broke the ham-mock you were using; where is Cora Jean going to sleep?" Mom also sent a shower kit with shampoo and deodorant. I guess she didn't want me smelling like a hiker for the big date! I clean up real good.

The 45th Parallel, Rangeley, Maine, is exactly hallway between the equator and the North Pole, with a 3,107-mile distance to each. Cora Jean called from Portland Airport. Huge problem. She prepaid for a rental car online, but didn't bring the credit card she used, not know-ing it was required to release the ride. We considered taxis, buses, li-mos, even floatplanes. As a last resort, I tried the Chamber of Com-merce. Very helpful, they put me in touch with a local shuttle driver and 5 minutes later, we were off to the rescue. After a three hour drive, it was exciting meeting Wildcat for the first time and she even wore a necklace matching the one she had given me. Because of the unex-pected shuttle cost to get here (the ride was not cheap), the new plan was to get dropped off in Monson, Maine, and hike 40 miles south to Caratunk and figure out the rest later. Wildcat has played in the out-doors her whole life, but this was her first long distance hiking expe-rience. I didn't want her to hate it.

There are 2 hostels in Monson. Shaw's Hiker Hostel, the more fam-ily oriented of the two, was already full. Shaw's opened in 1977 and the new owners, Hippie Chick & Poet (Class of 2008), are well known for a $10, all-you-can-eat breakfast. Next, we tried Lakeshore House on Main Street - a cute, white and blue, 2-story overlooking picturesque Lake Hebron. Decks were packed with happy hikers, the largest gath-ering I'd seen in months. Someone at the bar yelled out my name. It was Loophole! I hadn't seen him or his bud Sleeping Beauty in over a thousand miles! Voltron was setting up his tent outside and now ap-peared to be hiking alone, but persevered and was about to complete his thru-hike.

Rebekah, the owner of the boarding house, made me feel welcome right away by making sure to ask my trail name before talking business. Looking through a binder with papers and post-it notes sticking out everywhere, she found us a room and actually wrote "Loner and his woman" on my receipt! Then, I came back to find a drunk SOBO, simply named Kevin, hitting on "my woman!" He was so drunk, neither of us understood what he was mumbling.

Relegated to a hallway couch (sorry bro!), Weezy gave me a big bro hug. He and Aisha had already been here for a week doing odd jobs around town to raise some cash. Oddly, our room had a harp on the wall for decoration but was cozy, just don't lock the door. Weezy had to climb along the outside porch railing and into the window like a jewel thief to open it. Bunks $25, privates $40-50.

Maildrops (free for guests, $5 otherwise) were piled up to the celling in the upstairs hallway, including a long cardboard tube (trekking poles) and a black ball with address tied on a string (sleeping bag). Per their quirky website, they also keep an obscure collection of cell phone chargers on hand. Bottom floor of the hostel was a full service laundromat with rows of washing machines, turtle tapestries on the ceilings and the interesting history of Monson told by pictures on the walls. One B&W photo showed Lakeshore House in the old days, a honkytonk since the late 1800's. The marquee out front read "Rest in Pease Parkside," who was still on everyone's mind. Wildcat and I explored the beautiful town with buildings built right over the water. Then, ordering pizza at the A+E store, we got yelled at for acting like a couple of teenagers.

Shuttles to the trailhead are provided at designated times, otherwise I was told, "You're on your own." The shuttle was like a clown-car with at least 6 hikers, their gear, a dog and the driver, all squeezed into the tiny compact car. The trail was harder than the guidebook let on, but Wildcat handled everything it gave us. In her yellow backpack she carried a Boy Scout mess kit, HEET and a fleece blanket. Watching my videos, she was shocked by how I prepared meals (room temperature) and decided she would make campfires every night and do all the cooking. She even hung a container of pancake mix off her pack! We made our first camp near a river about 5 miles in. The Grand Trunk Ultralight hammock was a tight fit, but very cozy for both of us.

> HIKER TIP: Couples hiking together can split up gear to save weight, but I suggest both carry some food, water, a sleeping bag and tarp - just in case of emergency while you're apart.

"It's not about the miles, it's about the smiles." While we were having chocolate chip pancakes for breakfast, we heard several hikers walk by and I'm satisfied we just missed Fatherman because his name was in the next logbook. Busy beavers had dammed up several streams, making fun detours right across the tops of their lodges. I let Wildcat test them out first. I loved every second we hiked together, we talked about all sorts of things and

got along great. The only time it was stressful for me was making decisions for both of us. Getting dark, erring on the side of caution I chose not to hike any further that night because of increased elevation. Without any good camping sites, we made our own as Wildcat knocked over a deadfall tree with her bare hands! This time she cooked sitting in a dry streambed. Chocolate pretzels and taco mix burritos. She confessed to me later that this was the only time she was uncomfortable the whole week, as it was bitter cold.

Wearing extra clothes the next day, we summited Moxie Bald, 2,936'. On top, my first look at the ultimate goal, Mount Katahdin could be seen in the distance, still 130 miles away as the crow flies. A gentleman here bribed us with candy bars, into doing a survey. Something to do with windmill farms. I had seen several along the way, with dozens of tall, white windmills along tops of ridgelines. I couldn't tell which side of the debate our tester was hired to prove.

We stopped at Bald Mountain Brook Lean-to, and this time Wildcat cooked Mac & Cheese with a dessert made of Ritz crackers and pancake mix. I sure was eating better! We camped next to the beautiful brook, not knowing the woods would come alive when the sun went down. Like something out of a horror movie, mice, 2 - 3 at a time, climbed onto our tarp and ran along the ridgeline doing acrobatic jumps and sliding down the side. We could even hear them scratching around our cook kit, which was sitting on a tree stump. In the morning, we found hundreds of mouse pellets in the pan and never used it again.

The next morning, Wildcat warned me I was in big trouble. She had run out of coffee, cigarettes and mashed potatoes! Without a store in sight, to ease her withdrawals I brewed up some hot tea. And when that ran out, hot Crystal Light. Great weather the entire week, dragonflies were out in abundance and we navigated several calm stream crossings by skipping over stepping stones. Camping halfway up Pleasant Pond Mountain, we climbed to the top so we could have dinner watching the sunset through the trees. Getting creative with what was left in the food bag: She flavored beans and rice with crushed up Grippo's BBQ chips!

Hanging out at Pleasant Pond, Wildcat found an interesting rock with tiny fossil shells embedded into it. We later met Texas Pete (named after a hot sauce) and his mother at the lean-to. They had started their hike together in Georgia, but she caught Lyme disease and had to leave the trail. Now she was back to finish with her son.

Hiking an impressive 15 miles that day, we made it to town before heavy rain rolled in. Wildcat tore a small piece off one of her hiking sticks to keep as a souvenir and left them at the trailhead. She lost ten pounds, had a few blisters and was dying for real coffee, but never complained the whole time. A cool thing about going south for this section was that she got to meet lots of hikers: Canecutter, ezNOMAD, DK, Bubble Foot, The Big "E", Perch, Roboticus, Crochunter, Gumby, Lost, Renaissance Man, Joe Fore and others.

Caratunk was a very small town. How small was it? It was so small, the latest census only counted 69 people, even less during harsh winters when snowbirds fly south. Hundreds more than that hike through every year, giving local businesses a financial boost. I was also amazed to read in the guidebook that the elevation here was only 490'.

Wildcat and I spent her last night at Sterling Inn Bed & Breakfast. A 200-year-old stagecoach stop, this large white house was the most charming hotel on the trail. Each room was decorated with antique furniture and beds were adorned with country style quilts. No TVs, but there's one in the common room. Dining room tables had glass tops with vintage pictures of the town underneath. Shared rooms $25/person, privates/$40 and up. All include breakfast buffet.

Eric, the innkeeper, was very helpful and called the postmaster to ask if we could get our maildrops after-hours. The postwoman lives across the street from her office and even had fresh baked cookies for us! Outside, there was the biggest hiker box you've ever seen. *Update. In 2014, two houses in Caratunk burnt to the ground and the post office was closed due to water damage.*

Wildcat had bounced herself real clothes to wear in town and my laptop was here, but the Wi-Fi only worked well enough to reply to messages. Sorry, all my faithful viewers would just have to wait. Some wrote messages on old videos, "Where are you Loner?" & "Are you still on the trail?" Several folks asked if I had seen Fatherman, as he had also been off the radar. We did watch a recent video by fellow YouTuber Frenchy, from Pennsylvania. He was very excited and about to finish his thru-hike. I followed along with his blog: 'Journey North.'

> HIKER TIP: Most hiker's "live" video blogs have dead spots near the end where there is little to no signal, then upload a big chunk of videos all at once, after they finish.

As part of our stay, our host shuttled us to Northern Outdoors/Kennebec River Brewery. Focusing on cross country skiing, ATV riding and river rafting, there is hiker bunkhouse and popular restaurant, as YouTuber MedicineMan03 commented, "...well known for Blueberry beer and a humongous hot tub." A game room had foosball, pinball, video games and a crane machine with candy prizes. Wildcat got very aggressive whipping my tail at air hockey! I joked that I let her win. The food was good; service not so much.

The postmaster's husband was also a long-distance shuttle driver and drove us back to Portland Airport the next day to fly Wildcat home. We had a wonderful time together and made plans for after the trail. She said she was going to paint a white blaze on the back of her shirt so that I'd follow her around. It was a sad goodbye. Not enough shuttle money left to get back to Rangeley, I restarted from Caratunk and did that section all over again, retraced my steps going north.

There was also a new deadline - finish in time to visit my grandparents before they left Maine in a couple of weeks. By accident, I left my hiking ski poles at the Inn and instead used Wildcat's walking sticks, one brown, one white, still leaning against the tree where she left them. This made me feel closer to her.

Along the way, Firefighter John saw me and said, "Loner? Man, when you got out of the Smokies, you were just gone!" Last time we saw each other was at Standing Bear, way back in Tennessee. His large group had now dwindled down to only a handful. Samson was a thin guy from Dover, New Hampshire. He now sported a red beard, and I'll always remember him because he glued a Catholic medallion of St. Jude, patron saint of lost causes, to his walking stick. When we last spoke he seemed incredibly shy, but had gained a ton of confidence and was even cracking jokes.

Show & Tell! Taking a drink of water during the night, I lost my cap in the dark and placed the bottle on the ground, standing up. Next morning, picking it up for a sip I saw something grey floating in my bottle! It had been about half full of crystal light and a mouse had climbed in after it and drowned. Poor little guy. Of course I showed the bottle and its puffy passenger to several hikers I crossed paths with, but now could only carry one liter of water. I still covered the 40 miles between Caratunk and Monson in 2 nights.

Chapter 24. The Greatest Mountain

Roboticus climbing Mount Katahdin. Notice her full pack and knee braces.

115 miles to go... The final section felt like the last days of school. Soon, I would no longer wake up in the woods or breathe crisp New England air. Some friends had already summited and returned home. Back into Monson, the path led over a foggy rock face where a photographer had his camera set up on a tripod with a giant lens wrapped in clear plastic. With a poncho tight over my head, I didn't stop to chat, but would have loved to see that photo.

My last mail magic of the trip was from fellow YouTube friends, Sassafras & Kaboose. For inspiration, they even sent a photo of them both on top of Mount Katahdin. I carried it the rest of the way and still have it. Filling my pack, bowl and pockets with food, I hoped it would be enough. Entering the 100-mile wilderness, a threatening sign warned...

"CAUTION, there are no places to obtain supplies or get help until Abol Bridge, 100 miles north. Do not attempt this section unless you have a minimum of 10 days supplies and are fully equipped. This is the longest wilderness section on the entire A.T. and its difficulty should not be underestimated. Good hiking! MATC."

Next to the sign was a sign-in box. Late in the trip, hikers were tagging everything in sight and many left their name directly on the box itself. I'm sure it must be repainted every year. Miles in, Little Wilson Falls emptied into a deep granite gorge and its power was awesome. Rusty metal parts along the trail were remnants of Bessey Lumber Camp, 1949. Harvesting lumber of their own, beavers had changed the landscape and detours were marked with bright pink streamers.

> HIKER TIP: Entering the 100-mile wilderness, bring enough cash to camp at The Birches on the other side. Also, consider filling a waterproof bucket with resupply to be dropped off halfway. $20 at Lakeshore House.

Reaching Big Wilson Stream late in the day, I decided to ford it now instead of the next morning when it would be colder. Plus, more rain could raise the water level. This "stream" was about the width of your average 2-lane highway. There was a rope to hold onto, but I wished someone else had been there in case anything went wrong. After tying my shoes on tighter, making sure the pack liner was rolled up and securing my camera in double Ziploc bags, I went for it. Fighting strong currents over knee high, I made it safely to the other side, quickly changed out of wet clothes and got into my sleeping bag to warm up. Only six more fords to go!

> HIKER TIP: Even shallow fords can be dangerous because rocks hidden underwater are usually slippery. Skipping over stones? Take your time because some rock back and forth.

The mission now was just to make it to the end. Knowing how much food it takes to walk 100 miles, I used my mad yogi skills on four Golden Girls (one with a G.I. Joe action figure tied to her hiking stick) each offering up apples, cheese and raisins. Thanks girls! On top of Barren Mountain, 2,660', the skeleton of an old fire tower stood while its cabin lay destroyed in a pile on the ground. I still climbed the rung ladder high as I could. My Kung Fu improving, I yogied a couple

SOBOs, a guy named Efron and a girl named Warrior. Score: A pound of nuts and a Pop Tart - and you know how hard it is to get a hiker to let go of a Pop Tart! I even tried to yogi a squirrel out of a pinecone, but he was wise to hiker trash tricks.

After making camp, I went to nearby Carl Newhall Lean-to and signed the logbook. There, I found 2 sketchy SOBOs and their dogs, basically homeless people living on the trail (but aren't we all?). Both men immediately started trying to yogi - ME. I'm the last person who should say a word, but they were working it really hard to the point I felt uncomfortable. They even complained how hard it was to make the fire, as if they should be compensated. Being polite, in the a.m., I went to say goodbye when I was bitten by one of their dogs - a big white and gold, Siberian Husky-looking dog.

I should have been more careful. The night before, the younger man had told me his dog was protective, but it walked toward me without any sign of aggression, like it wanted to be petted, then lunged at me! Latching onto my upper leg, I was shocked and yelled out. The owner only got the beast to release his grasp with a firm yank of his collar. He then immediately hooked the dog to a leash, already tied to a tree, and put a muzzle on him. **If you know your dog needs a muzzle, it shouldn't be anywhere near the AT.** The owner asked if I was ok, but not a word of apology. Luckily, the dog had grabbed onto the water bottle in my shorts' pocket and didn't break the skin. It could have ended my hike, but without complaining, I left and even put a Mickey D's gift card where they would find it. I've always been leery of dogs, and since this scary episode, even more so.

On the bright side, Waldo, a NOBO from Illinois, left funny illustrated cartoons in each shelter log in the 100 Mile Wilderness:

• You've met Baltimore Jack and/or Miss Janet in at least four states (suggesting they were clones).

• Your cellphone contacts make you look like a drug dealer (list with trail names: Dirty D, Fire Fox, Disco, etc.).

• You've mastered the art of tripping over a rock into either... a dance move, some crazy triple-axle ice skating maneuver, or a convincing, 'I'm going to start running for no apparent reason.' (I cracked up laughing, because it's true!)

73 miles to go... White Cap Mountain, 3,644', was the last big climb before the end. On top, someone carved "Katahdin" onto a rock pointing at the greatest mountain. Standing tall among the others, it was as beautiful as it was intimidating. Visually seeing the finish line in front of me, I was tired and ready to go home. Wanting to tell Wildcat the good news, because of a bad signal we wasted 10 minutes of phone time only getting to talk 20 seconds. How frustrating!

East Branch Pleasant River was another uneasy ford. I checked the logbook at the preceding lean-to, and heavy rains had made this one impassible for several days. With more and more hikers arriving, but unable to advance, at least 30 were held up here until the water level resided. The congestion causing a massive hiker bubble.

> HIKER TIP: River fords are a great place for poor people (like me) to find FREE socks! Placed on tree branches to dry out, many are forgotten. Twice, I traded up to lightly used, already dry, matching pairs!

Camping at Mountain View Pond after a 23-mile day, I emptied everything out of my pack to survey my gear and found a lost Slim Jim. Jackpot! Otherwise my food bag was looking skimpy, while the Ziploc in which I kept trash was almost full. Other hikers were getting lazy and burning their garbage. Also, I was now carrying one Smart Water bottle and a found, Mountain Dew bottle to hold H2o.

The next day, trail maintainers were clearing deadfalls after the recent storms. One large tree directly on the walkway, was leaning over and pulling up duff (the top layer of soil and roots.) A hyper chainsaw man, fully decked out with helmet, face shield and ear protectors, stood on top of the stump while cutting and the tree dropped with him on it. Panicked, he ran for safety still holding the running chainsaw. The tree shook the ground with a crash. Another volunteer, wearing red flannel, was tall like a lubber jack. As the fallen tree was cut into sections, he picked huge pieces up over his head and tossed them like twigs. His trail name should have been "Paul Bunyan!" After my hike I learned from Mountain Squid that AT chainsaw operators take certification classes with the US Forest Service.

56 miles to go... Jo Mary Road (gravel) was busy with huge 18 wheelers barreling by at full speed, creating dust storms through the otherwise peaceful forest. Cold temps and the fever pitch my hike had taken on were burning calories faster than I could replace them. I hung out here hoping to see Texas Pete. Unfortunately, his mother had to get off trail again, still suffering from Lyme disease. They had bought a food drop bucket and had it stashed here. Now by himself, Texas Pete told me he wouldn't need it all. After an hour, I still hadn't seen Texas Pete, but I did yogi a section hiker out of a teeny-tiny honey bear! About 2 inches tall, it was a fun souvenir that I carried all the way home. I also met Zero, an Asian thru-hiker with a big smile.

Jo Mary Lake was beautiful and surrounded by colorful trees. Now fall, pastel yellows, oranges and reds changed before my eyes. I had started popping "Vitamin I" first thing in the mornings as preventive maintenance, but with only 2 nights to go, a blister developed on my foot and my back was hurting. Everyone said this 100-mile stretch was smooth sailing and elevation graphs in the AWOL guide resembled a flat line. Buying into this I envisioned a wide, flat trail, padded with beach sand, but was disappointed to find tall ridges still bouncing up and down, and as usual, only rocks and roots to walk on.

> NOT SO FUN FACT: Blisters hurt, but even worse, many long-distance hikers lose multiple toe-nails, usually caused by shoes or boots that are too tight. Nails grow back, but can take over a year.

Hoping to visit Whitehouse Landing Wilderness Camp, I walked a mile and a quarter off trail (each way) to a rundown, wooden boat dock where a SOBO was waiting patiently. He had already used the powerful air-horn (tied to a tree) to summon a motorboat from the other side of Pemadumcook Lake. The sign was adamant: "Only blow horn once!" and the owner was notorious for being moody. Of course, for all the trouble they hope visitors will stay the night (bunks $39). I didn't see anyone coming anytime soon, so I cut my losses and turned around. I still hiked 22 AT miles that day.

> FUN FACT: Want to own a hostel? Over 100 years old, Whitehouse Landing was recently for sale: 3.5 acres with vegetable gardens, fruit trees and "the biggest blackberry bushes you will ever see." Solar panels and a windmill power the lodge, 4 cabins and bunkhouse. Accessible by vehicle, boat, snowmobile, ATV, floatplane, or by foot. Asking price: $985,000.

38 miles to go... The next morning, Texas Pete caught up and gifted me a rice side, granola bars and oatmeal. I was super thankful, but he left most of his extra food at the road. With incoming weather, we briefly discussed using the buddy system to push each other, the started running. We had fun jumping over logs and rocks as we went. At one point, we leaped down an unseen drop-off at full speed. After 20 long miles, a day's work in itself, I was running on fumes while Texas Pete, boney and dangerously thin, was still raring to go. Shaking hands, he took off to complete his goal. Later, I learned he made it all the way to The Birches, hiking an incredible 40 miles in 1 day!

21 miles to go... Rainbow Ledges is a beautiful rock face covered with mosses of all colors. Through the trees, I had a perfect view of Katahdin. I bet thru-hikers were on top celebrating at that very moment. Then my fingertips went all tingly. I didn't know if it was the cold, from gripping my walking sticks too tight, or if I was having a stroke. But the uncomfortable sensation went away after taking a break. I wanted to make it to Abol Bridge where I could get some FOOD, but had to be there before 8:00 p.m.

I almost gave up at Hurd Brook Lean-to, but ran 4 more miles and made it to the road with 15 minutes to spare. Jogging over the bridge made of galvanized highway barriers, I had to stop and stare at Katahdin, now even closer, towering over Penobscot River.

Reaching the campground store, I bought $7 worth of junk food. Classy place, there was a full-sized oven for sale out front, $50: "Will not work but will help load." I couldn't afford a campsite ($15) and stealth camping is prohibited within Baxter State Park, so I crawled back into the woods with my pretzels and Pop Tarts. My last night sleeping on the AT, I was exhausted but proud after a 28-mile day, my new personal world record.

15 miles to go... Headlights piercing the fog like laser beams, the first logging truck of the morning woke me up. I had a frenzied 20 miles ahead (10 to the base of the mountain, 5 up, and 5 down - the 5 down don't count.) Crossing Abol Bridge again, I found it to be slippery with frost. Upon entering Baxter State Park (BSP), all thru-hikers (defined here as walking 100 miles or more) must register at a triangle-shaped kiosk to reserve a spot for Birches Campground: two 4-person lean-tos and 4 tent spaces/$10 cash/1 night only. Most hikers stage there for their ascent the next morning. If all spots are filled (as they were today), you're asked to retreat and wait until another time. Posted weather forecast for today: clear and cold; tomorrow, 90% chance of rain. It's not safe to climb Katahdin in the rain and I didn't have food or money enough to wait around. Today was the day.

I spotted a deer, the first in several states, its coat a dark brown. I wasn't running today, but still walking double time. White birch trees brought back memories, as I remembered tearing off thin sheets of bark I called "Indian paper," as a kid. Rationing my food carefully, I had breakfast at Big Niagara Falls and watched a man trout fishing. It was bitterly cold, and I was wearing all my raingear to help me keep warm. My excitement grew with every step. One more mountain to go! I didn't see any other hikers.

> FUN FACT: In 2011, Christie's auction sold Frederic Edwin Church's oil on canvas, a Hudson River School style landscape of Katahdin, titled "Twilight," for $3,218,500!

The first reported summit of mile-high Mount Katahdin was in 1804. Dangerous, over 60 lives have been lost in the BSP since records have been kept. Common causes of death: exposure, heart attack, lightning, drowning, falls, etc. More bizarre reasons: avalanche, plane crashes, dog sled accidents, a woman shot - mistaken for a bear, draft dodgers shot by authorities (and vice/versa).

5.2 miles to go... Arriving at Katahdin Stream Campground, I found a small bridge that led to the Birches and a primitive ranger station. To be honest, for the most prominent place on the entire AT, I thought it would be nicer; there wasn't even a vending machine! Inside, a ranger wearing a hunter orange toboggan welcomed me, but rummaged around his messy desk as if he'd never had a thru-hiker in his office before. After a few moments, he handed me a green leaflet of rules (dated 2 years old) and issued me a hiker permit. I was officially thru-hiker #583 for the season. At noon, rangers can enforce a

10:00 a.m. cutoff time, but he didn't say anything. P.S. - BSP doesn't accept mail drops and no dogs allowed.

Many hikers borrow "loaner" packs to carry just the essentials and make climbing easier, but purists carry their full packs all the way to the top. My pack was already lighter than the daypacks. We were also told hiking poles wouldn't be use-  ful. Five miles to the top, I had half a guidebook page, $3 in change, one Snickers bar, a pack of oatmeal, my beard was blazing and it was time to climb Katahdin!

3.9 miles to go... Katahdin Stream Falls was beautiful, but a strange place for the last privy on the AT. Boulder jumbles and rock climbing begin soon after, but these were just a teaser. Katahdin was the most technically difficult section of the whole trail, by a long shot. Climbing got increasingly challenging and white blazes could be hard to follow, but when in doubt - the AT always go up! Don't let all this scare you - plenty of senior citizens, and even little kids, were scurrying up and down the rocks. The only good thing about getting a late start was meeting friends on their way down, each smiling ear-to-ear, having just completed months of effort. It was nice to see them one last time...

- **Castaway:** Last seen playing croquet at Ice Cream Man's house.
- **Perch:** Recent sighting, in a minivan headed to Gorham.
- **Renaissance Man:** Decked out in a dayglow outfit and black sunglasses. Summited 2 days in a row - just for fun.
- **Kevin & Brooke:** I met this couple taking pictures of a dead mouse in my water bottle.
- **Croc Hunter:** We've known each other since Pennsylvania.
- **Roboticus:** Seeing me, she yelled "Loner!" and I got some great shots of her navigating a tricky obstacle.
- **Chameleon:** Reunited with Roboticus for the last day.

• **Detective & Wild Bill:** We had met only once before, at the Georgia/North Carolina state-line, over 2,000 miles ago!

• **Ultra Violet, Ass Rash, Blitz, Falls, Dream Walker, L.C. (Last Call)** and **Golden** were also on the mountain.

1.5 miles to go... After a deceiving false summit, I reached an area called "The Table Lands." From this treeless, relatively flat surface, I could see the real peak. Little dots, moving around on top, were thru-hikers rejoicing in their accomplishment at Baxter Peak. Only days after I walked over this surface, a woman with a military background got lost here. She emerged - scratched and bruised, from the woods near Abol Bridge a day and a half later.

30 feet to go... Everyone else had descended the mountain, either by way of the AT or the even more rigorous Knife's Edge Trail. Alone, I walked slowly toward the battered brown sign. I was flooded with emotions as I ran my fingers over the rough, carved letters on its surface. It was physically warm to the touch, and I tried hard to keep my composure, but my knees started to shake. With no one else here, I took my traditional summit pictures with the sign - selfie style. I made a video, my voice cracking, as I thanked everyone I could think of including my Babchie, Mom and my sister, mail angels and viewers for their support. Then I put the camera away. Sitting down, I enjoyed the last Snickers bar I had been saving, even sharing some nuts with a high attitude chipmunk, guardian of the mountain.

Friday, September 28th. After 5 ½ months striving to reach this exact spot, I only spent 15 minutes here. Some hikers spend hours and hours, but darkness was coming, and grey, spooky clouds blew-in over the mountaintop. I took in one last view from the tallest peak in Maine - 5,270' - with stellar views in every direction, then turned around and started back. Ten minutes later, the summit was completely obscured by thick fog.

> **FUN FACT:** *Official summit signs are replaced from time to time, most recently in 1999, 2009 and 2016. Cold and rain take their toll, not to mention all the people who carve their names into them. The most recent sign to be removed can be seen (and touched) at ATC HQ in Harpers Ferry.*

A thru-hiker's adventure doesn't end when we touch the sign. You still have to get back down! Skies had become completely dark with 2 miles to go, when I came across 2 day hikers, Kevin & Leigh, marathon runners who underestimated the mountain's difficulty and turned around without reaching the top. Agreeing to hike the rest of the way together, we used our combined headlamp power. Taking our time, it still took us another hour to get back to the campground. Their car was the only one left in the small parking lot and I was surprised to find a park ranger woman waiting for us, holding our hiking permits. Sternly, she asked how I was going to exit the park. Thankfully, my new friends offered to drive me to Millinocket, the closest town, 25 miles away, then to Bangor the following morning. I honestly don't know what I would have done otherwise.

Chapter 25. Easter to October (Post Script)

Craig gave me a ride across the Kennebec.

Still flying by the seat of my pants, I stealth camped in Millinocket, then road with Kevin and Leigh to Bangor, Maine. There, I waited at Mickey D's for the cavalry to arrive. With no warning, my Babchie dropped everything to come pick me up and along with her husband Sam, my Aunt Kathy and her husband Mike, we all went to Texas Road House to celebrate.

As you already know, my Babchie is a remarkable woman. Although we only see each other every few years, I have very strong memories hanging out with her. When I was a child, she'd sing in her Polish accent, 'How Much is that Doggie in the Window' before tucking me in at night. Then the next day, we might go to China Town and watch Chinese dragons dance. She always knew the best restaurants, even the "secret" ones in Boston. We'd walk between giant Cadillacs then knock on some non-descript backdoor. Letting us in, a bouncer would seat us across from mob bosses playing cards and counting money. "Don't stare, Jeffrey." Funny how kids remember stuff like that.

After Katahdin, I spent a wonderful week with Babchie and Sam at their summerhouse overlooking the harbor. We even drove to the local marina and bought live lobsters right off a fishing boat. One feisty little guy bit (pinched) me! Grandma took me on a shopping spree and bought me all new clothes. She suggested a haircut and shave, but I wanted to wear my trail beard home. Another day, Uncle Mike took me for a fun ride on his boat and even let me drive. My father called to congratulate me and was the first to suggest I write a book. It was good talking to him. I didn't know it at the time, but that would be the last time we spoke.

In addition to getting caught up uploading videos, I needed to send tons of "thank you" emails. After seeing my grandparents off at the airport - back to their home in Las Vegas - Uncle Mike drove me to the Greyhound station. I still had some unfinished business.

Back in Caratunk, dark and raining, I made camp on the shore of the Kennebec River and waited till morning. Not considered aquablazing, crossing the 400-foot wide Kennebec River by canoe is free and officially sanctioned by the ATC. The ferry is available late May to early September 9:00 to 11:00 a.m., and till 2:00 p.m. during peak season. Friendly dogs welcome.

I was really looking forward to meeting Steve "The Ferryman" Longley. Over 26 years, he safely transported over 19,000 hikers in his red canoe with a white blaze painted on the bottom. In the DVD, '2000 Miles to Maine,' The Ferryman was tall, hyper, well-spoken but straight forward. A wild man who loved the outdoors, the AT and its travelers, he often stood up in his canoe as he crossed, defying currents both wind and water. I was let down when some other dude was manning the boat that day. "Craig" didn't even have a trail name.

> FUN FACT: Many hikers who rode in the Ferryman's boat never knew he was son of James B. Longley, Sr. Independent Maine Governor (1974-1978). Also straight forward, once called his State legislators "pimps."

Still thankful for the ride, even though the weather was with us I really had to help muscle us across. I can't imagine fording this powerful waterway in any conditions, but several have died trying. The last log book entry by Alice Ference...

"8-25-85. Rain during night has slowed up. On to the Kennebec and an early morning swim. George & Alice Ference Brunswick."

Alice drowned fording the river. Her husband survived. The ferry was organized soon after. (Incidentally, Warren Doyle was the next hiker to sign the register.) Another hiker, Smiling Coyote, was washed away in 1998, choosing not to use the provided service.

Buses and shuttles. I don't recommend skipping sections to make up later. It was a huge production to finish up those 49.1 miles I skipped because of rental car red tape when Wildcat came to visit. Very late in the season, it was lonely only seeing hikers every now and then, equally gloomy, trudging one direction or the other. I also lost my trusty cook stove, a bummer even though I didn't have much that needed cooking. About all I had was leftover cereal and crackers my grandparents were tossing out before leaving for the winter. Painted blazes were more important than ever as damp leaves blanketed the ground, making it impossible to find the trail without them, or spot rocks and mud holes under the disguise. Dehydrated, I fell several times and only made 8 miles that first day back.

Now October, a jack-o-lantern greeted me at Peirce Pond Lean-to, but this was a somber place. Fellow thru-hiker Parkside drown here a few months earlier. A piece of wood had his name carved onto it and I sat on the shore a long time, looking over the moving water.

One night, I was woken up when a car stopped on a nearby road, then a LOUD gunshot! Hearing men laughing, I had no idea if they were shooting at moose, me, or what. Scared, I rolled out of my hammock and laid on the ground until they left. I was woken again when two night hikers walked by with their headlamps, making time to reach the river ferry, as it would stop for the season in a day or so.

Not by design, I saved the hardest bit for last. The Bigalows. Here, my goal each day was to scale up and over a few big bumps on the elevation chart and camp as low as possible. The biggest was North Crocker, a hefty 4,288', much of it steep rock climbing, grabbing roots and tree limbs to pull myself up, then friction sliding on my butt going down. There were 2 or 3 steep spots with no safe way around where I just let myself drop.

A season later, 66-year-old Geraldine Largay, "Inchworm" to her trail friends, went missing in these parts. She had started her hike in Harpers Ferry headed North and was last seen July 23th, smiling and happy. Later that day, she simply stepped off trail to use the bathroom and got lost. Desperate, she made phone calls for help and sent multiple text messages that never went through. Her husband reported her missing a few days later, but massive searches during the coming months found no trace. Missing person flyers were posted throughout the area and a makeshift memorial of walking sticks and wildflowers accumulated at the trailhead near Stratton, Maine.

Further confusing investigators, this poor woman's identity was stolen while she was missing, raising questions about foul play. Even her husband was questioned. Over 2 years later, Inchworm's remains were found in her tent just 3,000 feet off the trail, by a surveyor. According to clues in a journal she kept, she survived for almost a month before passing away due to starvation and exposure. The story drew national attention and was documented on the reality show 'North Woods Law.'

Soon, I was back in civilization on another Greyhound coach. The trip lasted 23 long hours! Police mistook me for a homeless man during a 3 hour layover at New York's Port Authority, so I left my ticket in plain sight. It was still fun getting New York hotdogs and checking out Times Square. Total sensory overload for someone living in the woods for almost 6 months. Not to mention the never-ending parade of yellow taxis jockeying for position, each trying to gain an inch advantage over dozens of others.

Funny, you can spot a thru-hiker anywhere. Bushy beards and backpacks give them away. I met Tiny Dancer for the first time at a bus stop hundreds of miles away from the trail. Re-enacting his summit photo, he let out a loud "Whooo" surprising everyone in the terminal. Amazingly, he was one of the hikers held hostage by a mad gunman on Beauty Spot, and like me, also found love on the AT. When we arrived in Ohio, Wildcat brought him a bag of snacks as trail magic. Poor guy, he still had 9 more hours to get back home to Texas!

I lived with Wildcat in Dayton, Ohio, for 3 weeks while she worked her notice at Victoria's Secret's call center. Thinking I would be having hiking withdrawals, she took me to a trail as a surprise. But at the first hint of an incline, I laid down on the path like a spoiled child and re-fused to move. Me, and my body, were spent. After spending another week or so visiting her family in Kentucky and several friends along the way, all wonderful people, we moved to South Carolina together. It was nice to see my mother, sister and nieces again after almost 7 months away. Mom made me an awesome collection of handmade scrapbooks while I was hiking. This was good therapy for her and I'll keep them forever.

> *FUN FACT: Wildcat the computer hacker? Once, she needed photos trans-ferred from a disk to a modern SD card, went into a thrift store, booted up an old PC on display with both functions, and made the conversion.*

Almost unrecognizable with scruffy beard and a big smile on my face, I came home 170 lbs. and much too thin for my sturdy frame. Wildcat was an awesome cook and after 6 months of conserving every resource and eating cold oatmeal, I just couldn't let anything go to waste. It didn't take long to find the 80 lbs. I lost, and then some. Writing this a few years later, I'm up to an all-time high, 350 lbs.

> *HIKER TIP: Post trail weight gain. No other activity can match the calories burnt hiking up and down mountains all day. After you hike, plan to stick to a "normal" diet and continue being active.*

Most friends who followed along with my videos were happy I made it back alive. Others criticized me for staying in hotels and accepting food and rides, thinking I should have hunted helpless squirrels with a sling shot, like a 'Naked and Afraid' reality show contestant. Not be-lieving I went anywhere at all, one accused me of filming videos in the woods behind my house, like conspiracy theorists say NASA faked the Apollo moon landings. Geez, I wasn't out to impress anyone, but give me a little cred! On the other hand, there was positive feedback, too...

• **15 minutes of fame?** Mom lined up interviews with newspapers and even a 'Today Show' clone hosted by a local TV weatherman/ma-gician. She also planned public speaking engagements.

• **Sponsorship?** A gear manufacture wrote: "If you ever do another thru, make sure and get a hold of us. We would be a proud sponsor."

• **Employment?** A mail angel who admired my determination, of-fered to get me a job at the large company where he worked.

- **Donor?** A lesbian couple asked my mother, to ask me, if I would be a sperm donor for their baby. True story!
- **TV star?** A producer for the TV Show, 'Hotel Impossible,' asked to source some video showing the "Magic Fingers Vibrating Bed."
- **Travel?** An outfitter in England offered to fly me over the pond to hike a trail there, documenting it on YouTube, as I had the AT.
- **Talking head?** My buddy Tear Drop - hiker and controversial shock jock - did a fun interview with me for his YouTube channel.

Most of the offers above, I politely declined. I was just happy to be home, hit my favorite arrowhead hunting spots, get back to work and enjoy the new relationship. The week in Maine with Wildcat was our first date. Our second lasted almost 2 years (my world record!) Adapting to my nomadic lifestyle, traveling around in an RV selling collectibles at flea markets, Wildcat and I had lots of fun together. But admittingly, I'm very hard to live with and sometimes things just don't work out like we think they should. In the end, I have good memories of the time we shared and wish her all the best.

Year of the reaper. Heartbreakingly, Mom got sick a year after I came home. Fighting through surgery, rounds of chemo, radiation and even stone healing, she passed away of brain cancer on Saint Patrick's Day, 2016. We lost my mother, father and Grandpa Sam all within a nine month period. I miss them all very much.

Can thru-hiking the AT change your life? Yes! Everyone finds something different on the trail. For me, important things seem more important now, and trivial things, are just that. I'll never forget walking into a grocery store after hiking to buy (and enjoy) a bag of chilled, green grapes as the couple next to me got into an argument about what kind of lightbulbs to use in a closet. Lightbulbs. I never want my life to be so mundane. Otherwise, I still scan trees for pairs to hang my hammock, and sometimes when I feel lost, catch myself looking for white blazes to show me the way. The trail will always be a part of me. I'll never forget the things my eyes saw, always remember the high and lows, miss all the interesting people I met and be thankful for everyone who helped me along the way.

The AT never closes and will always be there, but if this is a dream of yours, make plans now. No matter if you live to be 128 years old, every night when we go to bed is one less night we have on Earth. If there is anything you want to do, the AT or otherwise, put it on your

TO DO LIST - not your bucket list. Don't put it off until the kids are moved out, until you have extra money, or until after you retire. Guess what? Kids make little grandkids. You might think you'll be free after you retire, only to find your house has turned into a daycare center.

Start preparing, get your gear together, hike near home or visit the AT. Even if only for a small section, you'll be able to say you hiked the Appalachian Trail! It's my wish that this book will inspire you to "Get out and hike!" for health and spirit. Happy hiking! And don't forget...

Find some adventure - in your adventure!

Appendices

Charlie's Bunion in the Smokies. Look close, Firefighter John is standing on top!

Appendix A. *Acknowledgments*

Mail drops waiting for me in Dalton, Massachusetts. The bottom package is my laptop.

- **My mother.** I will always be very grateful for the food drops, paying my bills and keeping me updated with news from home and the trail.
- **Babchie and Sam.** Without their help, I would have surely left the trail just past halfway.
- **My sister Beth**, who along with her daughters Kendall and Deven, supported me with new shoes and most of all, by looking after my worrying mother while I was away. Kendall also helped a lot with the drop boxes.
- **Kath.** My "secret sponsor," who sent several mail magic boxes and gifts to make sure I made it all the way.
- **My "mail angels."** Too many to list; you know who you are!
- **Thanks to the ATC**, trail maintainers and volunteers who work tirelessly to maintain and protect the AT.
- **To all the trail angels** who brighten thru-hiker's days with cold drinks, warm food, rides...and in a hundred other ways.
- **Whiteblaze.com** and **Hammockforums.com** for lots of info.
- **Thanks Andrea Phillips, Juliana Martin and Lisa Kopel** for proofreading help.
- **Everyone** at the Pickens County Library, Village Branch.
- **YouTube vloggers:** Spielberg, Apache, and TD for shout-outs.
- **And, to the AT community on YouTube** for supporting hikers - just by watching and posting encouraging messages. You walked right along with me!

Appendix B. *What's in My Backpack*

Weighing my backpack at Amicalola Falls Visitor's Center. Total pack weight: Only 13.5 lbs. Most are 35+.

In preparing for my trip, I became what's called a "gram weenie," obsessed with packing as light as possible and found a YouTube video series, 'Only the Lightest,' hosted by ultralight expert Steve Green. Mostly budget minded, I spent a year studying, shopping and testing. Most items were bought on sale or lightly used. I was also willing to sacrifice some comfort to be more efficient, while still being safe.

BACKPACK

• **Terra Nova** Laser Elite 20 liter. 7 oz. List $90/Amazon $50. Two of this model was cheaper than just one of the popular brands, with weight savings a bonus.

> HIKER TIP: Made in England, Terra Nova equipment is a regular sight on Mt. Everest. Double the price, their 20 liter Superlite weighs only 3.9 oz.!

CLOTHES

• **Vest:** Montbell Thermawrap. 6.6 oz. Poly. List $120/demo $90.
• **(2) Basketball Shorts.** 7 oz. Poly. Dollar store $10.
• **Poly Shirt:** 6.5 oz. On sale $10. Worn over 2,000 miles.
• **Rain Poncho:** 5 oz. $6. I went through four. Cheap and light.
• **Fleece Beanie:** Z-Packs. 0.9 oz. $13. My favorite piece of gear!
• **Poly Socks:** 1 oz. Dollar store $3/3 pair. Replaced as needed.
• **Poly Beanie:** 0.5 oz. $7. Duplicated item but wore it a lot.
• **Alpaca Wool Socks:** 2 oz. $4 flea market find. Sleep socks.
• **Mid Layer Thermal Underwear:** Rocky. Poly. 4 oz. $20 at gas station.
• **Base Layer:** Silk. -0.05 oz. List $40/$20 bargain box find. Very warm!

> HIKER TIP: An old hunter's trick is to wear woman's silk stockings on cold days. "When the wind blows, go with the hose." (I never tried it.)

SLEEP SYSTEM

- **Hammock:** Grand Trunk Nano 7. 8.2 oz. +straps. List $70/eBay $55.
- **Sleeping Bag:** Western Mountaineering down 32° Summerlite. 18 oz. List $395/bought a returned item $225. Kept me warm to 17° (fully clothed).
- **Under Quilt:** Wilderness Logics ¾ down 20°. 17.5 oz. New $195/used $155.
- **Tarp:** Wilderness Logics Tadpole. 11 oz. $90 custom. Waterproof silnylon.

> *HIKER TIP: Hammock or tent? Comparing quality set ups, you'll find both are around the same price and total weight. It's each hiker's preference.*

COOK KIT

- **Cup:** Snow Peak Titanium 600. 2.8 oz. List $34/sale $25. Holds 2 cups water.
- **Stove:** End-to-End Trail Supply (E2E) 'Thru Hiker.' 0.4 oz. $12. Boils 2 cups of water in 5 minutes using 1 oz. of alcohol. Easy to use, durable and light.
- **Bear Bag:** Z-Packs. 0.25 oz. $15. Cuban fiber.
- **Plastic Bowl** with lid. Dollar store $4.

> *HIKER TIP: E2E has morphed into Loco Libre Gear, but the 'Thru-Hiker stove' has been discontinued. Search DIY videos on YouTube to make your own!*

FOOTWEAR

- **1:** New Balance 101 MT Trail Runners. $75. Springer to Pearisburg. 630 miles.
- **2:** Van's knockoffs. Dollar store $8. Pearisburg to Daleville. 93 miles.
- **3:** New Balance Nergy Trail Runners. $59.50. Daleville to Kent. 739 miles.
- **4:** ETONIC Stable Pro III sneakers. On sale $40. Kent to Manchester. 185 miles.
- **5:** INOV-8 ROClit 295. $100+/Gift. Manchester to Katahdin. 538 miles.

> *HIKER TIP: Weigh gear on a scale to make changes if possible. Cut off extra straps, tags, etc. Also, you don't need backups if you don't lose your stuff!*

MISCELLANEOUS

- **Trekking (Ski) Poles:** 12 oz. each. Accepted weight penalty for sentimental value (gift from friends). Unbreakable.
- **Belt:** I used a nylon strap, drilled and trimmed for length as I lost weight.
- **Extras:** Fingerless gloves, duct tape wallet (made by Don Don), lip balm, spare change, FM/AM radio (or MP3 player), batteries, 2 Smart Water bottles.
- **Didn't Carry:** Gaiters, pack cover, briefs, compass, map, dry bags, bug net.

Appendix C. *Trail Names*

Left to right: Kevin, Brook, Brad, Jonathan and Samson. Most of this crew never took trail names. I referred to Jonathan as "Firefighter John," but many more were suggested: Jolly, Crispy Critter, Ice Man, Cool-Aid, Bluey, Big Cat, Bugsy... Kevin & Brook didn't adopt trail names, either, but the trio took to calling themselves "Les Résistance." Finally, "Samson" might sound like a handle, but is his given name.

Here are some names I handed out...

- **8ᵗʰMile:** Name my mother earned because that's how far she could walk!
- **Almost an 8ᵗʰMile:** My niece, she didn't even make it as far as my mother.
- **Big Red:** Nickname for a kid with bushy red hair. Half of the High School Crew.
- **Team Dreadlock:** Guy and girl with dreadlocks and smelling of reefer.
- **Ski Pole Twin:** Dude who used the same brand ski poles as me. He actually called me "Ski Pole Twin."
- **Rasta Girl:** A girl hiker wearing dreads and a long dress. I never knew her real trail name and always referred to her as Rasta Girl.
- **Billy the Bear:** I don't know if anyone else has given wild animals trail names (trail dogs are), but this actual bear lived on the AT. With fondness and respect for letting me pass safely, he deserved a trail name. I had been listening to the Smashing Pumpkins on my radio. The lead singer's name is Billy Corgan, hence the name.
- **The GA Gang:** YouTube buddies who sent mail magic to keep me going.
- **All Star:** Given to a trail angel refilling his trail magic cooler in PA, and who wore Converse All Stars. He grinned, happy I thanked him with a trail name.

- **Old School:** This man thru-hiked the AT back in the 1980's. He said my backpack looked like a toy and he was leaving the trail because of people like me. I didn't tell him he had a new trail name - he was already mad enough!
- **Frostbite Challenge:** I made up this moniker after watching videos of SOBOs and early birds struggling with the famous Half-Gallon Challenge, in the winter.
- **Dayglow Crew:** Not an official trail name, just a term I called a group of four hikers, each wearing neon orange or green shirts.
- **Wilson the Propane Cylinder:** I bonded with this green propane cylinder-like Tom Hanks and his volleyball "Wilson" (from the movie, 'Cast Away'). In retrospect, it may have been funnier to name my cylinder "Coleman," but still got a few laughs.
- **Rembrandt:** Clay, the artist I met on Bear Mountain Bridge, who packed up his stuff and drove me to Wally World so I could buy a new camera. Otherwise, my video series would have missed important sections.
- **Mama Fratelli:** The most (and only) unfriendly lady laundry in Kent, CT. She had a striking resemblance to the character from the 1980's movie, 'The Goonies.'
- **Michael McDonald:** Jim, my host at a machinery museum, who after showing me around and giving me a ride in a mini-train, let me stealth camp on the property. With white hair and beard, he closely resembled the famous piano rocker.
- **Secret Sponsor:** A mail angel who sent lots of food drops, gift cards and cash. She didn't want her name used publicly, but has helped other hikers besides me.
- **Psychic:** Given to a young man that proclaimed, "Your trail name must be Munchie," after seeing the name painted on my hat. I jokingly replied, "Your name must be... Psychic?" He was quite pleased.
- **Overtime:** One half of a long-distance section hiking team from India. This fellow was always the late one, with his friend, Halftime, always having to wait.
- **Crazy Dude:** A slightly foreign man who gave me a ride, going the wrong way, and basically kidnapped me. We ultimately got into a car crash.
- **Flower Child:** My name for Karen, who I met atop Mt. Killington, VT. I didn't learn her real trail name was "One Up" until years later. Kirk was named "Weirder," but I knew him as "Guitar Man."
- **Mr. Serious:** I met this gentleman at Heaven Hill Shelter in VT. He wouldn't even crack a smile when I took his group's picture. I found out later his name was Zenith.
- **Golden Girls:** Phrase I coined describing groups of seniors hiking together.
- **Wildcat:** My then girlfriend, Cora Jean, came to visit me in Maine and needed a trail name. I decided on "Wildcat" while climbing up Wildcat Mountain in NH. Born and raised in KY, she was also an avid fan of Wildcat basketball.
- **Paul Bunyan:** This tall trail maintainer lifted huge logs over his head and tossed them like twigs! All he was missing was a blue ox.

Appendix D. *Lexicon of the Trail*

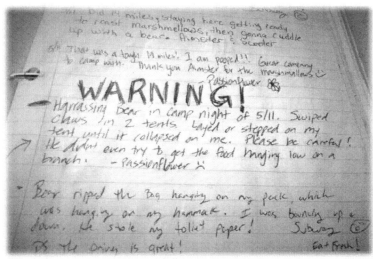

Every subculture has its own vocabulary, including the hiking community.

2000 miler: One who has hiked the entire AT in sections, or all at once.
Aquablaze: Traveling by canoe, kayak, etc. Not counted as official AT miles.
AYCE: All you can eat. **EAP:** Each additional person.
Baseball bat floor: Lean-to floor lined with round sticks.
Bear bag: Waterproof bag in which to carry your food, and hung out of reach.
Bear cable: Device, found at some shelters, for hanging food bags at night.
Bear spray: Pepper spray designed as protection from aggressive bears.
Beaver Fever: Illness caused by parasites in dirty water. (Credit Brooksy.)
Blue blazing: Taking shortcuts (some blue blazes lead to water or shelters).
Bounce box: A box you mail to yourself holding items used in town (and the name of Miss Janet's shuttle van.) Sometimes called a **bump box**.
Brown blazing: Hiking from one privy to the next, or tree-to-tree.
Cairn: Stacked rocks marking trails or landmarks.
Camel up: Drinking lots of water before a section with sparse water sources.
Camp shoes: Comfortable shoes carried to wear around camp.
Career hiker: A person who hikes every season, or hikes multiple trails.
Cat hole: A hole you dig into the ground to use as a bathroom.
CDT: Continental Divide Trail. 3,100 miles from Mexico to Canada.
Charmin daisies: Toilet paper marking human waste. (Credit Shutterbug.)
Cowboy camping: Sleeping on the ground with no tarp or tent.
Croo: AMC hut employees.
Damascathon: Hiking 26 miles, in one shot, into the trail town of Damascus.
Day hiker: Anyone out for a hike, but not camping overnight.
Deadbeat hiker: A hiker who bums everything, beyond acceptable yoging.
Deli blazing: Hiking to delis, pizzerias, or food stands. Common in NY & NJ.

Drop box: Resupply mailed by a support person; also **food drop,** or **maildrop**.

Duff: Layer of topsoil, or partially decomposed leaves. Used in privies.

End-to-end: A hike from one end of a trail to the other.

Extra-credit: Backtracking or hiking miles not counted toward the official AT.

False summit: A peak that appears to be the top of a mountain, but isn't.

Fastpacking: Attempting to hike a trail's length in record time, unassisted.

FBS: Frozen Butt Syndrome, caused by lack of hammock insulation.

Fence stile: Stairs or ramps over farmers' fences.

FKT: Fastest known time, referred to in record attempts.

Flip-flop: Hiking a section of trail, then hiking back from a different spot.

Floaties: Bits floating around in unfiltered water. Also called **amoebas**.

Frog water: Water sources in which frogs live.

Funemployed: Being laid off or quitting a job. (Credit Tarzan.)

Gaiters/gators: Worn to prevent pebbles, or mud, from getting inside boots.

Gold blazer: High rollers with expensive gear and gadgets; also **fancy hikers.**

Golden girls: Groups of grey haired retirees often seen hiking in groups.

Gorge tats: Bruises and scrapes from going off trail. (Credit SHUG.)

GORP: Good ole raisins and peanut butter.

Gram weenie: Hikers obsessed with making their gear as light as possible.

Grazing: Taste testing different foods in a grocery store.

Half-Gallon Challenge: Eating ice cream to celebrate the AT'S half-way point.

Hike your own hike: Do what you want. Let others do what they want.

Hiker box: A place for hikers to put unneeded things for others to use.

Hiker bubble: Big groups nomadically hiking together; also called a **herd**.

Hiker challenge: Usually retrieving food or alcohol within a time limit.

Hiker famous: Only known, or famous, to hikers.

Hiker feed: Trail magic usually provided by churches or other groups.

Hiker midnight: Eight o'clock dark, or after you get done setting up camp.

Hiker perfume: Bug spray. **Hiker porn:** Pictures of food.

Hiker rate: A lower room price at hiker friendly hotels.

Hiker trash: Thru-hikers. **Hiker TV:** Watching campfire flames.

Hobo bath: Washing up in a stream or bathroom sink.

Hobo hiker: People actually living on the trail, or who beg food or money.

Hobo wrap: A tortilla dish made with inexpensive ingredients.

HOJO: Howard Johnson Hotel.

Hostel: Places budget-minded hikers spend the night, get a shower, etc.

Hot spots: Places on the body where blisters are forming.

Iceberg: Large rocks blocking trailheads, or campsites, from being used.

LASHER or **Long Ass Section Hiker**: Someone hiking big chunks of trail.

Leap frog: Passing the same person several times, but not hiking together.

Logbook: Notebook for hikers to sign and read; also called a **register**.

LT: The Long Trail in Vermont. Hikers on the LT are called **LTs**.

MacGyver: Fixing stuff with whatever you can find.

Mail magic: Trail magic through the mail. Usually sent by a friend.

Moat: A hole at the front of a shelter to keep animals from getting inside.
Monkey butt: Painful rashes caused by chaffing or dehydration.
Mouse trapeze: A hook, hung from shelter rafters, to hang food or packs.
My Bear: Commonly referred to as the first wild bear a hiker sees.
Nature boy: Someone against phones, computers, GPS, etc. on the trail.
Nero: A day with very little hiking. Usually going in, or coming out of town.
Night hiking: Hiking, by headlamp, at night.
Ninja replacement: Replacing an item with an exact copy.
NOBO: Northbound. **SOBO:** Southbound.
Noro: Norovirus, transferred by infected person or contamination.
Outfitter: A store specializing in outdoor equipment.
Parkitecture: Architecture built by the Civilian Conservation Corps (CCC), usually incorporating local materials; also called **Park Service rustic**.
PCT: Pacific Crest Trail. 2,663 miles.
Peak bagging: Goal of reaching all worthy summits in a state or range.
Peak-a-view: Tiny views you can see through the trees. (Credit Harper's Terry).
Pink blazing: Rushing or skipping miles, to follow a potential love interest.
Post hole: Hiking in deep snow or mud into which your feet sink.
Privy: A bathroom or outhouse, usually found near a shelter.
PUDs: Pointless ups and downs. Small mountains - one after the other.
Purist: Hikers who insist on walking by every white blaze. Most don't slackpack.
Ramen bomb: Mixing Ramen noodles with something (anything) else.
Red blazing: Hiking while bleeding or injured.
Rescue blazing: Having to be rescued or helped off trail, to safety.
Ridgerunner: ATC employees who hike sections, interacting with hikers.
Rigor mortis: Taking a break so long that your muscles stiffen up.
Rock profile: Rocks or mountainsides, naturally resembling a person or thing.
Rockhound: People who look for, or collect interesting rocks.
Safety meeting: Code for taking a break to smoke pot; also called **green blazing**.
Section hike: Hiking from one point to another, but not a complete trail.
Self-rescue: Having to save yourself after getting into a dangerous position.
Shakedown: Short hikes to test gear you plan to use on a longer hike.
Shelter pet: Animals living at shelters.
Shelter: Trail structures where hikers sleep; sometimes called **lean-tos** or **huts**.
Shoe goo: Thick, glue-like substance used to repair shoes or boots.
Slackpack: Hiking without the full weight of your pack, or no pack at all.
Snake skin: Nylon mesh sleeves to keep a tarp bunched up when not in use.
Snake: Taking something before someone else does, or cutting in line.
Social ceremony: An act repeated over time, by members of a subculture.
Stealth camp: Camping off trail, usually hidden from view; also called **wild camping**, (Credit Tough Girl.)
Stunt double: A person who looks just like someone else, but not quite.
Superman Complex: Feeling indestructible, often resulting in injury.
Support person: A person, not on the trail, that sends drop boxes or money.

Switchback: Zigzags in a trail to prevent erosion or lessen grade.
Tagging: Signing or writing your name on things you're not supposed to.
Thru-hike: Hiking an entire trail in one calendar year, or in one attempt.
Top quilt: A sleeping bag used like a blanket, in hammocks.
Town clothes: A nice pair of clothes, just to wear around town.
Townies: Town's people or non-hikers. **Unfriendlies** don't like hikers.
Trail angel: A person who helps hikers. **Trail devils:** slow hikers down with beer.
Trail beard: Beards grown over the duration of a hike.
Trail legs: Legs conditioned after weeks of hiking.
Trail magic (TM): When hikers are surprised by acts of kindness. Usually hiker feeds, or coolers of drinks and snacks; also called **trail grace**.
Trail name: A nickname given to or adopted by a hiker. Earned from a character trait, funny happening, resemblance to a famous person and so on.
Trail town: A town directly on, or nearby, the trail. Usually hiker friendly.
Trailmance: A romance between people on the trail; also known as **trail love**.
Tramily: Trail family; friends with whom you bond on the trail. (Credit Darwin.)
Tree hugger: Webbing that protects hammock trees from damage.
Tree line: Alpine elevations where trees are less than eight feet tall.
Triple crown: Thru-hiking the AT, PCT and CDT.
Trolls: Hikers who camp under bridges. Also, people who harass video blogs.
Turtle patrol: Moving turtles from the trail or roads, to safety.
Under quilt: A sleeping bag hung below a hammock, for insulation.
Vehicle support: Hiking with assistance from a resupply vehicle.
Virginia blues: When hikers become bored or depressed on the long VA section.
Vitamin B: Beer. **Vitamin I**: Ibuprofen. **vlog:** Video blog or journal.
Water buffalo: Trailers with a water tank on top, sometimes left for hikers.
White blaze fever: Being obsessed with the AT, or feeling the urge to hike.
White blaze: A painted 2 x 6, inch white rectangle marking the AT.
Whoopie slings: Strong suspension cord for hammocks.
Widow maker: Dead or loose tree branches that could fall.
Windbreak: Trees or rock walls used by hikers as shields from the wind.
Wooly booger: A hairy, rough looking mountain man (or woman).
Work for Stay (WFS): Doing chores or other work, for free or reduced rates.
Wreck-spotting: Curious hikers looking for known plane wreckage.
Yardsale: Spreading out all your gear to let it dry out.
Yellow blazing: Riding in a vehicle to shortcut trail miles.
Yogi: The act of mooching or asking for stuff - without asking directly.
YO-YO: Hiking to the end of a trail, turning around, then doing it again in the other direction; also called a **roundtrip** or **Forest Gump**.
Zero: A day with no miles hiked - in town or on the trail.

Appendix E. Hiker Updates...

Crocatowie: You remember him pointing a bird toward the Smokies and their strict rules. Riding on a Greyhound together months later, he showed me his summit pic. Notice he's still dressed in the same clothes. I knew he'd make it.

- **Lone Star:** Thinking he left the trail with an injured foot, I was very happy to see his name on the official list of 2012 thru-hikers.
- **Firefighter John:** Summited the same day as me. In 2016, I saw him and his girlfriend at Trail Days and reported that he and his AT buddy Kevin had explored Iceland and were planning their next trip.
- **Rocket Man:** Unfortunately, he no longer works at Standing Bear Farm. Story is, he was hiking out west when he found some trouble and was incarcerated. Now you'll find a tall, jovial man there named Lumpy.
- **Miss Janet:** She still shuttles stinky hikers and will always be a part of the trail. She is currently driving the longest Dodge van you've ever seen.
- **JK & Navigator:** Reading their blog, "Not Quite Thru," this couple completed 550 miles before foot trouble and overcrowding ended their thru-hike. They continue working as outdoor writers in Florida.
- **Six-Six:** I met this tall fellow in Hot Springs, but he had to get off trail at Glasgow, Virginia, to recover from Plantar Fasciitis, pain in the heel and bottom of the foot.
- **High Life & Red Fury:** This couple abruptly stopped updating their Trail Journals in Virginia. I could only assume they had given up, but found out much later they made it all the way!

- **Apache:** AKA Joe Brewer, went on to complete "The Triple Crown." AT '12, PCT '14, and CDT '15. During his year "off," he was a ridgerunner at Baxter State Park. His YouTube vlogs of the PCT and CDT are of the highest quality.
- **Lt. Dan:** Suggested I use my digital camera to take photos of his guidebook. He recovered from a sprained knee and finished the trail.
- **The GA Gang:** Sent me my first mail magic. We've hung out several times since and they are awesome people.
- **Slow Foot:** This determined little German, broke his leg but cut his cast off with a hacksaw and still summited Mt. Katahdin the next day.
- **Socks:** She survived knee problems to finish 9/17.
- **Johnnie Walker Red:** On ATC's list of 2000 milers. **Johnnie Walker Black:** Is not.
- **Mr. Breeze:** I'll always remember him because he badly sprained his knee climbing out of Damascus, then later reinjured it enthusiastically reenacting Rocky Balboa's triumphant run up all 72 steps in front of the Philadelphia Museum of Art. He still finished the AT, and sends me messages from time to time.
- **Squatch:** He returned the next year to finish the AT and still makes documentaries. Next, he hiked around the country of Iceland, but didn't get to meet Bjork.
- **Fatherman:** My buddy FM summited on 9/25. After a bout with cancer, he tackled the PCT. Continuing his walking talk show, he reported having to "turn down the FM" and that Dr. Pepper was hard to find. Unfortunately, he broke his foot and hiked 420 miles with a plastic boot. The injury and forest fires ended his hike. He's doing fine and still enjoys riding his Harley.
- **Coach:** He made a documentary about his AT hike that I helped upload to YouTube. Still hiking, he has summited nine - 14,000 footers in CO and peak bagged all 115 - 4000 footers in NY, VT, NH and ME! Coach is a special person.
- **Rembrandt:** The artist I met who saved the video series by driving me to get a replacement camera. He's still teaching art and dipping brushes whenever he can.
- **Otto:** The hiker who tried to help me near Mt. Washington never stopped hiking until he died from cancer in 2015. His real name was Ray Douglas.
- **Voltron & Passion Flower:** These two friends summited on the same day.
- **Weirder & 1up:** This couple finished the LT, then found jobs and an apartment in Vermont. They even used a screen shot from my video for their 'save the date' announcement! Also, Weirder (Kirk) recently released his first album, 'Lesson One.'
- **Masshole:** He went on to thru-hike the PCT and is still hiking strong.
- **Ice Cream Man:** Dr. Bill Ackerly passed away in 2016 at the age of 87. His last wish was to thank all the hikers who stopped by for a visit: "They are the greatest."
- **Animal:** Made it all the way! But his goal of doing the whole AT for 50 cents a mile didn't come to pass, although he still insists it can be done. The AT Hall of Fame museum wants to add his drywall bucket to their collection.
- **Baltimore Jack:** Named after a Bruce Springsteen song, he thru-hiked the AT 8 times - and called Bill Bryson a "Candy Ass." He also coached many potential thru-

hikers, including me. Sadly, Baltimore Jack passed away from heart complications at age 57, while hanging out with his friend Ron Haven in Franklin, NC. Ron renamed one of his hostels "Baltimore Jack's Place."

• **Joseph Joe Fore:** "That summer was the BEST time of my life. When I got to Maine I fell in love with it. So much that I moved here. Also, thinking of retiring next year or so. If I do, I'm going for a triple crown."

• **"BOB spelled backward is still BOB."** Beginning in 2006, he finished his hike of the whole AT, climbing Katahdin "in heavy fog and gale-force winds," on Oct. 6th, 2012. He sent me a Christmas card and thanked me again for the cookie I left him.

• **The Ferryman:** Unexpectedly, he died in his sleep in 2013. He was only 56 years old. I regret not meeting him.

• **Sassafras & Kaboose:** Mail angels. They attempted a thru-hike after getting permission for Sassafras (thirteen) to miss school. A rainy season, she suffered foot trouble but still made it to NY. Kaboose returned to finish in 2016.

• **Tangled Roots Farm Stand:** Lucas and Maeve have since moved on from the farm but are doing well. The farm continues, now run by Maeve's mother, Clare. I was happy to hear Penny, the Australian Shepherd, is still greeting visitors.

• **Parkside:** Friends carried his ashes to the summit of Mt. Katahdin, completing his journey. After appealing to the ATC, he was named an honorary 2000 miler.

• **Sam I Am and Red Hot:** These guys watched my videos, and when their turn came in 2015, I followed theirs. Inviting me to visit, a month later I was on a plane to Maine - we even camped together while I did a 50 mile "vacation" hike. Today, Sam I Am does public speaking presentations about the Appalachian Trail.

Frenchy, Loophole & Sleeping Beauty, Pocahontas, Gluten Puff, Yosemite, Blue Sky, Gumby, Lost, EZ Nomad, B1, Late 4 Dinner, Mr. Breeze, Canecutter, Prophet, Shaggy, Lt. Dan, Ranger Bill, Count Chocula, Knief, Oak, Talloaf the Trail Ent, Murph, Cheesewater, Slim Pilgrim, Boomer, Samson: All are on the official ATC list of thru-hikers. Many more also finished, but didn't register with the ATC.

*Hike in 2012, or is your name in this book? Please send me an email with any updates or corrections to be included in future editions. Email: <u>Loner@ShadowArcherPress.com</u>

HIKER TIP: Beginning in 2014, AT hikers can order their own copy of "The Hiker Yearbook." Each class year includes headshots, profiles, hiker directory (both trail names and "real" names), trail angels and more. Cost $60.

About the Author

Loner, enjoying the view atop Mount Killington, Vermont.

Jeffrey "Loner" Gray, although born in Lowell, Massachusetts, has made South Carolina his home for many years. Working as a flea market nomad most of his life has afforded him time to pursue other interests: Racing cars, kayaking, studying Native American artifacts and producing hundreds of YouTube videos about diverse subjects.

Skateboarding competitively since he was ten years old, Jeff later formed his own skateboard company (Snake Session Skates), and sponsored team riders from the US and around the world. But hiking the Appalachian Trail has been his biggest accomplishment and **Painted Blazes,** about his trail experiences, is his first book.

After his mother passed away, he is continuing her independent publishing house, **Shadow Archer Press,** and hopes her name will live on by publishing books from a variety of authors.

Write to Loner: Loner@ShadowArcherPress.com.

Please visit: www.PaintedBlazes.com.

Please visit: www.ShadowArcherPress.com.

Other Books by Shadow Archer Press

Shamon Circus, is available from, All Things That Matter Press.

More praise for *Painted Blazes*

This book is full of helpful tips for those planning to hike the AT - tips I don't imagine you would find anywhere else. I appreciate that the tips are honest and do not sugar coat details about stops along the trail, even those that are somewhat negative. There are companion stories and fun facts to go with almost every stop. Some serious, some funny, but all enjoyed. I really appreciated the pop culture descriptions used to talk about people that Loner met along his way. **Supadiscofly**

Jeffrey's laid back attitude and down to earth style sets the tone for this enjoyable book about his A.T. adventure! **Remo**

There are many books about hiking the Appalachian Trail (AT). I have read about a dozen of them. What sets Painted Blazes apart is the depth and breadth of knowledge Loner gives the reader. You get the running commentary you expect from a trail journal. Discussion of the miles hiked, interactions with other hikers, town stops and interesting events along the way. But Painted Blazes goes deeper than that. Hiker Tips are included throughout the book to help anyone venturing into the woods. The appendices in Painted Blazes are also a good resource. Also included is a large glossary of hiker terms.   **Chad W Wesselman – Hiking with the Wesselmans**

Another thru hike journal...I woke up...I ate oatmeal...I walked I ate lunch I met zippy from bama bla bla bla NOT!!! Thank you Loner for putting some more meat on the bone with all the local history and background. **Yoda**

One of the best book about a thru hiker hiking the AT in 2012. Great read! **Kerry Young**

To learn more about the Appalachian Trail...

Appalachian Trail Conference

P.O. Box 807

Harpers Ferry, West Virginia 25425-0807

(304) 535-6331

www.appalachiantrail.org.

Made in the USA
Columbia, SC
25 April 2018